Friction

....

Friction

An Ethnography of Global Connection

Anna Lowenhaupt Tsing

Princeton University Press

Princeton and Oxford

Copyright ©2005 by Princeton University Press

Published by Princeton University Press,
41 William Street, Princeton, New Jersey 08540

In the United Kingdom: Princeton University Press,
3 Market Place, Woodstock, Oxfordshire OX20 1SY

Library of Congress Cataloging-in-Publication Data

Tsing, Anna Lowenhaupt.
Friction : an ethnography of global connection /
Anna Lowenhaupt Tsing.
p.   cm.
Includes bibliographical references and index.
ISBN 0-691-12064-1 (alk. paper) —
ISBN 0-691-12065-X (pbk. : alk. paper)
1. Intercultural communication.   2. International
economic relations.   3. International relations.
4. Ethnology.   5. Globalization.   I. Title.

GN345.6.T75 2005
303.48′2—dc22   2004043422

British Library Cataloging-in-Publication Data is available

This book has been composed in Janson and Frutiger

Printed on acid-free paper. ∞

pup.princeton.edu

Printed in the United States of America

10   9   8   7   6   5   4   3

Contents

....

Preface

....

From the perspective of many foreigners, Indonesia in the last thirty years of the twentieth century was a bustling yet quiet place, known for its beaches and its business opportunities. Then—suddenly—around the turn of the century, the country appeared to fall apart. Stories of financial crisis, political scandal, ethnic and religious conflict, and resource struggle filled the news. Even a slightly closer look, however, reveals that these outbreaks of unrest and disaster built directly on the policies and practices of the preceding thirty years of imagined peace and progress. Consider the terrain of Indonesia's famous rainforests and indigenous cultures. The New Order regime of General Suharto (1966–1998) made business a predator, born from the mix of nepotism, international finance, and military muscle, and feeding on cheap resources ripped illegally from rural communities. No wonder that after Suharto's resignation in 1998, villagers grew bold enough to assert their local rights. And, given the violence that had accompanied corporate expropriations, no wonder too that local complaints of all sorts entered a dangerous melee. Community groups fought and merged with illegal loggers, corporate security guards, gangsters, advocacy groups, religious factions, district officials, police, and army men.

This book describes the cultural processes in which certain kinds of predatory business practices, on the one hand, and local empowerment struggles, on the other, came to characterize the rainforests of Indonesia. Large pieces of my story draw on fieldwork in the mountains of South Kalimantan, but this is not a story that can be confined in a village, a province, or a nation. It is a story of North American investment practices and the stock market, Brazilian rubber tappers' forest advocacy and United Nations environmental funding, international mountaineering and adventure sports, and democratic politics and the overthrow of the Suharto regime, among other things. In reaching across these terrains, I offer an ethnography of global connection. The term "global" here is not a claim to explain everything in the world at once. Instead, it introduces a way of thinking about the history of social projects, including "business" and "local empowerment." First, such projects grow from spatially far-flung collaborations and interconnections. Second, cultural diversity is not banished from these interconnections; it is what makes them—and all their particularities—possible. Cultural diversity brings a creative friction to global connections. The topic of my book is this friction.

I first became excited by the possibilities of studying environmental connections across difference when I stumbled upon a curious misunderstanding during 1994 fieldwork in Indonesia. Although it was good to see old friends and adopted family, it was a disturbing time to be in the Meratus Mountains of South Kalimantan, the site of my on-going research. Timber companies had made new inroads into the Meratus landscape. Many of my Meratus Dayak friends were depressed by the destruction of the forests that had formed the basis for their livelihoods as shifting cultivators and forest foragers. As I traveled around the countryside listening to Meratus views of the logging crisis, a number of people reminded me of a moment of hope: a successful campaign to remove a logging company from one Meratus village in 1986. I decided to find out about this campaign, which was organized by village elders working together with a nature lovers' group in the provincial capital as well as national environmentalists from Jakarta. By chance, I knew, or knew of, many of the key players, and I was able to interview the leading participants. Of course, I wasn't there for the original campaign. But this only heightened my appreciation of the storytelling about it. For something very odd emerged in the stories: They all seemed to describe different events. When presented with other participants' stories, each respondent found the others fantastic, unreal. I couldn't help but notice the systematic misunderstandings that separated village elders, provincial nature lovers, and national environmental activists. And yet these misunderstandings—far from producing conflict—had allowed them to work together!

These incommensurable interviews clarified for me a central feature of all social mobilizing: It is based on negotiating more or less recognized differences in the goals, objects, and strategies of the cause. The point of understanding this is not to homogenize perspectives but rather to appreciate how we can use diversity as well as possible. (I discuss the story of this Meratus anti-logging campaign and its analytic significance in more detail in chapter 7.) The interviews also confirmed the practical usefulness of the kind of patchwork ethnographic fieldwork I had been doing on these issues. On the one hand, I was unwilling to give up the ethnographic method, with its focus on the ethnographer's surprises rather than on a pre-formulated research plan. On the other hand, it is impossible to gain a full ethnographic appreciation of every social group that forms a connection in a global chain. My experiment was to work my way back and forth between the Meratus Mountains—where I had a long-term ethnographic background—and the places implicated in the chains I traced.[1] My knowledge is variously ethnographic, journalistic, and archival, and it is formed in discrete patches. I search for odd connections rather than seamless generalizations, inclusive tables, or comparative grids.

How does one do an ethnography of global connections? Because ethnography was originally designed for small communities, this question has puzzled social scientists for some time. My answer has been to focus on zones of awkward engagement, where words mean something different across a divide even as people agree to speak. These zones of cultural friction are transient; they arise out of encounters and interactions. They reappear in new places with changing events. The only ways I can think of to study them are patchwork and haphazard. The result of such research may not be a classical ethnography, but it can be deeply ethnographic in the sense of drawing from the learning experiences of the ethnographer.

Many ethnographic learning experiences shaped this book. One of the most important came early in my research in the Meratus Mountains: The forest landscape is *social*. I originally entered the Meratus forests with the eyes of a naturalist. I marveled at the diversity of species, and I admired the forest views from many a mountain ridge. It was only by walking and working with Meratus Dayaks that I learned to see the forest differently. The forest they showed me was a terrain of personal biography and community history. Individuals and households tracked their histories in the forest: House posts resprouted into trees. Forest trees grew back from old swiddens. Fruits and rattans were planted in the growing forest. Forest giants were cleaned and claimed for their potential for attracting honeybees. People read the landscape for its social as well as its natural stories. Communities were constituted in these overlapping histories, as well as in shifting communal places, the old ones marked with enriched islands of trees. (This landscape is described in chapter 5.) Yet almost all scholarship and policy continues to portray forests as wild, natural spaces outside society. If Meratus forests were recognized as social, the predominant forms of both resource exploitation and conservation that have been imposed on the area would seem very odd indeed.

By the time I got back to the Meratus Mountains to continue research on this, something new had happened that took precedence. Logging companies had moved in, bulldozing orchards, rattan plantings, and old community sites. The people I knew best were angry and disturbed; a few years later they were resigned and depressed. (Later still, the economic crisis and a new anti-logging campaign reawakened anger.) I found myself caught up in their emotions and—quite properly, I think—unable to produce a dispassionate account. But what was I to write? On the one hand, activist accounts of corporate rip-offs of indigenous people were becoming so common that perhaps my story would be superfluous—and easy to dismiss. On the other hand, my academic colleagues, unhappy about the simplifications of these accounts, reminded me that many people benefited from the timber economy and the ensuing mining and plantation booms. I knew city people, migrants, and even ambitious locals who had made good money. But the farmers and foragers whom I knew best had shaped my perspective. I wanted to tell their story. To do so, I concluded that I must put the question of distress center stage rather than trying to avoid it: to focus on the most distressed area, to write specifically about distress, and to use an ethnographic writing style to make its contours as vivid as I know how (see chapter 1). If this is a story that should be told, it deserves an "audible" track.

My ability to think through Meratus dispossession was aided in large part by the blossoming of the Indonesian environmental movement in the late 1980s and 1990s (see chapter 6). Despite military rule, censorship, and public fear, here was a movement that endorsed the importance of democracy, the rights of marginal peoples, and the inseparability of conservation and justice! I have been thrilled to have this interlocutor for my research. Yet I also understood that any dialogue in which I participated required me to take some responsibility for my fieldwork and writing. Indonesian environmentalists work within an international culture of science and politics; they are sensitive about the power of U.S. scholars to say anything they want without thinking about its local implications. My ethnographic involvement with activists taught me habits of restraint and care: There are lots of things that I will not research or write about. I do not mean that I have whitewashed my account, but rather that I have made choices about the kinds of research topics that seem appropriate, and, indeed, useful to building a public culture of international respect and collaboration.

From 1966 to 1998, Indonesia was ruled by the authoritarian regime of President Suharto. Following massive student demonstrations, Suharto stepped down, and an era of reform and transition slowly began. Much has changed in the nature of politics, the relationship of city and countryside, the role of nongovernmental organizations, and the culture of natural resource management. Although I have continued my research to learn about these new conditions, I have focused my book on the period from the late 1980s through the 1990s, when resource exploitation was centrally mandated, rapid, and irresponsible, and the environmental movement, opposing this, was at its most heroic. The forms and categories set down in this period continue to shape more recent policies and political struggles.

Regime changes in other parts of the world have also influenced my writing. The global ambitions of the United States have shaped popular understandings of culture and politics in and beyond North America, particularly through two large and dangerous concepts. The concept of "globalization," at its simplest, encourages dreams of a world in which everything has become part of one single imperial system. The concept of "terrorism," at its most frightening, allows that all difference is really savagery aimed to torture decent folk. It is tricky, and more important than ever, to write about cultural difference where public debate is dominated by these two misleading concepts and the theories of universality and civilization to which they have given birth. It requires a perhaps-unreasonable optimism that the differences that simmer within global connections will be more curious and creative than anything imagined by these theories of suffocation and death.

....

This book has drawn from many collaborations. For my continuing research in the Meratus Mountains of Kalimantan, I am particularly grateful to the adopted siblings I call Uma Adang and Ma Salam, who have offered me so many insights. In South Kalimantan, the families of Hasan and Zainab and Iyan and Anisyah have been invariably kind hosts. The late Professors Koesnoe and Radam were most generous interlocutors. My more recent work has been facilitated by many activists and engaged scholars. I am particularly grateful for the multiple acts of assistance and hospitality of Emmy Hafild, Sandra Moniaga, Bambang Widjojanto, Arimbi Heroepoetri, Tri Nugroho, Agus Purnomo, Dea Sudarman, Chalid Mohammad, Professor Abdurrahman, Professor Abby, Professor Budairi, Rahmina, and all the activists of the Lembaga Pembelaan Masyarakat Adat. Ford Foundation Program Officers Jeffrey Campbell, Philip Yampolsky, and Mary Zurbuchen were most helpful hosts in Jakarta. Judith Mayer and Stephanie Fried extended contacts and discussed my research.

Various parts of the book required specialized research assistance. The chapter on nature lovers was made possible by working with Mercedes Chavez P., who helped set up the project in Yogyakarta through her own contacts there. One of the most exciting aspects of doing research on nature lovers is that they themselves are fascinated by research. As soon as I introduced my questions, my informants ran out to interview their friends, to offer me newspaper articles and nature lover newsletters, and sometimes even to write short essays on nature loving to help me out. For what I report here, then, I am very much indebted to the coordinated research of everyone I spoke with about nature loving. My particular thanks go to "Ceplies" Dyah Sutjiningtyas, Bambang Ponco Soewanto, and Sigit Murdawa. Conversations with Peter Adeney were also helpful. I hope that I have not distorted the gist of what I was taught by such an enthusiastic crew.

Scholars and friends in and beyond the United States have also contributed to this book. As with all scholarship, indeed, it is hard to know how to separate one's own insights from the ideas of others. I have benefited from readings of earlier drafts of my chapters by Warwick Anderson, Arjun Appadurai, Kathryn Chetkovich, Timothy Choy, James Clifford, Paulla Ebron, Lieba Faier, Susan Harding, Michael Hathaway, Eben Kirksey, Tania Li, Celia Lowe, Jitka Maleckova, Nancy Peluso, Lisa Rofel, Daniel Rosenberg, Shiho Satsuka, James Scott, and Mary Steedly. Some of these colleagues have been exceptionally patient, reading multiple drafts and offering advice over many years. I hardly know how to thank them enough. Conversations with Itty Abraham, Peter Brosius, Carol Gluck, Donna Haraway, Gail Hershatter, Renato Rosaldo, Michael Ross, Ann Stoler, Toby Volkman, Sylvia Yanagisako, Charles Zerner, and the SSRC Regional Advisory Panel on Southeast Asia have also helped me think.

During the years I have been working on the book, I have benefited from research assistance from Julie Beck, Benjamin Bray, Karen Ho, Mora McLagen, Scott Morgensen, Rheana Parrenas, Bettina Stoetzer, and Yen-ling Tsai. Susan Watrous offered her skills and enthusiasm to pull together all the details. I am grateful.

The time I spent at the Institute for Advanced Studies at Princeton in 1994–95 allowed me to find my footing in environmental studies. A residential seminar at the University of California Humanities Research Institute in 1997 allowed me to draft chapter 1. A fellowship at the Center for Advanced Studies in the Behavioral Sciences, Stanford, in 1999–2000 allowed me to fill in the book. I am grateful too to the students and faculty at the universities that have invited me to talk about the work as it has come into being.

The personal names of ordinary people who make an appearance in this book are pseudonyms, as are the names of villages. For major public figures and major cities, I use real names.

Versions of the first half of chapter 1 appear in *Economic and Political Weekly* (38[48, 2003]: 5100–06) and in *Histories of the Future*, edited by Susan Harding and Daniel Rosenberg, Duke University Press. A version of chapter 2 appears in *Public Culture* (12[1, 2000]: 115–44).

The lists on the endpapers at the beginning and end of this book are based on a discussion with a single individual, who recalled these life forms from memory, without the benefit of material stimulation. They are not intended as a master list. The making of this list is described in the interlude before chapter 5.

The photographs that precede part I and part II were taken by the author in 1994 and 2000, respectively. The photo that precedes part III is of a poster reproduced with permission from the Aliansi Meratus.

Friction

....

Introduction

....

Global connections are everywhere. So how does one study the global?

This book is about aspirations for global connection and how they come to life in "friction," the grip of worldly encounter. Capitalism, science, and politics all depend on global connections. Each spreads through aspirations to fulfill *universal* dreams and schemes. Yet this is a particular kind of universality: It can only be charged and enacted in the sticky materiality of practical encounters. This book explores this practical, engaged universality as a guide to the yearnings and nightmares of our times.

Post-colonial theory challenges scholars to position our work between the traps of the universal and the culturally specific.[1] Both conceits have been ploys of colonial knowledge, that is, knowledge that legitimates the superiority of the West as defined against its Others. Yet in studying colonial discourse, social scientists and historians have limited themselves to the cultural specificity side of the equation. There has been much less attention to the history of the universal, as it, too, has been produced in the colonial encounter. Here a specific valence for the universal has been produced; the universal is what, as Gayatri Spivak has put it, we cannot not want, even as it so often excludes us.[2] The universal offers us the chance to participate in the global stream of humanity. We can't turn it down. Yet we also can't replicate previous versions without inserting our own genealogy of commitments and claims. Whether we place ourselves inside or outside the West, we are stuck with universals created in cultural dialogue. It is this kind of post- and neocolonial universal that has enlivened liberal politics as well as economic neoliberalism as they have spread around the world with such animation since the end of the Cold War. Nor is scholarly knowledge exempt; every truth forms in negotiation, however messy, with aspirations to the universal.

This book is not a history of philosophy, but rather an ethnography of global connection. The specificity of global connections is an ever-present reminder that universal claims do not actually make everything everywhere the same. Global connections give *grip* to universal aspirations. Working through global connection, the book is an exploration of ethnographic methods for studying the work of the universal. As soon as we let go of the universal as a self-fulfilling abstract truth, we must become embroiled in specific situations. And thus it is necessary to begin again, and again, in the middle of things.

....

Something shocking began to happen in Indonesia's rainforests during the last decades of the twentieth century: Species diversities that had taken millions of years to assemble were cleared, burned, and sacrificed to erosion. The speed of landscape transformation took observers by surprise. No gradual expansion of human populations, needs, or markets could possibly explain it; besides, the products of these forests had been globally marketed for hundreds of years. Corporate growth seemed unaccountably chaotic, inefficient, and violent in destroying its own resources. Stranger yet, it seemed that ordinary people—even those dependent on the forest for their livelihood—were joining distant corporations in creating uninhabitable landscapes.[3]

Within Indonesia, this ugly situation came to stand for the dangers of imperialism and the misdeeds of a corrupt regime. Opposition to state and corporate destruction of forest-peoples' livelihoods became a key plank of the emergent democratic movement of the 1980s and 1990s. An innovative politics developed linking city and countryside, bringing activists, students, and villagers into conversation across differences in perspective and experience. The insights and vicissitudes of this mobilization have not been much appreciated outside of the country. Yet they speak to central dilemmas of our times: Why is global capitalism so messy? Who speaks for nature? What kinds of social justice make sense in the twenty-first century?

None of these questions can be addressed without an appreciation of global connections. Indonesian forests were not destroyed for local needs; their products were taken for the world. Environmental activism flourished only through the instigation and support of a global movement. Yet popular stories of global cultural formation are of little help in understanding these phenomena. There is no triumph of global integration here; both the chaotic melee of landscape destruction and the searing protests of radical critics are forged in dissension, fragmentation, and regional inequality. We see the unexpectedly persistent effects of particular historical encounters. A villager shows a North American miner some gold; a Japanese model of trade is adopted for plywood; students banned from politics take up hiking; a minister is inspired by a United Nations conference on the environment: These narrowly conceived situations lay down tracks for future "global" developments. Rather than tell of the evolutionary unfolding of a new era, my story inquires into the makeshift links across distance and difference that shape global futures—and ensure their uncertain status.

This book shows how emergent cultural forms—including forest destruction and environmental advocacy—are persistent but unpredictable effects of global encounters across difference. This proposition extends my earlier research, in which I explored how even seemingly isolated cultures, such as rainforest dwellers in Indonesia, are shaped in national and transnational dialogues (Tsing 1993). Scholars once treated such cultures as exemplars of the self-generating nature of culture itself. However, it has become increasingly clear that all human cultures are shaped and transformed in long histories of regional-to-global networks of power, trade, and meaning. With new evidence of these histories entering the academy from every direction, it has become possible for scholars to accept the idea that powerless minorities have accommodated themselves to global forces. But to turn that statement around to argue that global forces are themselves congeries of local/global interaction has been rather more challenging.

The challenges arrive from several directions. Some powerful conventions of thinking get in the way of research on this theme. Most theories of globalization, for example, package all cultural developments into a single program: the emergence of a global era. If globalization can be predicted in advance, there is nothing to learn from research except how the details support the plan. And if world centers provide the dynamic impetus for global change, why even study more peripheral places? Creative studies of the periphery are also hamstrung. Powerful social science directives catalogue and compare developments in the global south under a distancing imperial gaze, keeping us out of the arena where cultural outcomes really matter. If Indonesia is only a scrap of data, it might inform cosmopolitan readers, but its global encounters can never shape that shared space in which Indonesians and non-Indonesians jointly experience fears, tensions, and uncertainties. In this shared space, the contingency of encounters makes a difference. To guide us there, I must clear a theoretical path that extends far beyond Indonesia's forests. Yet can one gain an ethnographic purchase on global connections? Where would one locate the global in order to study it? Even those who are determined to conduct this kind of research still struggle to figure out how it is done.

To address these challenges, this book develops a portfolio of methods to study the productive friction of global connections. What happens when Japanese traders buy Indonesian trees, when army officers make deals with nature lovers, or when university students sit down with village elders? I begin with the idea that the messy and surprising features of such encounters across difference should inform our models of cultural production. In reaction to popular over-enthusiasm for programmatic global predictions, I emphasize the unexpected and unstable aspects of global interaction. To enrich the single-mindedness of cultural explanation focused only on internal blueprints for reproduction and growth, I stress the importance of cross-cultural and long-distance encounters in forming everything we know as culture (e.g., Clifford 1997). Cultures are continually co-produced in the interactions I call "friction": the awkward, unequal, unstable, and creative qualities of interconnection across difference. Each chapter of this book develops a method for learning about such aspects of contingent encounters.

While the situation in Indonesia is distinctive, it can also take us to the heart of the liveliest debates and discussions in contemporary scholarship. Thus, scholars of the Left have worried through how best to describe post–Cold War capitalism, with its global pretensions. Humanities scholars and social scientists tend toward opposite poles: Where the former often find the universalizing quality of capitalism its most important trait (e.g., Jameson 2002), the latter look for unevenness and specificity within the cultural production of capitalism (e.g., Yanagisako 2002; Mitchell 2002). Where the former imagine mobilization of the universal as key to effective opposition to exploitation (e.g., Hardt and Negri 2000), the latter look for resistance in place-based struggles (Massey 1995) and unexpected linkages (Gibson-Graham 1996).

The contribution of each of these works is stunning; yet placed in conversation they seem to block each other. There is a cross-disciplinary misunderstanding of terms here; as Jameson (2002: 182) explains, "the universal is [not] something under which you range the particular as a mere type."[4] Social scientists have often done just that. But rather than rectify the disciplines, my goal is to grasp the productive moment of this misunderstanding. At this confluence, universals and particulars come together to create the forms of capitalism with which we live. There is no point in studying fully discrete "capitalisms": Capitalism only spreads as producers, distributers, and consumers strive to universalize categories of capital, money, and commodity fetishism. Such strivings make possible globe-crossing capital and commodity chains. Yet these chains are made up of uneven and awkward links. The cultural specificity of capitalist forms arises from the necessity of bringing capitalist universals into action through worldly encounters. The messiness of capitalism in the Indonesian rainforest exemplifies the encounters in which global capital and commodity chains are formed.

A related set of debates characterizes discussion of the new social movements that arose in the late twentieth century as vehicles of protest: human rights, ethnic identity politics, indigenous rights, feminism, gay rights, and environmentalism. Scholars are divided: Some see these movements as expressions of a frightening new force of global coercion, while others portray them as carrying hopes for freedom. The split here is not across disciplines but rather across audiences. Those who address themselves to cultural theorists stress the formation of new kinds of disciplinary power (e.g., Rabinow 2002); those who include activists in their audiences stress such movements' potential (e.g., Keck and Sikkink 1998).[5] The former explain the universalizing logic of liberal sovereignty and biopower; the latter tell us of the urgency of particular cases. Again, these commentators talk right past each other; and, again, their intersection could be more productive. It is essential to note how protest mobilizations—including the Indonesian democratic movement of the 1980s and 1990s—rely on universalizing rhetorics of rights and justice. Through these, they make their case to the world; through these, too, they are shaped by liberal logics. Yet they must make these rhetorics work within the compromises and collaborations of their particular situations. In the process, new meanings and genealogies are added to liberalism. This does not mean people can do anything they want; however, it changes our view of liberal sovereignty—with its universals—to imagine it in concrete purchase on the world.

Both these discussions can benefit from a focused look at global connections. In the historical particularity of global connections, domination and discipline come into their own, but not always in the forms laid out by their proponents. On the one hand, this work can avoid the idea that new forms of empire spring fully formed and armed from the heads of Euro-American fathers. On the other hand, this work avoids too eager a celebration of a southern cultural autonomy capable of absorbing and transforming every imperial mandate. Instead, a study of global connections shows the grip of encounter: friction. A wheel turns because of its encounter with the surface of the road; spinning in the air it goes nowhere. Rubbing two sticks together produces heat and light; one stick alone is just a stick. As a metaphorical image, friction reminds us that heterogeneous and unequal encounters can lead to new arrangements of culture and power.

The metaphor of friction suggested itself because of the popularity of stories of a new era of global motion in the 1990s. The flow of goods, ideas, money, and people would henceforth be pervasive and unimpeded. In this imagined global era, motion would proceed entirely without friction. By getting rid of national barriers and autocratic or protective state policies, everyone would have the freedom to travel everywhere. Indeed, motion itself would be experienced as self-actualization, and self-actualization without restraint would oil the machinery of the economy, science, and society.[6]

In fact, motion does not proceed this way at all. How we run depends on what shoes we have to run in. Insufficient funds, late buses, security searches, and informal lines of segregation hold up our travel; railroad tracks and regular airline schedules expedite it but guide its routes. Some of the time, we don't want to go at all, and we leave town only when they've bombed our homes. These kinds of "friction" inflect motion, offering it different meanings. Coercion and frustration join freedom as motion is socially informed.

Speaking of friction is a reminder of the importance of interaction in defining movement, cultural form, and agency. Friction is not just about slowing things down. Friction is required to keep global power in motion. It shows us (as one advertising jingle put it) where the rubber meets the road. Roads are a good image for conceptualizing how friction works: Roads create pathways that make motion easier and more efficient, but in doing so they limit where we go. The ease of travel they facilitate is also a structure of confinement. Friction inflects historical trajectories, enabling, excluding, and particularizing.

The effects of encounters across difference can be compromising or empowering. Friction is not a synonym for resistance. Hegemony is made as well as unmade with friction. Consider rubber. Coerced out of indigenous Americans, rubber was stolen and planted around the world by peasants and plantations, mimicked and displaced by chemists and fashioned with or without unions into tires and, eventually, marketed for the latest craze in sports utility vehicles.[7] Industrial rubber is made possible by the savagery of European conquest, the competitive passions of colonial botany, the resistance strategies of peasants, the confusion of war and technoscience, the struggle over industrial goals and hierarchies, and much more that would not be evident from a teleology of industrial progress. It is these vicissitudes that I am calling friction. Friction makes global connection powerful and effective. Meanwhile, without even trying, friction gets in the way of the smooth operation of global power. Difference can disrupt, causing everyday malfunctions as well as unexpected cataclysms. Friction refuses the lie that global power operates as a well-oiled machine. Furthermore, difference sometimes inspires insurrection. Friction can be the fly in the elephant's nose.

Attention to friction opens the possibility of an *ethnographic* account of global interconnection. Abstract claims about the globe can be studied as they operate in the world. We might thus ask about universals not as truths or lies but as sticky engagements.

Engaging the Universal

It is impossible to get very far in tracing global connections without running into claims about universals. The universal is at the heart of contemporary humanist projects: Scientists, economic reformers, and social justice advocates all appeal to the universal. Yet universals, taken at their face value, erase the making of global connections. This raises a disturbing question: How can universals be so effective in forging global connections if they posit an already united world in which the work of connection is unnecessary?

Scholars have not much addressed this question because the idea of the universal suggests abstractions, which turn them away from the practical successes and failures of universal claims. Neither those who place their ideas inside the universal nor those who discredit it as false pause to consider how universals work in a practical sense. To move beyond this it is important to see generalization to the universal as an aspiration, an always unfinished achievement, rather than the confirmation of a pre-formed law. Then it is possible to notice that universal aspirations must travel across distances and differences, and we can take this travel as an ethnographic object.

Ethnographers are supposed to study their objects with respect. Yet cultural anthropologists have had a curmudgeonly suspicion of universals. Empowered by the notion of cultural relativism, anthropologists have argued that universals are folk beliefs, like gods or ghosts, with efficacy only within the cultural system that gives them life. I was brought up as a scholar in this creed, and it has taken me a long time—and a lot of frustrating interchanges with nonanthropologists—to decide that it is not a good place to enter the conversation. Universals are indeed local knowledge in the sense that they cannot be understood without the benefit of historically specific cultural assumptions. But to stop here makes dialogue impossible. Furthermore, it misses the point. To turn to universals is to identify knowledge that moves—mobile and mobilizing—across localities and cultures. Whether it is seen as underlying or transcending cultural difference, the mission of the universal is to form bridges, roads, and channels of circulation. Knowledge gained from particular experience percolates into these channels, widening rather than interrupting them. We must step outside the boundaries of locality to ask what's meant by "universal."[8]

One place to begin is with the accomplishments of the universal. Consider environmental politics. Environmentalists pioneered transboundary approaches in the 1980s and 1990s, drawing recognition to problems—pollution, climate change, species loss—that could not be contained in a single country. Transnational groups of scientists, with a common universalist faith in environmental objects of knowledge, were sometimes—against so much precedent—able to overcome national politics to work together and forge common standards. The most successful transnational mobilizations, it turned out, have been culturally and politically delimited, as when scientists working on transboundary acid rain collaborated with politicians to solidify the European Union (Rotmans 1995a).⁹ They have also been productive in relation to particular historical moments, as environmentalism in Eastern Europe and the former Soviet Union worked to popularize opposition to the state in the late 1980s (Jancar-Webster 1993). The universalism of environmental politics articulated widespread desires for knowledge free from state regulation and for ties with the cultural heritage of Western Europe. Freedom and science augmented each other's universal claims. After the breakup of the Soviet Union, environmental politics all but disappeared as the politics of citizenship rather than universalism took precedence.

Environmental politics in the disintegrating Soviet Union of the late 1980s was interpreted abroad as anti-Communist agitation. This association smoothed the way for Indonesian environmentalists, who had to find their way within a violently anti-Communist state. Where charges of Communism blocked other social movements, environmentalists were able to appeal to universal ideals of science and modernity. As in socialist Europe, universals opened possibilities for reform and even social criticism by articulating a larger frame of reference than state-led patriotism.¹⁰ But, as in Europe, this combination of appeals to science and politics worked best in the shadow of an authoritarian state. When the regime fell, politics took off in multiple new directions.

The universals that mobilize people, then, do not fulfill their own dreams to travel anywhere at any time. But this does not make them wrong-headed and irrelevant. Critical environmental scholars who address the problem have often taken us directly to the local, endorsing local or indigenous knowledge as the counterpart to universalist expertise. This reaction draws attention to cultural specificity but again misses the point. The knowledge that makes a difference in changing the world is knowledge that travels and mobilizes, shifting and creating new forces and agents of history in its path. However, those who claim to be in touch with the universal are notoriously bad at seeing the limits and exclusions of their knowledge. That's where my challenge enters.

Universals are effective within particular historical conjunctures that give them content and force. We might specify this conjunctural feature of universals in practice by speaking of engagement. Engaged universals travel across difference and are charged and changed by their travels. Through friction, universals become practically effective. Yet they can never fulfill their promises of universality. Even in transcending localities, they don't take over the world. They are limited by the practical necessity of mobilizing adherents. Engaged universals must convince us to pay attention to them. *All* universals are engaged when considered as practical projects accomplished in a heterogeneous world.

To study engagement requires turning away from formal abstractions to see how universals are used.[11] Universalisms have not been politically neutral. They were deeply implicated in the establishment of European colonial power. In the context of colonial expansion, universalism was the framework for a faith in the traveling power of reason: Only reason could gather up the fragments of knowledge and custom distributed around the world to achieve progress, science, and good government. In the matrix of colonialism, universal reason became the mark of temporally dynamic and spatially expansive forms of knowledge and power. Universal reason, of course, was best articulated by the colonizers. In contrast, the colonized were characterized by particularistic cultures; here, the particular is that which cannot grow. The universal, however, opens the way to constantly improving truths and even, in its utilitarian forms, to a better life for all humanity. These contrasts continue to structure global asymmetries.

At the same time, this history does not encompass the variety of claims of universality that characterize our times. Actually existing universalisms are hybrid, transient, and involved in constant reformulation through dialogue. Liberal universals mix and meld with the universals of science, world religions (especially Christianity and Islam), and emancipatory philosophies including Marxism and feminism. Moreover, the embrace of universals is not limited to just one small section of the globe. The West can make no exclusive claim to doctrines of the universal. Radical thinkers in Europe's colonies long ago expanded Enlightenment universals to argue that the colonized should be free, thus establishing doctrines of universal freedom at the base of Third World nationalisms.[12] The universalism of rights and reason continues to inspire critical post-colonial theory. At the same time, universal claims that justify coercion into internationally mandated standards of progress and order are at the center of neocolonial disciplinary programs— just as they were to colonialism.[13]

This brings to light a deep irony: Universalism is implicated in *both* imperial schemes to control the world and liberatory mobilizations for justice and empowerment. Universalism inspires expansion—for both the powerful and the powerless. Indeed, when those excluded from universal rights protest their exclusion, this protest itself has a twofold effect: It extends the reach of the forms of power they protest, even as it gives voice to their anger and hope. Political theorist Etienne Balibar refers to "normalization" and "insurrection" as equally inspired by universals (2002). This duality brings us back to the facility of universals for travel. Universals beckon to elite and excluded alike.[14]

The concept of friction acknowledges this duality and puts it at the heart of our understanding of "modern" global interconnections, that is, those that have developed under the aegis of Enlightenment universals. Friction gives purchase to universals, allowing them to spread as frameworks for the practice of power. But engaged universals are never fully successful in being everywhere the same because of this same friction. This book tells the story of how some universals work out in particular times and places, through friction.

The book is divided into three parts, and the title of each corresponds to a universalist dream: prosperity, knowledge, and freedom. These labels, however, should not mislead readers to assume that the book tells the story of philosophy or policy. Instead, my tale descends directly into the realm of historical experience. What is prosperity? In Kalimantan, Indonesia, in the 1990s, prosperity ripped up the forest landscape and dispossessed its human inhabitants to offer quick profits to a privileged or tricky few. The first section of the book asks just how aspirations for prosperity and progress produced this situation. What did it mean to be an entrepreneur in this historical landscape? The universals of market rationality are hardly a sheltering guide in entering this zone of robbery, violence, and confusion. Friction is all around.

What is knowledge? It would be easier for everyone if rational deliberations always converged in common understandings. But even those of us who believe that some knowledge claims are better than others have difficulty in denying that even the best ones retain a certain incommensurability. This is because knowledge claims emerge in relation to concrete problems and possibilities for dialogue—the productive features of friction. The second section of the book considers how friction morphs both knowledge of the globe and globally traveling knowledge.

And freedom? Throughout its history, freedom has refused to stick to predictable principles; it has blossomed and set into a multitude of previously unknown fruits. Even during the Enlightenment, the fact that the freedom of property ownership could not be reconciled with the emancipation of the dispossessed kept advocates busy devising contradictory schemes. The environmental politics of the late twentieth century was inspired by many divergent meanings of freedom—and they intrigue me as forms of freedom precisely because they do not jump to mind as its purest forms. Here rights discourse is extended beyond the limits of its humanism. Might not other species—and perhaps even landscapes and ecosystems—have rights with a status above and prior to human social conventions? The jurisdiction of modernity is turned inside out: Indigenous cultures deserve Enlightenment rights and liberties precisely because they have managed so far to do without them. It is within these jumbled and utopian causes that concepts of freedom are invigorated and made worthwhile for our times. My third section considers the accumulation of meanings and genealogies of freedom that has placed forest protection at the forefront of causes for making a livable world.

These concerns bring me back to the questions I raised earlier in this introduction: Why is global capitalism so messy? Who speaks for nature? What kinds of social justice make sense in the twenty-first century?

Beyond Globalization

The great insight of the protests against corporate globalization that gathered force at the turn of the twenty-first century was that current forms of capitalist expansion are not inevitable. Despite the reassurances of public oratory, the spread of capitalism has been violent, chaotic, and divisive, rather than smoothly all-encompassing. Observers laughed at protesters for lacking an appreciation of the force of global integration, and, indeed, for not seeing their own "globalization." Yet the protesters proved more insightful than sophisticated social theorists, who have been caught up in showing the programmatic advance of an integrated globalism of everywhere-flowing money, people, and culture.

To grasp the enormity of global changes in the last decade, social theorists drew a picture of evolutionary change on a planetary scale. Particularly influential were optimistic popular accounts of the spread of the market economy and Western liberal democracy (e.g., Fukuyama 1992; Friedman 2000). However, scholars on both the Left and the Right portrayed globalization as the worldwide advance to a global era.[15] Their stories share a commitment to a coordinated world transition, emerging from global centers and extending—through the technological collapse of distance—across the earth.

After the 2001 Al Qaeda attack on New York's World Trade Center and the ensuing U.S. leadership in worldwide re-militarization, the story of an inevitable, peaceful transition to global integration has seemed more and more like the dream of a particular historical moment. This is not because the force of global connections has disappeared—but it no longer looks so neat. Ten years ago social analysts were impressed by the size and power of newly emergent global circulations, so they focused on global coherence, for better or worse. Now it is time to turn attention, instead, to discontinuity and awkward connection, as this proves key to emergent sources of fear and hope.

On capitalism: In the last two decades of the twentieth century, capitalism was transformed by the establishment of new international rules of trade that offered tremendous advantages for the world's most powerful corporations. Capital whizzed around the globe. Free-trade zones and new technologies of communication encouraged companies to spread their operations to ever-cheaper locations. Transnational specializations—such as currency traders, energy traders—flourished. Privatization initiatives and free-trade regulations dismantled national economies, making once-public resources available for private appropriation.

Social analysts were awed by the scope of this project. Perhaps the most important responses were those that reminded readers that capitalism is a structured social system and not just the amassment of individual desires. Such responses necessarily stressed the internal coherence of capitalism. They showed the dangers not just of excesses of corruption but of basic principles of exploitation. It was this return to basics that made analysts focus on the global replication of new configurations of capital, labor, and technology. Yet now such simplifications seem inadequate. The idiosyncrasies of regional histories and persistent issues of violence and racial stratification have become pressing. War has reemerged as a central force for capitalism. Cultural genealogies no longer seem epiphenomena of economic change.

Most Marxist cultural theory of the late twentieth century focused on those forms—such as postmodernism—imagined at the forefront of the evolution of a monolithic capitalism.[16] Yet, once we abandon this evolutionary view, we can attend to the experiences of those whose stories "fall away" from the official ladder of progress (Tadiar forthcoming). New projects of connection and hegemony are emerging here. We see this for example in the importance of rural areas—completely ignored in evolutionary cultural theories—in key capitalist realignments and anti-globalization struggles. But this is the realm of friction: Unexpected alliances arise, remaking global possibilities.

Rather than assume we know exactly what global capitalism is, even before it arrives, we need to find out how it operates in friction. Chapters 1 and 2 develop this idea. Instead of rushing toward global spatial compression, I examine the links between heterogeneous projects of space and scale making, as these both enable capitalist proliferation and embroil it in moments of chaos. In tracing the connections through which entrepreneurship operates, the cultural work of encounter emerges as formative.

On nature as knowledge: Late twentieth-century excitement about global integration gave new impetus to those who hoped to use advances in scientific knowledge as a force for global progress. This has been nowhere more evident than in the field of environmental conservation. Conservationists have been eager to promote global knowledge and agreement, which might save endangered species and environments before it is too late.

Yet conservationist efforts have been impeded by the rise of other forms of globally circulating knowledge. Transnational political and informational networks have allowed public criticisms of conservationist projects to circulate widely. Even environmental activists may or may not agree with the established truths of conservation science. Meanwhile, public relations companies have made it possible to counter conservationist campaigns by spreading "alternative" science as well as self-conscious misinformation. As a result, political leaders and courts, as well as ordinary citizens, have been flooded with competing environmental perspectives. Each of these sources of criticism has forced conservationists to recall that global knowledge is neither monolithic nor settled.[17]

Many commentators move from this observation to what has been called the "science wars," the debate over whether science is a privileged form of truth or a political imposition.[18] Yet it seems better to explore just how knowledge moves. For this, it is important to learn about the collaborations through which knowledge is made and maintained. Conservation inspires collaborations among scientists, business, forest dwellers, state regulators, the public, and nonhumans. Through the frictions of such collaborations, global conservation projects—like other forms of traveling knowledge—gain their shape.[19]

Collaboration is not a simple sharing of information. There is no reason to assume that collaborators share common goals. In transnational collaborations, overlapping but discrepant forms of cosmopolitanism may inform contributors, allowing them to converse—but across difference.

Attention to collaboration moves discussion beyond the eternal standoff between opposing interest groups (e.g., the south and the north; the rich and the poor), but not because it assumes that compromise is always imminent. Collaborations create *new* interests and identities, but not to everyone's benefit. In standardizing global knowledge, for example, truths that are incompatible are suppressed. Globally circulating knowledge creates new gaps even as it grows through the frictions of encounter.

Drawing from the insights of science studies and environmental history, chapters 3, 4, and 5 develop these ideas. Here I explore in more depth the relation between collaboration and generalization to the universal.

On social justice: The possibilities of thinking globally have inspired social movements of all kinds to imagine global causes. Yet global politics creates special problems. Social justice goals must be negotiated not only across class, race, gender, nationality, culture, and religion, but also between the global south and the global north, and between the great mega-cities of the world and their rural and provincial hinterlands. Coalition politics is essential. Yet what does it mean to work in coalition? The twentieth-century class-based solidarity model asks coalition allies to line up as parallel equivalents. Allies rarely line up that well. Without even intending to break the line, they push in new directions. Their friction changes everyone's trajectory.

Furthermore, without the unifying frame of the state, what politics do transnational allies have in common? Post–Cold War social justice movements have tended to solve this problem by invoking the universal language of the Enlightenment, with its concurrence of justice and freedom. Human rights, feminist, and environmental causes have been influential across the world in part because of their language of universal rights. Whatever attempts activists have made at building politically sensitive coalitions have had to take place within this commitment to universal rights.

Yet, does this language offer its own political conditions, neutralizing meaningful coalition? Teaching a language of universal rights can foreclose other trajectories. Participants may be drawn into a framework of global observation and classification in which cultural difference becomes yet another brick of administrative data with which to be walled in. The importance of liberal frameworks in global social justice politics raises a number of issues for research. How do activists use globally circulating political rhetorics to devise and manage coalitions? How do logics of classification order differences among coalition partners even as they make it possible for them to work together? At the same time, how do encounters across difference exceed their disciplined boundaries to make new forms of politics possible? Chapters 6 and 7 explore these features of politics-in-friction.

It Didn't Have to Happen That Way

A bit of history offers a concrete illustration of friction and sets the stage for the chapters that follow. As inevitable as the story of resource exploitation may seem in hindsight, it is important to note that Indonesian tropical rainforests were not harvested as industrial timber until the 1970s. Situated at the confluence of the deep-historical commerce of the Indian Ocean and the China Sea, the Indonesian islands are hardly newcomers to world trade. Products from Indonesia's rainforests have spread around the world for many centuries. Yet the very biological productiveness that made these forests rich sources of commodities also blocked their use for industrial timber. Large-scale loggers prefer forests in which one valuable species predominates; tropical rainforests are just too biologically diverse. While colonial loggers prized Java's semi-tropical teak forests, they pretty much ignored the wetter and more heterogeneous tropical rainforests of the islands of Kalimantan, Sumatra, Sulawesi, and Papua.[20]

All of this changed rather suddenly in the early 1970s, when Japanese general trading companies, the *sogo shosha*, hooked up with the New Order regime of President Suharto, which had come to power in the blood of a great massacre. The New Order promised to solve the country's economic problems through the magic of foreign investment and loans.[21] The government threw its weight into logging; a flood of foreign investment followed.[22] State-making soon became entangled with logging as concessions were distributed to political clients, who made "voluntary" contributions to the regime's favored development initiatives.[23] The sogo shosha, which aimed to control trade, not production, offered loans and arranged trade agreements. Hungry for large quantities of cheaply produced logs, rather than for quality control, they were comfortable with ecological shortsightedness. In 1971, they cut from the Japanese trade all logs produced by nonmechanized (and ecologically less harmful) logging, thus cementing the new logging regime. By 1973, Indonesia was the world's largest tropical timber exporter (Ascher 1998).

Stories of the disastrous projects of transnational corporations and corrupt politicians have become commonplace, and this encounter perhaps just seems an ordinary link on a global chain. My point, however, is that the specific features of the link have ramifying effects. New trajectories for business practice, natural resource management, and class formation gelled from these specifics. Three features of these trajectories are especially relevant to my story. First, the rainforest was magnified in importance, simplified, and mischaracterized as a sustainable resource in the encounter between Japanese trading companies and Indonesian politicians. Forest simplification became a model for resource management and the organization of business more generally. Industrial tree plantations were later planted in place of natural forests. (Consider in contrast the no better but quite different trope of productive forest conversion, as in Brazilian cattle ranching.) Second, the adoption of the trading company model of amassment and market control accommodated forms of state-making in which public and private became hopelessly confused. (In contrast, the U.S. model of privatization continually converts public goods to private ones.) Third, the complicity of legal and illegal entrepreneurs, working at different scales, displaced indigenous rights and fueled regional boom-and-bust economies. I elaborate briefly.

The link between Japanese trading companies and Indonesian politicians created a new way of seeing the forest. Instead of biodiversity, loggers now saw only one family of trees, the dipterocarps. Dipterocarps are remarkable giants emerging out of the lower canopy to tower over the forest. But dipterocarp species are diverse, and individuals grow among many other families and species; there are no pure stands. Only in the peculiar circumstances of the Japanese-Indonesian connection were loggers able to imagine the rainforest as if it were a pure stand.[24] Dipterocarps—remade as disposable plywood for the Japanese construction industry—all looked alike, and the rest of the trees, herbs, fungi, and fauna became waste products. This change also emptied the forest, conceptually, of human residents, since the fruit orchards, rattans, and other human-tended plants of forest dwellers were now mere waste. Logging companies were free to harvest these newly "uninhabited" forest landscapes.

In the 1980s, Indonesian businessmen turned against the export of profits to Japan, but in a particular way: by mimicking the sogo shosha. Indonesia banned the export of raw logs and built its own plywood industry.[25] Under the leadership of the President's close friend, Mohamad "Bob" Hasan, the Indonesian Wood Panel Association, or APKINDO (*Asosiasi Panel Kayu Indonesia*), formed as a national marketing apparatus with control over plywood exports. APKINDO self-consciously adopted the Japanese trading model: forcing particular trading chains; taking over all middleman functions; controlling volume, price, and low-cost finance; and using government backing to maintain dominance. All plywood firms had to participate. From this position of control, APKINDO flooded world markets with low-cost plywood.[26] Most dramatically, it broke into the Japanese market, underselling Japanese manufacturers despite protective tariffs. "We're the only guys in Southeast Asia who fight the sogo shosha," boasted Hasan.[27]

After the fall of the New Order, APKINDO became a symbol of corruption: Hasan had used his connections to force a whole industry into submission, and he had made a fortune in the process.[28] But during the New Order, his success formed a model for building the nation. Other products were organized into similar cartels and monopolies. In his brief moment of glory as Minister of Finance and Trade in 1998, Hasan explained this business-oriented patriotism: "Monopolies are okay. As long as the monopoly serves the interests of many people, it's okay."[29]

As the identity of the nation became entangled with forest destruction, logging concessions became a clear sign of regime connections.[30] The state depended more heavily on the off-budget finance obtained from such favors. The forests became even more badly degraded. The encounter between Japanese trading companies and Indonesian politicians had been effective. The sogo shosha model held sway even though Indonesian cronies had replaced the Japanese. And the simplification of the forest as an uninhabited dipterocarp stand—the product of that encounter—formed the basis for a national economy based increasingly on what post–New Order Indonesians call "KKN," that is, corruption, collusion, and nepotism (*korupsi, kolusi, nepotisme*).

By the 1990s, KKN was distributed from top to bottom. As state rhetoric turned from communal development to private entrepreneurship, small businessmen, village leaders, ambitious youth, migrants, thieves, police, and petty gangsters all got involved in rerouting public resources as private gain. Where resource extraction licenses were not obtained through national channels, they were faked or fixed locally; illegal logging and mining became the systematic adjunct of legal exploitation. Illegal extractions proceeded as scaled-down versions of legal ones. In logging, district officials made arrangements with private operators, obtaining off-budget financing for their projects. Village heads were sometimes brought inside these arrangements, exchanging permission to log village forests for their own off-budget funding.[31] The 1998 fall of the New Order did not improve the situation. The decentralization of natural resource permits in 2000 spread the possibilities for corruption.[32] Illegal resource extraction rocketed out of control.

Ties between illegal and legal enterprise have been close. Most importantly, their collaboration undermines pre-existing property rights and access conventions, making everything free. Either official or unofficial alone could be challenged, but together they overwhelm local residents, who generally have been unable to defend their lands and resources against this combination of legal and illegal, big and small. Together, they transform the countryside into a free-for-all frontier.

The same period I have just reviewed saw the rise of a vigorous national environmental movement.[33] In the 1980s and the early 1990s, a period of serious government repression, environmentalism was essentially the *only* pluralist social justice movement that flourished across Indonesia.[34] As such, it drew social reformers of many sorts and became the vehicle for many, sometimes contradictory, hopes. The movement was an amalgam of odd parts: engineers, nature lovers, reformers, technocrats. Modernizing experts and romantic populists rubbed shoulders there. Social justice advocates made plans with sympathetic regime bureaucrats. In the repressive political climate of those years, even the bravest activists were cautious about what they said and did. Still, questions of freedom welled up, and activists argued against the hegemony of centralized development with ideas of human rights, farmers' rights, and indigenous rights.[35] In the mid-1990s, the easing of state vigilance allowed other causes to take the public spotlight, including democracy, labor, student activism, freedom of speech. However, environmentalism played a role in articulating dissatisfaction with the state—especially in regard to rural issues—through the decisive mobilizations that led to Suharto's resignation in 1998.[36]

In the 1980s and 1990s, the movement was organized around difference, within the framework of nationalist advocacy. Rather than build a single centralized policy board, the movement was committed to negotiating among small groups organized by place, issue, or campaign. For most of this time, the movement imagined itself as coordinating already existing but scattered and disorganized rural complaints. Activists' jobs, as they imagined it, involved translating subaltern demands into the languages of the powerful, including English. They offered themselves to document injustice, meet with ministers, and bring forward court cases. Translating back to let people know their rights—in barefoot legal clinics, meetings, or vernacular versions of international agreements—was equally important on the agenda. In their public representations, activists perhaps underestimated the messiness of the work of translation, but their practices jumped into the middle of it. (The prominence of women in leadership positions was explained to me in relation to women's facility with languages.[37]) Rural campaigns in particular required engagement across differences not just of language but of multiple registers of life experience.

Within the links of awkwardly transcended difference, the environmental movement has tried to offer an alternative to forest destruction and the erosion of indigenous rights. The second half of this book explores this theme. To get there, I begin in the first part with the social links and cultural practices that made deforestation a destructive "business-as-usual." I then turn to a wider interplay of transnational, national, and regional forms of knowledge about the forest. When I describe the environmental movement, I place it in relation to two of its persistent interlocutors: student nature lovers and village leaders. I show how the environmental movement came to depend on links with these groups, even while developing its own distinctive perspectives. In the last chapter, I consider a case in which these three groups reached across their differences to reclaim "community forests." Their collaborations—like those of legal and illegal businessmen—rearrange property. Just as the encounter of Japanese trading companies and Indonesian politicians produced simplified dipterocarp forests, these activist-inspired encounters may yet produce new kinds of forests. This theme—the possibilities of friction—is explored and extended in all the chapters that follow.

Prosperity

Better you had brought me a bomb . . .

"Better you had brought me a bomb, so I could blow this place up"

[The unseemly viewpoint of despair]

Development has been portrayed as a great machine for manufacturing prosperity in poor countries. In New Order Indonesia, development was the state religion. President Suharto was the "father of development."

In the 1970s, development looked to technopolitics: the transformation of tradition into modernity. Big dams would water dry fields; the Green Revolution would make rice spring up; natural resources would enrich the nation. In the 1980s, the miracle of a growth-based nation arose. Indonesia became a "tiger" with its own dynamic capitalism. In the 1990s, privatization spread like wildfire around the world. In Kalimantan, privatization took a particular form: the intertwined growth of legal and illegal resource extraction. Together, big and small operators advanced privatization through military and political force, displacing earlier residents' resource rights. As in a war campaign, a few heroes were raised and many sank unnamed—collateral damage.

After the economic crisis of 1997–98, development experts rushed to criticize 1990s' practices as improper market discipline. If only they hadn't distorted the market! Surely there would have been prosperity. The experts imagine the perfect market, pure as one of Plato's universal forms. Yet markets are made in the friction of political and cultural circumstances.

The 1990s' frictions in Kalimantan moved in multiple directions. Centralized reform chased well-publicized fiascoes; less remarked-upon scams materialized at every level. Perspectives fragmented as people found themselves in diverse circumstances. Privatization was experienced as a multiplication of private fortunes as well as communal losses interpreted as personal woes. To ask about this heterogeneity does not require that we reduce all development to unabated greed. My goal is to channel attention to the unevenness of expectations and fortunes within this political economy of development, violence, reform, despair, and prosperity. Prosperity is best understood through its disparities.

Prosperity is formed in friction. Prosperity separates haves and have-nots within local conditions for the enforcement of property rights. These local conditions shape market economies, whose universals cannot transcend politically managed questions of access.

1997. My activist friends in Jakarta are optimistic. The regime's grip is loosening. New forms of mobilization seem possible. One activist explains to me the "generations" of Indonesian advocacy: the first generation spawned charity organizations; the second, development organizations; the third, issue-oriented activism. The fourth generation is democratic agitation. Its time has come.

The news of the Asian financial crisis has not yet hit.

Everyone is talking about community-based natural resource management. No one can resist it. The foreign foundations are pushing it. The government is interested. The corporations will have to deal with mobilized communities, who know their resource rights.

Jakarta friends warn me that the level of activism in South Kalimantan is currently low. There is not much going on other than "second generation" development work.

When I arrive in Banjarmasin, the capital of South Kalimantan, I find myself in another world. There is quite a bit of activism, more than I have seen before. But most is conducted in a regional Muslim idiom that might make it unrecognizable in Jakarta. Furthermore, I sense an enormous confusion about how to proceed. Not so long before, rioters burned down the downtown shopping areas, along with churches and offices. My friends blame the people; angry and aroused, without discipline, they created their own hell. To many, piety seems a better goal than democracy.

The situation in the countryside is even more confusing. Resource extraction has reached a feverish peak, with corporations as well as ordinary people fanning across the land to pick up what they can. No one is talking about community-based resource management. It is hard to identify "communities." Every man seems out for himself. No one cares to protect the environment, activists tell me, because greed now rules the land.

Pak Arman is particularly sensitive to these issues because he has just returned from studying in Jakarta. He has been energized by Jakarta optimism, and he doesn't yet know what to do in Banjarmasin.

"We are only spectators," he says with frustration. "We can only watch what is happening. First they take the trees. When the trees are finished, they come for the gold. When the gold is finished, they come for the coal. When the coal is finished, they come for the marble. When the marble is finished . . . they'll take whatever is left."

I don't know if he knows of the famous lines about the Holocaust.

Pak Arman details for me the resource extraction projects that have been initiated in the region. There is the government. The government plans to open one million hectares of wet rice paddies in Central Kalimantan, using transmigrants from Java as their labor force. "One million hectares, one million problems," Pak Arman explains. On those lands live Dayaks, who make a decent living raising water buffaloes. What will happen to them? The lands, too, will be damaged. The regional ecology is regulated by sensitive blackwater swamps. Pak Arman was not yet aware of the worst of this experiment. The rice was a disaster. The residents were resettled and their livelihood destroyed. By 2000, the project had made lists of the worst environmental disasters of all time (WALHI 2000: 2).

But we are in 1997, and this is not the most severe of Kalimantan's problems. The devastating forest fires have not yet begun. Pak Arman explains that gold mining has penetrated deep into the Meratus Mountains, spreading mercury through the waters. Trucks of coal and marble move constantly at night. He has joined campaigns and prepared legal cases against mining-related cultural and environmental destruction, but his cause is losing. And it is not just companies. Individual miners spread out over the land, looking for new sites. It is "our people," he says, not anyone else. It is hard to differentiate the bad guys from the good. "There are so many problems, we don't know how to address them."

"Kalimantan is being destroyed," he says. He is not optimistic. "This is the end of Kalimantan. We have become nothing but spectators."

....

On my way into the countryside, it is not difficult to find more optimistic individuals: the entrepreneurs and migrants who are hoping to gain from the flow of natural resources. Everyone assumes that I, too, am looking for resources; can my survey team offer a job? What about a loan for a really promising scheme?

Sutanto is a Javanese who moved to Kalimantan with nothing; now he has a lot going. The youngest of ten siblings, he moved first to a transmigration camp, where he was given a one-year supply of food and seed, tools, a house, and agricultural land. After a year, the transmigrants received title to their property. They were expected to become farmers and work on nearby plantations, but this was not a lucrative alternative. Like many of the others, Sutanto sold the house and land to other Javanese migrants, and he moved to a Meratus Dayak village to become an entrepreneur in the resource extraction boom.

Since then, he has participated in every resource scheme—logs, ores, forest products, even sand. For the moment, he also has opened a food stall and he is using it as a transport terminal to haul resources out of the region. He has brought other Javanese transmigrants into the village to help with his schemes, and now there is a lively Javanese community there. "This area will never progress without Javanese," he says. "They must bring in transmigrants for real development." The government is planning to start a housing and farm location program for "local transmigrants," and he plans to participate again in this government handout, acquiring more property to sell for his businesses.

He is enthusiastic about the prospects, and he urges me to join in. "Lend me twenty million rupiah," he says, "I'll buy a truck. You can make Rp. 200,000 a day with your own truck here. You can carry sand, stones, wood. If you carry a cubic meter of wood, you get Rp. 25,000; if you carry four cubic meters, isn't that Rp. 100,000? You can do this many times a day. If you buy the truck on credit, it's only fifteen million down. I'll give half your money to [my adopted sister] and put the rest in the bank for you when you come. You won't have any trouble when you are here. You'll just need the expenses for your trip.

"Kalimantan is rich with valuable things. Stones [e.g., coal]. Wood. Marble. The companies haven't taken out any of these materials here! Move here and build a house. It's a great place to trade. There are all kinds of fruits that aren't even eaten; you won't have to buy anything at the market. You can get lots of money!

"So you're a teacher: There's an opening at the elementary school. You can teach a little and have plenty of time to trade as well. You would only have to teach a few hours, and you could trade and see your family. It's a good life making money here."

....

An asphalt road has just been built to the village of Kalawan. It is only about four feet wide, but trucks take it constantly, right up to Sutanto's food stall. Not knowing about the road, I had been looking forward to the hike to the village after a long bus ride. But a motorcyclist takes me, charging me double the customary price when he realizes I am surprised to see the road. On the side of the road are piles of rubber and sand, waiting to be transported. An official convoy speeds by toward a newly formed county seat, in the heart of Meratus resource lands. The neat homes of new Javanese migrants line the entrance to the village. A laborer in dirty clothes sings a refrain: "Wherever the money is . . ."

At Sutanto's food stall, I ask for my sister and Meratus Dayak mentor Uma Adang and I learn that she is living away from the road, in the forest. She never comes in, people say.

Indeed, she has cast herself as an old woman. Ten years ago, she was a respected leader, consulted by all about custom, religion, and culture. Now she is strong enough to clear a field or lead a survey team for a wage, but not, it seems, to hike a level twenty-minute trail to the road. What is out there anyway, except trucks shipping out the wealth of the land? Uma Adang tells me that every tree is coming down, including fruit and honey trees. You can get up to Rp. 150,000 for giving permission to fell a tree on your ancestral lands; you might as well give permission, because they will fell the tree whether you give it or not. You hear the sound of the chain saw; by the time you get there, the tree has been felled. Javanese migrants are moving in; sometimes they buy land, but usually they just take it. Everyone worries about whether to sell. But it doesn't matter because the police commander is selling land, claimed or not, for his own profit. Property signs have sprouted up along the main road. If you go to the main road, she says, you must have money. The Javanese are even carting out sand, at Rp. 40,000 a *ril*.

There is a lot going on for those who are ambitious enough to take it. For the rest, she says, there is almost nothing left. There is no more customary law and no more culture, she says. I will be disappointed in my stay, she tells me.

I draw out a bag of presents. Hers is a set of nesting containers to store dry foods; I have wrapped its big, rectangular box in bright paper, and it takes her a few moments to get it open. Before she has opened it, she has already registered her disappointment. "Better you had brought me a bomb, so I could blow this place up." I think at first she is joking. But later, she repeats the refrain. I realize she is seriously angry.

There are times that the only solution one can think about is bombing everyone.[1]

....

It takes me a long time to figure out whether and how to write about the deteriorating conditions I saw in Kalawan, not just in 1997, but throughout the 1990s and into the beginning of the twenty-first century. What are the stories that can be told about this place? There is no point in telling a story no one wants to hear.

People don't want to hear about victims. Many people benefit from resource booms. And why privilege indigenous residents over migrants? Cultures never sit still; it is nostalgia to speak out for what is being lost. Anthropologists have been especially cautious to avoid stories of "disappearing cultures": Those stories seem too caught up in a discredited connoisseurship of culture. In my own work, I have endorsed the promise of intercultural hybridity. But hybridity is not all promise, and neither is agency. Destruction too requires agency. To tell its stories, we cannot avoid the viewpoint of despair.

Others have, and will tell of the pleasures of resource booms. The need to understand capitalist expansion, however, inspires me in another direction: I will not erase the conditions of terror in which agency is sometimes formed. I will tell stories of destruction.

1 Frontiers of Capitalism

....

Clusters of red earth push up in broken bits,
as if asking in an angry fit:
   "Why did you let my humus flee?
   Why weren't forests replanted on me?
   How much longer must I endure,
   more than two decades and still no one cares?"

South Kalimantan gasps
Your breath, your life, sucked out, lapsed.
Who is ready to claim this disaster?
Which big man is prepared to answer?

My protests flare up, my blood boils
Is this true, the real face of Kalimantan?
Was it a lie, my vision of a vast great forest?
          —from Victor Roesdianto,
            "The Forests of South Kalimantan"[1]

proliferation: *1. Pathology, etc. The formation or development of cells by budding or division. 2. Enlargement or extension; an increase in number (of); now esp. of nuclear weapons.*[2]

What do cancer and nuclear weapons have in common? Their expansion, proliferation, is always already out of control. Proliferation, too, is a key principle of capitalist expansion, particularly at capitalist frontiers where accumulation is not so much primitive, that is, archaic, as savage. Frontiers are not just edges; they are particular kinds of edges where the expansive nature of extraction comes into its own. Built from historical models of European conquest, frontiers create wildness so that some—and not others—may reap its rewards. Frontiers are deregulated because they arise in the interstitial spaces made by collaborations among legitimate and illegitimate partners: armies and bandits; gangsters and corporations; builders and despoilers. They confuse the boundaries of law and theft, governance and violence, use and destruction. These confusions change the rules and thus enable extravagant new economies of profit—as well as loss.

The late twentieth century saw the creation of new "resource frontiers" in every corner of the world. Made possible by Cold War militarization of the Third World and the growing power of corporate transnationalism, resource frontiers grew up where entrepreneurs and armies were able to disengage nature from local ecologies and livelihoods, "freeing up" natural resources that bureaucrats and generals could offer as corporate raw materials. From a distance, these new resource frontiers appeared as the "discovery" of global supplies in forests, tundras, coastal seas, or mountain fastnesses. Up close, they replaced local systems of human access and livelihood and ecological dynamics of replacement and replenishment with the cultural apparatus of proliferation, out-of-control interstitial capitalist expansion, the frontier. This chapter explores the making of a resource frontier in the eastern part of South Kalimantan in the 1990s.

My goal in this chapter is both practical and poetic. To allow readers to feel the rawness of the frontier is also to make it less sensible and ordinary. Sensory absorption can, with luck, sweep away the "common sense" of resource exploitation and leave us with the moving force of anger. The poet Taufiq Ismail is said to have inaugurated the Indonesian environmental movement in a public reading of a poem containing the following lines in 1971 (Ismail 1971, discussed in Aditjondro 1991a, my translation):[3]

> *I want to write a poem that resists the probability that Japanese traders will plunder the wood of the forests of Kalimantan, that prohibits the oil drillers and foreign investors from feeding spiritually weak officials, and forbids bribes to customs officers and judges.*

My chapter shares this same goal.

The chapter is divided into two parts. First I tell of how the frontier and its resources are made. This section is based on ethnographic observation from the mid-1990s. Second, I turn to the post-1997 crisis, when frontier-making spiraled out of control.

I. How to Make Resources in Order to Destroy Them (and Then Save Them?) On the Salvage Frontier

A frontier is an edge of space and time: a zone of not yet—not yet mapped, not yet regulated. It is a zone of unmapping: even in its planning, a frontier is imagined as unplanned. Frontiers aren't just discovered at the edge; they are projects in making geographical and temporal experience. Frontiers make wildness, entangling visions and vines and violence; their wildness is *both* material and imaginative. This wildness reaches backward as well as forward in time, bringing old forms of savagery to life in the contemporary landscape. Frontiers energize old fantasies, even as they embody their impossibilities.

Most descriptions of resource frontiers take for granted the existence of resources; they label and count the resources and tell us who owns what. The landscape itself appears inert: ready to be dismembered and packaged for export. In contrast, the challenge I've set myself is to make the landscape a lively actor. Landscapes are simultaneously natural and social, and they shift and turn in the interplay of human and nonhuman practices. Frontier landscapes are particularly active: hills flood away, streams are stuck in mud, vines swarm over fresh stumps, ants and humans are on the move. On the frontier, nature goes wild.

The place I describe is a mountainous, forested strip of southeast Kalimantan. My companions in traveling and learning this landscape are Meratus Dayaks, old inhabitants whose livelihood has been based on shifting cultivation and forest foraging.[4] For Meratus, the frontier has come as a shock and a disruption; it is with their help that I experience the trauma of transformation. My account begins in the mid-1990s, when the New Order regime still seemed to stretch forward endlessly. By this time, privatization had become a regime watchword, in practice further concentrating economic power in the hands of the president's family and cronies. Huge tracts had been assigned to logging companies, mining companies, and pulp-and-paper as well as oil palm plantation companies. The military played an important role in transferring these tracts from previous residents to their corporate owners; military men also took their own interest in resources. This seminal period has shaped the wildness of the twenty-first century.

An Abandoned Logging Road Has Got to Be . . .

An abandoned logging road has got to be one of the most desolate places on earth. It doesn't go anywhere, by definition. If you are walking there, it is either because you are lost or you are trespassing, or both. The wet clay builds clods on your boots, if you have any, sapping your strength, and if you don't have any boots, the sun and the hot mud are unmerciful. Whole hillsides slide down beside you into the stagnant pools where the mosquitoes breed. Abandoned roads soon lose their shape, forcing you in and out of eroded canyons and over muddy trickles where bridges once stood but which are now choked by loose soil, vines crawling on disinterred roots and trunks sliding, askew. Yet, ironically, the forest as a site of truth and beauty seems so much clearer from the logging road than anywhere else, since it is the road that slices open the neat cross-section in which underbrush, canopy, and high emergents are so carefully structured.

In 1994, I walked on a lot of abandoned logging roads in southeastern Kalimantan between the Meratus Mountains and the coastal plains now covered with transmigration villages—Block A, Block B, Block C—and giant, miles-square plantations of oil palm, rubber, and acacia for the pulp and paper trade. In the 1980s, despite the logging, local villagers were asserting customary resource rights, and transmigration here was just a gleam in one engineer's eye, and he wasn't in charge. Now, the region had been overwhelmingly transformed. Even beyond the newly planted industrial tree plantations lay miles of scrub and vines. These were landslides of slippery red and yellow clay, with silt-laden excuses for water. The logging roads had eroded into tracks for motorcycles, water buffalo, and the still-streaming mass of immigrant and local blood and sweat that the government calls "wild": wild loggers, wild miners, and bands of roving entrepreneurs and thieves. Something easy to call degradation rode through the land: Human presence was leaving the terrain all but bare.

Such destruction is not just human nature or the nature of resources. In the violent clarity of the abandoned logging road, irreverent questions come to mind. How does nature at the frontier become a set of resources? How are landscapes made empty and wild so that anyone can come to use and claim them? How do ordinary people get involved in destroying their environments, even their own home places?

These questions can only be addressed by getting inside our daily habits and our dreams. Freeing "resources" opens the landscape in complementary nightmares. The frontier emerges in the intertwined attraction and disgust of their engagement. Order and progress banish imagined wildness; wildness emerges in a parody and recuperation of the worst dreams of order and progress. Monocrop plantations are the flip side of the wild resource frontier. Each calls the other into existence: On one side, endless rows of silent symmetry, biopower applied to trees; on the other side, wild loggers, miners, and villagers in the raucous, sped-up time of looting. Each solves the problems put in motion by the other. Each requires the same entrepreneurial spirit. In that spirit, gold nuggets, swallows' nests, incense woods, ironwood posts, great logs destined to be plywood, and whole plantations of future pulp are conjured. Here is a first answer to my questions. Resources are made by "resourcefulness" in both plantation and wild frontier. The activity of the frontier is to make human subjects as well as natural objects.

The frontier, indeed, had come to Kalimantan. It hadn't always been there. Dutch plantation schemes mainly bypassed Kalimantan in the colonial period before World War II, allowing colonial authorities to treat their natives as subjects of kingdoms and cultures. Kalimantan's Dayaks, while to them patently uncivilized, were still seen as having law and territorial boundaries, not a wilderness that needed to be filled up. In its first years the postcolonial nation maintained Kalimantan's villages, fields, and forests. Commercial logging only got underway in the 1970s. Administrative expansion and resettlement followed, with the goal of homogenizing the nation. In the 1980s, conflicts broke out between villagers and commercial loggers. Massive fires and waves of immigration disrupted emergent localisms. Through the 1980s, however, it was possible to see rural Kalimantan as a landscape of villages, small cultivations, and traditional agro-forestry, with discrete patches of estate agriculture and large-scale logging and mining here and there.

The late 1980s and 1990s witnessed a national wave of entrepreneurship. Spurred on by economic liberalization with its international sponsors, and a consolidating regional capitalism, entrepreneurs shot up at every level from conglomerates to peasant tour guides. In this great surge of resourcefulness Kalimantan became a frontier.

The frontier, then, is not a natural or indigenous category. It is a traveling theory, a foreign form requiring translation. It arrived with many layers of previous associations. "Indonesian Miners Revive Gold Rush Spirit of 49ers," crowed a headline in the *Los Angeles Times* (Williams 1988: 1). "Kalimantan at this time is part of the Wild West . . . like parts of America in the 19th century," despaired the Minister of the Environment (Gellert 1998: 82). Indonesian frontiers were shaped to the model of other wild times and places. Nor was the American West the only moment to be reworked and revived. There is the dark Latin American frontier: a place of violence, conflicting cultures, and an unforgiving nature driving once-civilized men to barbarism, as Domingo Sarmiento, soon to be president of Argentina, argued in 1845 (Sarmiento 1998). This savage vision of the frontier has continued to percolate through later frontier optimism. There is the nation-making frontier, as famously articulated by Frederick Jackson Turner in his 1893 address, "The Significance of the Frontier in American History" (Turner 1994). Wild, empty spaces are said to have inspired white men to national democracy and freedom in the United States. Amazing for its erasures, the power of this formulation is suggested by the fact that U.S. historians remained in its thrall for nearly a hundred years.[5] Furthermore, the story of frontier progress was remade in an internationally colonizing form after World War II in the concept of the technofrontier, the endless frontier made possible by industrial technology. The closing of national borders need no longer just lead to nostalgia; the technofrontier is open and expanding. In the guise of development, the technofrontier dream hit Indonesian centers hard in the late 1960s. By the 1990s, it had dragged its older frontier cousins, those entangled stories of the wild, to the rural peripheries.

Frontiers are notoriously unstable, and it is fitting that Kalimantan landscapes should have a role in forging new frontier conceptions. The frontier arrived in Kalimantan *after* environmentalism had already become established not just among activists but also in government and corporate public relations. No one could be surprised this time to find that frontier-making is destructive of forests and indigenous cultures. Susanna Hecht and Alexander Cockburn wrote that in the Amazon, heroic development plans unexpectedly turned to smoke, mud, and violence: "The generals had unleashed forces beyond their control, and now the Amazon faced its apocalypse" (1990: 141). But in New Order Kalimantan, the Amazon apocalypse was already known. Plans were set in motion to save the environment in the process of destroying it. Tree plantations were introduced to restore deforested and degraded land. Only then was the landscape deforested and degraded to make way for the restorative tree plantations. Giant mining conglomerates were licensed to save the land from the depredation of wild miners, yet legal and illegal prospectors were inseparable. "They go where we go," a Canadian engineer explained, "and sometimes we follow them" (Williams 1988: 1). Indonesian timber and plywood tycoon Bob Hasan hosted a 10K "Run for the Rainforest" and raked in international environmental prizes.[6] "Indonesians don't destroy their forests," he told reporters, "We are just given a little time to manage [the forest] for others" (Vidal 1990). This is the salvage frontier, where making, saving, and destroying resources are utterly mixed up, where zones of conservation, production, and resource sacrifice overlap almost fully, and canonical time frames of nature's study, use, and preservation are reversed, conflated, and confused.

By this point it should be clear that by frontier I don't mean a place or even a process but an imaginative project capable of molding both places and processes. Frederick Jackson Turner describes the frontier as "the meeting point between savagery and civilization" (1994: 32). It is a site of transformations; "the wilderness masters the colonist. . . . Little by little he masters the wilderness" (33). It is a space of desire: it calls; it appears to create its own demands; once glimpsed, one cannot but explore and exploit it. Frontiers have their own technologies of space and time: Their emptiness is expansive, spreading across the land; they draw the quick, erratic temporality of rumor, speculation, and cycles of boom and bust, encouraging ever-intensifying forms of resourcefulness. On the Kalimantan salvage frontier, frontier intensification and proliferation lurch forward in a hall of mirrors, becoming showy parodies of themselves. Time moves so quickly that results precede their causes, and the devastation expected behind the line of frontier expansion suddenly appears, as it seems, ahead of its advance.

The Kalimantan frontier is not the enactment of a principle of commodification or conquest. The commodification of forest products is centuries old in this area, and while the new frontier draws on the earlier trade, its appearance is not a logical intensification. The frontier is not a philosophy but rather a series of historically nonlinear leaps and skirmishes that come together to create their own intensification and proliferation.[7] As these kinds of moves are repeated, they gain a cultural productiveness even in their quirky unpredictability. Thus, Marianne Schmink and Charles Wood (1992) describe frontiers in Amazonia as a series of ironic twists. Planned communities lead to unplanned settlement; resource nationalization leads to private control; land titling leads to forgery; military protection leads to generalized violence. Such twists are more than irony: They predict and perform their own reversals, forming productive confusions and becoming models for other frontiers. In Kalimantan, related paradoxes produce frontier degradation and salvage. The frontier is made in the shifting terrain between legality and illegality, public and private ownership, brutal rape and passionate charisma, ethnic collaboration and hostility, violence and law, restoration and extermination.

Legal, Illegal

Shifting cultivation is illegal in Indonesia, despite the fact that it is the major subsistence technology for many rural people, including Meratus Dayaks. Perhaps that is why, as I hiked down the Meratus Mountains into the eastern coastal plains with Meratus friends, the lines of legality were not clear to me, and I was hardly aware that the immigrant loggers I passed were out of bounds, wild men. As soon as we hit the old logging roads, we found them, singly or in groups of three or four, each with a small chain saw or a water buffalo to haul out the logs. Their living places were bed-sized bamboo platforms along the road with only a sheet of plastic hung over to keep out the rain; they seemed to have no possessions but a coffee pot and a can of mackerel, poor man's sardines. We stopped to drink sticky, thick coffee, loaded with sugar, and to talk of the pleasures and dangers of the forest world they knew. They chanted the prices of wood, the names of logs. They spooked themselves, and us, with tales of stolen chain saws and armed men on the roads. They were always planning to leave in a few days, when the earnings looked good, and before fiercer men arrived. Even as quick-moving transients, they gave us a human face for the frontier.

My friends thought the men worked for Inhutani, a government timber company, and while this turned out to be technically wrong, they were right that lines between public, private, and criminal were unclear. These loggers have both legitimacy and access. They sell their logs to the big logging companies or to small but perfectly legal wood processers. Where environmental regulations keep the companies off mountain slopes or village claims push them back, that's where the wild loggers go. They fill out logging economies of scale, and their earnings are the only prosperity logging is likely to bring to the province. Their chain saws come to them through networks of renting and profit-sharing that cross local, ethnic, and religious lines. They tap the slender ends of arteries flowing with capital from rich urban entrepreneurs, conglomerates, and—at that time—the family of the president branching in thinner and thinner capillaries out into the forest. Usually, the police and the army do not bother them, although the police and the army can be unpredictable. Many pay fees to Meratus village heads to give them permission to cut in village forests, and while villagers complain that village heads keep it all for themselves, this privatization is common, even proper for village subsidies.

And yet, both despite and because of all this respectability, these lonely loggers carry and spread the wildness of the frontier. Even in sitting with them, chatting with them, we partook of that wildness. They encouraged our fears of armed men; oh, no one will attack you, they joked, because they will assume you are carrying a lot of guns. And who can tell the difference between a logger and an armed thief? Each time we came upon another man, another logger/thief, we stopped, hoping to domesticate him with our chatter. Perhaps he wouldn't attack us; perhaps he would alert us to the presence of other logger/thieves. Soon our nerves were jangling from all those cups of coffee, and by then my friends and I formed a silent pack, each huddling in his or her own unspoken fear.

They modeled frontier behavior for us, teaching us the value of wood until my Meratus companions looked at familiar forest trees with eyes like cash registers. Oh, that one could bring me a million rupiah, Ma Salam sighed, interrupting our conversation about environmentalism. In writing their names or initials on the logs they cut, the wild loggers had introduced the new practice in this area of writing one's name on trees—to claim the tree, to hold it or sell it to a logger with a chain saw before someone else did. The proliferation of naming brought new identities for trees and men, wrapping both in fearless assertion and violence, for, people said, armed men came by and cut the name off the tree, or cut the tree above the mark, and wrote their own names on the logs. If you confront them with five men, my friends said, they will come at you with ten or twenty. Sell quickly and move on to write your name again.

Who were these men, so human and yet so transiently identified? They came from everywhere and spoke the common language of trade and calculation based on the hope of a quick windfall. They were called *penyingso*, "chain saw men," or *pembaluk*, "square log men," after the shape of their logs. No one knew them as wild, but they were men without ordinary culture. Appendages to their equipment and their products, they had names but no houses, families, meals, work schedule, or ordinary time. In this stripped-down human form, they communicated across cultures, arranging ethnic collaborations. They offered a hot human connection to still the chills of fear. This thrilling connection was an anesthetic, blocking out the damaged world in which they operated—a world already left behind by bigger frontier makers, the soil sloughing off the hills, trees falling, waters muddied. Entering that damaged world, can't you see the resources waiting to be claimed?

It is difficult to find the words to discuss this kind of transethnic, translocal collaboration and the regional resource dynamics it sets in motion. Resource economists and bureaucrats recognize no localisms; to them, the world is a frontier. There is no point in asking how frontiers come to be; they are nature itself. To counter that perspective, anthropologists, rural sociologists, and geographers have drawn attention to non-frontier-like (or even anti-frontier) environmental social forms, such as common property, community management, and indigenous knowledge. They have returned attention to the cultural specificity of capitalism and state bureaucracy.[8] This important and quite wonderful work has come to dominate local and regional analyses of environment and society in Kalimantan; scholars point to the long-term social making of the rainforest, to a community "ethic of access" that sustains forest commodities, and to the bizarre stereotypes of government planners.[9] My own work has developed within this dialogue.

Yet in contrasting community conventions with state and corporate schemes, there is little room for discussing the call of the wild, with its regionwide collaborations for aggressive resource grabbing and the seemingly unstoppable spread of the frontier. One might call this "the tragedy of the tragedy of the commons," that is, the tragic result of state and corporate policies that assume and enforce open-access conventions as the flip side and precondition of private property.[10] By refusing to recognize alternative forms of access, these policies will alternatives to disappear. But this is a tragedy that cannot be well described with the vocabulary of management, property, and access rules. From the perspective of the abandoned logging roads, the divide between community and state-corporate standards feels nostalgic: too little, too late. The logging road and its illegal-legal loggers from everywhere call me toward more dangerous country.

One look back: Grand schemes never fully colonize the territories upon which they are imposed. If the frontier is an environmental project, not a place, it can never fill the landscape. Away from the logging road, there are trees, fields, and villages. The frontier could move on; the forest might regenerate. Still, those industrial tree plantations are truly huge, and through them the frontier claims powerful national and international players.

The Public Private

Riding from the provincial capital up the east coast and toward the mountains in an airless, overcrowded van with the music so loud it closes down my senses, there is more than enough anesthetic; yet the difference between legal resource concessions and the wild is perfectly visible here. The road runs for miles through land without underbrush or animal life but only neatly planted tree stock, row on row on row. The transmigration villages placed here to provide the labor force for these future trees are similarly orderly, blank, and anonymous; in striking contrast to everywhere else I've been in Indonesia, the passengers get on and off at these nameless stops without looking at us or speaking. Sometimes we stop in noisy frontier towns, full of gold merchants, truckers, and hungry, aggressive men. But soon enough we are back among the silent army of young trees. This is the discipline that boosted Indonesia—for awhile—among the emerging Asian tigers. Under the banner of political stability, discipline made economic indicators soar.

Appearances are important here. No weeds, no trash timber. It is unclear to what extent appearances were the New Order economy's most important product. Oil palm, the darling of the export-crop set, was sponsored by foreign and domestic plantation subsidies; perhaps the companies will have moved on before the oil is pressed.[11] The pulp plantations were financed by the national reforestation program, the answer to environmentalists' concern for the rainforest. New international agreements offered plantation timber as the solution to rainforest destruction; timber companies put in plantations, sponsored by the government, to earn the right to cut down more forest, useful for future plantations.[12] Meanwhile, the young trees await future pulp factories. And as they wait, what will befall them? Many of the acacias are cloned from the same parent stock, making them highly vulnerable to disease.[13] They are affected by a rot that causes hollow boles, an apt image for an economy of appearances.

There have been government corporations here, and there have been private ones, but most fall awkwardly across this distinction. The oil palms were said to belong to the wife of then president Suharto, Mrs. Tien Suharto, who died in 1996 but before her death was widely parodied as Mrs. Tien (Ten) Percent, after her voracious interest in the economy. The loggers told villagers who complained about the invasion of village forests to "go ask Mrs. Tien." The president's family served both a material and a mythical role in the plantation economy. The capital they controlled was both public and private. It was the confusion of these categories that allowed frontier investment to flourish. Here national interest merged with that of the president, the army, and the corporations.

Even the staunchest of neoclassical economists admit that it was difficult to distinguish among domestic, foreign, and government ownership in New Order Indonesia, given the mix of investors, the central importance of patronage, and the slippage back and forth between military and private enterprise. The confusion proliferated at every level. Foreign was domestic: Foreign aid formed a major portion of domestic revenue, and foreign firms worked through domestic partners. Public was private: The explicit goal of the government was to sponsor entrepreneurship at every level. Even peasant subsidies in the 1990s were individual entrepreneurship loans. Licenses and concessions were both public and private. Civil servants were paid a low base salary and expected to gain the rest of their living from perks and benefits of their discretionary authority.

You could call this corruption, or you could call it, as one North American corporate executive, gracefully submitting to government demands for a share of his company's enterprise, dubbed it, "Indonesia's political, economic, and social environment."[14] One must also consider these public-private arrangements in relation to the worldwide post–Cold War infatuation with the market. In the 1990s, most every country redoubled its endorsement of the market, and New Order Indonesia was exemplary. The bureaucracy was the market; its goal was to promote entrepreneurship. The military was the market; soldiers had the muscle to make the best deals. Environmental management was the market, offering another chance to claim resources and promote trade. The fluidity between public and private was a fertile space for the capital, the deals, the plans, and the appearance of the economy itself. The president's family and friends were exemplars of what every citizen was supposed to be doing; their capital flowed out through transregional networks in complementary small and large deals.

This dynamic was said to speed up development, and speed things up it did. Secrets passing through personal ties encouraged speculation in which investments preceded contracts; for those tracking money and resources, an impatient anticipation emerged, speeding up time. A boom-time excitement was stimulated by the fluidity of deals, trickling down and then streaming between official coffers, foreign firms, and those-in-the-know. Rumors spread the excitement, and the wild men flocked to the frontier following or anticipating news of gold strikes and quick timber harvests, before the plantations rolled in. In this productive space, quick, erratic, anticipatory frontier time intensifies and spreads, ricocheting back and forth between centers and peripheries, and getting ahead of itself in death-defying leaps. Here alternative, appearance-based scams—disciplined or wild—are born, and the only promise that must be kept is of fabulous, unearned wealth.

Roads That Empty the Territory

Between the tree plantations and the mountains are networks of more- and less-maintained logging roads, with their heavy cargoes of legal logs by day and illegal logs by night. For bosses and managers, the roads shrink and simplify the territory, making it quicker to get from here to there. For most everyone else, the logging roads expand landscape emptiness, separating off- and on-road sites and creating obstacles between once-connected forest places even as they speed the trip to town. The roads are also conduits for migrants, fugitives, and thieves, who expand both danger and wildness for everyone who lives or visits there.

Natural treasures themselves become fugitive in this landscape of movement and flight, just as once, people said, a man stumbled over a nugget of gold as big as a rice mortar and marked the place oh so carefully to come back later with help—but when he did, nothing was there. Masculine magic and charisma are required, for even safe in one's possession, treasures disappear. Thus, every man on the road with a splinter of gaharu incense wood or a palmful of immature swifts' nests unwraps it from its plastic bag, shows it like a secret talisman, wraps it, stows it carefully in his pocket, chants the price, pulls it out again to rewrap it, trying thereby to stabilize its presence on his person. And how much more flighty are the incense trees and swifts themselves.

Take the swifts. The saliva nests they build in limestone caves are the key ingredient of Chinese birds' nest soup and fetch startling prices even locally: a million and a half rupiah for a kilo of the white clean ones and 800,000 for the debris-filled black.[15] In this area, they have long been associated with fugitive luck and danger. In the 1980s, people told me that the only way to find birds' nests was to bring a freshly sacrificed human head to the spirits who could reveal them. Now, with armed men on the roads, the birds' erratic flight has intensified beyond the reach of headhunters, as have attempts to hold them in place. Where military men have found productive caves, they have posted guards and signs: "This is the property of the army." Meratus who consider themselves traditional owners hurry to guard remaining caves, building their homes and clearing swiddens in the dark glens facing the caves, never leaving them. Still, they are outmaneuvered by the men on the roads, who come around with guns and flashlights and demand entry. They peel off the birds' nests before they are fully built, ensuring that the birds will not return. Quick harvesting leads to quicker harvesting, and nests the size of kidney beans are removed, depriving the birds of any place to raise their young. In this fugitive landscape, armed men are the best part of the law, and parodies of property appear. One Meratus man who had moved in front of a cave to guard it showed me the letter written by the most recent gang to have come by to rob the cave, which warned off future gangs on the principle of this group's precedence. My Meratus host got nothing, as did the swifts, who could only fly to other fugitive locations.

Men arm themselves with old war stories, and invulnerability magic from the 1958 rebellion has been revived, with its metaphors of penises as weapons and semen as spent bullets. As much as I tried to avoid too simple an ecofeminism, it was difficult not to conclude that an emergent masculinity fueled this regionally spreading dynamic, with its ability to unite men across lines of local culture and religion in a competitively intensive virility. Men arouse each other on the roads with stories of women who will do anything ("and then," he said, "she tore off her bra"). They work themselves and each other into a constant state of masculine anxiety, forever talking deals, opportunities, and prices in the sped-up time of the chase. They forget day-cycles, lifecycles, and seasons. They talk back and forth and challenge each other to greater efforts.

Hiking the logging roads in the hot sun, I find it difficult to refuse a ride from the men in the truck. But crammed into the cab with the crew behind a windshield covered with stickers of busty naked ladies and my male Meratus friends stuck in the back with the water buffalo, fear hits me like an avalanche. Within 30 seconds, they are feeling my arms and legs and breasts, and I must concentrate on how to get them to let me off at the next crossroads, where I heave a sigh of relief that I made it out, again, this time. Yes, says a wizened Meratus friend, they grab your breasts even if you are a wrinkled old woman, they must have no eyes, and every woman must learn to jump out of the truck. But a younger friend replies to my stories with bravado: Why didn't you do it? Weren't they handsome enough? I had heard similar bravado from young men when a peer was cowed by soldiers: If they had come at me, I would have shown them something! Indeed, one's only choices are to hide or to play. Women can be resourceful too, and prostitution brings new resources to the frontier. But this is a world formed by an intensive, peculiar, exaggerated masculinity.

This is a masculinity that spreads and saturates itself with images and metaphors, amulets, stickers of naked women, stories based on the confusion between rape and wild sex. Its moving force is perhaps best seen in the imagistic effects of the "water machine," the high-pressure hydraulic pump, small enough for one man to carry and connect to any local stream, but whose power in the spray emerging from the taut blue plastic piping can gouge a hole four feet deep into the land and thus expose the gravel underneath the clay, gravel mixed, perchance, with small flakes or nuggets of gold. What charismatic force! And what possibilities it unveils.

The water machine, introduced in this area around 1990, is the key technology of small-scale or "wild" gold mining. It is much too expensive for an ordinary Meratus man, but networks of renting and share splitting, with borrowed funds and imagined profits split among more and more men make it possible for many ambitious men to join a mining group, or more aggressively yet, to bring the machine and a team upstream toward home. Nor are Meratus the only players. The miners, like the loggers, come from everywhere, building makeshift settlements along the logging roads with names like "Kilometer 105 and a Half." At their excavations, they erect camps of bamboo platforms hung with plastic sheets; they have coffee pots, sugar, mackerel cans. But I know some of these people; they are Meratus farmer-foragers. I know they are perfectly capable of stopping anywhere in the forest and, in half an hour, building a cozy, rain-tight shelter of bamboo, palm leaves, or bark. I know, in other circumstances, they would carry rice; they would hunt and fish and gather wild fruits and vegetables and make a tasty meal. But here, surrounded by familiar forest, they observe the proprieties of rain-soaked plastic sheets and a nutrition of coffee and rancid fish. It feels like nothing so much as "culture" in its most coercive, simplistic form: a way of life that draws us in, ready or not, sensible or not.

Among the huddled mining shelters, men and women disagree. Women join the profit-sharing groups, panning the gravel with men until their own jealous menfolk arrive, sending them back to the village. The men attack the land with new vigor, sharing the washing with other women, and women sneak back to join the gold parties of strangers.

But what is the result of all this passion? Despite obsessive attention to secrets and signs, much of the gravel exposed yields no metal at all; and when it does, the gold flakes are quickly spent in the extortionate prices of coffee, sugar, and cigarettes. No one I heard of had made much money; meanwhile, water machines broke and huge debts were accrued. Most strikingly, the land lay pock-marked and deeply eroded beyond recovery. Those trees that remained clung tottering by the tips of their roots, their bases airily exposed. Broken streams formed muddy pools; even grass was banished. "They have ruined the land for many generations," said the old people. But perhaps it doesn't matter, if the industrial tree plantations and their transmigrant labor force are coming anyway. Their mission is to make and restore degraded lands; why not get started?

....

Frontier men and resources, I have argued, are made in dynamics of intensification and proliferation. Confusions between legal and illegal, public and private, disciplined and wild are productive in sponsoring the emergence of men driven to profit, that is, entrepreneurs, as well as the natural objects conjured in their resourceful drives. These men and objects are contagious, recharging the landscape with wildness and virility. The frontier then appears to roll with its own momentum.

II. Crisis—and the Confusion of the Senses

In 1997 and 1998, the economy of Indonesia was hit by a great financial crisis that spread across Asia. The internationally evocative term *krismon* (*krisis moneter*, "financial crisis") was coined in the newspapers, but the term *krisis* also spread on less sophisticated channels. By the summer of 2000, the term krisis had reached remote South Kalimantan villages. I heard it used to refer to all kinds of bad-news events, from family breakups to entrepreneurial failures to regional political upsets.

In the village of Kalawan, times have been bad indeed. These are not the bad times broadcast around the world to portray the Indonesian "crisis": the fights over imported food, the violence against Chinese shop owners, the empty urban real estate. The crisis in Kalawan is deeper, at least in the sense that it could not be solved with the stabilization of the rupiah or even a change in the regime. Since the late 1980s, logging had "opened" the region: to armed men, legitimate and illegitimate; to entrepreneurial schemes, big and small; to migrants and transmigrants, with their superior citizenship claims; to proselytizing Pentecostals; to the destruction of subsistence livelihoods and the voiding of local rights; and, indeed, to panic and despair. Since the early 1990s, oil palm and pulp-and-paper plantations have spread closer and closer, drawing surveying lines through Kalawan people's orchards and fields, and unloosing waves of imported transmigrant laborers to further denude the Kalawan landscape. Then the fires of 1997 burned down everything on one side of the road and much on the other, leaving a charred scar. Since then the rice has failed three times, and Kalawan people have become accustomed to discussing the distressing prices of those bottom-of-the-barrel rices, broken and red or black from improper storage, that have emerged as the staple. There is not much hope here, except, for some, in heaven . . . and for others, in the latest resource scam.

The krisis in this area, then, has been long in brewing. Indeed, there is a basic continuity between "development" here and "crisis." Development required the making and using of "resources," and resources cannot be made without violent upheaval. But frontier proliferation can get out of hand. Post-1997 frontier dynamics have challenged investors. The withdrawal of the New Order army as the guarantor of corporate greed has had drastic results. Community groups and gangsters have seized mines and timber camps. Illegal resource extraction suddenly overwhelms the legal. All but the bravest investors have considered backing out.

....

Crisis is a time for realignments within capitalism. Things are out of control; individual firms, and perhaps whole sectors, will go under, even if capital as an abstract idea may move on, unscathed. Fortunes hang in the balance. Capitalists must make big decisions: Can they take advantage of the confusion? Should they pull out?

Everyday processes of frontier-making become crises when, in contingent concert with regime disintegration and international "loss of confidence," frontier violence and destruction take on a new magnitude. The business-as-usual obfuscations and confusions that make up frontier dynamics are magnified. Investors become vulnerable to frontier instability in the same way that residents and immigrants have been. What was "development" and "opportunity" in Kalimantan when trauma remained a small distraction is "crisis" when it emerges larger than life.

Media representations play a part in making crisis by changing focus from figures of rosy profits to landscapes of disruption. They reverse the scale of each: Frontier wreckage that looked small in the shadow of bright economic forecasts now takes up the front page of the newspaper. Kalimantan is lumped with Africa as a sacrifice zone. Let them kill each other, the authorities say: Tribes will be tribes. Their subtext reads: Capitalists beware!

It makes no sense to blame disruption on its poorest participants. If fingers must be pointed, let us begin with corporate and military elites. Yet their provocations have been effective: An apparatus has been put into motion that mobilizes chaos. There are no more anesthetics; confusion and pain are now free to show their faces. Suddenly powerful, they reach out to touch the ruling classes. Will the frontier rock the center, revealing global capitalism in its dirty underwear?

Chaos: a frontier spun out of control, its proliferations no longer productive for the authorities. This section explores the technical, sensuous features of such chaos. In chaos, sense disorientation itself becomes a historical agent, drawing people and landscapes in its path. How might we track the agency of the senses?

Smoke

The smoke of the fires of the 1997 El Niño drought year and beyond created a crisis of visibility.[16] What should be visible and what should be invisible? Proper standards of visibility were contested and overlaid. Should Indonesia be responsible when airplanes in Singapore cannot fly because of the haze? Is corporate responsibility proved when environmentalists with satellite photos and Global Positioning System technologies make visible the smoke that emerges from plantations? Is the government creating more haze by blaming swidden farmers for the fires? And have the corporations successfully clarified property law by making the space of their plantations visible—by burning down their village competition?

As Emily Harwell (2000) has noted, most of the arguments about the fires stayed resolutely at a very high scale: the aerial view of the landscape. Opponents disagreed about the causes and consequences of the fires, but nobody cared much about the view from the ground. No one demanded that villagers affected by the fires become participants in the debates. Yet, perhaps such a demand would have made the situation only more difficult to decipher. Smoke created no clear perspective from above or below; the only difference involved the set of potential arsonists most available to blame. Many villagers have testified that corporations started the fires hoping to burn village forests for plantations. But often they used this story not to protest, but rather to catalyze more stories: about how village neighbors burned each other's forests down, about how villagers burned plantations.[17] No breathing space emerged for solidarity. Some stories were realistic; others ranged into the fantastic. Rumors were everywhere, and suspicions aroused. Smoke itself was the protagonist.

In Kalawan, my friends told me, the fires came from the south, from the Kodeco plantation complex. Yes, the company had started the fires, they thought; it was clearing land for *sungkai* and *damar* plantations. Then carelessness and jealousy fanned the flames. Three men on a fishing trip must have left coals in their campfire; the fires had gone out when they started again in that area. A young man they knew had gone hunting and must have dropped a cigarette, for the flames took off there. Certainly, it was dry. But then, jealousy flared. People who saw their own forests burned were jealous that other people still had fruit trees; they took fire to them. Our conversation took on a new intensity here, as my companions vied to tell me of the meanness of neighbors. I was unclear if we were still talking about carrying real coals or whether we had moved into the realm of sorcery. At the same time, stories poured forth of people dousing their houses in water brought up, bucket by bucket from the river, hour after hour. There was hard work and courage here. And suspicion and anger. The fires were not a natural occurrence, they said. Only through happenstance, more gracious than human plans, had the rain come to put the fires out at last—at the doorway of the house where we now sat. Even then the smoke and soot obscured the view.

The karst formations where the swifts build their expensive nests had burned in the fires. Even if the birds were still there, my friends said, you couldn't get to them; there were no handholds now that the trees were burned and the karst had turned to dust. Yet even as we spoke thus, a young man in the household went out to gather nests. You can't see them; you can't get to them; but, yes, people gather them every week, smaller than a fingernail clipping and worth almost nothing: an economy of the invisible.

Smoke and soot: a challenge to visibility and planning at every level, from the humble to great. When times were good in the national and international gaze, it seemed that investment ushered in clarity. For the first time, we—the self-proclaimed global management—knew where those resources were: We could count them; we could know their potential; we could talk about caring for them; we could use them. It was said that plywood tycoon Bob Hasan had a computer program that showed every harvestable tree in Kalimantan. "Computers, robotics, contour interpretation, satellite technology, can all help identify what trees are where," he told a reporter (Vidal 1990). Yet these tools only show certain things. Human residents and their rights became invisible. In 1997, however, this trick collapsed, and obscurity became the common complaint. At the bottom of the heap, villagers struggled to survive within the smoke. Above them, contrary regimes of visibility openly competed.

Why did the plantation companies burn down the forest when they had been warned by the government that drought would make the fires spread out of control? Imagine for a moment a contradiction between capital and governance. Governance requires rationalization, clarity, and order. Capital, in contrast, thrives where opportunities are just emerging. The exceptional profits that allow a firm or corporate sector to get ahead are made where bureaucratic visibility is not yet firmly in place. In the deregulation zones where government is at the end of its tether, capital can operate with the hyperefficiency of theft. Capital cooperates in the spreading of governance measures that facilitate and legitimate this theft; some visibilities and rationalizations develop rapidly, while other economic standards are fluid and even purposely muddy. In the midst of contrasts between clarity and haze, discipline and free-for-all are uncannily bundled together. Obfuscation appears as a state plot, and as a people's uprising. Either way, proliferation is the result. Whose side should we be on?

No one, I think, wanted the fires to be so big and so destructive. But what is to stop proliferation from getting out of hand?

Poison

> Klerat Pellets: 0.005% w/w brodifacoum pellets.
> Klerat is the original single feed anticoagulant rodenticide.
> Klerat Pellets are active against rats and mice, including those resistant to first-generation anticoagulants, such as warfarin. A lethal dose can be ingested as only part of a single day's food intake. Rats and mice normally die several days later, so bait shyness does not occur as the rats do not associate the symptoms with the food they have eaten. As multiple feeding is not necessary, "Klerat" can be used most economically and safely when small quantities are applied with an interval between applications.
>
> —http://www.sorex.com, "International"

After the fires of 1997, the rice plants grew healthily enough and flowered, but the grains never developed. There was no harvest. By the next year the rats had come out of the forest. They infested the fields and ate everything before them. The plantation company sold the people rat poison, telling them to spread it on their fields at least three times every month. My friends said, "It kills the cats; it kills the dogs. But it doesn't affect the rats. They come back every night in greater numbers."

Some rats come in great clans, spreading over the fields as evening arrives. They cry "oi, oi, oi." Mouse traps are not effective. Cats are not enough.

"What kinds of rats?" I asked. My friends were using the Indonesian *tikus* rather than the Meratus *wagang*, and thus it was easy for them to avoid the biological specificity of Meratus wildlife classifications. "All kinds of rats," they said. "Tiny ones no bigger than your toe, and giant ones as big as your calf; white ones and grey and black." With the burning of the forest and the clearing of the plantations, there was nowhere else for them to go but the village fields and orchards. Indeed, I had never seen so much wildlife there. In every trip to relieve myself in the trees, I would scare a mousedeer or watch a colorful tree shrew scamper away. I was reminded of a flood I witnessed in Florida: On every mound of dry land, armadillos and rabbits and mice shared space with birds and foxes. There was no place else for the animals to go. They wouldn't last long.

The plantation, they say, sells rat poison named "kill a rat." I hear overtones of death, sweeping from the English-speaking north. At home, I find the poison "Klerat" on the Web, from the British firm Sorex, a product of its international line. This is a second-generation anticoagulant poison, formulated for rats that have become resistant to warfarin. Elsewhere on the Web, I find complaints that it is killing British owls and California wildlife, even as the rats become resistant again. I'm sure it is effective in killing off a broad spectrum of Bornean tropical rodents and other small animals, possibly sparing the cosmopolitan Norway rats, who seem quick to adapt to almost anything.

Fires that sweep across the forest; rats that sweep across the fields; poisons that sweep across the rats: They have called up the plagues. Each plague follows the simplifications and reductions of the last to leave the landscape more barren.

After the rats, a pestilence of tiny grasshoppers appeared.

Seizures

Little signs had begun sprouting in Kalawan. On each signboard appeared a man's name and two numbers: the length and width of his plot. These were not Kalawan men. They were newcomers, arriving to claim property. Their plots were tracts of forest, brush, or grass; all that showed of them were the little signs.

Yet these plots had not been unclaimed. There is no unclaimed land in Kalawan; that's what makes it a settlement. But the technologies of "claiming" are not those recognized by the Indonesian state or regional authorities. No one, for example, had thought of Kalawan land as a series of ownable plots. In the 1980s, the village as a collective had claimed a territory in which elders must be consulted to determine rights of use. Newcomers asked for permission to move into the village; elders negotiated disagreements about land use. Personal territories were marked by the plantings and histories of old users and claimed by their descendants. Some of these territories overlapped and supported diverse kinds of claims, reflecting the variety of ways that fields, brush, and forest could be used. This was not considered a problem.

In the 1990s, the Korean Development Company (Kodeco) put a logging road through Kalawan, and the village was forced into greater regional visibility. The police began to sell plots of land to immigrants, and particularly to Javanese transmigrants brought to work on the tree plantations but eager to move off-plantation to enter the more profitable trade in natural resources. Kalawan residents protested. The land was Kalawan orchard land, tended by its owners and charted for eventual reuse as farms. They asked customary leaders to intervene. But no one dared to go against the armed forces. " 'State land,' the soldiers said. If you disagree they shoot you. What could we do? Life is for a moment; death lasts until the end of time." The land was sold out from under them.

Kalawan became an attractive site for immigrants, and old Kalawan residents began selling land themselves before others could sell it for them. But who had the right to sell which land? The man who married in from another village sold the land of his wife's family. The neighborhood head sold his neighborhood. Who could interfere? Meanwhile, two different plantation companies drew their property lines through the village, separating "Korea" and "Indonesia," as residents put it. Some of my Kalawan friends worked for the survey teams, showing them the trails, and losing their lands for a few days of cigarette money.

A paroxysm of greed seized the village. Young men rushed to sell local resources, and, when they ran out, to join the army. Men in army uniforms, real or fake, ransacked the houses, stealing valuables. "If you don't wreck and rampage, your rice pot will be empty," someone said.

"If there's money in it, people will do it," Uma Adang grumbled. "If they have one million, they want two million. If they have two million, they want three million. Up to tens of millions. They don't stop to think. They just want it to multiply: gold, clothing, anything 'modern,' electric motors, motorcycles, motor vehicles. Kalimantan is sick."

Sin

Property regimes come into being with domestic realignments. In Kalawan, family values were asserted in a defensive spasm of fear. When most everything has been lost, it is easy to demand more and more control over less and less.

Misah had sex with her boyfriend. I knew because everyone was talking about it. Their teacher had caught them. When they had not shown up in class, he had left the other students to their own devices. He spent the afternoon stalking the couple, following them silently to Misah's house and peering through a window as they chatted. When they lay down, he pounced. He called an emergency village meeting in which he described in the most excruciating detail everything that he had seen. His report provoked a crisis. The couple must be married off immediately, and in acknowledgment of sin. They had disgraced their community.

In Kalawan, there are only two kinds of teachers: Muslims and Christians. Both hold themselves above the local community of pagans. Both sit in chairs and eat pastries with their coffee, while others sit on the floor. Both send the children home if they are a few minutes late to school, even if they have hiked through the jungle for an hour in a storm to get there. My friends used to make fun of them, gently and with respect for their willingness to teach the children. But in the light of krisis the villagers saw themselves in the gaze of others, and they seemed poor, backward, and without protection. Sinful and without civilization. There were no more jokes about the teachers then.

"Misah is an animal," her kin said, "she's not even human." Women's sexuality has so often been posed to configure battles between kindreds and communities. But here the teacher's accusation had turned the battle into a defensive siege. Either Dayaks were capable of moral standards or they were not. There would be no kin supporting Misah; she must be an icon of disrespect. My friends raged about her bad behavior. And I marveled: These were the same women with whom I had joked so often about sexual matters and otherwise. How had they become such small-town moralists?

A few years before, Uma Adang had mimed how the pious at prayer peeked out from under closed eyes to see what others were doing. She demonstrated how a tone-deaf chorus sang "Hallelujah" while bemused villagers lined up for post-service refreshments. We had laughed. Now, civilizational disciplines didn't seem so funny. Under the circumstances, everyone must learn piety.

"At least she could have finished class 5," my friends said. I wasn't sure that the memorized inaccuracies of the school texts would have done her much good, but the sizzling atmosphere suppressed such irreverence. "Why can't she continue school anyway?" I ask with false naivete. "Of course the teacher throws these students out," they reprimand me with finality. "It is sin." We would have no more parody of the teacher's discipline. If he says it is sin, it is sin.

"Dayaks must have a higher standard than others," says Uma Adang. "It's different for [Muslims and Christians] who live in the city; they are sophisticated. Dayaks are the older sibling [of Muslims and Christians]; our law is higher." In the confrontation of ethics, local custom is left a role as a defensive standard of value.

"There are three *suku* [groups]," explains Rusli, "Dayaks, Muslims, and Christians. The Javanese are Muslims. 'Indonesia' is the same—Muslim." Now Dayaks have become a minority in Kalawan. Propriety is what they have. People should keep their houses clean and obey their parents. Teenagers who go to school should mind their virtue.

"I don't think you'll come back," said Uma Adang. "There is no more culture here." *Kebudayaan*, the official state term for "culture," had become a code word between us some years ago for our shared work in savoring the revitalization of customary law and the resurgence of community. But by 2000, customary law was a remnant. The spreading frontier had buried such nonproliferation regimes.

When there is nothing left, there is still the shadow of civilization, inspiring pious disciplines. And, while trouble is unlikely to come out of Kalawan, even the piety of the powerless can get fiercely out of control.

Body Odor

By 2000, indeed, whiffs of pious violence could be detected across Indonesia, pitting ethnic and religious groups in new, morally inspired hatreds. Even in Kalawan, people knew that Dayaks in West Kalimantan had mobilized to protect the reputation of their women from the disrespectful gestures and violent intrusions of migrant Madurese. Dayaks were driving Madurese out, killing them if necessary.[18] People in Kalawan have identified as Dayaks for a long time. But this was an exotic version of ethnicity: charismatic, passionate, and frightening.

My closest Kalawan friends heard about the Dayak-Madurese clashes from relatives who had moved to West Kalimantan and who had come back, briefly, to visit. I heard their stories some weeks after the visitors left, but the tales were still fresh as they detailed the tellers' sense of a breath-stopping fear—and the need for a brave response.

By the time I heard the stories, there was one detail that stood out, to be repeated over and over: The Dayaks of West Kalimantan, my friends said, could identify Madurese by smelling them. Madurese and Dayaks mixed in public spaces, such as transport buses. It was difficult for strangers to tell one from the other. But when buses were stopped by militants during these wars, Madurese and Dayaks were separated, despite attempts on each side to disguise their names, their clothes, and their language abilities, because they could not change their body odor. My friends showed me what it might have been like, touching me and one another with a finger and sniffing—and then laughing in amazement at the very idea. The children caught on to the game, wiping a finger on first one and then another, and smelling. They ran around giggling, giddy with the new idea, practicing. The adults were equally intrigued. Imagine, sniffing out your enemies in a literal sense!

Body odor as ethnicity was too powerful an idea to fade. In the mass of strangers conjured up by frontier culture and intensified by krisis, how else might one identify one's friends and enemies? Everything else could be mimicked, or so it was said. A poor man's DNA testing, and no authority could standardize the results. This was a technology of identity that could reach out across separate strands of fear and discontent to conjure some common ground of discomfort: It's them.

Body odor ethnicity reappeared in the 2001 Dayak-Madurese violence in Central Kalimantan.[19] It accompanied ethnicity-making ritual and fashion: The "red bowl" of blood and feathers passed from village to village to mobilize a Dayak force; the red head scarves and rattan bracelets of Dayak combatants. All were codes to make mass ethnic conflict legible. Yet, of these, smell is the most intriguing. Smell is elusive. It is difficult to describe. It arouses inchoate emotions and carries deep and often confused memories. Smell brings emotional force to difference: Some body odors make us relax; others offend us. Yet smell is not easy to categorize. The *one* smell that opens the door of recognition has no cognates; it is unique. No two people offer that same smell, however closely they are related. Smell is not a good guide to social status. Smell undermines the mirage of category accuracy even as it provides it a close-to-the-body story.

Smell, like smoke, draws our senses inside obscurity. Something is going on but we don't know what it is. We immerse ourselves in it, engulfed in its unknowns. We steer loose from familiar distinctions and commitments, joining the flow of the frontier.

From afar it is easy to see the destruction, the violence, the consolidation of property rules and ethnic boundaries, and the rise of new political disciplines. Observers wonder how people could have been induced to join this madness. I have argued here for the importance of an assault on the senses: the frontiers of capitalism, spun out of control.

Still Alive, But Captured by the Enemy

Looking up from the confusion, one can only grunt, struggling to remember the precision of mathematical symbols, the numbers of the dead.

One: Natural resources are not God given but must be wrested from previous economies and ecologies in violent extractions.

Two: Such violence leaves none of us unscathed.

Three: This assault is no neighborhood storm. It gathers force from afar, entangling multiple local-to-global scales. For more on this, dear reader, please read on.

"They communicate only in sign language"
[Friction in the commodity chain]

Everyone knows a commodity: It is the material good of capitalist production and the object of consumers' desire. Commodities seem so familiar that we imagine them ready made for us throughout every stage of production and distribution, as they pass from hand to hand until they arrive at the consumer. Yet the closer we look at the commodity chain, the more every step—even transportation—can be seen as an arena of cultural production. Global capitalism is made in the friction in these chains as divergent cultural economies are linked, often awkwardly. Yet the commodity must emerge as if untouched by this friction.

A lump of coal travels from a mine in Kalimantan to a power plant in India. Before it achieves an existence as a lump of coal, it is part of the landscape under a village field. Somehow it must be coaxed or coerced out of this landscape. Once mined, it still must travel to a warehouse and from there to a port city, where the coal ships can dock. It must be sorted and graded, and managers will have to make sure no one mixes the poor-quality coal with the good. It must meet specifications. If it sits too long in the warehouse, or in the ship at harbor, it will lose all its value to storage and docking costs. At the other end of its journey, it must convince the power plant managers that the contract has been met. All along the journey this lump is "coal." Yet at each stage it is appraised for different properties; if it will stay in this commodity chain, it must be ready to meet these varied demands. It requires not a vague and transcendent "coalness" but rather a step-by-step negotiation of the possibilities at hand—for digging, sorting, transport, and so on. It is transformed as coal-the-diggable, coal-the-sortable, coal-the-transportable, until it eventually becomes coal-the-burnable. In these shifts the lump of coal rubs up against other participants in the chain: unhappy villagers, conveyor belts, contracts. In its shape, its cost, and its composition, coal is made in the friction of the commodity chain.

The managers who facilitate this process can tell us: To produce a commodity is the work of the translator, the diplomat, and the power-crazed magician.

2000. In Banjarmasin, I happened to meet Mr. Krishnan, a business manager from Singapore, who represents United Power, which trades in coal. Mr. Krishnan, according to his business card, received his MBA in the U.K.; he is the assistant manager for exports at United Power. He speaks English, Tamil (his mother tongue), and a "smattering of Malay," on which he gets by in Indonesia. We spoke in English; later, I wrote down what he said.

Mr. Krishnan was in Banjarmasin to supervise the loading of a coal ship. Each day the ship sits in the harbor, United Power pays U.S.$10,000 in harbor fees. He was able to reduce the time to five days; otherwise it would have been at least two weeks. In Australia, he said, loading would have taken one and a half days.

United Power buys coal directly from the mine, which means they are responsible for trucking it to the stockpile, located three hours from Banjarmasin. From there, they transport it to the jetty, and then on to the ship. Each of these transport stages is contracted to different groups. The ship itself is on contract. Mr. Krishnan's job is to make sure transport at each of these stages moves smoothly and efficiently. This is not a simple task: Each stage presents its own cultural, political, and technical complications.

From the mine, the coal is loaded on to trucks and brought to the stockpile. A regulation requires the trucks to take an outer ring road rather than the regular roads. But the ring road is sandy and it damages the trucks, so the drivers take the main roads anyway. Meanwhile, coal trucks have caused the deaths of several children, and people are angry.

From the stockpile, the coal is trucked to the jetty, loaded on a conveyer belt, and dumped on to barges. The barges, pushed by tugboats, take six hours to get out to the ship. There the coal is loaded into the ship's hatches. If you put coal into standard shipping containers, it burns up, so you must use bulk loading. This job was further complicated by the fact that the buyer, in India, wanted two grades of coal, and these needed to be loaded into separate hatches.

Coal of different grades has separate uses. South Kalimantan produces a good deal of "environmentally friendly" coal, which is clean but of a low grade, less than 5.9. It causes power outages if you use it for power stations because it can't burn long enough. Indonesia, like India, has a lot of low-grade coal, and one must mix it with a higher grade coal, for example the 7.0 coal from China, to keep power stations running. Indian politicians always want to use Indian coal in the power stations, and as a result they always experience power outages. Low-grade coal is only good for uses such as cement plants.

Different parts of a mine may produce different grades of coal. The suppliers try to mix the lower grade into shipments that are supposed to be higher grade. The differences are not actually visible, so Mr. Krishnan performs random checks at the conveyor belt. He tests the coal on the belt at least every two hours. If the grade is 6.4 or above for a 6.5 order, he lets it go; if it is below 5.9, he stops the belt.

Each coal company has a separate character. Mr. Krishnan thinks A__ is the most professional company. (I recall that the newspapers have been full of A__'s refusals to restore mining areas. Professionalism is not the same as environmental or community responsibility.) He says Indians are worse than Indonesians in requiring bribes and kickbacks. At least in Indonesia you can sit down with the company people and talk. Mr. Krishnan comes to Banjarmasin two days before the ship arrives to discuss arrangements, including the schedule. He talks particularly to the mining engineers, who can speak a little English. If he didn't come, they would work much more slowly. For example, they would all take lunch breaks together instead of taking turns. If something breaks and no one is there, no one fixes it. Everyone waits for authorization before doing anything. Mr. Krishnan is there to make them change their attitudes.

That week, for example, he went out to the ship, where the stevedores were loading very, very slowly. He saw a barge of watermelons going by; he had it called over. He bought the load for U.S.$100 and distributed the melons to the workers. They sped up the work, and he saved two days.

The ships are contracted for the course of the voyage. This ship has an Indian captain and two officers, and the rest of the crew is Indonesian. They have been sailing together now for one year. The captain and his officers do not speak Indonesian, so the crew and the officers have no language in common. They communicate only in sign language. When the captain wants coffee, he puts his hand to his mouth to signal drinking. When he wants a meal cooked, he goes to the kitchen and points to each of the ingredients he wants and mimes how to cook them. They will travel that way to India.

United Power used to buy Australian coal. Now the rupiah is so low that Indonesian coal is irresistible. But if they don't send a manager to make the process move smoothly, they will lose more money in delays than the coal is worth.

....

What a lot of work to make sure the coal is delivered! After talking to Mr. Krishnan, I imagine myself an ethnographer on that coal ship, watching the crew go about the daily business of the ship without being able to take orders or explain difficulties to the ship's officers. But each stage of the process is similarly plagued with recalcitrant cultural difference. Mr. Krishnan must negotiate every step of the labor process because there is little agreement about how each task must be done.

In this case, indeed, there is outright conflict. I've heard about the coal truck drivers, described by Banjar friends as fiends who don't care for the lives of children; meanwhile, the drivers accelerate to avoid angry residents. At the mines, things are no better. Since the army stepped back as guarantor of the coal companies, community groups, gangs, and entrepreneurs have been taking over mines by force. After all, the coal companies appropriated the land themselves only through the force of the army. Not that this does the miners much good, since then coal production proceeds without even the meager benefits the company provided. As for the engineers negotiating with Mr. Krishnan about delivery schedules, they are nice to him, I think, because they are hoping he will be a resource to leverage a better position somewhere else, out of what they imagine as a backwater assignment. Each of these little worlds forms part of the production of South Kalimantan coal. Mr. Krishnan's job is to make this jostling work together—at least well enough to deliver something recognizable as a market load to India, and in enough quantity to make his company a profit.

2 The Economy of Appearances

the unemployed become murderers
  with uniforms and badges of rank
vast forests are torn apart

It is necessary that I emphasize
  the problem of power
that tends to turn people into bandits
    —Pramoedya Ananta Toer, as reworked by
      Peter Dale Scott, in "Minding the Darkness"

scale. *Relative or proportionate size or extent.*[1]

Indonesia's profile in the international imagination changed completely at the end of the 1990s. From the top of what was called a "miracle," Indonesia fell to the bottom of a "crisis." In the middle of what was portrayed as a timeless political regime, students demonstrated, and, suddenly, the regime was gone. So recently an exemplar of the promise of globalization, overnight Indonesia became the case study of globalization's failures.

The speed of these changes takes one's breath away—and raises important questions about globalization. Under what circumstances are boom and bust intimately related to each other? Might *deregulation* and *cronyism* sometimes name the same thing—but from different moments of investor confidence? Such questions run against the grain of economic expertise about globalization, with its discrimination between good and bad kinds of economic policy. Yet the whiggish acrobatics necessary to show how those very economies celebrated as miracles were simultaneously lurking crises hardly seem to tell the whole story. A less pious attitude toward the market may be necessary to consider the specificities of those political economies, like that of New Order Indonesia, brought into being together with international finance.[2]

This chapter brings us back to the months just before Indonesia so drastically changed, to canoe at the running edge of what turned out to be a waterfall. It concerns a set of incidents that can be imagined as a rehearsal for the Asian financial crisis as well as a minor participant in the international disillusion that led to the Suharto regime's downfall. In 1994, a small Canadian gold prospecting company announced a major find in the forests of Kalimantan. Over the months, the find got bigger and bigger, until it was the biggest gold strike in the world, conjuring memories of the Alaskan Klondike and South Africa's Witwatersrand. Thousands of North American investors put their savings in the company called Bre-X. First-time investors and retired people joined financial wizards. Whole towns in western Canada invested (Eisler 1997). The new world of Internet investment blossomed with Bre-X. Meanwhile, Bre-X received continuous coverage in North American newspapers, especially after huge Canadian mining companies and Indonesian officials entered the fray, fighting over the rights to mine Busang, Bre-X's find.[3] The scandal of Indonesian business-as-usual, opened to public scrutiny as corruption, heightened international attention and garnered support for Bre-X. But, in 1997, just when expectation had reached a fevered pitch, Busang was exposed as barren: There was nothing there. Gasps, cries, and lawsuits rose from every corner. The Toronto Stock Exchange changed its rules to avoid more Bre-Xs.[4] Bre-X lawsuits set new international standards.[5] Several years later, Bre-X investors still hoped and complained across the Internet, as they peddled the remains of their experiences: jokes, songs, and stock certificates (as wallpaper, historical document, or irreplaceable art, ready to hang).[6] Meanwhile, Indonesian mining officials and copycat prospecting companies scrambled to free themselves from the Bre-X story, even as they reenacted its scenes, hoping to revive its investor enthusiasm.[7]

The Bre-X story exemplifies popular thinking about the pleasures and dangers of international finance and associated dreams of globalization. The story dramatizes north-south inequalities in the new capitalisms; it celebrates the north's excitement about international investment, and the blight of the south's so-called crony capitalisms: business imagined not quite/not white. Depicting southern leaders as rats fighting for garbage, the story also promises new genres of justice for the northern investor who dares to sue. Finance looks like democracy: The Internet, they say, opens foreign investment to the North American everyman. But the Bre-X story also narrates the perils of the downsized, overcompetitive economy: the sad entrepreneurship of selling worthless stock certificates. As one writer put it, mixing metaphors, "The Bre-X saga will come to be known as the demarcation of the Internet as the weapon of choice for investors" (Zgodzinski 1997).

Most salient to my concerns about the working of global capitalism is the genre convention with which Bre-X started its own story, and by which it was finished off. Bre-X was always a performance, a drama, a conjuring trick, an illusion, whether real gold or only the dream of gold ever existed at Busang. Journalists compared Busang, with its lines of false drilling samples, to a Hollywood set.[8] But it was not just Busang; it was the whole investment process. No one would ever have invested in Bre-X if it had not created a performance, a dramatic exposition of the possibilities of gold.

Performance here is simultaneously economic performance and dramatic performance. The "economy of appearances" I describe depends on the relevance of this pun; the self-conscious making of a spectacle is a necessary aid to gathering investment funds. The dependence on spectacle has not been peculiar to Bre-X and other mining scams: It is a regular feature of the search for financial capital. Start-up companies must dramatize their dreams in order to attract the capital they need to operate and expand. Junior prospecting companies must exaggerate the possibilities of their mineral finds in order to attract investors so that they might, at some point, find something. This is a requirement of investment-oriented entrepreneurship, and it takes the limelight in those historical moments when capital seeks creativity rather than stable reproduction. In speculative enterprises, profit must be imagined before it can be extracted; the possibility of economic performance must be conjured like a spirit to draw an audience of potential investors. The more spectacular the conjuring, the more possible an investment frenzy. Drama itself can be worth summoning forth.[9] Nor are companies alone in the conjuring business in these times. In order to attract companies, countries, regions, and towns must dramatize their potential as places for investment. Dramatic performance is the prerequisite of their economic performance.

Yet conjuring is always culturally specific, creating a magic show of peculiar meanings, symbols, and practices. The conjuring aspect of finance interrupts our expectations that finance can and has spread everywhere, for it can only spread as far as its own magic. In its dramatic performances, circulating finance reveals itself as both empowered and limited by its cultural specificity.

Contemporary masters of finance claim not only universal appeal but also a global scale of deployment. What are we to make of these globalist claims, with their millennial whispers of a more total and hegemonic world-making than we have ever known? Neither false ideology nor obvious truth, it seems to me that the globalist claims of finance are also a kind of conjuring, a dramatic performance. In these times of heightened attention to the space and scale of human undertakings, economic projects cannot limit themselves to conjuring at different scales—they must conjure the scales themselves. In this sense, a project that makes us imagine globality in order to see how it might succeed is one kind of "scale-making project"; similarly, projects that make us imagine locality, or the space of regions or nations, in order to see their success are also scale-making projects. The scales they conjure come into being in part through the contingent articulations into which they are pushed or stumble. In a world of multiple, divergent claims about scales, including multiple, divergent globalisms, those global worlds that most affect us are those that manage tentatively productive linkages with other scale-making projects.

Analytic tools with which to think about the global picture are still rudimentary. Many ethnographers find ourselves with data about how a few people somewhere react, resist, translate, consume, and from here it is an easy step to invoke distinctions between local reactions and global forces, local consumption and global circulation, local resistance and global structures of capitalism, local translations and the global imagination. I find myself doing it. Yet we know that these dichotomies are unhelpful. They draw us into an imagery in which the global is homogeneous precisely because we oppose it to the heterogeneity we identify as locality. By letting the global appear homogeneous, we open the door to its predictability and evolutionary status as the latest stage in macronarratives. We know the dichotomy between the global blob and local detail isn't helping us. We long to find cultural specificity and contingency within the blob, but we can't figure out how to find it without, once again, picking out locality.

This chapter suggests that we address these dilemmas by giving attention to the making of *scale*. Scale is the spatial dimensionality necessary for a particular kind of view, whether up close or from a distance, microscopic or planetary. I argue that scale is not just a neutral frame for viewing the world; scale must be brought into being: proposed, practiced, and evaded, as well as taken for granted. Scales are claimed and contested in cultural and political projects. A "globalism" is a commitment to the global, and there are multiple, overlapping, and somewhat contradictory globalisms; a "regionalism" is a commitment to the region; and so on. Not all claims and commitments about scale are particularly effective. Links among varied scale-making projects can bring each project vitality and power. The specificity of these articulations and collaborations also limits the spread and play of scale-making projects, promising them only a tentative moment in a particular history. The performative dramas of financial conjuring offer one perspective from which to appreciate the specificity and contingency of particular niches within capitalist scale-making.

One of the chief puzzles of globalist financial conjuring is why it works. We've all seen ads for hamburgers, express mail, or computers bridging cultures across the globe. But it's one thing to offer a stylish picture of diversity, and another thing to figure out how entrepreneurial projects actually manage to affect people who may not pay them any mind. Conjuring is supposed to call up a world more dreamlike and sweeter than anything that exists;

magic, rather than unsparing description, calls capital. The puzzle seems deeper the more the material and social worlds to be reshaped and exploited are geographically, culturally, and politically remote from financial conjuring centers. How do the self-consciously glossy and exaggerated virtual worlds conjured by eager collectors of finance become shapers of radically different peoples and places? My frame highlights contingent articulations in which globalist financial conjuring links itself with regional and national scale-making projects, making each succeed wildly—if also partially and tentatively. It seems likely that successfully conjuring the globe is possible, at least now, only in thick collaborations with regional and national conjurings; certainly financial conjuring has been deeply implicated in promises of making regional and national dreams come true.

Globalist conjuring sometimes supports the most bizarre and terrible of national and regional dreams. Certainly this was the case in the Bre-X story. Finance capital became linked with greedy elite dreams of an authoritarian nation-state supported by foreign funds and enterprises; this is a nation-making project I call franchise cronyism to mark the interdependence of corruption and foreign investment. These in turn became linked with migrant dreams of a regional frontier culture in which the rights of previous rural residents could be wiped out entirely to create a Wild West scene of rapid and lawless resource extraction: quick profits, quick exits. To present this rather complicated set of links, I offer a diagram (fig. 1). Diagrams by their nature are oversimplifications, and this one is certainly no exception. To acknowledge this, I have named each of the three scale-making projects

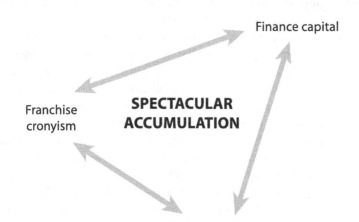

Finance capital

SPECTACULAR ACCUMULATION

Franchise cronyism

Frontier culture

Figure 1. F-C Articulations in the Economy of Appearances. This diagram is both serious and a joke.

I discuss in a self-consciously joking manner. Yet the playfulness is also a serious attempt to focus attention on the specificity and process of articulation. Finance capital is a program for *global* hegemony; franchise cronyism is one particular *nation*-making project; frontier culture is an articulation of a *region*. Each is a scale-making project with its sights set on a different scale: global, national, and regional. The links among them cross scales and strengthen each project's ability to remake the world. At the same time, none of these three projects is predictable or ubiquitous in the world. Coming together as they did for a moment, they created a great fire. Looking back on them now, we see they didn't create an evolutionary ladder to the stars. Isn't this sense of engagement and contingency what scholars and social commentators most need to bring into view?

"Yes, We Are Still in Business"

Bre-X was the brainchild of a Canadian stock promoter named David Walsh. Walsh dropped out of high school at the end of tenth grade and soon joined a Montreal trust company, rising quickly to become the head of the investment department. After thirteen years, Walsh left to try to form his own trust company. Three unsuccessful years later, he agreed to start an office in Calgary for another firm, only to quit the next year. From then on, Walsh worked to set up his own companies: first, the oil-oriented Bresea Resources Ltd. (named after his sons Brett and Sean), and then, in 1985, Bre-X Minerals Ltd., which from the first aimed to find gold.[10]

Gold mining had become a profitable industry in the 1970s, when the United States ended the Bretton Woods standard of fixed exchange rates, and the price of gold, which had been held constant at $35 per ounce for many years, skyrocketed, hitting $850 per ounce in 1980.[11] Canadian companies rushed to take advantage of the new gold prices by exploring not only in the Canadian West, but around the world. Junior mining exploration companies, whose goal is to find the minerals that can be exploited by major companies, sprouted by the dozens. Toronto became the world's mining finance capital. In 1997, there were 1,225 publicly traded mining companies in Canada, and mining stocks represented 21.5 percent of all trades on the Toronto Stock Exchange (Francis 1997: 24). In this industry, the line between various kinds of expertise is thin: geologists (with salaries supplemented by stock options) must be promoters to raise the money to finance their mineral finds, market analysts must be geologists to evaluate those finds, and stock promoters must explain their offerings in geologically convincing terms. Canadian preeminence in mining depended on both its mining history and its position as a center of mining finance.

For a stock promoter like David Walsh to become president of a gold exploration company was not unusual in this climate. Consider the trajectory of the president of Barrick Gold, Canada's biggest gold-mining company. Peter Munk is a high-flying but not always successful entrepreneur. In the 1950s, he founded a television and hi-fi company that crashed, leaving the government of Nova Scotia in deep debt; he went on to build hotels on South Sea islands funded by Saudi Arabian princes. Nothing in his background gave him expertise in minerals. In 1986, however, he bought a worked-over mine in Nevada. It turned out to be the most profitable gold mine in the world, pushing Munk's company into a leading position (Wells 1996). Peter Munk was "a dreamer who became a king" (Newman 1996). In this context, David Walsh's little enterprise made sense.

In 1988, Walsh listed Bre-X on the Alberta Stock Exchange at 30 Canadian cents per share. His wife Jeanette supported the household by working as a secretary. The family bought on credit, and, over C$200,000 in debt, both David and Jeanette Walsh declared personal bankruptcy in 1992. Bre-X shares sometimes fell as low as two cents; in his 1991 annual report, David Walsh wrote, "Yes, we are still in business." In 1993, however, Walsh pulled together some money for a trip to Indonesia. There he met Dutch-born geologist John Felderhof, who had achieved some fame in identifying the Ok Tedi copper and gold mine in Papua New Guinea in 1967, but suffered hard times in the 1980s. Felderof agreed to help Walsh find gold in Kalimantan and contacted Filipino geologist Michael de Guzman for the project. Filipino geologists had been in great demand in Indonesia because of their experience, education, and regional savvy.[12] De Guzman brought several Filipino associates to the team.[13]

Mining properties were cheap and available in Indonesia in the early 1990s because the Australians, who had come in some ten years before in their own wave of national mining speculation, were trying to get out. Felderhof had worked for some Australian companies and had witnessed the financial boom and bust in which mineral exploration was begun and then abandoned, promising or not. He convinced Walsh to form a partnership with an Indonesian entrepreneur to buy an old Australian claim around the creek called Busang in East Kalimantan, and Walsh raised the money to drill some holes. The results were disappointing, and by December 1993 they were about to close the property. Then, early in 1994, de Guzman struck gold. Walsh was quick and effective in informing investor newsletters and brokerage firms. Felderhof's estimates grew bigger and bigger. In 1993, Bre-X was trading at 51 Canadian cents a share; by May 1996, stocks were trading at C$286.50, accounting for a ten-to-one split. In April, Bre-X had been listed on the Toronto Stock Exchange; in August, the stock was listed in the United States on NASDAQ; in

September, it was also listed on the Montreal Stock Exchange. By then the company's market capitalization was over C$6 billion (Goold and Willis 1997: 64–65). Awards started to roll in: Mining Man of the Year for Bre-X President David Walsh; Explorer of the Year for chief geologist John Felderhof. On March 9 and 10, 1997, Bre-X officers and geologists were feted in awards dinners and ceremonies at the Prospectors and Developers Association of Canada meetings. They were at the height of their success.

Conjuring

On March 19, 1997, Michael de Guzman fell 800 feet from a helicopter into the rainforests of Kalimantan. Although up to that point he had been considered little more than the Filipino sidekick, at the moment of his death, de Guzman became the company, his face displayed everywhere in the news media over charts of the company's finds and stock prices. If Bre-X had been a big story before, it was truly dramatic now.

Mysteries abounded. A suicide note was found in which de Guzman wrote that he couldn't stand the pain of hepatitis; but he was an optimistic man and in quite good health. What happened to the third man the other Filipino geologists had seen enter the helicopter? Rumors circulated like wildfire. One Philippines scholar confided to me, "When I heard about the watch found in the helicopter, I had to find out what kind it was. When they said 'Rolex,' I knew he was murdered. No Filipino gangster would dispose of his victim without first removing his Rolex." A sign, a trophy. The trouble was, the scene was cluttered with signs, clues, false leads. Wives of de Guzman who knew nothing of each others' existence cropped up everywhere: in Manila, Jakarta, Manado, Samarinda. Rumors circulated that de Guzman had parachuted into Zurich. When a corpse was finally found, the face and much of the body had been devoured by wild pigs. Multiple autopsies failed to establish the identity of the body beyond controversy: Could Bre-X have changed the fingerprint on his employee identity card? Did the dental records match? And where were his geologist friends when it was time for the funeral?[14]

It was at this period, too, that the gold deposit at Busang came to seem just as mysterious. Bre-X had been drilling core samples at Busang since 1993; by 1997, some sites looked like "Swiss cheese" (Hajari 1997). As Busang became famous, industry professionals came to visit. Bre-X President Walsh later complained, "Virtually every mining geologist, analyst went to the site, but I never received one letter or phone call during that whole period that something was amiss over in Indonesia" (*Calgary Sun*, October 12, 1997). The "analysts" Walsh refers to were mining stock analysts, and, indeed, dozens visited the site, each fueling investors' attraction with more glowing reports. But in March 1997, the U.S. company Freeport McMoRan sent their assayors as the "due diligence" element of their agreement to become partners with Bre-X at Busang. Freeport found nothing. Furthermore, they claimed that the kind of gold in Bre-X's samples was inappropriate for the site: It was stream-rounded alluvial gold instead of igneous gold. Bre-X's assay methods were now open to question. Rumors flew of plots and cover-ups, and the price of Bre-X stocks roller-coasted. Perhaps Freeport was making false claims to take over the property. Perhaps Bob Hasan, an Indonesian partner, was buying up cheap stocks at a bargain-basement price. Why else had he taken out a bank loan to log just in this area, just at this time? Perhaps New York investors were trying to beat out Canadians. The gamble drew stock speculators into the fray and on April 2, the trading was so intense that it closed down the computer system at the Toronto Stock Exchange.[15] On May 3, however, the independent test report arrived. Its finding: *no* economic gold deposit. The ballooning stock swap immediately deflated; Bre-X stocks were officially worthless.[16] Yet what are we to make of the mysteries?

I am not a journalist, and my concern does not involve just which gold miners and which Indonesian government officials and which stock market participants knew about or participated in various conjuring acts. I'm more interested in the art of conjuring itself, as practiced not only by Bre-X officers and employees but also by the analysts, reporters, investors, and regulators who formed their retinue. I am struck by two counterintuitive observations. First, mystery, rumor, and drama did not come to Bre-X at the tail end of its ride; these qualities marked the Bre-X story from its beginnings. Rather than closing Bre-X down, mystery and drama kept Bre-X alive and growing; it was only when an official report stopped the show that the company died. Second, Bre-X is not the only company that has required spectacle to grow. Bre-X seems typical of the junior Canadian mineral exploration companies that it has helped usher into the international spotlight—except, of course, it was more successful at first and later more despised. Junior companies don't have the equipment or capital to take their mining ventures very far. They must make a big splash, first, to attract enough investors to keep prospecting, and, second, to bring in big mining companies to buy out their finds.

One can draw the net wider. The mystery and spectacle Bre-X cultivated is representative of many kinds of companies in which finance capital is the ruling edge of accumulation. Such companies draw investments through drama. And the importance of drama guarantees that it is very difficult to discern companies that have long-term production potential from those that are merely good at being on stage. The charismatic and dramatic attraction of international finance capital was a key feature of Southeast Asian development strategies during the "economic miracle." After the 1997 financial crisis, we were told to distinguish between the real and the fake, but does not the whole design of these accumulation strategies work against our ability to draw this line? As in a beauty contest, artistry and drama are necessary to compete; spectacle and mystery, playing equally across the line of the real and the fake, establish the winning reality of performance.[17]

Bre-X initially attracted investors because of the excitement of the reports coming out about Busang. From the very first, Bre-X was in the news, and journalists constantly wrote about Busang. The success with which Bre-X attracted investors depended on these reports, and particularly on the ways they used and elaborated tropes that brought the Bre-X find into other circulating stories of wealth, power, and fulfillment. Some of these stories were colonial adventure tales: the search for hidden, uncounted riches in remote places. *Maclean's*, a Canadian magazine, wrote: "Two, four, and then maybe six million ounces will be pulled from Busang annually. There has never been an El Dorado like this" (Wells 1997c: 40). Other stories told of frontier independence and the promise of wealth "at the end of a miner's rainbow," as the *New York Times* put it, where "independent-mindedness" led miners to "forbidding jungles" in search of the "century's greatest gold strike" (DePalma 1997: A1). There were stories of science in the service of human innovation. There were stories of war and conquest—"the battle for Busang"—recalling the French and the United States in Vietnam, and Bre-X became, repeatedly, a "rumble in the jungle," and then, eventually, a "bungle" or a "jumble" in the jungle.[18]

There were also pervasive stories of underdog charisma. After announcing the Busang find, Bre-X had to fight for the rights to mine it. The story of little Bre-X up against the big North American mining companies and the big Indonesian establishment generated an overwhelming response, ushering in Bre-X's greatest period of popular investment. When U.S. ex-President George Bush and Canadian ex-Prime Minister Brian Mulroney put pressure on Jakarta at the request of a big company, Bre-X's David Walsh, with his high school education, his beer belly, and his ineptness, looked like David up against Goliath. He made such a convincing "little guy" that after the scam was exposed, many refused to imagine him responsible. As *Fortune* magazine's reporter wrote, "Even now I have trouble believing that Walsh participated. ... Walsh looked more like some poor schlemiel who had just won the lottery and couldn't locate his ticket" (Behar 1997: 123).

Stockholders, too, contributed to the stories swirling around Bre-X.[19] Bre-X established an Internet presence early on, with stories posted on their Web site; meanwhile, investors' chat lines buzzed with Bre-X news.[20] The more controversy swirled around Bre-X, the more investors talked and exchanged rumors, extending, too, dreams of wealth, conspiracy theories, reinterpretations of the mining geology and engineering, and romances of unexpected underdog advantage. On the Internet, dramatic presentation was often clearly the point. As one *Silicon Investor* contributor wrote about the Bre-X Internet thread, "The theater is open. The stage is set 24 hours a day. There is always an audience" (Zgodzinski 1997).

One Internet contributor signed herself "Ole49er," reminding readers that the Wild West is never far from discussion of Bre-X. A Canadian shareholder with whom I spoke explained that Canadians were excited about the chance to invest in minerals in Indonesia because of the symbolic importance of mining in Canada as well as a national anxiety about the closing of the frontier. Environmental regulations in Canada, he explained, made it difficult to mine profitably in the last wide open spaces of the Canadian West. Yet those open spaces might be pursued abroad in foreign lands. As a substitute frontier, Bre-X's Kalimantan continued the excitement of the frontier story of Canada's development.

But what of Kalimantan in this story? In the moment of frontier making, financial conjuring runs up against the landscape, but not quite as in its dreams. At this trick in the magic show, an opportunity presents itself to ask about how the magic works, and how it doesn't.

Frontiers

Let me return to the beginning of the Bre-X story, or, at least, *one* beginning, in Kalimantan. A brave man is hacking his way through the jungle, alone and surrounded by disease and danger. There is nothing there but mud, malaria, leeches, hepatitis, and the pervasive loneliness of the jungle trek. But one day . . . he discovers gold!

This is an old story, told not only about Borneo, but about many a jungle or lonely rock cliff. But it is also what the Bre-X miners told the press. According to the *Far Eastern Economic Review* (McBeth 1997: 42–43):

The story of how Felderhof and de Guzman unearthed Busang's golden secret is the stuff that fables are made of. Mostly it is a human saga—about two quiet, very ordinary men from opposite sides of the world who persevered for years in the face of tropical illnesses and some of the harshest terrain in the world. . . .

Felderhof first landed in Indonesia in 1980. . . . [H]e worked his way from west to east across the centre of the vast Borneo island. . . . Those were hard times. He lived in jungle villages, eating whatever was available, carrying what he needed on his back, and hacking his way through some of the remotest rain forest in Asia.

De Guzman has gone through similar hardships. . . . He's had malaria 14 times since he met up with Felderhof in 1986. . . . Travelling alone, de Guzman took a seven-hour boat ride up the Mahakam River, then trekked 32 kilometers. . . . During a week of old-fashioned prospecting, he recognized a geological setting he had come to know well in the Philippines.

The story has come close to the moment of discovery. The *New York Times* tells that moment succinctly: "1994. Michael de Guzman, a mining geologist, is trekking through the Busang site doing work for Bre-X when a bit of yellow rock on a river bank catches his eye. 'Check it out,' he writes on a plastic strip and tacks it to the rock. His assistant follows with a more detailed analysis and writes: 'Checkmate'" (DePalma 1997: C10). One might be suspicious of this sudden appearance from nowhere of an assistant, but let's let that pass and move on to the second act in the discovery, the scientific theory that lets the miners know that a glitter of gold might be the tip of an underground hoard. Without science, de Guzman is just a Filipino guy playing with rocks; with science, he is the translator between nature and North American industry.

Working alone at 3 o'clock one morning, it suddenly became crystal clear [to de Guzman]. Bounding upstairs, he woke Puspos [the assistant] and explained his theory: that Busang, with its dome-like geological structure, lay at a fault-line crossroads. Together on that January morning, the two spent eight hours in "nonstop technical brainstorming." (McBeth 1997: 44)

It is a lovely story, but it bears a very odd relationship to everything else one might want to say about mining in Kalimantan. By the time de Guzman arrived at Busang, foreign prospectors, migrant miners, and local residents had all combed the landscape for gold. Yet his "discovery" story does not reflect the interdependence of his knowledge with that of other miners. Local residents, government regulations, mining camps, churches, markets, bus schedules, army officers, village heads, property disputes: all are missing. The frontier story requires that de Guzman wander alone on an empty landscape.

The story of lonely prospectors making independent discoveries in a remote jungle moved North American investors and stimulated the capital flow that made Bre-X rich. These images are repeated in the portfolio of every North American prospecting company working in Kalimantan. Consider the exploration of a Canadian prospecting company called International Pursuit, as reported in *Gold Newsletter's Mining Share Focus*. International Pursuit was prospecting in the wake of the Bre-X drama and needed to distance itself from Bre-X. Yet the frontier story is precisely the same. The company has sent its prospectors to the empty, wild landscape of Kalimantan, where, through a combination of luck and science, they stumble on precious metals. They are especially in luck because in late 1997 the devastation brought about by El Niño drought and forest fires had given the landscape some of the wild loneliness of which they dreamed. El Niño, they say, was a godsend because the streams dried up, revealing hidden minerals. "[I]t was as if Mother Nature had lifted a curtain, exposing the secrets below" (Lundin 1998: 4). Ignoring local residents' hunger, fire damage, smoke inhalation, and displacement, he bragged, "International Pursuit's exploration teams were among the relative few left on the ground" (ibid.).

I first began to think about gold mining because of the spread of desolation and wildness across large swathes of the Kalimantan landscape. A new landscape had developed in resource extraction areas: Quiet scenes of forests, fields, and houses had become wild terrains of danger, urgency, and destruction. The mad rush for gold joined and stimulated mad rushes for logs, birds' nests, incense woods, marble, and even sand.

As I discussed in chapter 1, three developments were essential to this transformation of the terrain. First, big and small entrepreneurs were interdependent. Transnational companies and transregional migrants from all over Indonesia complemented each other. In mining, big companies have official permits; independent miners are illegal. Independent miners lead company prospectors to the best spots. The companies displace them but then employ them for prospecting. The companies complain about the illegals, blaming them for environmental problems, thus protecting their own reputations. The illegals supply everyday services for the companies. The companies follow the small miners and the small miners cluster around the companies; they become codependents.

Second, nature had to be made into loot, free for all. In the 1980s, logging companies worked hard to extinguish local rights to resources. "This place belongs to Indonesia, not to you," the logging bosses said when residents complained. The military followed and supported their claims, creating an authoritarian lawlessness that made resources free for those who could take them. By the mid-1990s, local residents said, "We still know our customary rights, but no one cares about them." The roads invited migrants. Violence became key to ownership. Swarming miners escalated the terror, the risk, and the urgency of taking everything out, right away.

Third, frontier migrants arrived at the end of long chains of culture and capital. Small miners rarely owned the hydraulic pumps with which they removed topsoil; they contracted them from urban entrepreneurs in profit-sharing arrangements. Often, they subcontracted with local residents, dividing imagined profits even further. Migrants and local residents learned to share cultural practices of entrepreneurship that reached from distant cities deep into the forest. Local residents brought mining activities up the rivers, through their familiar forests, close to home, spreading frontier standards of rapid resource extraction. They have been drawn into the competition and violence of frontier relationships, taking on even the superficial trappings of migrant-oriented subsistence. In these entrepreneurial chains, a spreading frontier culture is created. It is a culture dedicated to the obliteration of local places, local land and resource rights, and local knowledges of flora and fauna. The makeshift camps of the miners proliferate across the landscape, mixing migrants and local residents in an anti-local regionality in which commitment to the local landscape is as useless as the gravel residue left after gold has been picked out and taken away.

Frontier culture is a conjuring act because it creates the wild and spreading regionality of its imagination. It conjures a self-conscious translocalism, committed to the obliteration of local places. Such commitments are themselves distinctive and limited—and thus "local" from another perspective. Yet they break with past localisms in self-conscious regionalism. This is a conjuring of scale, and frontier resource extraction relies on it.

A distinctive feature of this frontier regionality is its magical vision; it asks participants to see a landscape that doesn't exist, at least not yet. It must continually erase old residents' rights to create its wild and empty spaces where *discovering* resources, not stealing them, is possible. To do so, too, it must cover up the conditions of its own production. Consider the contrasts between the features of the story of the frontier that must be told and the frontier conditions I observed: The lone prospector replaces swarming migrants and residents, searching the landscape. The excitement of scientific discovery replaces the violence of expropriation as local resource rights are extinguished and armed gangs enforce their preeminence. The autonomy of the prospector's find replaces the interdependent negotiations of big companies and illegal miners, each leading the other to new sites and trading political and material assets as they form complementary players.[21]

Why does the frontier story have any power at all, considering what it erases? How can it imagine the Kalimantan landscape so wrongly? These trompe l'oeils became possible because of national discipline: the violence of the military, which spreads a regional lawlessness; the legal regulations that privileged company rights and profits yet allowed illegal migrants to accumulate in the spreading wildness; the confusion between private entrepreneurship and public office that forged the national government. This is not the only kind of nation-making that can exist. To explore its specificity, it is useful to turn our attention to CoWs.

CoWs

CoWs are Contracts of Work. No mining company can extract minerals in Indonesia without one. Like animals, CoWs come in generations. The first CoW was a much revered and singular ancestor, granted to Louisiana's Freeport McMoRan to mine in West Papua.[22] Succeeding generations of CoWs have become more differentiated, more limited, and more finely detailed.[23] Yet as they develop, they continue to be icons, even fetishes, held up to show the relationship between the Indonesian nation and the world. Ideally, they guarantee that resource extraction activities work in the interests of the Indonesian nation as well as the mining company. They specify the conditions that create mutual benefits shared between the nation and its foreign investors.

CoWs have been magical tools of the national elite. Although merely paper and ink, they conjured a regular income for the Indonesian nation-state. Their terms must be secure and attractive by international standards, or they will not draw capital. But if they meet these standards, they can conjure the funds that allow the nation-state to produce itself as what one might call a "miracle nation": a nation in which foreign funds support the authoritarian rule that keeps the funds safe. I have called this "franchise cronyism." In exchange for supplying the money to support the national leaders who can make the state secure, investors are offered the certainties of the contract, which ensures title to mineral deposits, fixes taxation rates, and permits export of profit.

The CoW guarantees that investors are not working with "dictators." As one Canadian Bre-X investor explained to me, in investing his modest funds he always avoided the countries of dictators. This was the reason the Bre-X investment seemed reasonable. I was confused: What is a dictator? As we talked, I realized that a dictator is a foreign ruler who interferes with Canadian investment. Indonesia's President Suharto was not a dictator, at least before Bre-X. As Bre-X president David Walsh put it, his company—like other Australian and Canadian mining companies in the 1980s and 1990s—targeted Indonesia "by virtue of its geological setting, favorable investment climate and political stability" (Wells 1997c: 42).

Other nations could be and were imagined in Indonesia. Suharto's New Order emerged violently in 1966 from an earlier scene of diverse and competitive programs for making the nation, and from the start the regime depended on the repression of other Indonesian national visions through censorship and militarization. Political quietude was nurtured, too, through internationally sponsored "development," which came to refer to programs of state expansion dedicated to convincing diverse local people of the unified national standards of state power. Through "development," the state conceived a legal framework to claim the nation's resources and make them available for foreign expropriation, thus amassing the materials through which its version of the nation could prosper.

When investment capital began to circulate wildly across national boundaries in the 1980s, the Indonesian elite was ready for it. They beckoned to the mining sector, saying: "There are still vast tracts of unexplored land in Indonesia. For those who dare to venture, Indonesia offers immense possibilities."[24] The Australians came. One Indonesian ex-mining official candidly admitted that these were "irresponsible investments" with "rubbish technology." When the Canadian companies followed in the 1990s, it was more of the same: "It's a repetition of history. It's not really a gold rush. It's rather a stock market rush."[25] Yet the government transformed the stock market rush into a gold rush by offering it regional frontiers in the making. The regime gave the companies Contracts of Work, despite their irresponsibility. The CoWs wrote away local rights. Military men deployed to enforce CoWs felt encouraged to start their own entrepreneurial schemes, creating a model of government in which administrators by definition doubled as entrepreneurs who, supported by kickbacks, freed up resources for investors, including themselves. Civil servants became franchise entrepreneurs too, learning to conjure the miracle nation locally. It was they who sanctioned the mass migration of illegal small loggers and miners that kept the regional economy afloat while bigger investors took out bigger resources and profits. In this escalating mobility and lawlessness, the mysteries of the search for buried treasure became possible. Whether there was gold or not, the economy could grow, spurred on by fabulous dreams.

By the 1990s, the Suharto regime began to take for granted its domestic stability and international support. The work of disguising official kickbacks as sound investment policy seemed already complete. Perhaps this will help to explain how the set performance of the miracle nation could have been allowed to deteriorate into dramatic excess. Drama ultimately embarrassed the Suharto regime, allowing investors to label it corrupt. At the same time, it provided a moment of opportunity for investors, who could maneuver within the new embarrassments of national performance to gain a better position for themselves. No investors did better than Bre-X and its rivals in opening up those dramatic cracks and making them visible on international news screens. However unself-conscious the manipulation, it seems clear that the over-the-top drama of franchise cronyism set off around Bre-X allowed the Bre-X investment bubble to last far longer than it could have otherwise, drawing out the drama from the 1994 announcement of gold to the 1997 death of de Guzman. This drama popularized the Bre-X story, vastly enlarging investment.

In January 1994 Barrick Gold offered to buy a stake in Bre-X. Barrick was involved in an aggressive campaign of acquisitions in an attempt to become the world's biggest gold mining company. As mentioned previously, Barrick's CEO, Peter Munk, was a risk taker who had made his fortune from the lucky purchase of a Nevada mine, which turned out to be a fabulous mother lode. Furthermore, Barrick had targeted Indonesia as a possible site for high-profit, low-cost mining. Bre-X's Busang was just Barrick's kind of buy (Goold and Willis 1997: 99–100).

When Bre-X turned him down, Barrick moved into the cracks of the Indonesian regime, working the connection between greed and vulnerability that their nation-making performances had themselves produced. The high-powered politicians on Barrick's advisory board pressured the minister of mines and energy, and even President Suharto.[26] Barrick then approached the president's daughter Tutut, a tycoon in road construction contracts. Barrick offered her Busang's construction contracts, and she pushed the minister of mines to negotiate a Barrick Bre-X split in which the government would control 10 percent of the mine, Barrick 70 percent, and Bre-X 20 percent. Bre-X was vulnerable because they had begun drilling without a CoW; now the ministry pulled out even their temporary exploration permit to clinch the deal (Wells 1997c).

Bre-X stockholders went wild with anger. In the glare of their dissatisfaction, the drama escalated. Placer Dome, another Canadian company, made a better bid.[27] Meanwhile, Bre-X made a spectacular play by approaching the president's son, Sigit, and offering him 10 percent of the mine plus an eye-catching $1 million per month to push their case. Whether naive, as read at the time, or unimaginably clever, this move took the performance of franchise cronyism to its extreme limits, offering the investment drama a new life. Now Suharto's children were pitted against each other publicly.

Barrick continued to have government support until it gained a new opponent: entrepreneur Bob Hasan, the long-time friend and golfing buddy of the president, and the man who best knew how to mimic foreign investors' ploys to enlarge his own empire. Hasan played the patriot of the miracle nation, arguing passionately that the enrichment and empowerment of national elites is the first principle of national interest. Barrick irritated him by sending in North American politicians, and he railed against their "cowboyisms," which made Indonesia look helpless under the American thumb.[28] Meanwhile, too, he managed to acquire a 50 percent share in Bre-X's Indonesian partner.[29]

The game was almost over when President Suharto asked Bob Hasan to work out a solution for Bre-X, and yet, this too was a moment of momentous drama. Bre-X stockholders were at the edge of their seats. Activist stockholder George Chorny wrote a public letter to Hasan, reminding him that it was Bre-X that discovered the gold. "It's not any of the guys at Barrick or Placer. It's not the Indonesian government. All the Indonesian government did was to welcome the people of Bre-X to come into their country with open arms to explore this jungle, this desolate jungle in the middle of nowhere" (Wells 1997b). For Chorny, the frontier is always already empty. But Hasan had a different perspective; making the frontier was a national responsibility. Hasan dismissed both Barrick and Placer Dome and brought in the regime's favorite company, Freeport McMoRan. In Hasan's solution, Freeport McMoRan would take 15 percent of the mine and become sole operator; the Indonesian government would take 10 percent; Hasan's companies would take 30 percent; and the remaining 45 percent would remain with Bre-X. Backed into a corner, Bre-X signed gracefully.[30]

Freeport, unlike Bre-X and even Barrick, was not in the business of spectacular accumulation, the economy of appearances. Freeport worked with its own cultural logic of investment and development, which, at least at this period, differed from that of Bre-X. Freeport was no mining junior, amassing capital to finance further exploration. Instead, it had established itself as a big, solid outpost of "American civilization" in Indonesia. As CEO Jim Bob Moffett put it, "We are thrusting a spear of economic development into the heartland of Irian Jaya [West Papua]" (Marr 1993: 71). Freeport built residential neighborhoods in West Papua reminiscent of U.S. suburbs; Moffett performed Elvis Presley imitations during Christmas visits. Freeport's culture of business, then, offered Americanization rather than "frontier discovery" as a model of profitability.

Freeport had long since gained its miracle deal from the Suharto regime. Its personal Contract of Work far exceeded the benefits of all other investors. In turn, Freeport was the largest source of investor tax revenue for the Indonesian government. It had spent an enormous amount of money developing its Grasberg mine in West Papua, where it depended on the army to keep local residents in line. In 1995, however, riots closed the mine; in 1996, West Papuan tribal leaders sued the company for environmental destruction and human rights abuses, and the Overseas Private Investment

Corporation (an agency of the U.S. government) cancelled the company's risk insurance because of its environmental policies. In 1997, then, Freeport was busy living down international accusations of environmental and social irresponsibility in West Papua. It needed a green profile and solid production results, not an economic miracle.[31] In this spirit, Freeport sent in a sober team to assess the gold at Busang. There was nothing there. "It makes me sick every time I think about it," said Jim Bob Moffett, Freeport's CEO (Behar 1997: 128). After a few most impressive last gasps, the spectacle wound down and collapsed. Said Bre-X President David Walsh, "Four and a half years of hard work and the pot at the end of the rainbow is a bucket of slop" (*Calgary Sun*, October 12, 1997).[32]

On Spectacular Accumulation

What does this story allow us to learn about transnational finance and its globalist aspirations? In the midst of their dramatic roles, the major players usefully remind us of the stage they have laid. Like Bob Hasan, I am struck by the North American character of the dreams and schemes of investment that swirled around Bre-X. With Bre-X stockholders, I marvel at the ability of Indonesian nation makers to usurp an economic process that has been imagined as so independent from national controls. And as for the Kalimantan landscape, it is hard not to mourn: The pot at the end of the rainbow is a bucket of eroding mud, damaged forests, and mercury-poisoned rivers. Slop indeed.

It was the Canadian imagination of the combined frontier of investment and mining that made this drama possible. The mining industry has been historically important to Canada's economy and identity. By the 1980s, its locus had shifted from mining *in* Canada to mining *for* Canada. It represented opportunity, initiative, and the potential prosperity in national character. Bre-X's run from the bottom of the Alberta stock exchange to the top of the Toronto exchange and into the world was a source of pride for many Canadians. As much as for profits, Canadians invested for reasons of national pride.[33]

Yet the national specificity of attraction to investments disappears in the excitement of commitments to globalism in the financial world. When one thinks about finance in the Bre-X case, there was nothing worldwide about it at all; it was Canadian and U.S. investment in Indonesia. Yet it was easy to assimilate this specific trajectory of investment to an imagined globalism to the extent that the global is defined as the opening-up process in which remote places submit to foreign finance. Every time finance finds a new site of engagement, we think that the world is getting more global. In this act of conjuring, *global* becomes the process of finding new sites. In the force field of this particular globalism, Canadian national dreams are reimagined as transcendent, circulating, beyond culture.

Despite the enormous coercions and seductions of financiers, which aim to make the whole world ready for investment, there is great particularity not only in the reasons a Canadian might want to invest but also in places where he or she can invest. In the 1990s, when the dreams of the Indonesian elite linked with those of Canadians to jointly conjure the promise of gold, Indonesia became one of those places. Images of remote wild places that could make independent-minded Canadians rich and free touched Indonesian visions of a miracle nation, a nation that could come into being in the arms of foreign finance. Flying in the face of financiers' fantasies of making the nation disappear for the greater mobility of capital, the magic of the miracle nation, waving its CoWs, asserted itself as the only door to North American investment. CoWs, as I have argued, are not merely mechanical adjustments of economic affairs. They are fetish objects, charged with conjuring the miracle nation in the face of competing alternative visions, which unless warded off might come to control the apparatus of the state. From investors' perspectives, they are charged, too, with the security of profit and property. As a gift, they remake the identities of both giver and receiver, vitalizing the miracle nation and its globalist speculators.

For the aspirations of international investors and national elites to emerge as more than a moment's daydream, however, they must be made tangible on a regional landscape. They must engage people, places, and environments. The anti-local culture of Kalimantan frontier regionalism nurtured and raised up both the miracle nation and Canadian speculation. Here is a truly cosmopolitan scene, where varied dreams are jumbled together, naming and renaming creeks, valleys, routes, and towns. The dreamers jostle, fight bitterly, and patronize each other. As they make their own new places, these too are knocked away. Old residents become aliens as the familiar landscape is transformed by trauma, danger, and the anxiety of the unknown. Here mystery can flourish, and unexpected discoveries can be made. Unimagined riches can be found because the layout of wealth and poverty is unsettled, un-imagined. Impossible promises cannot be ignored. On this landscape, the economy of appearances seems so real that it must be true.

When the spectacle passes on, what is left is rubble and mud, the residues of success and failure. People with other stakes and stories will have to pick up the pieces.

....

At the intersection of projects for making globes, nations, and regions, new kinds of economies can emerge. In the Bre-X drama, globalist commitments to opening up fresh sites for Canadian mining investments enabled Indonesian visions of a miracle nation at the same time as they stimulated the search for mining frontiers. The program of the miracle nation offered speculators security as it also forced potential frontier regions into lawless violence and abolished customary tenure. When Kalimantan responded by developing a wild frontier, its regional reformation confirmed the proprietary rights of the miracle nation. The Kalimantan frontier could then appeal to globalist speculation, offering a landscape where both discovery and loss were possible. Three scale-making projects came into conjunction here: the globe-making aspirations of finance capital; the nation-making coercions of franchise cronyism; and the region-making claims of frontier culture (see fig. 1). Globalist, nationalist, and regionalist dreams linked to enunciate a distinctive economic program, the program of spectacular accumulation.

Spectacular accumulation occurs when investors speculate on a product that may or may not exist. Investors are looking for the appearance of success. They cannot afford to find out if the product is solid; by then their chances for profit will be gone. To invest in software development requires this kind of leap: Software developers sell their potential, not their product. Biotechnology requires a related if distinctive leap of faith to trust the processes of innovation and patenting to yield as-yet-unknown property rights and royalties. Real estate development requires an assessment of desirability and growth, not demonstrated occupancy; it sells investors attractiveness. In each of these cases, economic performance is conjured dramatically.[34]

I use the term *spectacular accumulation* mainly to argue with evolutionary assumptions in popular theories of the ever-changing world economy. According to regulation theorists, "flexible accumulation" is the latest stage of capitalism. Flexible accumulation follows Fordist production as barbarism follows savagery, that is, up a singular political-economic ladder. David Harvey's writing (1989) has made this conceptualization influential among anthropologists, who suggest correlated changes in culture, spatiality, and scale to go along with this evolutionary progression. Thus, too, scholars imagine evolutionary changes in the making of space and time. Theories of globalization have us imagine a worldwide condensation of space and time in which spaces grow smaller and times more instantaneous and effortless. Consider, however, the space-time requirements of Bre-X's spectacular accumulation: Space is hugely enlarged; far from miniature and easy, it becomes expansive, labored, and wild, spreading muddy, malarial frontiers.

Figure 2. APHIDS. This acronym is both serious and a joke.

Time is quickened but into the rush of acceleration, not the efficiency of quick transfers. It is not effortless; if you can't feel the rush and the intensity, you are missing the point, and you'll keep your money at home. Moreover, this spectacular accumulation does not call out to be imagined as new. It is self-consciously old, drawing us back to the South Sea bubble and every gold rush in history. In contrast with flexible accumulation, its power is not its rejection of the past, but its ability to keep this old legacy untarnished.

This is more than yet another classificatory device in the annals of capitalism. My point is to show the heterogeneity of capitalism at every moment in time. Capitalist forms and processes are continually made and unmade; if we offer singular predictions we allow ourselves to be caught by them as ideologies. This seems especially pressing in considering the analysis of scale. Since the 1990s, every ambitious world-making project has wanted to show itself able to forge new scales. Nongovernmental organizations, ethnic groups and coalitions, initiatives for human rights and social justice: We all want to be creative and self-conscious about our scale-making. We want to claim the globe as ours. In this context, rather than ally myself with globalist financiers to tell of *their* globe, I trace how that globe comes into being both as a culturally specific set of commitments and as a set of practices. The investment drama of the Bre-X story shows how articulations among globalist, nationalist, and regionalist projects bring each project to life. In the spirit of serious but joking diagrams, I offer an acronym to refocus your attention (fig. 2). The particularity of globalist projects, I am arguing, is best seen in the contingent articulations that make them possible and bring them to life: These are "aphids," Articulations among Partially Hegemonic Imagined Different Scales.

Often we turn to capitalism to understand how what seem to be surface developments form part of an underlying pattern of exploitation and class formation. Yet before we succumb to the capitalist monolith called up in these analyses, it is useful to look at the continual emergence of new capitalist niches, cultures, and forms of agency. For this task, Stuart Hall's idea about the role of articulation in the formation of new political subjects is helpful (1996). New political subjects form, he argues, as pre-existing groups link and, through linking, enunciate new identities and interests. Social processes and categories also can develop in this way. I have used this insight to trace the spectacular accumulation brought into being by the articulation of finance capital, franchise cronyism, and frontier culture. While each of these linked projects achieved only a moment of partial hegemony, this was also a moment of dramatic success.

Soon after the story I have told, Indonesia precipitously collapsed as a celebrated site for investment; the miracle nation was discredited, and the articulation fell apart. Afterward, analysts scrambled to tell the difference between good and bad investments. They recognized that the Busang saga had contributed in a small way to the Indonesian crash. But they ignored or refused its allegorical quality: Bre-X offered a dramatic rendition of the promises and perils of the economic miracle attributed, in Indonesia and beyond, to globalization.[35]

How might scholars take on the challenge of freeing critical imaginations from the specter of neoliberal conquest—singular, universal, global? Attention to the frictions of contingent articulation can help us describe the effectiveness, and the fragility, of emergent capitalist—and globalist—forms. In this shifting heterogeneity there are new sources of hope, and, of course, new nightmares.

Knowledge

Global vision 1955

"Let a new Asia and a new Africa be born"
[Global vision]

Stories of the Enlightenment often pair knowledge and vision, in two senses: the privileging of the sense of sight, and the importance of planning. Vision has energized knowledge of the globe by condensing it in a friendly visual icon and normalizing its futurist aspirations. Yet global imagery is contested and tentative. Knowledge that travels today is haunted by the disappointments of past visions. Haunting disturbs our reliance on vision. Double vision gives us a headache, reminding us of our frailty. Authoritative knowledge is forced to shore up its boundaries. "Experts" are those who have trained themselves to see with a singular vision. In contrast, the public is troubled by haunting. Only by excluding the public can knowledge be kept pure.

None of this means that any knowledge is as good as any other. Continued life on earth depends on getting our knowledge into as good a shape as possible. But this can mean paying more rather than less attention to the multiplicity of knowledge claims. Both global knowledge and knowledge that travels around the globe are improved by dialogue across difference. Hauntings sometimes open the way to such dialogue: What visions have we been formed by, yet forgotten? What visions have we let shrivel, fester, or fall away?

1955. On April 18, in the town of Bandung, Indonesia's first president welcomed delegates from across Asia and Africa to what promised to be a momentous occasion: the Asia-Africa Conference. The theme of the president's opening remarks ("Let a new Asia and a new Africa be born") was freedom. Freedom was spreading across the globe.

Sisters and Brothers, how terrifically dynamic is our time! I recall that, several years ago, I had occasion to make a public analysis of colonialism, and that I then drew attention to what I called the "lifeline of imperialism." This line runs from the Straits of Gibraltar, through the Mediterranean, the Suez Canal, the Red Sea, the Indian Ocean, the South China Sea and the Sea of Japan. For most of that enormous distance, the territories on both sides of this lifeline were colonies, the peoples were unfree, their futures mortgaged to an alien system. Along that lifeline, that main artery of imperialism, there was pumped the life-blood of colonialism. '

And today in this hall are gathered together the leaders of those same people. They are no longer the victims of colonialism. They are no longer the tools and playthings of forces they cannot influence. Today, you are representatives of free peoples, peoples [of] a different stature and standing in the world. (Sukarno 1983: 5)

In 1955, the American Revolution still stood as a beacon of freedom—at least in Indonesia, where U.S. influence had helped the independence struggle. President Sukarno reminded his audience that on April 18, 1776, Paul Revere rode at midnight through the New England countryside warning of the approach of British troops in "the first successful anti-colonial war in history" (1983: 7). Sukarno quoted Longfellow:

A cry of defiance, and not of fear,
A voice in the darkness, a knock at the door,
And a word that shall echo for evermore![1]

Yet the echoing U.S. voice was also known for its menace. The atom bomb had been unleashed, and the escalating Cold War threatened the very existence of the world. As Sukarno explained: "War would not only mean a threat to our independence, it may mean the end of civilization and even of human life. There is a force loose in the world whose [potential] for evil no man truly knows. . . . [I]t has been made clear that the weapons of ultimate horror will certainly be used. . . . No task is more urgent that that of preserving peace" (1983: 8).

What can we do? We can do much! We can inject the voice of reason into world affairs. We can mobilize all the spiritual, all the moral, all the political strength of Asia and Africa on the side of peace. Yes, we! We, the peoples of Asia and Africa, 1,400,000,000 strong, far more than half the human population of the world, we can mobilize what I have called the Moral Violence of Nations in favor of peace. We can demonstrate to the minority of the world which lives on the other continents that we, the majority, are for peace, not war, and that whatever strength we have will always be thrown on to the side of peace. (1983: 8).

Thus opened what would become known as the Third World, here imagined as a nonaligned block of emerging nations whose united presence could stop the Cold War. Their unity would define them as a global force. Their freedom would sponsor global peace. Peace and freedom would work together to remake the globe.

The guest list at Bandung was a roll call of the celebrities of post–World War II nationalism. Besides Indonesia's leaders, the sponsors were India's Jawaharlal Nehru, Burma's U Nu, Pakistan's Mohammed Ali, and Ceylon's Sir John Kotelawala. Gamal Abdel Nasser represented Egypt; Chou En-lai represented China; Prince Sihanouk represented Cambodia; Kwame Nkrumah sent his deputy from the Gold Coast. Ministers from Afghanistan, Iran, Iraq, Jordan, Lebanon, Libya, Saudi Arabia, Sudan, Syria, Turkey, and Yemen came from the Middle East. Leaders still working for independence came from sub-Saharan Africa. Two delegations represented Vietnam, North and South. In a gesture of solidarity, novelist Richard Wright and U.S. Congressman Adam Clayton Powell came as "unofficial delegates" representing African Americans. Racism was an important conference topic. As Sukarno put it, "This is the first intercontinental conference of colored peoples in the history of mankind" (1983: 3).

In Bandung, national sovereignty seemed full of promise. Colonialism was on its way out; freedom was sweeping the globe. Unity among the emerging nations could be a new source of political power, thwarting racism and nuclear war. Solidarity could make peace possible, and peace could guarantee freedom. How many times the world has turned since then! How few today remember the meeting in Bandung.

....

In April 2000, I visited the Museum of the Asia-Africa Conference in Bandung with an international group of scholars. The museum itself is a New Order creation, inaugurated in 1980. It trains our eyes with a "conference hall in miniature" exhibit, reducing the conference's success to its pomp and discipline. It is careful to excise President Sukarno, who was deposed by the New Order, from too much praise. Yet the mythic world of post–World War II nationalism rushes upon us as soon as we see the black-and-white photographs of the delegates. Nasser, Nehru, U Nu: the names themselves resound with the promise of post-colonial development, Third World nations on the move. How young they look—as beautiful as movie stars—how full of optimism and hope! How possible it still seemed that the nations over which these young men had come to preside would overcome colonial legacies to build new worlds of freedom and opportunity. For a moment we can taste the promise that the clasped hands of rising Third World leaders offered. A map of the world, covered with radiating lines, fills one wall: the connections among developing nations will cover the earth.

Meanwhile, we peer at dusty typewriters and telex machines in glass cases: these are the machines that ran the conference. How old and obsolete they seem. This dream of a rising Third World has not lasted. Instead of unity blocking the Cold War, the Cold War blocked the unity of nonaligned nations. Radical nationalists were deposed and murdered; the Cold War was exported to countries across the world. Militaries and development budgets took over. Nationalism lost its promise, as imperially mandated authoritarian rule came to define the Third World. As the future has shifted, the past contorts, confused. In one cabinet featuring conference pamphlets, the curators have included an engineering report on an airplane crash in another city. No explanation is offered.

This past is ours, but through a glass, mythical, and dusty.

....

In 1955, the Bandung conference was commemorated on an Indonesian postage stamp, an enlarged version of which adorns the museum wall. On the lower right side, Asians and Africans raise their hands to release scores of doves. The doves are flying to a great, round, moonlike rising globe, which forms the focus of attention of the crowd. This globe is the earth, illustrated with its Asian and African countries in prominent view.

This is not the globe whose image we naturalize in the twenty-first century. The space shots of the fragile blue-green orb, wrapped in clouds, had not yet been produced. This is still a globe of international maps. Most strikingly, the people are not standing on it. They face it with admiration and hope; they send doves to it. It shines on them, offering them light, but it does not appear to trap them in its vulnerabilities and disciplines.

In Bandung, the globe was a symbol of what might be possible: national sovereignty and world peace. This global dream space was made possible by other mid-twentieth century uses of the globe, for example in the United Nations. The bridge to this dream space was that of universal truths, such as science, modernization, and political freedom. This was a time when science seemed more than a neutral set of truths. Science was the antidote to ignorant racial stereotypes and misguided imperial impositions. International cooperation among scientists formed a model for coexistence and respect. Similarly, modernization and development might allow each nation to fulfill its dreams while entering cooperative arrangements with others. Human rights might form a peace-loving common language. The doves set off in the

Bandung commemorative stamp are universal truths, which forge a bridge to the dream space of global peace and freedom.

When we consider the importance of the Bandung dream of peace and freedom, the inadequacy of the bridge seems hardly a good enough reason to have abandoned the quest.

....

The universal bridge to a global dream space still beckons to us. The bridge might take us out of our imagined isolation into a space of unity and transcendence: the whole world. We find ourselves like a man looking out from his parochial island toward the vast but hazy world of the mainland. The bridge of universal truths promises to take us there. Yet we walk across that bridge, and we find ourselves, not everywhere, but somewhere in particular. Even if our bridge aims toward the most lofty universal truths—the insights of science, the freedom of individual rights, the possibility of wealth for all— we find ourselves hemmed in by the specificity of rules and practices, with their petty prejudices, unreasonable hierarchies, and cruel exclusions. We must make do, enmeshing our desires in the compromise of practical action. We become hardened, or, alternatively, we are overcome with grief and anger. The bridge we stepped off is not the bridge we stepped upon. Yet to cast away the memory of the first bridge denies desire. To pretend it is the same as the second bridge is the baldest lie of power. It is only in maintaining the friction between the two subjectively experienced bridges, the friction between aspiration and practical achievement, that a critical analysis of global connection is possible.

Science, modernization, and freedom were simultaneously dream bridges for the development of Third World nations and real-life programs within the contingencies of Cold War politics, elite power grabs, authoritarian regimes, religious wars, ecological disasters, and bureaucracies of expertise. Their ability to mobilize national support and their failure to deliver on their promises are intermeshed in these histories.

....

Since the mid–twentieth century, the global dream space has been kicked around like a football claimed first by one team and then another. Environmentalists have wanted it badly, but so have human rights activists, religious sects, and marketers. In the 1990s, corporate public relations took hold of the image of the globe and carried it away. "Globalization" came to mean corporate consolidation, the standardization of world markets, and the deference of national governments to transnational business demands. This global dream space also required a bridge of universal truths, involving neoliberal economic principles and the standardization of property law. Yet even the urgent stridency with which such standards were imposed could not keep other versions of truth from having their say. By the turn of the century, "anti-globalization" politics had begun to gel. The confrontation between demonstrators and police guarding the deliberations of the World Trade Organization in Seattle in 1999 opened a new era of globe-making politics.[2] The motley demonstrators—like the national representatives at Bandung—hoped that the force of their unity might form a block against dangerous giants.

Seattle and Bandung could not be more different. Anarchists and children dressed as turtles in the street, versus negotiating heads of state. Police fomenting riot versus police on display. The refusal of the hegemony of nation-states, versus the proud assertion of nation-state autonomy. The critique of development, versus the endorsement of rights to develop. In Seattle, official representatives of Third World nations were notorious for refusing to discuss labor standards: Too many accepted that their power as nations now rested on their ability to offer the cheapest labor and the worst working conditions.

Yet both Bandung and Seattle were sites for reclaiming the dream space of the globe. Both offered a bridge of doves to make the dream of a livable globe real. The globe, however, was not the same. In Seattle, the globe could not be projected as a sphere of hope. No one would argue that the world's problems were caused by a lack of global unity. Instead, demonstrators argued that corporate giants had seized the globe; it was up to transnational activists to take it back. The globe could not be imagined rising hopefully like the full moon; it presented itself as already divided between the discipline of military and machines, on the one hand, and the hopes of resistors, on the other.

The universal truths that might form a bridge to global dreams were also contested in Seattle. The momentary unity among labor activists, environmentalists, anarchists, and anti-imperialists did not disguise the lack of common principles that guided their critical assaults. Is the destruction of property a progressive or a destructive strategy? Is the problem for labor refractory countries such as China, or power-hungry ones such as the United States? Would environmental management be improved or worsened by placing its concerns integrally inside free trade? Is Christian prayer a good basis for cosmopolitan solidarity? Each position can be argued with a universal truth, but with different results.

These disagreements are not a reason to give up on anti-globalization politics; they are what make it lively. However, they require a new kind of attention to universal truths, our bridges to global dreams. The principles of justice are multiple and contested: Those who feel the effects of injustice continually stretch the categories through which justice is understood. The play among multiple, contested universals can be described as one kind of friction. Knowledge of the globe, and globally traveling knowledge, depend on this friction.

3 Natural Universals and the Global Scale

To see a World in a Grain of Sand
And a Heaven in a Wild Flower,
Hold Infinity in the palm of your hand
And Eternity in an hour.
      —from William Blake,
        "Auguries of Innocence"

Generalization. The action or process of generalizing, i.e. of forming, and expressing in words, general notions or propositions obtained from the observation and comparison of individual facts or appearances; also, an instance of this.[1]

Many things are said to be universal: freedom, money, love. But the two most historically successful universal claims—which continue to form exemplars for all universality—are still God and Nature. The universality of God and the universality of Nature are historically connected; in the European Renaissance, the stirrings of modern science conceived the latter on the model of the former. Only because God was known to be universal could Nature be depicted that way. The connection between God and Nature has continued to inspire the musings of theologians, scientists, and naturalists, reminding us of the importance of reason and mystery in appreciating each domain. Yet readers interested in how God came to be universal will have to consult other texts. This chapter enters the story midway to ask about the universality of capital-N Nature, that is, the awe-inspiring, lawlike systematicity of the cosmos and of life on earth.

Nature and the globe have helped make each other. Today's most powerful claims about the nature of the globe refer us to global Nature: If universal laws of Nature can be established, then the globe forms an orderly part of them. The globe is a node for the expression of universal logic. Scale-making, in turn, is a foundational move in establishing the neutrality and universalism of Nature; only if observations are compatible and collapsible across scales can they be properly described by a universal logic. Yet to "think globally" is no easy task. To recognize the globe as the relevant unit for our imaginations requires work. Moreover, establishing Nature has never been simple.

How does the universality of Nature operate in a world of friction? I approach this question through looking at the process of "generalization," in which small details support great visions and the universal is discovered in particularities. Two features of generalization intrigue me. First, generalization to the universal requires a large space of compatibility among disparate particular facts and observations. As long as facts are apples and oranges, one cannot generalize across them; one must first see them as "fruit" to make general claims. Compatibility standardizes difference. It allows transcendence: the general can rise above the particular. For this, compatibility must pre-exist the particular facts being examined; and it must unify the field of inquiry. The searcher for universal truths must establish an *axiom of unity*—whether on spiritual, aesthetic, mathematical, logical, or moral principles.

Second, tentative and contingent collaborations among disparate knowledge seekers and their disparate forms of knowledge can turn incompatible facts and observations into compatible ones. Just as tiny convergences in incompatible testimonies at a criminal trial can establish a line of truth, the founding lines through which we learn to recognize Nature are often established in convergent opinions. Convergences offer legitimacy and charisma to nascent categories. They offer bridges over unrecognizable difference. Convincing universals must be able to travel with at least some facility in the world, and this requires negotiations across incompatible difference. Upon occasion, these give rise to collaboratively agreed upon Natural objects. The unfamiliar becomes the familiar through this process, and generalization can occur.

What is most striking to me about these two features of generalization is the way they cover each other up. The specificity of collaborations is erased by pre-established unity; the a priori status of unity is denied by turning to its instantiation in collaborations. Buoyed by axioms of unity, collaborations create convincingly agreed upon observations and facts that then appear to support generalization *directly*, that is, without the prior mediation of the collaboration. The contingency of the collaboration, and its exclusions, no longer seem relevant because the facts come to "speak for themselves." The pre-evidential status of the axiom of unity fades into the background, too, when facts naturalized through collaboration can be called on as the natural basis of generalization.

Generalization to the universal is at the heart of much analytic work; it makes it possible to devise market principles from particular transactions, to interpret events within Biblical prophecy, to mobilize class struggle, and to make scientific observations speak to general laws. No one I know wants to accept every claim made through generalization—or to dismiss them all out of hand. To characterize the process of generalization is not to reject all its products. I am not making fun of this procedure in studying it; I have no interest in ironic dismissals. I write here only about generalizations that I care about.

In this chapter, I illustrate the interplay of the two processes of generalization I have introduced in defining the global scale together with universal Nature. For this, I have chosen discrepant examples: the emergence of botanical science, American nature loving, mathematical climate modeling, and an international forestry accord. Each offers a different axiom of unity through which individual observations are made available for generalization. Botanical science first generalized on the basis of God's will, and only later substituted evolutionary process. American nature loving proposed a spiritual and aesthetic unity for Nature. Climate modeling has offered systems logic. Forest management advocates turned to international politics. Each project, in turn, has built from a divergent history of collaborative relations, such as those that connect botanical collectors across the world, or link nature lovers and promoters of tourism, or join scientists and policy makers. I show how these contingent collaborations are necessary to the process of generalization even as they are covered up by it. Axioms of unity and collaborations both need each other and hide each other; generalization—with its particularistic exclusions and biases—is produced as the product of this interaction.

Naming God's Creations

> [T]he world is a great library, and Fruit trees are some of his Bookes wherein we may read and see plainly the Attributes of God his Power, Wisdom, Goodness, etc.
>
> —R. Austen, *The Spiritual Use of an Orchard*

Botanical classification had a privileged role at the beginning of modern science. Botany pioneered understandings of Nature, showing the potential of a universal science. Botany was perhaps the first science concerned with uniting knowledge from around the globe to create a singular global knowledge. The global scale and the universal were developed and demonstrated for science in this emergent field.[2]

European voyages of discovery in the fifteenth and sixteenth centuries stimulated interest in the diversity of plants around the world. The folk botanies of Europe could not incorporate the wealth of unfamiliar plants that were being described from Asia, Africa, and the New World. In the ensuing excitement about new plants, a universal logic was put forward for the task of ordering global diversity: the logic of God's creation. Plants formed a unified set because God had created them according to His plan. The insight of botanical science was to imagine from this plan a universal *system* of classification. In the nineteenth century, the strength of the system allowed insights about an evolutionary history linking organisms, and only then did a logic *within* Nature usurp God as the unifying source of order of global biology. But by then, plant classification had begun its descent to the lowly scholarly status it occupies today: data collection. Today, newly discovered plants are members of a pre-established scientific set: the plant kingdom, with its constituent families, genera, and species. They are self-evident elements of Nature and thus of little abstract interest. This success in reducing mysteries to facts speaks to the transformation of consciousness involved in making universality, and the global scale, self-evident. Botanical classification was an important catalyst for this transformation.

A key feature of this transformation was the erasure of the collaborations that made global knowledge possible. European botanical knowledge in the sixteenth and seventeenth centuries was gained by learning from Asians, Africans, and indigenous Americans who introduced Europeans to their native plants. Botanical treatises from this period acknowledge the centrality of these knowledge exchanges. As European power grew around the world, however, European botanists came increasingly to imagine themselves as communing directly with plants—and the universality of science—without the mediation of non-European knowledge. The very collaborations that had made this science possible were covered up, and the plants were asked to speak for themselves as elements of Nature. In the history of systematics (the science of classification), universal premises and collaboratively established facts hid each other's work. Given its importance in establishing Nature, it is worth elaborating this story in a little more detail.

Let me return to the moment when plant classification became a site of intellectual discussion throughout Europe—the second half of the sixteenth century. World travelers brought news of unknown and exotic plants from foreign lands. European herbalists were overwhelmed. Thus arose an exciting reconsideration of knowledge, which lasted for two centuries. During this period, plant classification was at the forefront of the development of science. Scholars of the diversity of life worked particularly from two resources: classical treatises, especially the work of Aristotle, and Christian teachings about the workings of God. Both taught of a universal Nature, accessible through reason and by studying life-forms; both suggested the possibility of a singular global system uniting all life. Scholars debated about which was more important: the logical, rational system through which diversity could be charted, or the empirical study of organisms, through which the system could be inductively built. Andrea Cesalpino, a professor at Pisa and papal physician, is known for his early attempt at a universal taxonomy of plants. He relied on Aristotle, as well as his Catholic faith, to construct a rational system to account for diversity. He also developed a dichotomous key to identify plants: On the one hand, it depends on the logic of dichotomy; on the other, it follows the identifying characteristics of real plants, rather than exhausting logical possibilities (Atran 1990: 157). Not much later, Gaspard Bauhin, a Huguenot who presided over the botanical garden at Basel, sought a system of classification through tracing relationships of thousands of plants from around the world (Drayton 2000: 16). Cesalpino has been criticized for being too much of a rationalist; Bauhin has been criticized for not having enough of a logical system. But the concerns about creating a system to understand empirical diversity are clear in each.

Basic to this discussion was the search for universal order, that is, God's order. Cesalpino, for example, classified plants by the organization of their flower and seed parts, not, as modern biologists might, because of the role of these organs in reproductive biology, but rather because he thought these parts were the best exemplification of God's plan (Atran 1990: 152). It turned out that classification through flower and seed worked very well to order global plant diversity; it is because of the effectiveness of this framework that botany was so significant as an emergent science. (Zoology, in comparison, was a mess at the time.) Classification by flower and seed showed the potential of systematization.[3]

God could be known through reason or through observation, but there was no question about the underlying divine plan that would be revealed. Catholics and Protestants had their differences, but both read the world as God's book. Among botanists, differences between those who stressed reason versus empirical study were expressed in arguments about the relative priority of the "genus"—a classificatory category that grouped closely related types of plants—versus the "species"—the basic plant type. But arguments for each depended on the stability of God's plan. He created the species, and told humans to name them. He created the logic of genus, which allowed species to develop, each to its proper place. "The Creator of all things, who gave us the faculty for giving names to plants, places in the plants themselves signifying marks" (Tourefort 1719: 54, quoted in Atran 1990: 166).

This search for the universal—in marks on the plants themselves, and in underlying logics of plant relationships—drew attention away from the knowledge about plants that was learned in dialogue between Europeans and non-Europeans. It might have been possible for Europeans to learn about plants merely by stumbling upon them, but, in fact, they took the easier route of learning about them from other people.

Historian Richard Grove has described two books about plants in India that drew explicitly from such interactions. Garcia de Orta, a Portuguese doctor in Goa, wrote a treatise on botany in 1563; it was quickly translated into Latin and incorporated into European natural history. The treatise is written as a dialogue between Orta, speaking for the importance of the indigenous knowledge of Goa, and a skeptical interlocutor. Grove writes: "In general the text is remarkably subversive and even hostile to European and Arabic knowledge, regarding it as superfluous in the face of the wealth of accurate local knowledge" (1995: 81). European knowledge was not globally dominant at this period. "Far from imposing European systems of classification and perception on South Asia, the invention of printing and the collation of regional botanical knowledge actually provided an opportunity for the diffusion of indigenous South Asian methodologies of classification throughout the European world, rather than the reverse" (Grove 1995: 80). When the Dutch botanist Hendrik van Reede tot Drakenstein made a new compilation of useful plants of Malabar a century later, he assumed a similar respect for indigenous knowledge. His botanical illustrations were annotated in five languages, including the local Malayam, Arabic, and Latin (Drayton 2000: Plate 3). His text discusses his special reliance on Ezhava collectors of the "toddy-tapper" caste, who were adept at medical knowledge as well as identification of plants. His classifications, which feature Ezhava knowledge, were readily absorbed into European discussions.

Yet discussions among Europeans refused to acknowledge this global sharing of knowledge. Instead, they focused on the formation of a universal system of classification. John Ray, known for his "grammar" of botany (Atran 1990: 61), obviously read van Reede: "Who could believe that in one province of Malabar, hardly a vast place, there could be three hundred unique, indigenous species of trees and fruit?" (Ray 1686: sig. A3v quoted in Drayton 2000: 18). Yet he attributed no importance to the Ezhava dialogue that brought those species to him. The system itself was knowledge, not its component parts.

Carl Linnaeus, known as the father of modern biological classification, explained the importance of the system in unifying and ordering a singular global knowledge:

The system is for botany the thread of Ariadna, without which there is chaos. Let us take, for example, an unknown plant of the Indies, and let a botanophile leaf through descriptions, figures, every index; he will not find it unless by chance. But a systematist will determine it straight away, be it old or new. . . . The system indicates the plants, even those it does not mention; this, the enumeration of a catalog can never do. (Linnaeus 1751: sec. 156, quoted in Atran 1990: 170–71)

The system takes precedence over the plant, as well as the process through which that plant was gathered "out there." Linneaus unself-consciously adopted van Reede's Malabar classifications without noting them as foreign (Grove 1995: 90). For him, all correct knowledge could be united through the use of a universal method. The method is the key to Na-ture. "Nowhere has the Supreme Creator exposed as many objects to the senses of man as in the Plant Realm, which covers and fills the globe we in-habit. Thus, if there be anywhere a proper method, it is that whereby we may hope to obtain a clear idea of Plants" (Linneaus 1737, quoted in Atran 1990: 151). Since it uncovers the handiwork of God, the system of classifi-cation must form a unified, homogeneous whole. There is no understanding here of knowledge as gained in dialogue—and certainly not dialogue be-tween Christians and non-Christians.

As European hegemony grew, European knowledge increasingly directed global programs. If botanists came to see themselves as alone with Nature, it was because of this political power as well as the insight of "the system" in which all knowledges could be absorbed. Scholars of colonialism have pointed to the texts of eighteenth- and nineteenth-century European botanists, gathering plants in non-European locales, as models for imperial consciousness. In contrast to the earlier period, European botanists wrote of the plants but not the people. Their texts emptied the landscapes they stud-ied of human inhabitants, making them appropriate for European settle-ment and conquest (Pratt 1992; Carter 1987). In the process, they sup-pressed attention to the practices in which at least some of their knowledge was gained.

Contemporary efforts to describe plants around the world continue to rely on this emptying out of Nature: Although they often depend on folk ex-perts familiar with local flora, they disavow collaboration except among sci-entists. Celia Lowe (1999) has studied the species-collection activities of a conservation organization in the Indonesian Togean Islands. She found that English-speaking foreign volunteers objected to learning native names; they imagined their task in finding Nature to be the direct matching of organisms and internationally recorded Latin species names. Their Indonesian hosts and guides juggled local, national, English, and Latin species names, and they used their familiarity with multiple systems to identify species. But

they, too, favored Latin names to show their affinities with international science; in their reports, only Latin names counted. This use and disavowal of
cross-cultural collaboration also characterizes commercial bioprospecting.
In her study of pharmaceutical bioprospecting in Mexico, Corinne Hayden
(2003) found that researchers depended upon folk knowledge of plants to
acquire biologically active samples. The researchers she studied bought
plants from market vendors, who described for them herbs used within
Mexican folk medicine. However, it was protocol that samples forwarded to
their North American partners for further testing be divested of this folk
medical information. To count as scientific samples, the biological material
was purified from the history of its discovery.

This is a very specific Nature. As the touchstone of biodiversity discourse,
it is a resource for environmental politics, and it is one way of encompassing
the local within the globe. It also can be criticized for its imperial gaze.
Might it be possible to attend to Nature's collaborative origins without losing the advantages of its global reach?

Meanwhile, there are other possibilities for uniting God and Nature. I
turn to a different way to the universal, and to the local in the global.

Nature Located—in a Global Gaze

> [W]hen we contemplate the whole globe as one great dewdrop, striped
> and dotted with continents and islands, flying through space with other
> stars all singing and shining together as one, the whole universe appears
> as an infinite storm of beauty.
>
> —John Muir, *Travels in Alaska*

Nature soared in Europe and North America in the second half of the nineteenth century—in the gaze of educated travelers, in amateur and professional natural history, in emergent natural sciences, in philosophy, and in
poetry. Looking back at this period, contemporary environmentalists single
out Scottish-American nature writer John Muir as a prophet of Nature.
Muir was a master of rhetoric who conjured reverence for Nature and zeal
in protecting its significant wild places. In these wild places, he argued, the
global force of Nature is condensed and made available in all its beauty and
power for the appreciation of the cosmopolitan pilgrim.

This vision of a condensed and located global Nature moved a public,
who, like Muir, imagined themselves as travelers in a wide and astonishing
world. Muir's rhetoric galvanized an emergent movement of nature appreciators, bringing together natural scientists and lay people to create a new
kind of public advocacy. Together with businessmen who promoted tourism

and patriots who imagined U.S. wilderness as an equivalent to European monuments, these nature appreciators invented the idea of national parks, an idea that proved charismatic enough to spread around the world. The national park idea catered to a model of citizenship that privileged those who imagined themselves as cosmopolitan and civilized travelers, and thus potential park visitors. Wild nature would teach and refresh the cosmopolitan heart. Without a coalition of public forces, this vision would never have flourished. Yet its focus on personal inspiration in the encounter between an individual and Nature denied all social mediation.

As in my previous example, the collaborative construction of Natural facts—here including inspiration—was shrouded by an axiom of unity in which individual experiences and observations could be referred directly to the universal. Here, too, the axiom of unity depended on the interplay of Nature and God. Yet Muir's God was personal and pantheistic, leading him to discover not the system behind all diversity but rather the totality in the local, the global at home. The collaborations on which it depended (and which it hid) did not cross oceans but instead forged a cosmopolitanism ready to rebuild the nation. This coalescence, with its wide-reaching effects on global nature loving (see chapter 4), is worth exploring in more depth.

John Muir grew up with a potent mixture of Nature and God. His father was a strict and zealous Christian who, in pursuit of religious mission, moved the family from Scotland to rural Wisconsin. Muir recalls his childhood there as full of discipline and pioneer challenges. As a young man, Muir spent some time at the University of Wisconsin, where he was introduced to transcendentalist philosophy and botany. Evading the draft, he spent two years in search of rare plants in Canada. He returned to the United States to work in a factory in Indianapolis, where an industrial accident blinded him temporarily. In his recollections, Muir credits the accident for turning his path more fully toward Nature—as God. "I bade adieu to all my mechanical inventions, determined to devote the rest of my life to the study of the inventions of God" (Lankford 1991: 46).

In 1867, at the age of 29, Muir traveled south, determined to see the grandeur of Nature in South America as described by world explorer Alexander Humboldt. "How intensely I desire to be Humboldt!" he wrote to a friend (Fox 1981: 47). But a bout of malaria in Florida convinced him to travel west instead of south. He took a boat to California and walked east toward the Sierra Nevada Mountains. When he recalled his first glimpse of the Sierras later, it was with that potent religious vision of Nature that characterized so much of his writing. Starting from the western mountains, he looked east over California's Central Valley, which at that time was strewn with flowers. "And from the eastern boundary of this vast golden flower-bed rose the mighty Sierra, miles in height, and so gloriously colored and so radiant, it seemed not clothed with light, but wholly composed of it, like the wall of some celestial city" (Muir 1988: 2). He was even more deeply moved upon finding himself in the spectacular Yosemite Valley. "I feel like preaching these mountains like an apostle," he wrote (Fox 1981: 12). Although he later settled in San Francisco, and, after his marriage, on a ranch outside Oakland, it was Yosemite that remained the center of his gaze.

Muir's descriptions of Yosemite helped others see Nature's power. Some of these were men of influence: philosopher Ralph Waldo Emerson; future president Theodore Roosevelt. Others were friends and colleagues. Muir cofounded the Sierra Club, bringing together nature lovers, scientists, and advocates for the preservation of nature, and thus crystallizing that amateur-professional-activist synthesis that still invigorates environmentalism today. Meanwhile, Muir's writing mobilized an American love of Nature. One result of this mobilization was legislation designed to protect Yosemite Valley—passed first by California and then by the federal government to designate it a national park. Muir, then, is credited with inspiring the national parks movement that spread in and beyond the United States.

Muir's message depended on dramatic, emotionally charged modes of expression, infused with religious rhetoric. Consider Muir's famous indictment of those who would dam Yosemite's Hetch Hetchy Valley for a water reservoir: "The temple destroyers, devotees of raging commercialism, seem to have a perfect contempt for Nature, and, instead of lifting their eyes to the God of the mountains, lift them to the Almighty Dollar. Dam Hetch Hetchy! As well dam for water-tanks the people's cathedrals and churches, for no holier temple has ever been consecrated by the heart of man" (Smith 1987: 177). This passage is characteristic of Muir's identification of Nature as a focus of religious devotion. It mobilizes an advocacy for the sacred, and for the locally sacred—our church—as well as the universal religion it represents. Nature is God, in Hetch Hetchy and beyond. Muir was a priest of Nature, bringing it devotees. On meeting Emerson, Muir wrote: "I invite you to join me in a month's worship with Nature in the high temples of the great Sierra Crown beyond our holy Yosemite. . . . With most cordial regards I am yours in Nature, John Muir" (Fox 1981: 5). Scholars of Muir have noted that Muir's identification of God and Nature is hardly Christian orthodoxy.[4] However, Muir's worship of Nature shares much with the heterodox Protestant Christianity he knew best. Nature, like God, forms the basis of a universal Truth, accessible through direct experience and study. To study a particular instance offers a window into the universal. The local enfolds into the global and the universal; our devotions must simultaneously know the local and its transcendence.

Muir worked back and forth between evoking global Nature and its local instances. One interpreter of his writing speaks of the ubiquity of "planetary passages," in which references to the "earth-planet" offer a heightened emotional charge to landscape descriptions (Lankford 1991: 35).[5] Yosemite thus instantiated global space and time.

> Yosemite temples will be the more enjoyed by those who have traced . . . the crystallization of the granite in the dark, thousands of centuries before development, and who know how in the fullness of time the sun called to lift water out of the sea in vapor which was carried by the winds to the mountains, crystallized into snow among the clouds, to fall on the summits, form glaciers, and bring Yosemite Valley . . . to light. (Muir quoted in Lankford 1991: 41)

Muir's Nature—and his Yosemite—are forged in a scale-making project in which the local and the global are wrapped together and charged by the principles of the universal. Yosemite stood for the possibility of individual contact, through study and experience, with the hugeness of a global and universal Nature. Not any individual, however, can achieve this gaze. The subject who can grasp Nature here is the cosmopolitan traveler. Muir's use of travel writing as the genre in which he conveyed his sense of Nature's wonders is not incidental. Like Humboldt who inspired him, Muir appeals to the free metropolitan intellect who can imagine him- or herself in global travel. It is tempting to identify this reader as white, male, and wealthy, but this is not historically accurate. White women were among the most enthusiastic audiences for Muir's writing, and women's clubs energized the movement to create parks and nature reserves (Smith 1987).[6] Moreover, Muir projected an ambiguous or androgynous gender identification in his writing, drawing female readers and gentle men (Jespersen 1997). Indeed, Muir's opponents weakened him by portraying his cause as feminine; some scholars have argued that this feminization of nature protection kept environmentalism at a low profile through the first half of the twentieth century (Smith 1987). Race and class are also ambiguously implicated. Rather than reduce him to a "type," it is useful to look at who joined this collaborative momentum.

Consider, then, Muir's most powerful allies: scientists, nature lovers, and a certain set of entrepreneurs and politicians. Each of these was invested in the cosmopolitan gaze upon Nature. In science, Muir's affinities were with scientists who themselves were working through the relation between local and global instances of universal Natural law. Muir's study of glaciation in Yosemite Valley was in direct dialogue with Louis Agassiz, a Harvard naturalist who studied the chronology of rock strata as evidence of a global era of glaciation. Muir also worked with evolutionary biologist Asa Gray in collecting Western flora. In studies of glaciation and botany, Muir's sense that Nature formed a book that could be read—a global/local instancing of the universal—brought him inside an important current of nineteenth-century naturalism.

Muir's most enduring fans have been nature lovers and environmentalists. It is only because of their efforts that his legacy continues to be important today. Even during Muir's lifetime, they came in different sorts, from the activist hikers of the Sierra Club, to the women's clubs already mentioned, to tourists, scholars, and publishers. Despite their differences, the Californians among these nature lovers shared certain orientations: California was a new state, still at the edge of being a colonial territory. Through much of the nineteenth century, "science" in California consisted mostly of military surveys, commissioned for the purpose of securing administrative control. Muir formed part of a change in which science and nature loving signaled a more civilian form of citizenship. The settlers became citizens through their love of the land. Muir's evocation of Nature helped to secure this form of settler consciousness (Smith 1987).[7]

The support of these groups only translated into political effectiveness, however, because of influential allies: the bosses of the Southern Pacific Railroad. Muir formed a friendship with railroad baron E. H. Harriman, who convinced the U.S. Congress to designate Yosemite a national park (Fox 1981). The railroad was interested in the development of tourism since tourists came to the western United States mainly by train. Larger issues of what it meant to be a citizen were also at stake. The railroad block promoted notions of citizenship in which cosmopolitan travelers—people on the move—were the quintessential U.S. citizens. These people could benefit from encounters with Nature; indeed, these mobile and malleable citizens could be made as such in encounters with Nature. The railroad bosses fought for a particular point of view in the making of the western United States, and Muir's version of Nature supported their struggle.

Muir's articulation also created opponents and areas of invisibility. Ranchers were Muir's most explicit enemies; ranchers *used* the wilderness rather than experiencing or studying it. They were cut off from the universal; they destroyed it through inattention. Ranchers became the icon of one side of a dichotomy dividing the exploitation of Nature from its study and protection.

This dichotomy forms the basis of the most well-known divide in U.S. environmental politics: the divide between "conservation" and "preservation." (These terms take on particular meanings for this debate; after discussing the debate I return to using the term "conservation" much more broadly.) Histories of U.S. environmentalism often begin with Muir's disagreements with Gifford Pinchot, who became the first head of the U.S. Forest Service.[8]

Pinchot, educated in the emerging European science of scientific forestry, believed that forests should serve economic and state-administrative interests. Ranching, timbering, and other forms of commercial use were a proper part of forest management; the goal of forestry was to maintain a national stock of forest lands precisely for such uses. Pinchot here stands for a view of the forests that combines utilitarian use and bureaucratic control, in this story called "conservation." Muir, in contrast, stands for the full protection of Nature for its own sake.

Both sides of this debate formed their momentum through culturally specific claims about the universal that blocked attention to the sometimes discordant collaborations that enlivened each agenda. Scientific forestry promoted universals of rationalism and profit. The uses of nature could be planned through a calculus of management. This agenda drew bureaucrats and businessmen. It also appealed to popular democracy: people should *use* forests. In this spirit, small as well as large users have been drawn to the resource management agenda. However, it is useful to remember that the legacies of both Pinchot and Muir articulate problematic universals and draw dangerous allies into the struggle for environmental well-being.

The debate reminds us why Muir's vision continues to inspire. In contrast to the resource managers, Muir tells us that Nature cannot be reduced to the needs of capitalism and the state. Nature deserves protection for itself. Here too are the shortcomings of the collaborative legacy of Muir's vision. The nature protection that Muir stimulated has not done well in forming alliances with local residents, who tend to be dismissed as users and therefore despoilers of nature. It has been easier to gain the support of distant corporate sponsors, who, like Muir's railroad friends, support nature tourism, rather than resident communities. As the national park idea spread around the world, parks advocacy formed even more problematic alliances with colonial heritages of resettlement and the displacement of indigenous residents. Residents have been evicted from nature reserves by force; local livelihoods have been disrupted. Recent environmental scholarship is full of documentation on the conflicts between residents and parks.[9] The challenges loom large.[10]

These alliances and enmities are the collaborative legacy John Muir set into motion. They form the power and the danger of this legacy; they set an awkward agenda. Yet nature lovers rarely acknowledge these issues; certainly Muir himself did not. Why? Muir's vision of Nature itself shut out the possibility that collaborations were important. Nature was knowable through direct experience. We need no conversations to make Nature come to life; we want direct access to the universal text. "The clearest way into the Universe is through a forest wilderness" (Muir quoted in Lankford 1991: 38). Environmentalists and nature lovers must struggle with this legacy, which offers both the transcendent power of Nature and the inability to know one's own collaborative positions.

Meanwhile, the United States launched other understandings of the globe. After World War II, U.S. military intelligence research was responsible for new kinds of globalisms, in which a mechanical vision of the relations of the parts to the whole replaces God as the author of universal laws. Cybernetics, systems dynamics, systems ecology, and circulation models were developed from the insight that systems create their own dynamics. Information about the interrelationship of elements within a system can generate knowledge of the whole. In contrast to Muir's endorsement of the global condensed in the local, these models bypass locality completely, except as an unmarked moment in scaling up and down. The system of flow and feedback takes precedence to any internal point. The global emerges as a node of systematicity. A key example is the model-making at the heart of public and scientific discussion of global climate change. My focus here is not the making of a universal logic but rather its use in the construction of a new kind of global scale. Collaborations across difference are both demanded and denied in this process.

Global Climate is a Model

Developing a predictive understanding of global environmental change
in order to provide a scientific basis for national and international
policy and decision making requires a comprehensive, interdisciplinary
approach to studying the total Earth system.
—SEDAC, Consortium for International Earth Science Information
Network, "a part of NASA's Earth Observing System Data and
Information System," 1993 brochure

In the 1990s, global climate change was the center of what environmentalists, and the interested public, thought about when they imagined environmental issues as global. When environmental organizations wanted to prove that they were tapped into transnational networks, they mentioned global climate change. Government officials and businesses pointed to global climate change to index the common problems of the world. One kind of globality, or at least multilocality, of climate change, then, is its multiple referencing by groups in varied social and physical locations.

Climate change seemed "global" to the public, too, because the issue was introduced during a period of concern about transboundary environmental issues: species loss, water pollution, acid rain, radioactivity. In the United States, a hot, dry summer in 1988 corresponded to the peak of public concern about the destruction of the rainforests in Amazonia. The emission of greenhouse gases (carbon dioxide and other gases whose increase in concentration is causing global warming) linked the U.S. climate and the loss of the Brazilian forest. The world was losing the carbon sink of the forests, while the burning of the forests produced more greenhouse gases. The idea of global climate change articulated the new realization that places far apart from each other were still connected for their basic survival, especially through the circulation of air and water.

The most easily identified "globality" of this realization, however, has been in the model that climate experts promoted to explain and predict climate change. General Circulation Models (GCM) use the laws of circulation of air and water to generate an abstraction we might call global climate. These models are self-conscious representations. They do not purport to describe the globe but rather to picture it in the model. They simplify and reduce the social and natural world to geophysical laws. In the process, they develop a globe that is unified, neutral, and understandable through the collection and manipulation of information.[11]

This is a specific—even a peculiar—kind of globe. The global scale is privileged above all others. In contrast to Linnean plant classification or Muir-inspired nature appreciation, the global scale is the locus of prediction as well as understanding. Local conditions can be predicted from the global model; that is the point of its globality. Local data may adjust the global model but never defy it. Its globality is all-embracing.

The model declares itself continually to be science. It is expert, neutral, rational, and empirically grounded. We know this, in part, because the model is complex and constantly under revision. It requires the computational prowess of computers because it integrates many factors. It admits to many uncertainties. Because of all the uncertainties integrated into it, using it requires great skill. Experts must train as part of a "community" of model users; they must develop common standards and trust. They should also communicate with the public. Experts use the models to tell the public about risks; public representatives can then debate what to do about these risks. "Uncertainties," "trust," "risk": These terms circle in the model's orbit. Through them, the model both secures its place as science and stimulates debate. The model unleashes its own dangers: This is its goal. Neither botanists nor nature lovers have used globality to push potential collaborators to the negotiating table, but climate modelers do just that.

It is my contention that the global commitments of the model are strategic: They are tuned to stimulate international dialogue. They also cover up dialogue through reference to the unified globe of the model. Model-building practitioners are self-conscious about the effects of their models on policy makers and the public. They want to create collaborations, and they know what kind they want. They want their models to show the way to global standards and structures of management. Their models show that only such standards and structures will promote survival. The model-makers want to bring policy makers into the modeling effort. They want policy makers to be future-oriented global citizens. The model is an attempt to make this happen by denying pre-existing interests and identities—and thus the necessity of negotiation within the collaborations they endorse. The global unit supercedes nations, classes, cultures, or specific business interests. The model's generalizations promote negotiation by making its necessity disappear into a seamless globe.

The models incorporate strategy through the forms of global Nature they delineate. To see this, it is useful to examine the culture of modelers. First impressions, imbued with the shock of cultural difference, can perhaps convey this culture's strangeness and specificity. I offer an ethnographic arrival story.

I had my first taste of global climate models, and their makers, at the "First Open Meeting of the Human Dimensions of Global Environmental Change Community" in 1995 at Duke University in Durham, North Carolina. This was a very specific segment of the "community": the meeting was organized by political scientists, who have their own global agendas; the modelers present were those most interested in socioeconomic rather than geophysical data. Yet if I ignore the political science and focus on the surprises of my first impressions of modeling, I can introduce some recurrent cultural features.

For me, everything seemed exotic: the incessant clicking of laptops in the lecture halls; the parade of computer projections; the use of acronyms; the programmatic nature of much of the research, in which results were just an example of potential. It seemed that U.S. modelers wore dark, drab suits and armed themselves with piles of overheads, while Europeans wore bright jackets and flamboyant ties and spoke of creativity and culture. Women appeared as representatives of official organizations; they hid behind charts. Used to the informality of scholars who imagine themselves as of little public importance, I could tell I had entered an unfamiliar scene of action and effectiveness. Details of dress and presentation were geared for particular policy audiences. More so the models, which, through the ways they surprised me, instructed me in fundamentals.

I recall my first surprise: *The global scale takes precedence—because it is the scale of the model.* A geographer showed us how to use climate models for social science research. We needed to understand the procedures for "down-scaling" from the global model to predict local environmental impacts. He used his computer to demonstrate for us how to predict the weather in one Swiss canton two hundred years in the future.

At first, I was just shocked by the temerity of predicting the local from the global. What happened to the social and natural landscape of that canton? Could it mean nothing? Then I did see that his demonstration was not just a direct downscaling. One can "nest" a limited-area atmospheric model within the global climate model, thus including a certain amount of local information. Smaller scale information can be incorporated in global climate models in a number of ways. "Parameters" are introduced into the global model from regional and local empirical studies; these keep the model closer to accepted descriptions of reality. Model users may add data from other sources to create regional and landscape scale predictions. There is considerable interest in "meso-scale" modeling. Finally, there is much discussion among modelers about problems of scale. In a special issue of *Science* on global environmental problems, for example, two scientists argue that neither "scale-up" nor "scale-down" research paradigms can provide reliable ecological assessments. They advocate "strategic cyclical scaling," which integrates regional and local empirical data into global models, correcting global projections with the results of smaller-scale monitoring and evaluation of actual effects (Root and Schneider 1995).

Within these nuances, a set of assumptions about scale remains. Scales ought to fit neatly inside each other, the small inside the large, each neutral and fully encompassed by the next scale up. If they don't, we must fiddle, looking for a more realistic fit. The incompatibility of scales is a practical problem. It does not challenge the principles of the model, which requires that the local disappear compatibly inside the global.

My second surprise: *Models breed more models.* One man lectured on the modeling of uncertainty. It was one of the more unusual kinds of social science I had seen. He discussed, for example, the degree of trust that different climate scientists had in the global climate model, based on a survey. He then correlated their trust with personal characteristics, such as whether they smoked. I thought at first it was a joke, but I hadn't been around the discussion of uncertainty, or modeling. Models are made more reliable by incorporating uncertainties into the model, that is, by modeling them.

Since the emergence of global climate models, much concern has been expressed about the fact that the GCM does not include social information: The world is reduced to physical laws. Modelers have responded by developing more extensive models that incorporate everything. This is called *integrated assessment* (IA), and it requires combining rather different kinds of models. Social features of the globe are usually modeled using systems dynamics models, which are then combined with geophysical circulation models. Other kinds of modeling may be brought in as well. Since it is not clear how to do this, many forms of integrated assessment compete for attention. Everyone wants to include population and land use, but there are many other categories; some have even tried adding "culture" to that which can be modeled. The common assumption is that everything can be quantified and located as an element of a system of feedback and flow.

"Uncertainties" pile up. One IA project admits, "In view of the accumulation of uncertainties, the interpretative and instructive value of the . . . model is far more important than its predictive capacity, which is limited by the incomplete science upon which it is constructed" (Rotmans 1995b: 3). Is modeling a teaching practice or a predictive science?

Another surprise: *Models must be charismatic and pedagogical.* One modeler compared the success of European modeling with the failures of U.S. counterparts. He explained that the first success of climate modeling in Europe occurred as a result of concerns over acid rain. The European Union was just emerging, with transboundary issues as its reason to exist. The modelers brought policy makers from the EU into their modeling efforts. They let them design simulations. The policy makers became involved; they integrated the models into their positions. In contrast, he argued, U.S. modelers have had much less success. Their models are too complex and too academic; policy makers aren't attracted to them. Modeling, he argued, is a tool, not a declaration of truth.

The embedding of smaller scales into the global; the enlargement of models to include everything; the policy-driven construction of the models: Together, these features make it possible that models can bring diplomats to the negotiating table. Indeed, the models have helped stimulate negotiations, as in Rio in 1992 and in Kyoto in 1997. Yet, rather than the consensus that modelers hoped for, these negotiations have been arenas of conflict. Two conflicts have dominated the field: differences between representatives of the global north and south, and differences between the United States and Europe. The former takes the unified globe of the models apart, dividing it into sectors with dissimilar interests. The latter disputes environmental science, arguing for other forms of knowledge. Each reveals the collaborative structure of modeling through claims of being excluded.

Spokespeople for the global south argue that global climate models are an articulation of northern interests. Global climate models show everyone invested in the same reductions of greenhouse gases; they cover up the fact that most of these gases are emitted in northern countries. In blaming southern countries for a share of the greenhouse gas problem, the models also obscure differences between northern and southern emissions. Many greenhouse gases emitted in southern countries are "subsistence emissions," in contrast to the "luxury emissions" of northern countries. Global modeling, they imply, is not neutral but rather positioned with those wealthy nations who can cut emissions—but want others to help them. In international negotiations before the 1992 Rio Earth Summit, this argument was convincing enough to be incorporated into the United Nations Framework Convention on Climate Change.[12]

This north-south separation was one reason anti-environmental politicians in the United States criticized climate change negotiations, and, in the face of international disapproval, withdrew from the Kyoto Protocol in 2001. U.S. politicians have advocated a different form of universals through which they imagine the globe: private property, free trade, and the entrepreneurial spirit. U.S. negotiators had already done their best to bring these business-oriented perspectives into discussions of climate change.[13] Yet the models of global change that informed climate negotiations still privileged the environment for itself. These environmental universals had not won over U.S. politics.

U.S. intransigence warns us against the glorification of incompatibility; when claims of difference are combined with unilateral power, they can be ugly. Whereas representatives of the south asked for revisions of the model, the most powerful nation of the north merely refused to discuss it. Powerful blocs have worked hard to stop global agreements based on international cooperation and amity. The expertise of modelers has formed defensive walls against such power plays, but generalizations more directly dependent on international politics have had fewer defenses.

The recognition of environmental crisis has brought nations to the negotiating table to talk about a variety of universal standards. But not all negotiations result in effective generalization. Negotiators must agree upon common objects. As long as they refuse all compatibility, generalization is impossible. The troubled progress of international negotiations illuminates the specificity of the generalization process, in which productive collaborations and sincerely endorsed axioms of unity are not easy achievements. I turn to these troubles.

A Universal Regime?

> The ITTO's underlying concept is to sustainable development of tropical forests by encouraging and assisting the tropical timber industry and trade to manage and thus conserve the resource base on which they depend.
>
> —International Tropical Timber Organization, "What Is the International Tropical Timber Agreement?"

The combination of trade promotion and conservation is a heady brew for international politics. Nowhere has this been more important than in the International Tropical Timber Organization, better known as the ITTO. With this combination brewing, the dream of a global management regime was born. Could forest protectors and exploiters, and wood producers and consumers, come together to form universal standards, governance procedures, and expectations about the use of forests?[14]

The ITTO's hopes for forming universal standards came to life around the concept of "sustainable forest management." Sustainable management emerged at the intersection of varied concerns about "protection": of wood supplies for consumer industry; of state forestry institutions; of wood prices for timber companies; of the reputation of the forest-products trade; and, of course, of forests themselves. Sustainable management showed the potential to reshape conservation, trade, forestry, and industry, so that they formed a common trajectory in a commitment to a managed global Nature. Sustainable management could be the cornerstone of a new governmentality. Yet the most exciting thing about the ITTO turned out to be its failure. Everyone saw quickly that "sustainable management" was an empty concept. The ITTO stayed on, but the action, emerging from other sites, swirled around it. The ITTO took up the defensive role of managing participants' agendas in the light of what was happening elsewhere.

This section, then, turns from relatively successful agendas for global Nature to consider a relatively unsuccessful one. A coalition politics continues to sustain the ITTO, but it is not a coalition that has forged effective collaborations. Some participants hang in, hoping to exert influence on other players and on international programs. They advocate global accord for the name, not the substance; they are most involved in their separate mandates. In their still-strident efforts, global Nature stutters, and falls silent. Why?

The ITTO was imagined as a forum in which compromises might bridge disagreements among dissimilar parties. Even while claiming to search for common ground, the organization worked assiduously to maintain these globe-ripping divides. The ITTO began as a Japanese dream, suggested to the UN Conference on Trade and Development in 1977. The Japanese representatives said they were concerned about the stability of the tropical timber trade, for which Japan was the most prominent consumer. Conservationists and foresters had pointed to evidence of rapid deforestation; supplies in key Japanese source areas, such as the Philippines, were already running out. The Japanese plan blocked other possibilities. Sporadic discussions among tropical wood producing countries had generated speculation that a cartel might form to influence supply and pricing. It also seemed possible that conservationists, concerned about the rapid loss of tropical forests, might themselves succeed in forming international forestry standards. In either case, Japan's business profits would suffer. These concerns informed several years of discussion of the proposal. In 1983, an International Tropical Timber Agreement (ITTA) was signed, to take effect in 1985. The agreement formalized the dialogue between tropical wood producing countries and consuming countries. It included conservation as well as trade promotion goals. The agreement also formed the ITTO.

Bureaucratic structure seems cut and dry; but much agonizing and struggle went into settling the structure of the ITTO. Who would participate? What global, national, or business commitments would dominate the agenda? These were questions hammered out in the organizational structure. The ITTA made a start. The organization would be divided into moities, consisting of representatives of nation-states, and identified respectively as "producers" and "consumers"—thus assuring that the ITTO would function neither as a price-setting cartel nor as a forum for global citizens. Votes were to be distributed in proportion to a nation-state's "involvement" with the tropical timber trade; countries that either bought or sold more tropical wood received more votes. As one critic points out: "The net result is that the more a country destroys tropical forests, the more votes it gets. The voting structure ensures that the ITTO's primary role of promoting the timber trade heavily outweighs its secondary conservation role" (Colchester 1990: 167).

These arrangements meant that the struggle over the organization's goals was played out in relation to the representation of different countries. Forest conservation objectives became identified with countries such as the United Kingdom and the Netherlands; the voice of the wood-products industry was heard from Japan; the defense of national sovereignty and rights to destroy the forests became identified with Indonesia and Malaysia. Thus, too, the struggle over which nation would supply the Executive Director and where the secretariat would be seated was a struggle over organizational definition. The battle was heated. Finally, the Japanese government offered to fund the ITTO in exchange for gaining the secretariat. Japanese support then boosted a Malaysian forester, Dr. Freezailah, to the post of Executive Director (Colchester 1990).

Despite this alignment of Japanese and Malaysian interests in rapid timber exploitation, conservationists hung on. Getting forest conservation goals into a mandate that had begun as a trade agreement was a victory; they were not about to retreat. For nongovernmental organizations, the goal of participating at all in ITTO negotiations seemed overwhelmingly important. In Indonesia, for example, environmental NGOs were just then struggling for a voice in the nation—in the legal system, in forestry, and in public culture. Indonesia was a major player in the ITTO, and NGOs wanted to be involved.[15]

In other arenas—including global climate change—agreement among experts has sparked intergovernmental cooperation. Not so for forest protection. Experts are differently aligned. Foresters have been trained to work with the timber industry, not the environmental movement; in contrast, conservation biologists, often spokespersons for environmentalism, may oppose logging. Anthropologists, who may speak up for forest-dwelling peoples, are rarely given credence by either foresters or biologists. Economists are given much credence although they may know nothing about forests. Agendas for forest management thus multiply. Most experts adopt a rhetoric of concern for forests, whether they propose to stay or hasten their disappearance. The 1992 UN Earth Summit at Rio produced a set of principles on forests that affirm state sovereignty and promote free trade; what does this have to do with forest protection?[16] Thus, too, the ITTO combines and juxtaposes agendas that, everyone admits, contradict each other.

Sustainable management holds the mix together. But it is not enough. The ITTO promotes sustainable management of forests. But, given the self-conscious reliance on contradictory programs, it is difficult for the organization to define the term substantively. Here is the organization's formal definition:

> Sustainable forest management is the process of managing forest to achieve one or more clearly specified objectives of management with regard to the production of a continuous flow of desired forest products and services without undue reduction of the inherent values and future productivity and without undue undesirable effects on the physical and social environment.[17]

This is obviously a compromise between sustainable *yield*—the foresters' dream of stable timber production ("a continuous flow of desired forest products")—and sustainable *ecological function*—the environmentalists' goal ("inherent values," "undesirable effects"). The product is almost incomprehensible. Furthermore, no one knows how to do it. No one, even industry experts, thinks that current tropical logging techniques are allowing the forest to regenerate—even for timber.

Two paths present themselves as ways out of this conundrum. One could use the term as public relations rhetoric to defend the reputation of current logging practices, taking them out of the opprobrium of environmentalist criticism. The advantage here is that it doesn't matter if the definition is incomprehensible. Alternatively, one could focus on *management* itself as the true objective. By rationalizing data collection and bureaucratic structures for forestry while at the same time highlighting technical training, one might achieve some goals, even if they might not be forest protection ones. After all, the definition says that sustainable management is meeting the specified objectives of management. It is management itself that must be sustainable. The ITTO has worked back and forth between these two paths.

Throughout the 1990s, the highest profile program of the ITTO was the "Year 2000 Objective," the promise to limit trade in tropical timber to supplies from sustainably managed forests by the year 2000. The promise was passed as a producer-countries' resolution in 1991, with participating environmental organizations, and even some representatives from consumer countries, bewildered about just what this promise meant. The first possibility that occurred to critics is that the promise meant nothing at all: "In fact, 'Target 2000' will present the timber industry with few difficulties, for, according to the rhetoric of the producers and traders, logging as practiced *already is sustainable*" (Colchester 1990: 169). As 2000 approached, the organization began to suggest that the Year 2000 Objective was rhetoric: "The . . . ITTO has done more in the 15 years of its existence than any other organization to advance the idea of sustainable tropical forest management" (ITTO 2000). Spreading the *idea* of sustainable management is enough.

Meanwhile, the organization sponsored a variety of technical studies and data collection exercises, some of which might lead to more, if not better, management. Guidebooks for standards of forestry are being published. "Reduced impact logging" offers the solution of managing timber industry workers to address the problem of logging's destructive impact. Other ITTO grants sponsor studies of illegal logging—one of the few evils on which state bureaucracies, the timber industry, and tree-counting conservationists can agree. These activities advance the bureaucratic ideal; however, little effort has gone into addressing the problems of *legal* logging, the loss of local livelihoods, and the opening of forests to destructive forms of settlement and mining. The technical solutions of ITTO programs do not address either ecological or social questions. Sustainable forestry management is self-contained—an "anti-politics machine" that converts social issues into technical ones.[18]

The machine asserts its globality mainly as a rampart against attacks from other transnational sources. The ITTO's major activity has involved neutralizing other initiatives for tropical forest management. It has been particularly active against environmentalist initiatives, such as tropical wood boycotts to protest destructive logging. ITTO fought the concept of wood-products labeling as well as certification, which environmentalists proposed as a way of identifying better and worse timber sources. When it became clear that labeling and certification were ideas that would not go away, the ITTO then rushed in to create its own profit-friendly programs.[19]

Meanwhile, the ITTO has taken a stand for particular governments against international pressure. In 1989, at the height of the international campaign against the logging of Sarawak, Malaysia, the ITTO sent an official mission to assess "the sustainable utilization and conservation of tropical forests" there (ITTO 1990: 2). The mission made no attempt to meet with indigenous protestors or environmentalist critics; instead it limited its vision to the formal aspects of forest management. "The mission inverts the priorities of Sarawak's forest policy, putting the production of timber above local needs," environmentalists proclaimed (Rowley 1990). Meanwhile, the Sarawak government touted the ITTO mission's regard as an endorsement of its sustainable forest management.

None of this is doing the tropical forests much good. The conditions of tropical forests have only deteriorated since the formation of the ITTO, and no amelioration seems in sight. Nor has there been much success in forming global accord. No mechanisms have been set for compliance with forestry standards, should meaningful standards be suggested. Everyone who knows about the problems of forestry on the ground—from local foresters, to residents, to spokespeople for wildlife—has been excluded. Practical forestry solutions would look quite different with their input.

These failures show the weakness of the process of generalization the ITTO put in motion. International cooperation did not prove a convincing axiom of unity. The ITTO's retreat to technical rhetoric is an exemplar of the weakness of contemporary international politics in forging a "universal regime." Yet, given its penchant for blocking more meaningful forest solutions, the organization's ineffectiveness is perhaps its best quality.

Nature and the Globe

Making the globe our frame of reference is hard work. This chapter has explored projects for making global commitments that rely on Nature as a set of universal, orderly, and inspiring laws. Looking at universals, I find that they include contrasting sources of knowledge and define varied kinds of participants in the knowledge-making process. Their quiet exclusions, and their heralded opponents, are equally varied. Yet they rely on a common process: Global Nature both facilitates and obscures worldwide collaborations.

Nature offers various kinds of commitment to a global scale. Global Nature can collate facts from around the world. In forming a plant classification system, global Nature made the knowledge of varied localities compatible. It offered a universal system to bring together local knowledges. Global Nature can inspire moral views and actions. In nature appreciation and the parks model, localities are charged with global insight; they are microcosms of universal knowledge. Global Nature can also form a common object for the formation of international standards. In global climate models, the material primacy of the globe seen in the model can impel the urgency of international negotiation. And global Nature can facilitate governance regimes, making technical standardization an international imperative. The sustainably managed forests of the International Tropical Timber Organization are leaky boats for Nature. But, like the other projects introduced here, they are claims about Natural universals that make the globe the relevant forum.

These forms of global Nature are resources for everyone involved in using or advocating for the environment. They make it possible to make claims for Nature, and for the globe. The cultural specificity of their universals does not, in itself, make them wrong. However, claims of universality do make it hard for us to see just who can imagine themselves inside, and who is out.

The projects for making nature and scale that I describe in the rest of this book draw on these cultural resources. You will hear more about botanizing as a moment of cultural sharing, about nature loving in the legacy of Muir, about the dreams and models of environmental science, and about heated debates over the protection of tropical forests. These projects are deployed and transformed in varied social contexts—making and remaking the variety of small-n nature.

For this task, however, I need a different approach than I have used in this chapter. To see practices of nature and scale-making in their variety, I can't just work with famous examples; I need to investigate more ordinary environmental politics. Instead of beginning with successful globe-making projects and ferreting out their collaborators, I must proceed the other way around. I must follow the articulative process, however partial and incomplete its results. I dip into the cultural resources I have introduced here, but I do not privilege their globe-making perspectives. Instead, I track globe-making interactions much closer to the ground.

"Dark rays"

[On environmental ethics]

Popular environmental knowledge is diverse and syncretic. It takes multiple forms of expertise and brings them down to size. This is not a one-way street, however. Individuals, including scientists, politicians, and activists, apply their eclectic perspectives in forming projects of nature-making.

It makes no sense to search for a singular "Indonesian" environmental knowledge or one divided neatly into ethnic groups or religions. Instead, we might begin by identifying distinctive confluences of knowledge, as well as the nodes of practice and discourse informed by these confluences.

1997. President Suharto is still in power, but the New Order regime is beginning to unravel. Oppositional voices are growing louder even in the provinces. In South Kalimantan, these voices are moral and religious in their tone. They raise a new question about the environment: What if nature is a moral question?

....

Late one night, in a provincial town in South Kalimantan, the guests had finally left the *mulut* gathering, and I found myself in focused conversation with the host, a batik merchant, who was smoking a cigarette.

"People say that smoking causes sickness; but actually it is the human heart [*hati*] that causes sickness. If you have only good deeds, cigarettes—or any foods—won't harm you. The important thing is what is in your heart. It is better to associate with thieves than with someone whose speech is different than his heart.

"Everything that a person does should have a use for others. Otherwise people are more stupid than rocks, more stupid than the sun, moon, and stars. How can people be as stupid as dead matter? God made humans to guard the conservation of the earth. But this can only be done by recognizing that people do not live alone, like Robinson Crusoe. We live in a world connected with others, and everything we do must be of use to others. It is useless to do meditation exercises alone on mountains or on a rock in the ocean: What use does this have for others? Everything we do must have use, and this can only be gained by losing one's ego, one's 'I.' We don't need to hate others, to be jealous, to be angry. Our sense of ego is what causes ruin in the world.

"People are worried about climate change. But it's not industry that causes climate change. It's the doing of people. Every action of a person causes a wave, and these waves meet and reverberate in the atmosphere. A good action causes a ray of brightness; a bad action causes a dark ray [cehaya gelap]. If there are many dark rays, the sunshine will not come through.

"There are many kinds of rays: ultraviolet; alpha; beta; x-rays. (They call them 'x-rays' because they don't understand them; so they say 'x.' Did you know this?) There are other rays caused by human conduct. These influence the world.

"There is electricity in the human body. It's not the same as electricity in the world, which lights the lamps. But how could a child form in the womb before it has received a soul? Only because of electricity. The man has positive electricity. The woman has negative electricity. The woman has elements of the earth; the man has elements of the heavens. These come together and a child is made from earth and sky, positive and negative electricity.

"Human actions affect atomic particles. There are two kinds of atomic particles: those under control, and those out of control. A bad heart makes things out of control. A good heart makes things under control. This is where science and religion meet. It's no different from what foreign scientists say, but they haven't given these things enough attention.

"God made the elements of the earth to stabilize the earth. There is iron, gold, silver, oil, coal: All give the earth stability. When people mine these until one element is gone, there will be no more stability to the crust of the earth. Inside the earth, lava flows in a more and more liquid form, and deep inside there is gas. It is very hot, perhaps 6,000 degrees or more. If the stability of the crust of the earth is disturbed, it will sink into the liquid and gas below. If you take out any of the elements of the earth until one is gone, the stability will be lost.

"Can you take this in, Anna?

"Every religion, whether Islam, Christianity, Judaism, or Buddhism, teaches us the effects of our hearts on our own world. Why do we pray? It's not just to praise God. Our prayers come back to us humans, to make us conscious of ourselves. That is the promise of prayer, to raise self-consciousness [*kesadaran diri*]. The conscience [*hati kecil*] has its own influence on the world, different than thoughts. For example, sometimes you have a feeling you shouldn't travel; you travel anyway and meet an accident. It is the conscience that should guide our actions. This is only possible by uniting microcosm and macrocosm, and by losing the sense of self.

"Have you ever seen water flow up? It always flows down. When you drop a rock, does it ever go upwards? It always falls to the ground. This is the way of nature. People are greedy and don't accept this."

....

Ahmad is an educated man. He spends most of his days seated at his stall at the market unfolding colorful sarongs for customers and supervising the young men who help him show his cloths. But he has been to college, and he has kept up particularly with natural science, philosophy, and religion. I have known him for a long time, and we often have these kinds of conversations when I see him. He knows me as a fellow scholastic, with whom he can share serious thoughts.

I didn't want to be a merchant. I wanted to study when I was still a bachelor. I studied so much my father worried I would go crazy, so he married me off. Then I had to make a living for my wife and children.

Ahmad reads voraciously. Most of what is locally available are pamphlets on various aspects of Islamic faith. He pulls these together with his thoughts on science to forge a synthesis between the world as known by science and as known by religion.

The Koran speaks of the seven layers of the earth and the seven layers of the heavens. Science has only begun to know the first layers. It is all written in the Koran, but we have yet to know about these things. For example, it will be found that there are fourteen planets, seven we know and seven beyond Pluto that we don't yet know.

The synthesis he offers is distinctive, but it does not make use of only local materials. Ahmad mentions Robinson Crusoe; when he talks about philosophy, he refers to Aristotle, Descartes, Hobbes, and Kant. After the conversation above, he recommended a book to me, which turned out to be the Indonesian translation of a treatise published by the State University of New York, called *The Tao of Islam* (Murata 1992). Ahmad is especially drawn to spiritual forms of understanding through which to blend religion and science.

Westerners rely too much on thoughts. If you use thoughts you can only take them in "one by one." If you meditate [*merenung*], you can take in the *global*. With contemplation, you can remember everything without writing it down. Your vitality is inspired.

Through this distinctive cosmopolitanism, he has put together a philosophy of nature—and, indeed, of nature conservation.

It never used to be so hot as this. This is probably due to cutting down the trees. Every movement has a sound. Now there are more sounds than movements, because of television, radio, chain saws, motorboats, and the like. The atmosphere is like a container; sounds are not lost from it. They travel from one place to another creating new influences. The relation between the earth and the sun changes as a result.

Ahmad's discussion of nature conservation would not be recognized by environmental activists in South Kalimantan as their kind of talk; they would consider him countrified, quirky, and out of touch. He does not share their access to international circuits of environmental information and action; he does not use their rhetoric. Yet his ideas are consonant in many ways with the spirit of engaged intellectual discussion of nature in South Kalimantan. Like better recognized intellectuals, Ahmad looks for nature in the confluence between modern science and Islamic precept. Ahmad does not think that science and religion offer alternate ways of approaching nature. There is no divide between faith and reason, as in Western tradition. Instead, modern science and Islam reveal the same truth. Apparent divergences are only temporary misunderstandings that will disappear as we learn more about God's world. The challenge of learning is to accept this.

Ahmad identifies the route to understanding nature as proceeding through personal spiritual experience, as well as ethical choice for right conduct. The microcosm of one's personal awareness must be brought into alignment with the macrocosm of the universe. Personal self-interest must be discarded so that a larger "global" understanding can enter one's consciousness. Although the personal character of awareness is essential in Ahmad's discussion, this is not the same personal spirituality that I heard about from the Javanese student nature lovers I describe in the next chapter. For cosmopolitan Javanese youth, personal spirituality is a break from the rigidity of established values; it is a world of insight that comes directly from mysterious sources, bypassing orthodox opinion. It recognizes equal ties to U.S. New Age spirituality, Islamic religiosity, and Javanese mysticism. In contrast, Ahmad's personal spirituality opens the self to the power of truth in religion and science. It does not require nonconformism; indeed, it rejects the goal of self-differentiation as self-aggrandizement. Instead of egotistically searching out mysteries, we must each ask ourselves about our willingness to accept God's universe, just as Ahmad asked me: "Can you take this in?"

Authoritative texts are an important way to open one's understanding of God's universe. These include the Koran and its interpretations, as well as the texts of modern science. Reading and rereading these texts, one can lose self-interest and approach the truth. This is the point of scholarship, whether religious or scientific.

These assumptions frame intellectual discussion of the big questions of nature and society in South Kalimantan. In the mid-1990s, activists, professionals, and professors developed these frames together with ordinary ethical men. The environment, along with democracy and justice, emerged as an object at the confluence of religion and science. The management of the relationship of humans and nature was best considered through the interpretation of authoritative texts, and the goal was to raise ethical standards of behavior.

In the mid-1990s, Professor N. was a teacher, a journalist, and a political activist in the provincial capital.[1] He was the founder of an organization that specialized in issues of law and the environment. Unostentatious and sociable, he was a popular teacher, and many of his students followed him into his NGO to pursue the interests he sparked in them concerning democracy and governance. "Usman" also wrote essays for the local newspaper. He became a political commentator in authoritarian times; he was brave but cautious in his opinions. In public seminars, he raised sharp and pressing questions. But he also quickly withdrew them if they attracted *too* much attention.

Usman did not come to environmental issues as a nature lover; he was a student activist. When we spoke in 1997, he admitted to me good-naturedly that he formed his NGO first and then looked around for some issues for it to address; he picked the environment because he thought he could make a difference with this issue, given its high public profile. His wife, however, was once a student nature lover. She had been an avid rock climber when they met. Now, he chuckled, their one-year-old baby loves to play with ropes. He forbids his wife to climb, he explained solicitously; it is too dangerous for women. Rock climbing is a better sport for men. They went camping, once, but the baby was angry and cried.

After inviting me to his house and introducing me to his reticent, pious, and polite wife, who, indeed, it seemed, had been domesticated by marriage, Usman opened the big notebooks that held the manuscripts of the essays he had written for the newspaper. The bulk of what he showed me were articles on environmental law. But I could see, interlaced with them, many articles on religion. He explained that these had become his two passions—each at the heart of political action. Each structured his approach to both scholarship and politics: the laws of God and the laws of society.

Law was at the center of Usman's moral world. He had written at least one essay about the nature of law itself. Law, he argues, is at the heart of our ability to choose right conduct. From law, cultural norms emerge, which help us negotiate the tension between ideals and realities. Laws are norms that challenge people to reach their ideals, within cultural standards. The abstract and systemic nature of law makes it available as a system of guidelines for human behavior. Through the careful study of law, it is possible to raise awareness about environmental and theological issues. Through awareness, people may make better choices.

> Norms, as a reflection of the will of society to guide the behavior of members of society, are put into effect to make choices among behaviors that are appropriate and those that are not. . . . Legal norms are a precondition of values.

In the 1990s, law was a key symbol in Indonesian democratic politics. Activists saw their role as pressing the government to rule through law, not arbitrary authority. To do this, one must make people aware of law. Usman offered one vantage point from which this progressive endorsement of law made sense: Law, like religion, is at the basis of ethical conduct; to train the nation in good governance is to train it in law.

Law defines things. It offers a rational frame. What is the role of humanity according to the Koran? Usman asks in one essay. His answer begins with the distinction between humans and other creatures. Like other living beings, humans sustain themselves, obtain foods, and reproduce; like other animals, humans have senses and desires; but, among all beings, only humans have the power to *reason*, and thus to contribute to shaping the future they would like. Humans are responsible to make their own fate. He quotes the Koran about human privilege: "And He made you to control the earth . . ." and reminds us of the human fall from grace. God taught Adam the names of all things, and thus raised him above even the angels. Now humans have the responsibility for themselves and for the natural world. Humans can choose God, or they face a bleak future. "God explains this matter in the Koran: 'Whoever is unwilling to remember Me, surely he will face a barren life and in the afterlife will be assembled with the blind.'"

Dark rays, indeed, I thought. For Usman, humans are rational, and thus we must make the right choices. We control nature, and we must manage it properly; the choice of outcomes is our human inheritance. We learn to choose properly through studying the law.

> Whoever purposefully does an action that causes damage to the environment or pollutes the environment as covered by this law or other laws, will be criminally liable with a criminal prison sentence of ten years and/or a fine of Rp. 100,000,000 (one hundred million rupiah).

This is, in fact, a section of the 1982 national environmental law, as quoted in one of Usman's essays. Imagine, an environmental law so powerful as to send polluters to prison for ten years! What if it were enforced against offending corporations? Usman's articles raised such matters carefully, referring to specific cases at most tangentially, but standing strong on general principles: There is law, and we should respect it. In some articles, Usman lists one law after another; in others, he pays careful interpretive attention to one chapter or verse. Usman does not mention religion in his articles on environmental law, except when God's presence is mentioned directly in the legal texts. But behind the law, I thought I could glimpse the Koran and its interpretations, setting an example for our reading of authoritative text. Law offers us a chance to reform social conduct.

Reform takes place through personal changes in awareness. Thus, an essay detailing the problems of forest destruction and the implementation of forestry law brings Usman back to personal choices: "All of this comes back to our own selves in how far our honesty will take us in managing the forest, both in our capacity as decision makers and as those who receive and implement and are affected by these decisions." As Ahmad put it, "Our sense of ego is what causes ruin in the world." Here, at the confluence of science and religion, we have the option for better behavior.

What did "nature" look like here? What kinds of environmental activism were possible in this space of reform and piety? South Kalimantan environmentalism in the late New Order flourished in a moral space that distinguished it from other times and places. For the activists I met, justice and right-doing were the priority. Biocentric nature conservation was promoted by several bureaus and organizations, but it was not a popular social cause. Pollution was an important issue for government-corporate negotiations, but it did not move young activists. Ethical behavior was the key political issue.

The environmental justice that flows from ethical behavior is not the same as the populist social justice I discuss in the third section of this book. Instead, it is an abstract justice based on moral principles. It is philosophical, legal, and committed to raising ethical standards through internal discipline.

Prayer and study are important methods. In 1997, the political meetings I attended were scholarly and prayerful.

Political change can sometimes be quite sudden. A few years later, the spirit of activism felt quite different: with the fall of the New Order and the rise of a more open national politics, secular and pluralistic stances became possible (see chapter 6). There have also been continuities. Banjar environmental activists continue to struggle within the moral economy of regional social justice. Yet the rapidity of change reminds me that every confluence of knowledge is tentative and ephemeral. Despite its commitments to timeless standards of truth, ethics is historical.

4 Nature Loving

....

My steps

I swing my feet exploring the forest
I throw my tiredness far away
I enjoy everything around me
And feel the load that hangs from my shoulders.

Then, at last—
The mist at the summit greets me
Offering me a beautiful view
Ten thousand happinesses overcome me, and—
This is my forest world.
    —from a nature lovers' club log book, 1997[1]

cosmopolitan. *Belonging to all parts of the world; not restricted to any one country or its inhabitants.*
specific. *Having a special determining quality.*[2]

It is not necessary to have traveled to imagine oneself as cosmopolitan. To be cosmopolitan is to cast off parochialism in order to reach out to the world. All over "affluent Asia," emergent classes of professionals, managers, and technical workers have fashioned themselves in relation to an imagined worldliness that reaches across oceans and cultures toward a beckoning global future.[3] During Indonesia's "economic miracle" years in the 1980s and 1990s, as foreign money flowed into the country, self-consciously cosmopolitan projects blossomed. Yet these projects were neither homogeneous nor variations on the same design. There were many reasons to reach for the cosmopolitan: for internationally effective political action, for wordly consumption, to facilitate foreign investment, to create charismatic personal identities, to reach transnational professional compatibility, or to achieve broad-ranging scientific or civilizational knowledge. Lawyers demanded internationally recognizable forms of law. McDonalds and Dunkin' Donuts became fashionable places to eat. Activists agitated for universal human rights. Corporations extended trade agreements. Rayon dresses and pants replaced sarongs in women's fashion. Environmentalists joined global networks. Nature lovers went camping with the latest outdoor equipment. These varied cosmopolitanisms spoke with and against each other, but not with a single voice. Each was caught up in the desires and promises of its own contingent formation.

The specificity of these cosmopolitanisms is an important object—even a model—for the cultural analysis of knowledge. Cultural analysis thrives on the description of specificity, for it is an appreciation of cultural specificity that best gives us a critical distance from the common-sense platitudes and everyday assumptions of our lives, as well as the powerful ideologies that keep us in their thrall. Yet classically the study of cultural specificity has been identified with the study of small, enclosed places: the diverse "cultures" of an imagined pre-contact world. For several decades now, scholars studying cultural specificity have moved away from a "tribal" model of cultural difference to look at much larger cultural units, such as nations, ethnic diasporas, and even international projects such as capitalism or human rights. Yet smallness was not the problem of studies of ethnic groups and "isolated" cultures; the problem was the assumption of the autonomous self-generation of culture, and this assumption can plague studies of large units as well as small. Even the most out-of-the-way cultural niches are formed in world-crossing dialogues (Tsing 1993). Cultures are always *both* wide-ranging and situated, whether participants imagine them as global or local, modern or traditional, futuristic or backward looking. The challenge of cultural analysis is to address both the spreading interconnections and the locatedness of culture. To study a self-conscious cosmopolitanism in all its energizing connections to the world *and* all its exotic distinctiveness models the inextricability of interconnection and location. It is in this spirit that I turn to Indonesian nature lovers, *pencinta alam*, and the both familiar and surprising ways they have learned to love nature.[4]

"Nature lovers" are members of student clubs devoted to outdoor activities, such as camping, mountain climbing, rafting, and scuba diving. As participants in internationally recognized adventure sports, they are self-consciously cosmopolitan in the fashioning of their identities. The nature they learn to love is not the fields and forests of ordinary, parochial, rural lives. As they learn to love nature, student nature lovers break away from the world of routine and authority to embrace the breadth and freedom of the outdoors. The outdoors is made modern, technical, and scientific; it must be taught in classes and taken into one's own practice through discipline and experience. The cosmopolitanism of nature lovers results from a training of internal agency, desire, and identity; it is a matter of crafting selves. Unlike tourists or migrants, most nature lovers have never been abroad; unlike scientists and other professionals, their work does not require certification. My questions

about the specificity of cosmopolitanism turn, here, to the formation of identities and desires. For this, I trace the lineages of knowledge and desire
through which the cosmopolitan appreciation or "loving" of nature comes
into being. I am also concerned with the cultural specificity of "nature."

I first became interested in Indonesian nature lovers when I interviewed
environmental activists, and many told me that they began as student nature
lovers. Aristides Katoppo, a well-known environmental journalist, told a
story that was echoed in various ways by many environmentalists:

> I am a journalist. I also used to be an avid hiker, associated with Mapala UI,
> the organization of student nature lovers of the University of Indonesia. . . .
> Well, climbing the mountains, hiking there: At that time the concept of envi-
> ronment was alien. But going up the mountain slope, it's quite different if you
> walk under the canopy, it's cool. If you walk through a devastated forest the
> same distance, say you walk half an hour, but it drains a lot of your energy be-
> cause you can feel the hot sun. I realized that the forest line was receding. I
> may have seen it for a long time, but at some stage it shocks you. It was re-
> ceding like the hair of my head! [He laughs.] And I realized that the camping
> sites where we used to camp where there was clean water available year round
> had begun to dry up, or else there was a big flood. And other things, such as
> the disappearance of birds. I think it was in the late 1960s or early 1970s there
> was a long spell of droughts, and I could see the water supply for the *sawah*
> rice fields dry up. Today [1994] you can also see the parched fields, which I
> knew from other times with water flowing and beautifully green. . . . Gradu-
> ally I became more aware of what is now called the environment.[5]

To become an environmentalist, Katoppo reminded me, one must learn to
recognize and care about "the environment." His story encouraged me to
ask myself, "What is this environment that activists recognize?" Katoppo
tells us: The environment is that form of nature that is vulnerable to human-
made devastation and disaster. He was able to recognize it because of *shock*:
The cool forests he had once known had been transformed into hot earth;
the streams were drying up. And he experienced the shock because he had
hiked through those cool forests and seen those green fields before, as a nature lover, an admirer of nature's beauty. The romance of nature gives
grandeur and autonomy to the natural world; those who appreciate that
grandeur are also able to feel the shock of nature's desecration and destruction. Is it possible, I wondered, that, even in Indonesia, the romance of nature is one important route to an appreciation of nature's fragility?

The idea that the romance of nature might be a significant feature of *Indonesian* national culture works against every stereotype of the difference be-

tween the global north and the global south. The notion of a transcendent nature, separated from culture, is often cited as a unique feature of "the West." Southerners are supposed to be practical users of nature, interested in feeding themselves but not in admiring wilderness.[6] Yet in the 1980s and 1990s, nature loving was one of the most popular activities of students all across Indonesia. In every city and provincial town I visited, I kept running into nature lovers without looking for them. Furthermore, there was a self-conscious national consistency about nature loving: student nature lovers across the country learned similar ways of talking about and being in nature. This national consistency was not intended to be indigenous; nature lovers strove to learn international ways of enjoying and appreciating nature. In the process, however, they made these international standards distinctly identifiable as Indonesian by incorporating them into Indonesian nationalisms as well as Indonesian internationalisms.

Indonesian nature loving thus raises questions about the ways widely circulating knowledges become local. If Indonesian nature loving draws, as it self-consciously does, from international figures and their legacies—Alexander Humboldt, Ralph Waldo Emerson, Sir Edmund Hilary, John Muir, Robert Baden-Powell, Teddy Roosevelt, and many more—how does it become Indonesian? This is the question of cosmopolitan specificity, the subject of this chapter. To address it, I first explore the concept: How does cosmopolitan specificity come about? This allows me to imagine Indonesian nature loving at the confluence of a number of cultural lineages that, taken together, give popular force to both its cosmopolitan yearnings and its locally distinctive features.

On Mt. Merapi

Above us rose the volcanic cone of Mt. Merapi. We passed through gorges lined with tropical vines where we touched heart-shaped aroid leaves as big as picture windows and exclaimed at blooming trees with monkeys jumping in the branches. Yet on both sides of the main trail, the trees were straightboled, evenly spaced, and park-like in their orderliness, with cleared ground between them. Pure stands of pines further interrupted my stereotypes of the tropics. I guessed we were in an old tree plantation. My fellow hikers, students from the city, didn't know. From the beginning, then, I felt disoriented, confused between the strange and the familiar in my appreciation of nature.

Every now and then we passed an elderly, wrinkle-faced peasant, bent over completely at the waist and balancing a load of grass or wood that far exceeded the size of his or her frail body. But my companions carried frame packs and wore hiking boots and fashionable trousers with extra pockets on the outside for gear. We had even brought a guitar so that we could sing folk songs, in Indonesian and English, at night under the stars. Like the other hiking parties we passed on the trail, ours included men and women. And in common with them too, our party included a young woman who wore the modest *jilbab* headcovering that signals a personal commitment to Islam. The jilbab covers the forehead and sides of the face and flows down over the shoulders so that no hair is revealed; it does not get in the way of hiking, camping in a gender-mixed group, or staying up late to lie on one's back to watch the night sky. Combined with jeans and T-shirts or colorful tie-dyes, it added to the self-conscious cosmopolitanism of our group. None of us—Indonesian or American—imagined ourselves to be anything like the peasant women we stopped to watch as they intoned communal chants in their hard labor of digging and carrying sand from the stream bed, with their skirts tucked up around their thighs. Watching but not joining them, we were *menikmati alam bebas*, enjoying wild and free nature.

Since the mid-1960s, students in Indonesia have been attracted to internationally popular outdoor activities. They have formed themselves into clubs that identify them as *pencinta alam*, nature lovers. By the 1990s, most every university had multiple nature lovers' clubs, organized by administrative units such that the law school, agricultural college, literature faculty, or biology department each had their own nature lovers. Many high schools and even middle schools had nature lovers' clubs. I took the camping trip I have been describing with an informal group of senior university-level nature lovers.[7]

Nature lovers' clubs recruit students through school activities' fora; they demand a rigorous training before the student can join as a full member of the club. Short courses are offered on outdoor activities: backpacking, mountaineering, rock climbing, spelunking, kayaking, white-water rafting, scuba diving, hang gliding, survival, orienteering, search and rescue. A course of reading assignments and lectures is followed by practical training under the supervision of seniors. The student initiates graduate as a cohort (*angkatan*) within the club; each cohort is given a distinctive name. Members then organize activities, ranging from weekend trips to month-long *ekspedisi*, expeditions. Expeditions combine research, exploration, and adventure. Sometimes the members participate in competitions or in joint training or research with other outdoor-oriented organizations, including the armed forces. When students graduate, they usually leave the group, although sometimes over a prolonged period. Some graduates have started private nature lovers' clubs for those not associated with schools; the majority of nature lovers, however, are students.

Nature lovers form tight-knit social groups and networks. The clubs try to locate themselves in an office space that they can use day and night, and members show up at all hours to socialize, sleep, play music, make new friends, and discuss upcoming and past adventures. They raise money together for trips. They survive harrowing experiences together, worry through problems of identity and spiritual focus, and make passionate attachments. For many students, nature lovers' groups become a home away from home. In their sociality as well as their adventures, nature lovers' groups open the possibilities of a new social and cultural world, unlike that of childhood. One young woman told me of her sense of self-awakening among nature lovers, saying, "I was quiet at home, but when I went to college, I was like a horse let out on a grassland, like an arrow released from a bow."

Some of the college students who join nature lovers' groups grew up in small towns or even rural areas. But when they leave home, they join a national student culture in which nature has a new form, a new magic. They remake themselves in relation to the beauty, the skills, the danger, and the leadership opportunities of nature loving. It is within this "bubble" context that nature loving develops both its cosmopolitan yearnings and its distinctive specificities. Indonesian nature loving blends characteristics of nature-making projects from around the world: It is part nature romanticism, part scout troop discipline and loyalty, and part commercially sponsored adventure campaign. Yet Indonesian nature lovers are also engaged with a *national* nature, and one that is further inflected by regional and ethnic nature-loving practices.

Nature loving is thus both cosmopolitan and situated. Like a city, it can be appreciated as the hub of many roads, stretching out to other places in every direction; it can also be experienced as an unforgettable and distinctive style, a pace, an outlook, a peculiar arrangement of neighborhoods and markets and parks and crime zones, a manifestation of a particular history that can never be exactly replicated. The closer one looks at any idiosyncratic feature of the city, the more one sees the tracks that lead to other cities in conjoined pasts and presents; the more carefully one follows these links, the more one is startled by the unique features they have given to the city.

Residents in the city imagine themselves as reaching out to others on many roads; the roads also bring the foreign to them, and they remake it as their own. In its confluence of roads, its bringing together of interconnections, the city becomes most local and specific. In this sense, the confluence is the mode of situating and specifying cosmopolitanism, understood spatially as an appreciation of ideas, things, and beings from many places.

Imagine, too, the history of this confluence over time. Roads have been rerouted, and neighborhoods have changed. The form of the confluence exists only because it is a node of articulation of varied historical trajectories.

Perhaps, in the drive for urban development, office buildings have replaced a neighborhood of squatters; yet the squatters have multiplied and moved into what, before the demise of manufacturing, once was a warehouse district. Looking back from the confluence as we know it today, we might call these shifting urban histories "lineages," that is, shards of genealogies through which present forms have emerged. Occasionally these lineages result directly from urban planning policies; most of the time, however, they come into existence through some haphazard combination of varied and contradictory planning, unpredictable negotiation, rebellious refusal, and unavoidable confusion. We might speak of "contingent lineages" through which the current form of the city has come into being. The city makes cosmopolitanism its own through these contingent lineages.

To return from the image of the city to my method of cultural analysis: cosmopolitan specificities can be studied through tracing their contingent lineages. Contingent lineages show us the world-embracing spread of cosmopolitanisms even as they bring us into the articulations through which these cosmopolitanisms become locally identifiable. Like the crossroads and neighborhoods of my city metaphor, the confluences of contingent lineages refigure imported ideas, migrants, and materials from all over the world as local. In these conjunctures, cultures are made and remade.

As I mentioned earlier, the cosmopolitanism of Indonesian nature lovers is a cosmopolitanism of identity formation. Nature lovers are trying to make themselves cosmopolitans. One way to understand this identity project is to consider their reliance on *youth* as a category through which they simultaneously approach identity formation and cosmopolitanism. Youth is often a time for forging new modes of agency and desire. For nature lovers, this is a resonant frame for creating cosmopolitan knowledge.

The Agency of the Young

Saturday night, 1/6/97

The most difficult thing for "youth" [*"pemuda"*] is the moment one has to separate one's rational thoughts from one's emotions. In an emotional register, I am never going to break free from MG [the nature lovers' club]. In a rational register, I have to use my time as efficiently as possible.

MG is a home and my first family in Yogya. This organization has already given me and my friends the meaning of comradeship, friendship, enmity, ambition, idealism, knowledge, insight, spirit, a place of protection, the meaning of growing up and of self-enlightenment.

Closeness to "nature" and all of its harmoniousness, its conceit as well as its grandeur, has already truly changed my views of the meaning of life, death, and self.

—nature lovers' club log book, 1997

Youth is a self-conscious attribute of the nature lovers I met. In contrast to the U.S. "outdoors" culture of the 1950s and 1960s that I knew from my childhood, Indonesian nature loving is not a family activity. After women have children, they stop participating in nature loving, even if they have enjoyed hiking and camping. In contrast to U.S. nature appreciation, Indonesian nature loving is not a way to bring young and old into the same space. When men graduate and find jobs, they "advise" nature lovers but do not join them in their activities. Although middle-class Indonesians of all ages sometimes engage in outdoor leisure activities, nature lovers' groups are perceived as bringing together and organizing youth (*pemuda*).

Benedict Anderson (1972) has described how pemuda emerged as a revolutionary force in the 1940s, as Indonesia struggled for independence from colonial rule. The radical youth he describes drew from Javanese traditions in which youth, for men, was a time of wandering in search of utopian and spiritual illumination before the responsibilities of adult status set in. At the end of World War II, youth organized to express the urgency of national independence; they forced their often-recalcitrant elders into stronger confrontations with the European armies and administrators who came to repossess the colony from Japanese occupation. The youth imagined themselves as responsible for the fate of the nation.

After Indonesia gained its independence, the youth movement dissipated, only to rise again in 1966, when students took to the streets calling for a radical change in national politics. Calling themselves "the Generation of 1966" in explicit dialogue with the revolutionary "Generation of 1945," they organized mass demonstrations and demanded a ban on the Indonesian Communist Party, a new cabinet, and a reduction in soaring prices. Working under the protection of the army, and particularly the elite army corps that later became known as Kopassus (at that time RPKAD), students played an important role in ending the regime of Indonesia's first president, Sukarno, and the transfer of power to then-General Suharto, with his ambitions to create a New Order for Indonesia (Douglas 1970: 153–74). Outside of the universities, Islamic party youth wings were mobilized in the mass killings of suspected communists in which a half million people were killed (Anderson 1999).

University students and Islamic youth were among the strongest supporters of the New Order in its early years. Slowly, however, their criticisms mounted. A decisive break for students occurred in 1974, when student demonstrations during the visit of the Japanese prime minister embarrassed the government, which responded by clamping down on students and the press. By the end of the decade, the government had decided to shut down all student politics. The 1978 Campus Normalization Law outlawed student organizations. A political quiescence set in that was to last into the early 1990s.

Meanwhile, James Siegel (1986) has argued, the lineage of youth nationalism passed into the public schools. "Whatever their inadequacies," Siegel writes, "there can be no doubt that schools today are the places where sentiments of nationalism are centered; when people view youth in terms of the future, as they do frequently and fervently, it is the schools they think about" (1986: 139). The nationalism of schooling is expressed particularly in the use of Indonesian, the national language, in place of regional mother tongues. The use of Indonesian, Siegel argues, writing of the Javanese city of Solo, creates a respectful distance between the student and his or her learning, turning repetitive recitations into revelations of the mystery of the future. Although there is no trace of the revolutionary politics of the 1940s, schooling creates a future-looking nationalism built around the possibilities of youth. Furthermore, by removing the political content of youth nationalism, Siegel argues, the New Order regime opened the way for other kinds of youth culture to emerge.[8]

The first nature lovers' clubs formed at the university level in the last years of the Sukarno regime, and as an explicit reaction to the tensions and struggles of the crisis-oriented student politics of the time. The founders of nature lovers' clubs at the University of Indonesia—many of whom were student activists—decided to create some activities that were decidedly nonpolitical, as they understood politics.[9] Yet what is nonpolitics? Their ideas for a new youth activity were formulated in the shadow of the youth politics lineage. Where politics was socially boisterous (*ramai*), they chose the quiet loneliness (*sunyi*) of nature. Instead of social contention, they chose natural harmony. Their object was shaped by the heritage of "politics" even as they chose to avoid it.[10]

Some of these early founders became critics of the Suharto regime; however, their idea was taken up and popularized by new cohorts of students in the 1970s, 1980s, and 1990s precisely because it helped to delineate the nonpolitical nationalism of the New Order. Nature loving mirrored the frame of radical youth politics by assuming an enthusiastic nationalism; yet it avoided politics. By turning the legacy of youth politics on its head, nature loving helped formulate what a youthful and cosmopolitan nationalism might mean outside of the contentious political struggles of the 1940s through the 1970s.

Nature lovers were not, however, concerned with the national political trajectory; they were self-consciously politically trivial. They would never have flourished except for the coming together of other meanings of youth from which they gained force. Three other emergent lineages of youthful agency have been important in popularizing nature loving. First, youth found themselves at the cutting-edge of class formation during the New Order. The new middle class depended on cultural *distinction*, in Pierre Bourdieu's (1984) sense, to give shape to their economic role as mediators for the influx of international money during the years of Indonesia's economic "miracle." Young people—and the education process itself—were credited as the formulators of these cosmopolitan distinctions, which would allow the young to move into a global future imagined as wealthy and successful. Nature lovers' relearning of "nature" as something transcendent and romantic has been a key distinction for cosmopolitan youth.

Second, nature lovers nationalized a once-foreign youth agenda: They domesticated international adventure tourism, making it their own. In the 1970s, Indonesia became a popular destination for northern tourists. One of the most distinctive forms of international tourism has been adventure tourism: trips to "wild" places imagined as involving physical challenges, unpredictable dangers, and new discoveries. In this spirit, Indonesia hosted foreign jungle trekkers, mountain climbers, and rafting teams. These activities displayed the challenge of youthful identity, as travelers overcame the unknown to find their essential selves. It did not take long for Indonesian students to master these activities and to plot out a domestic scene of adventure tourism that offered opportunities for personal growth without the necessity of foreign travel. By the 1980s, Indonesian nature lovers were mounting expeditions all over the archipelago, forging a new national geography that featured "wild" places and exotically "local" village people to surround their new cosmopolitanism.

Third, nature lovers became a particular species of youthful consumers. The students I knew joked and complained about nature lover consumerism. By the 1990s, they said, nature lovers could be identified by their fashionable flannel shirts, jeans, and hiking boots. The nostalgic reminisced about an earlier pre-commercial period; now, they worried, it's all about fashion, and people don't respect and care about each other. The freshmen, said the seniors, were too caught up in equipment. But all the nature lovers I knew loved equipment. Their introductory courses diagrammed and explained the importance of backpacks, tents, and camping stoves as well as more specialized climbing gear, kayaking gear and other such items. Small industries sprang up to supply students with Indonesian-made versions of international adventure sports gear. Both domestic and foreign companies began to see the potential of advertising using images of nature lover activities: They could show young, active people challenging the world with the help of their brand-name products.

National anti-politics; middle-class distinction; domestic adventure tourism; consumer culture: These four lineages came together to give meaning and practical substance to nature loving as a project for youth. Their routes toward youthful identity overlapped and intertwined, offering the excitement and stability of varied perspectives. Each provided a channel through which cosmopolitanism was made locally workable. These channels formed a confluence at which nature loving reached out to the world—and made worldliness its own. To see how this could be, I offer a closer look at each of these lineages.

National Anti-Politics

> Up and down, ravines and steep slopes, we became used to having
> our backs bent, while the load of our packs felt heavier because of
> the previous day's rain. A hard rain returned to join us as we put up
> the tents around 4:30 in the afternoon. On the 17th of August,
> Independence Day, we didn't forget to have a small ceremony after
> we finished packing up the camp, and it was affecting enough to have
> a 17th of August ceremony in the middle of the saddening and lonely
> forest far from civilization.
> —reminiscing about an expedition in a club log book

New Order nature lovers participated in a nationwide organizational network. They learned to love a national nature, that is, one that was made accessible through their national citizenship and schooling. In the process they learned to be Indonesians. As the opening quotation suggests, this was a heartfelt nationalism and not just a ploy to avoid state repression. Yet it was also a nationalism without either radical urgency or liberal criticism. It was self-consciously empty of a social change-oriented politics. It is perhaps useful, indeed, to think of New Order nature loving, iconically, as an Independence Day celebration in the "lonely forest far from civilization": an appreciation of the nation from the perspective of its resounding political emptiness.

The national frame of nature loving was produced and reproduced in nationwide meetings and training standards, in the everyday practices and assumptions of university student culture, and in dreams of participating in national and international competitions. Every August 17th, New Order nature lovers held demonstrations of agility and solidarity in celebration of Indonesian independence. Meetings, training, competitions, and displays of patriotism brought them into the form-and-routine-conscious world of the state bureaucracy. But many New Order nature lovers also imagined themselves as on the way out the door. For those who knew the freedom and wonder of nature, they told me, these organizational forms were the necessary formalities but not the content of nature loving. Nationalism in their hands became an experience-based love of countryside as much as country. To be outside of politics meant, to them, to be able to escape from regulation, even as state regulation was a necessary form.

"I don't follow any political activities or any forms of activism at all. With the circle of nature lovers, I run to the mountains." (DS)

"We were hedonists; we liked to play in free nature. . . . We learned from our friends. Our friends were rotten, extremists, 'against the law.' It was fun actually. . . . At that time, nature lovers were identified as 'outlaws' [English]: dirty clothes, never bathed, not caring, 'the important thing is I enjoy it' [refrain of a popular song]. I had a special uniform: scratched jeans and sometimes I just wore sandals. . . . We were long-haired; we smoked." (BPS)

In this vein, nature lovers gained a reputation as "hippies" (*kelompok hippies*) and drunkards who did not properly respect adult authority. One of the more popular stories about the origin of nature loving that nature lovers told me was that they took the international scouting model but divorced it from the discipline, regulation, and status hierarchy of scouting to experience nature in all its freedom.[11] Nature lovers were criticized for their lack of discipline, combined with their interest in activities, such as mountain climbing, that were seen as involving great risk. Students quarreled with their parents over nature lover activities; one of the most difficult moments in trip planning, they said, is getting parental permission.

Even the most compliant of nature lovers were forced into an awkward dance with state authority. In the late 1970s, when all student organizations were shut down as part of the military "normalization" of university campuses, nature lovers were shut down too. In Yogya, where the military raided the university, all student organizations, including nature lovers' clubs, saw their records burned. Slowly, nature lovers regrouped, this time even more carefully divorced from politics. As one participant of the time recalls, the groups reappeared on a "hobby" basis, avoiding student politics and incorporating regime-initiated rhetoric. By the 1980s, nature lovers' clubs had become quite popular across the country. But on every significant outing, they needed the permission of police and civil authorities. In the process, nature lovers learned to imagine themselves in a complicated relationship with the state, involving both respect and evasion.

It was in this political atmosphere that nature lovers developed ties with the armed forces. Some nature lovers I spoke to had participated in army-sponsored training or competitions, and they recalled the discipline they learned there with considerable pride. In this spirit, too, one contributor to a nature lovers' 1997 log book wrote an unfavorable comparison between the nature lovers' club and Kopassus, the elite army unit that only a year later became notorious for firing on student protesters.[12] The nature lover noted comparable features of nature lovers and Kopassus: Each trains initiates forming cohorts that face challenges together. Yet, the writer concludes, nature lovers suffer in the comparison. Kopassus, with its discipline, spirit, arrogance, and repeated practice, has succeeded in reaching Mount Everest—"something that gives pride to the Indonesian nation." In contrast, the nature lovers' club is caught in never-ending internal squabbles and can't accomplish anything. The entry is intended to revitalize club spirit.

The log book entry itself, intermingled with late-night stream of consciousness thoughts, reminiscences of past expeditions, romantic nature poetry, exhortations for better performance in competitions, words from popular songs, and caricatures of club members, is not very important. But it does evoke a major arena in which the "anti-politics" patriotism of New Order nationalism was promoted through the collaboration of nature lovers' clubs and the armed forces: mountain climbing. In international understanding, to scale a mountain peak is to conquer it for the nation. Mountain climbing as "something that gives pride to the Indonesian nation" is a good example of a nationalized cosmopolitanism, that is, a world-embracing standard that enters local notions of nation-making. Here, the armed forces and the nature lovers have needed each other. When the army first became interested in mountain climbing, they learned from the more experienced nature lovers. In turn, army sponsorship has guaranteed the finest equipment, the highest-level permission, and the most spectacular peaks for the nature lovers. Working together, nature lovers and army men have made the *national* scaling of mountain peaks their own.

Mountaineering was the favored sport of the country's most well known nature lover of the late 1980s and early 1990s, a University of Indonesia student and journalist for the daily paper *Kompas* who carried the already cosmopolitan-sounding name of Norman Edwin. Edwin popularized nature loving through his newspaper articles. In one series, he chronicled the climb jointly undertaken by the Kopassus mountaineering unit and a team of student nature lovers from Pagata University in April 1990 (Edwin 1990a, 1990b). The party climbed Mount Jaya, the peak in West Papua that had been designated "not only the highest in Indonesia, but also in Southeast Asia and the Pacific" (1990a: 13). The ascent was particularly historic because it recapitulated the first Indonesian climb of this peak in 1964, shortly after the Republic of Indonesia assumed administration of West Papua, in one of then-President Sukarno's more flamboyant nationalist moves.[13] As Edwin explains it, the 1964 ascent was part of national history as "the first time the highest peak in Indonesia was 'subjugated' by sons of Indonesia" (1990a: 1).[14]

The 1964 expedition to what then was called "Mount Sukarno" was plagued with difficulties, and, literally, bogged down in the mud. A forest-and-swamp transect that was supposed to take six days instead took six weeks. The party of climbers continued against all odds in part because Sukarno exhorted them over the radio to complete their task for the motherland. "Continue to advance! No retreat!" he admonished. When three officers stood at the summit to "offer their respect to the nation as a sign of their completed service" (the message they left in a bottle under the Indonesian flag), they felt that their prayers were miraculously answered. In contrast, the 1990 expedition was facilitated by "modern transport": buses, cable cars, and the dropping of food and supplies by helicopter. "This expedition is simultaneously a military training, so logistic supplies and equipment are carried out with military procedure," said a Kopassus spokesman. Furthermore, the Kopassus mountain climbing team—unlike the poorly prepared 1964 army climbers—had been in training since 1983, when the unit first contacted student nature lovers for technical assistance. Still, the party experienced their share of challenges. Because improved transportation allowed them to gain altitude so rapidly, many members of the party experienced altitude sickness. Rain and fog put an end to their first attempt to scale the highest peak. Yet on April 15, 1990, the thirty-eighth anniversary of Kopassus's founding, two Kopassus officers climbed to the top. On the 17th, Kopassus men and nature lovers stood on the peak to remember the earlier expedition: The 1964 climbers "opened the way; now we are continuing their efforts to become military officers who bring about our nation's national ideals" (1990a: 13).

Without a forced march through the mud, the 1990 party could enjoy an efficient and predictable nationalism bathed in the expectation of success. Edwin congratulates the officers on their discipline and camaraderie. Theirs is a success of national culture, which, unlike Sukarno's mass politics, needs no struggle. They are already dreaming of their next challenge: to go abroad to conquer foreign mountains. "Continue to advance, no retreat!" Edwin echoes Sukarno, referring to their dreams (1990a: 13). But the advances and retreats have changed. Under the protective shadow of the state, mountain climbing offers an opportunity not only for army spectacles but also for individual self-development: technical prowess, athletic strength, personal discipline, and even the admiration of beauty. The prerequisite is that one leave aside public criticism and debate.

The student nature lovers of the 1980s and 1990s came of age under this protective state shadow.

Urban Distinctions

> A story of disgust and village life: Nur went to Bali for a nature lovers' training, and stayed in a village. When she went down to the river to brush her teeth in the morning, she saw human feces [*shit*, English] floating by. Before this incident, they had laughed at a team mate who proposed to brush his teeth using bottled water. Afterwards, everyone on the team used bottled water to brush their teeth.
>
> —my notes from an interview
> (in Indonesian except for the word "shit"), 1997

Norman Edwin's journalism provides an entry point into other aspects of nature lovers' culture as well. Consider nature lovers' ideas about rural society. Some nature lovers come from rural backgrounds, but, whether urban or rural, they make themselves urbanites by re-learning nature as an object of modern technology, international standards of training, and transcendent romance. Nature lovers do not go fishing or hunting; those are activities of rural people. They explore, study, subjugate, and admire nature. In the process, they create a set of rural-urban distinctions. In the anecdote from an interview with which I opened this section, a nature lover tells me of her sense of abjection confronting the ordinary conditions of rural life. Through this abjection, she makes herself a stranger in her home country; she approaches the rural with the sophistication, resources, and sense of alienation of a cosmopolitan traveler. This is a process of class formation. Through these cultural distinctions, a cosmopolitan managerial class has fashioned itself.

One of Norman Edwin's most compelling series of articles concerns a seventeen-year-old high school student who was lost on Mount Kerinci, the highest mountain in Sumatra (Edwin 1990c, 1990d). Yudha Sentika had climbed the peak with six of his school friends. The fog was dense, and the wind was strong. Yudha snapped a photo of his friends at the peak and immediately started down. By the time his friends realized he had gone ahead, he had disappeared into the fog. They themselves couldn't find the trail. With difficulty, they maneuvered back to the base camp, but Yudha never arrived.

Edwin's first article focuses on the search for Yudha. Nearby residents and members of the local village safety squad began looking for him the next day. "This was well meant, indeed," Edwin writes. "But, alas, good intentions that are not guided by knowledge and the skill to look for a lost person in the mountains resulted in the fact that their effort had no immediate results" (1990c: 2). This is a mild rebuff compared to what follows. The searchers, ordinary local people without training, were incompetent. Their uncoordinated search muddied the trail for subsequent searches, destroying the possibility of finding footprints or other traces. They allowed rumors to circulate, spreading false information, such as the idea that Yudha's shirt and water bottle had been found, or worse yet, that he himself had been sighted at a location scores of kilometers distant. The searchers huddled in their tents, confused. Meanwhile, they knew that the boy had no preparations for surviving in the wild. The situation was serious.

Only during the second week were student nature lovers called in to help. The students, trained in up-to-date search and rescue techniques, came from Jakarta and Padang. They joined with an amateur radio operators' club to arrange proper communication. And they turned the search around, providing a clear structure and organization and precise work descriptions for volunteers from the closer cities of Jambi and Medan. Teams were deployed with exact directions and the directive to work with all due speed. Edwin's description (1990c) is illustrated with a photograph showing the nature lovers studying maps, with the following caption: "CLOSE STUDY: The search was carried out with close study and planning. Maps were deployed and data assembled to ascertain approximately where Yudha was lost." The next photograph, showing a tent just below the peak, is captioned: "CONTROL: Camp 3 (at 3,675 meters) was erected as the control center for the search operation. It is assumed that Yudha split off from his party near this location." Yet even with radio equipment and precise locational information, the search was not easy. The fog was still thick and the wind strong. "Sometimes we only advanced half a kilometer in a day, because the forest clumps at the base of the peak were so thick," explained one nature lover to Edwin. One search team was lost in the forest for five days. Edwin documents the ways the mainly male search parties kept up their spirits, from imagining food orders to admiring pin-up calendar girls. They used their radio link to find out the results of international soccer matches, and to bet with other team members on the various foreign teams. Yet after all this, Yudha was not found. Where had he disappeared? Edwin ends his article in English: "The answer, my friend, is blowing in the wind." Those of his readers themselves nature lovers, who tend to be avid fans of U.S. popular music, would surely understand the cosmopolitan sadness of the folksong.

In a second article (1990d), Edwin documents the interference the nature lovers felt from a second kind of searcher: traditional healers, *dukun*, who also came up the mountain to find Yudha. The article suggests that the nature lovers have ambivalent feelings toward what they imagine as traditional, locally rooted, mystic practices. Half-jokingly, they admit to similarities with these searchers by calling them *sarkun*, from SAR (search and rescue) plus kun (dukun), or *dupala*, du (dukun) plus pala (short for pencinta alam, nature lover). Yet, Edwin writes, they are embarrassed by these countrymen, who burn incense and sacrifice chickens to ask the spirit inhabitants of the mountain to return Yudha or his corpse. They have come, Edwin speculates, because a rumor has gone out that a Rp. 5 million reward is being offered for finding Yudha; they want the money. They are hypocrites, says one Jakarta nature lover, watching a dukun leave the head of a chicken for the spirits, while taking the body home to eat. They are fools who come up with excuses for why their magical rites do not work. They make irrational requests, asking the nature lovers to plant nodes of yellow bamboo across the mountain. They make the rational-minded nature lovers tense and irritable with their mystical practices. Worse yet, some are brought to the mountain by armed thugs who demand modern equipment, such as walkie-talkies, from the nature lovers.

Despite all these reasons to dismiss them, the nature lovers find themselves imagining that mystical practices might work. "All methods can be tried when hope is lost," writes Edwin. "The search and rescue operation, which was full of calculation and based on a healthy rationality, suddenly was infiltrated with dukun practices that were difficult to accept with a fully conscious intellect" (1990d: 2). He quotes the SAR mission coordinator, who spoke for many team members: "Whether you believe it or don't believe it," he says, lapsing into Jakarta slang, "I've also felt susceptible to black magic" (ibid.). Edwin tells of how the nature lovers' SAR operations became tinged with magical practices, such as the idea that all search teams must have an even number of members, since Yudha's unlucky party had an odd number. Worse yet, some search teams started to practice inexplicable rituals, such as sweeping the earth at the edge of the forest while putting a leaf behind the right ear. At the end of the article he returns to the tension between the dukun and the nature lovers, which sometimes resulted in open hostility. Yet he adds a final coda to his report: "It is only necessary to record these facts. So far, the methods cited above have not been proved true. Who knows about another time!" (ibid.). His studied objectivity underlines the ambivalence about traditional mysticism that he shares with most nature lovers.

I encountered this set of articles in a Yogya nature lovers' club office, where the nature lovers showed them to me to illustrate the conversation they were having about "paranormal" and "supernatural" events they had witnessed while out exploring nature. In their conversation, the occurrence of such events was a reasonable topic of debate: Some students declared not to believe in such things; some had not witnessed them but felt they were real, "whether you believe in them or not"; others had first-hand experience with forces they believed to be outside of ordinary rationality (*penalaran*; *masuk akal*). Despite these disagreements, the students appeared equally comfortable drawing lines between the rational and the irrational. Their discussion suggested that their ordinary lives were explicable by reason; they thus knew how to identify inexplicable events in the untamed wild that could not be explained by reason—and these were properly captured, they implied, in the ideas and practices of dukun healers, traditional mystics, and village customary beliefs. The very definitiveness of this codification of the supernatural made it possible for them to approach the subject from a distance, as questioning skeptics. Unlike rural people, they implied, they knew better than to mix and confound the ordinary and the mystical. Their ambivalence about the supernatural constituted it as a shadow world—behind ordinary rationality—that they could explore with either respect or playful doubt. And the terms of this ambivalence were proof, to themselves, of the distance they had traveled from village tradition.

As in late Victorian England, debates about the existence of the supernatural deepen the chasm between city and countryside by formulating the grounds of urban difference. When the supernatural is seen as rural and traditional, to argue about it, even as an advocate, establishes one's metropolitan credentials. Certainly these Yogya students, absorbed in learning the latest scientific methods for appreciating nature, could afford to look back at the countryside with wonderment as well as superiority. In their imaginations at least, they were bound for a future in which their cosmopolitan expertise would allow them a combination of disdain and nostalgia about rural society.

Adventure Geographies

> During trekking, you'll up and down the mountain chain, cross some rivers and hanging bridges, caves, waterfall and a great variety of flora and fauna with a beautiful panorama. Advisable you must take licensed tour guide, porter and a good personal equipment.
> —from *Come Experience to South Kalimantan*, tour pamphlet

After graduating from college, some nature lovers establish outdoor adventure clubs, through which they can become tour guides and activities facilitators for domestic and international tourists. I talked to the founder and some of the members of one such group in Banjarmasin, South Kalimantan, in 1997. They offered me the English-language tour brochure from which I have quoted above, and they urged me to send American travelers to them. So far, they admitted, they had had no success in finding international trekkers to guide. However, they were organizing trips for Indonesian trekkers from other parts of the country. Indeed, it seemed that their determination to attract international trekkers was an indirect route to organizing domestic trekkers. Indonesian nature lovers want to go to internationally attractive places. To make the jungles of South Kalimantan a prime destination for Indonesian students, the group felt it necessary to promote the area as an international destination—and, indeed, to advertise it in English; if international visitors showed up as well, so much the better. But most of the adventure visits in the 1990s came from domestic tourism.

Nature loving has domesticated international adventure tourism in Indonesia, that is, it has turned its dreams and destinations into sites for Indonesian national experience. Foreign adventurers still come to tackle Indonesia's jungles, rivers, caves, and mountains—and most continue to organize their trips through international channels and thus avoid contact with Indonesian nature lovers. Yet there are few wild spots in the country that have not been thoroughly challenged by Indonesians. The most active clubs mount expeditions all over the country. Enthusiastic individuals have visited many places across the archipelago. Here is one young man's list of the adventure and training trips he took with his Yogya nature lovers' club:

South Lampung, Sumatra, 1989 (training)

Lore Lindu, Sulawesi, 1989 (exploration)

Tulungagung, Java, 1989 (training)

Merapi, Merbabu, Sumbing, Sundoro, Slamet, 1990–93 (climbing)

Bandung, Java, 1990 (training)

Kuala Kurun, Kalimantan, 1991 (training leader)

Meru Betiri, Java, 1991 (training leader)

Tasikmalaya, Java, 1991 (training leader)

Kali Progo, Java, 1989, 1991 (rafting)

Batang Asai, Sumatra, 1992 (rafting)

Despite this profusion of places, I never heard nature lovers boast of their acquisition of various sites, in the way international tourists do all the time. ("I have been to Sulawesi, and I am on my way to Kalimantan.") Although club members could recite lists of their expeditions, the places themselves seemed unimportant except as sites for experiencing a rather generic untamed nature. Some nature lovers have fond memories of the challenge of travel in parts of the country with which they were previously unfamiliar. One young Javanese woman told me of her journey to climb a mountain on the island of Lombok by herself. She knew no one there, but she dressed in bulky clothing, rather like a man, to avoid harassment, and she was happily able to get directions from local people. Although the unfamiliarity of the place plays into her story of bravery and loneliness, it was not Lombok as a *place* that impressed her, but the wild beauty of mountain scenery: a hidden lake; a stretch of loose gravel that made it almost impossible to climb; a vast panorama. This was nature that transcended place. The adventure tourism of nature lovers differs in this way from the international tourism it follows: It does not sponsor a calculating accumulation of places, condensed into short, harrowing experiences that seem, to the tourist, to "capture" the meaning of the site. Instead, it is the distinction between home and the wild that is reiterated in these domestic tours. The trips affirm the homogeneity of the Indonesian nation even as they separate it into cosmopolitan centers and wild peripheries.

Nature lovers' expeditions involve research as well as adventure. Common kinds of research include surveys of vegetation or wildlife, as well as ethnographic surveys of "local people" (*masyarakat sekitar*). Most of the places that nature lovers explore have already been mapped by foreign and domestic surveyors. Still, survey research connects nature lovers with conventions of militarized science, including the science of colonial conquest and centralized state administration. The "local people" are further localized and contained by imagining them as objects of scientific inquiry; the researchers emerge, in contrast, as cosmopolitan travelers. The nature lovers take notes; the local people can merely answer questions. Yet this form of objectification can also, sometimes, lead to moments of identification. Those nature lovers who became political activists almost always spoke of learning about the social problems of the countryside from talking to village people during their nature lover trips. For example, a nature lovers' club in Banjarmasin told me how they traveled to the east coast of Kalimantan to check out caves as possible sites for exploration. The area they chose was being claimed by a coal mining company, and the local people were angry that they had received no compensation for their land; meanwhile, problems of erosion and pollution loomed. The nature lovers' club decided to form an advocacy group on the issue of mining. They hosted several informative seminars on the topic and joined with Jakarta-based activists to lobby the provincial government to consider social issues. In part due to their efforts, Banjarmasin became a center of mining activism.

Whether participants emerge as activists or merely as admirers of wild beauty, their expeditions remap national geography. Nature lovers offer a new cosmopolitan standard with which to separate Indonesian centers and peripheries: the wildness of *alam bebas*, untamed nature, becomes a form of peripheral "difference" that defines through contrast the worldly order of centers. Unlike other Indonesian measuring sticks of urban-rural contrast—such as "development," "modernity," or status hierarchy—this is a geography that allows for romance, inspiration, and advocacy as well as exoticization.

It is a geography that can only be maintained by the identification of Indonesian nature lovers and international travelers. This identification is furthered by the fact that a few nature lovers do get the chance to explore wild nature abroad. Even these few set the sights for the many who stay closer to home. For example, the nature lovers' club of the University of Indonesia sent representatives in 1990 to climb a mountain in Russia. The trip was joined by none other than Norman Edwin, whose newspaper report inspired other nature lovers—including the ones who showed the article to me—to imagine themselves in foreign climes (Edwin 1990e). Edwin's article suggests not only the force of foreign travel in reaffirming cosmopolitanism, but also the self-conscious openness of Indonesian nature loving to influences from the histories of international adventure sports.

The team went to what was then the Soviet Union to climb Mount Ebrus, the highest mountain in Europe. The mountain had only recently been opened to international climbers; the Indonesian team joined a cosmopolitan group in re-claiming the mountain for the world. The team was inspired, too, because in earlier years the mountain had been a center of the development of international mountain climbing as a sport. It had been used as a training area for ascents to Mt. Everest, and it was also a destination on its own. Edwin describes the 1920s as the "golden era" of international mountain climbing there. In the 1930s, a Soviet climbing sensibility had developed, beginning a period in which more than 600,000 "Soviet alpinists" trained for this "master sport."[15]

The Indonesian nature lovers' expedition—following international expectations of the mountain's challenge—required teamwork and self-sacrifice for its success. One of the four team members was struck with severe mountain sickness, and Edwin himself fell ill with altitude-induced pulmonary edema; they had to be evacuated to lower elevations. But they urged the other two team members to continue, and they reached the peak. From there they could inspire nature lovers across Indonesia.

Nor was Norman Edwin defeated by his failure to reach the peak. He continued to climb mountains, foreign and domestic. In 1992, he died in an attempt to scale a peak in Argentina.

Youthful Consumerism

> Hundreds of meters high, hanging from a cliff! Are you brave enough
> with a single rope? Prove you have the daring!
> —Marlboro cigarette advertisement seen across Indonesia, 1997[16]

Before Norman Edwin died, he made a different sort of national impression.
He signed a contract with Gudang Garam, Indonesia's largest cigarette
manufacturer, to become a cigarette advertising model. Gudang Garam billboards showed him on a mountain peak; as one nature lover quipped, he was
posed somewhere in Jakarta, but the photograph was made to look as if he
was climbing in West Papua. When Edwin died, there was an outpouring of
sentiment, and Gudang Garam, in respect for his memory, agreed to take
the billboards down. Soon, however, they had picked another mountain
climber model. I remember him on billboards across Indonesia in 1994,
standing on top of a high rock with a roll of rope over his arm that placed
him somewhere between a climbers' exercise and Marlboro country. Soon,
too, another Indonesian company had picked up the theme of adventures in
nature. Bentoel cigarettes began advertising with the slogan: "I love the blue
of Indonesia" and photographs of river-running sports. ("Blue" also referred
to the cigarette pack's color.)

Some time before this, nature loving had established itself as a small but
distinctive market niche for urban youth. There was room for small-scale
entrepreneurship in the making and marketing of daypacks, camp stoves,
and rock climbing grommets. However, the market status of nature lovers
expanded wildly with their entry into the cigarette advertising business; now
their image was selling one of the country's more profitable products. The
idea of nature loving became available at an entirely new level: Every cigarette smoker could imagine him- or herself a nature lover. The commercial
lineage of nature loving brought a new national notoriety and a new way to
become cosmopolitan through the fantasy of fulfilled consumption. No
company proved better at working this fantasy than Philip Morris, the makers of Marlboro cigarettes.

In the 1980s and 1990s, Philip Morris had embarked on an ambitious
globalization campaign (Barnet and Cavanaugh 1994: 184–207). Earlier in
the century, the company had focused on selling cigarettes in the United
States. But by the 1980s, U.S. cigarette health warnings and tobacco industry regulation had alerted the company to the need to expand its sights. The
company bought up grocery and household product makers and distributors; still, cigarettes remained their most profitable product. Watching rates
of smoking drop among middle-class white Americans, they moved to target

other groups of smokers: both minorities in the United States and the people of Asia, Africa, and Latin America.

Breaking into these markets was not simple. Many Asian countries controlled the importation of cigarettes, protecting the profits of domestic cigarette manufacturers. During the 1980s, Philip Morris took an aggressive stance against such protection, working together with then U.S. President Reagan's trade representative, Clayton Yeutter, to dismantle protective barriers against Marlboro. Yuetter used a U.S. trade regulation that allows punitive action against nations that practice "discriminatory" trade restrictions against U.S. exporters to attack the trade regulations of Japan, Taiwan, and South Korea, forcing each, in turn, to capitulate to U.S. cigarette companies. Thus, for example, the United States forced Taiwan to eliminate its tariffs on foreign cigarettes in 1988; within one year foreign imports had taken 21 percent of the market (Barnet and Cavanaugh 1994: 202). With the assistance of the U.S. government, Philip Morris was able to make its product popular across Asia.[17]

Philip Morris has always relied heavily on advertising. Introduced in 1954, the Marlboro man—the virile cowboy smoker—was an immediate success (Barnet and Cavanagh 1994: 189–95). The banning of cigarette advertising from U.S. television in 1970 worked to the advantage of the Marlboro man, whose celebration of freedom in the Great Outdoors looked particularly good on billboards. While company executives feel strongly that the Marlboro man has "global" appeal, they have also invested heavily in market research that makes the Marlboro image more appropriate to particular national markets. In Hong Kong, for example, the cowboy looked to local people like a menial worker; Philip Morris removed him but kept the horse, an appealing image for Chinese consumers.

In Indonesia, domestic cigarette producers were protected for many years by a national preference for clove cigarettes (i.e., tobacco cigarettes with cloves included as a flavoring). The challenge for foreign cigarette marketers was to create a new niche, with different tastes: The solution was an appeal to cosmopolitan youth, or at least their image, with its connotations of mobility, status, and urban distinction. In the United States, the public frowns on cigarette advertising directed toward youth. Yet Philip Morris was free to target anyone in Indonesia. And their market researchers had the examples of Gudang Garam's and Bentoel's advertising from which to develop their own billboard designs.[18]

It is in this context that Philip Morris created the "Marlboro adventure team" in 1994. Yearly contests picked national winners, not only from Indonesia, but also from Hong Kong, the Philippines, and Malaysia. Winners received a week of adventure sports in the U.S. West. While there was no direct rule against winners being female, all advertising, as well as photographs of past winners, showed men. As with Marlboro advertising in the United States, the contest evoked masculinity as the necessary prerequisite for the Great Outdoors; women were expected to consume as admirers of virile men.

In 1997, Marlboro adventure team billboards were everywhere. Each showed a dramatic photograph of an adventure sport and offered the challenge: "Prove you have the daring!" Filmic versions were screened before every movie showing. Advertising brochures collected the photographs and sayings, as follows (all in Indonesian):

> Face the obstacles of savage nature. [A photograph shows dramatic lightning striking the U.S. southwest desert.] Are you brave enough to take control? [Jeeps driving across the desert.]
>
> Prove you have the daring!
>
> Tossed against terrifying rapids! [A wild river.] Are you brave enough with just a paddle? [A paddler steers in the spray.]
>
> Prove you have the daring!
>
> Your arena is risk. [Steep canyons.] Are you brave enough to subjugate it? [Flying motorcyclists.]
>
> Prove you have the daring!
>
> Hundreds of meters high, hanging from a cliff! [A towering rock.] Are you brave enough with a single rope? [A climber hangs.]
>
> Prove you have the daring!
>
> Reach for a field without a master. [Desert.] Are you brave enough to break through? [Mountain bikers.]
>
> Prove you have the daring!
>
> Sprint swiftly between steep hills. [Horses in the desert.] Are you brave enough to race? [Racing horsemen.]
>
> Prove you have the daring!

The spirit of these advertisements does not quite fit the nature lovers I knew: The advertisements focus on virility and risk, rather than the contemplative freedom of nature more important to nature lovers. Some of the fantasies the ad campaign invokes may have set out to appeal to other Asian audiences, as well as the advertisers' own images of the outdoors. Yet it is hard to escape the connection between this campaign and the groundwork laid by Gudang Garam and Bentoel. Nature lovers were quick to tell me about these connections, as they formed a commercial lineage of selling nature lover identities.

Furthermore, nature lovers were excited by the popularization of their images in Marlboro advertising. Throughout the summer of 1997, Marlboro sponsored exhibitions in shopping malls advertising the adventure team campaign. The exhibitions were planned for twenty-six cities—with more than one in major cities—providing a reasonably precise map of Indonesia's cosmopolitan centers. The exhibitions sold Marlboro products and advertised the contest. They displayed the wonders of adventure sports, complete, in some cases, with a climbing wall and demonstration dirt bikes. In some cities, they also provided a forum for nature lovers to get together to advertise themselves. Around the central Marlboro station in the Jakarta exhibition I visited, nature lovers set up tables presenting their offerings. Private clubs advertised their outdoor trips and training. Distributors advertised nature lover paraphernalia. Student nature clubs, too, set up tables to attract new members and tell others about their activities. The Marlboro campaign had organized a new confluence of nature loving concerns, presenting nature lovers with the opportunity to be entrepreneurs. Surprisingly, even the Indonesian Environmental Forum (WALHI) joined the Marlboro exhibition. The WALHI representative was not there to talk about the environmental problems of tobacco growing or smoking. As a panel participant, he introduced environmental advocacy; he was hoping, he said privately, to politicize nature lovers. Within the range of interests the exhibition promoted, advocacy was possible, too. If wild nature was a site of fashionable consumer identity, perhaps new activists could be recruited, along with athletes, romantics, and smokers.

The commercialization of nature lover imagery forms a clear example of what I am calling a *contingent lineage* of cosmopolitan specificity. The cigarette advertising campaigns that invoked nature loving built upon each other, drawing nature lovers into their plans. Gudang Garam's initial success grew in large part from the chance event that Norman Edwin, as a widely read journalist and an admired mountain climber, was available to bring his personal charisma to the cigarette business. His accidental death increased his charisma, and gave a push to the second rock climbing ad campaign, as well as to Bentoel's river-oriented take-off. Philip Morris was able to draw from the success of each of these Indonesian campaigns in presenting their cigarette as an element of outdoor adventures. Meanwhile, each of these campaigns popularized Indonesian nature loving, and they created new opportunities for consumer-oriented identity formation for would-be cosmopolitan youth. The consumerist lineage of nature loving grew from one unpredictable, contingent development to another. It converged, too, with other contingent lineages of nature loving, including those I have identified as anti-politics nationalism, urban distinctions, and adventure geographies. Together, they mapped the ground on which nature loving seemed exciting, popular, and able to address cosmopolitan yearnings. Various images of the challenge of nature were confused and blended, ranging from masculine self-assertion to rural nostalgia, and from individual freedom to environmental advocacy. I have suggested the limitations of this ground—as well as its openings and possibilities—in describing the Jakarta Marlboro exhibition, with its fashionable products, its eager student club recruiters, and its hopeful activists, as well as its transnational cigarette hustlers.

Another of the Marlboro exhibitions of the summer of 1997 was planned for the city of Banjarmasin. It was never held; pre-election riots that spring burned down the main shopping mall and everything around it. At least one hundred and twenty-five people died in the burning shopping center, mysteriously piled into a heap; the government claimed they were looters. The commercial downtown was reduced to smoldering husks. It turned out that this event was a pre-figuration of things to come in Indonesia, as ethnic and political violence, often sparked by secret army provocations, spread. Neither commercial campaigns (like those of cigarette companies) nor individual voyages of self-discovery (like those of nature lovers) turned out to be as autonomous of state, regional, and ethnic politics as they imagined themselves under the protection of the New Order regime and its economic miracle. The convergence of contingent lineages that produced the nature loving I knew in the 1990s turned out to be tentative and unstable. Viewed through the hole in the Marlboro exhibition schedule left by the fires in Banjarmasin, one might see that its future was already unclear.

The Romance of Nature

> I don't know why,
> nature,
> you don't scare me,
> but you make me calm,
> without a sense of restlessness, dejection, or anxiety,
> I am happy, relieved, and free,
> I love you.
> —from a nature lovers' club log book, 1993

With this much context established, I can return to my initial questions about the shape and feeling of "nature" among Indonesian nature lovers. Rather than continue to map trends and decode representations, I turn to things I learned directly from particular nature lovers. The contingent lineages I have described lay the social framework for nature loving, but they do not express the force of the sentiment of loving nature. They do not tell us how and why particular people are moved by the romance of nature. This requires asking individuals, whose personal trajectories work within the confluence of cultural lineages but make something personally meaningful of them.

Let me introduce four nature lovers I had the chance to get to know in Yogya in 1997. Sri is a creative and energetic young woman, determined to find her personal path. Nature loving has opened her eyes to the wonder and majesty of the world. Budi is a mischievous young man, properly proud of his charm, his intellect, his openness to unconventional ideas, and his only-sometimes successful ability to get out of sticky situations. He offers his cheeky enthusiasm to nature lovers, inspiring the younger kids and keeping up the spirits of the old-timers. Dwi is serious, thoughtful, and religiously pious; he would like to see the nature lovers' club become well-organized, well-documented, and successful. Hamam is on a larger personal and social mission: How can we improve both ourselves and the world? Through nature loving he has found a taste for the responsibilities and challenges of NGO work, as well as those of a disciplined personal spirituality.

In many ways, these four young people, when I knew them, were no different than other students in Yogyakarta. They blended in easily: They were friendly, informal, good-looking, always ready to hang out and talk, and full of ideas and dreams. Like their outdoorsy counterparts in the United States and elsewhere, they were in excellent physical condition; they were articulate and upwardly mobile, at least in their imagination; if they had any potentially damaging eccentricities, they were still hidden behind the promise of youth. Like most nature lovers around the world, they are interesting not so much as personalities but as thinkers, organizers, leaders, or poets, able to articulate imagery or inspire activities that move others to appreciate the world around them. To meet them is to follow them into their ideas and projects. And so, I present them in the ethnographic present, and without much personal contextualization.

It is Sri who speaks most forcefully about awe and the magic of nature. She wrote for me about mountains: "For me, the word mountain makes me mesmerized; I have the image of beauty, vastness, power, intimacy, companionship, and the mystery in it. Why? In my thinking, a mountain is a miracle of nature that cannot be defeated. It can erupt; it can shake the earth in a quake; it can lose a person who takes lightly the procedures for working together on the mountain; at the same time, it also hides so many secrets that humans can never uncover. The height of a mountain, the density of its forests, the cold of a mountain, the high peak: these are things that astonish me."

I had asked Sri about the custom of climbing mountains at night to arrive at the peak at sunrise. She explained the stunning effect of the sunrise breaking over a vast panorama extended in time as well as space. "The moment I see the sunrise, the feeling in my heart is like being born again—and of meaning nothing as long as the world has existed. For the nature that exists at that instant was already there before I was born, and it will be there too after I die. Who knows from when and until when the sun has risen like that?"

Sri writes poetry inspired by her experiences in nature. She depends on nature to help her work through life's traumas and challenges. On the mountain, she explains, "I am like a student listening to my teacher who is telling me about how to live, a teacher who is instructing me but also a teacher who invites discussion, and I am given problems to finish myself, as well as perils." She learns about nature's needs as well as her own. "From the mountain I learn that it isn't necessary to try to subjugate or exploit nature, whatever one's purpose." The mountain puts our petty goals and troubles in nature's grand perspective. Nature is a site of wisdom and a source of healing. "From 'studying about nature' we should also 'study in nature' at the same time as 'studying from nature.'"

Studying from nature can also mean studying from the "local people," those closer to the natural world and its archaic, mysterious wisdom. I found Sri's story of her 1991 ascent of Mount Lawu in central Java particularly moving as it told of her awkward but intense engagement with a Javanese villager she met at the summit. Sri was able to engage this villager because of her romance with nature. Even as she processed the encounter through this romance, nature loving also became a way to reach out and to evaluate her cosmopolitan difference.

It all began, she explained, when she and a group of nature lovers climbed Mount Lawu on the first day of the Javanese month of Suro, the date of an important traditional festival for which many people gather on the mountain. "So many people were climbing Mount Lawu! At the summit of the mountain, there were people selling meatball soup and hot tea and coffee. They had stoves there and had been living there for a week!

"I became fascinated by the people who had climbed the mountain. They had come wearing regular jackets and caps. They sat there quietly, in reflection within themselves. And they were only wearing [thin cloth] sarongs! While we mountain climbers had come with large backpacks, with secure hiking boots, with camping stoves, with sleeping bags, with tents. And even then we moaned, 'Oh, this' and 'Oh, that' and every kind of 'Oh my.'

"But they had come only with their own bodies and maybe a bottle of water. So I ventured to ask—not really an interview, but I wanted to ask—one of the men, using Javanese:

'Why, sir, have you come here? Isn't it cold?'

'My dear, this is the way I can offer prayers for my children. So that my children can become someone. So that they can work well. So that they won't encounter difficulties. So that they will be able to get money for their work. Yes, it's only this that I can do for my children. So that nothing terrible will happen. I'm not a rich man. I can only make a plea for a blessing. I pray for all my family, my children, and myself for the gift of happiness.'

'But, sir, why are you only wearing a sarong?'

'My dear, if things are already as they are, what is one's body? Cold is also given by the Almighty. If we are warm, that is also given by the Almighty. This is what I have to enjoy. I have this sarong, and what else is needed?'

"All that I could think was, well, yes, I'm not embarassed, it's true I have a full load of equipment, and it gives me security. But like that—simple—I could carry just a little money—every day one only needs to eat maybe two times and drink tea or coffee one or two times—I would need perhaps only Rp. 1,000 to eat because they are selling food here. And, with just that, it would be enough for me.

"My heart's approach—I can't translate it into words. Well, I thought, this is a different approach to life. And I kept thinking: Next year, if I can, I want to join a ritual occasion like this. I want to have little, as they do. I won't be trifling. I won't climb the mountain for show, with a backpack and a full set of equipment."

The encounter continued to teach Sri about life. The next year she did re-climb Mount Lawu by herself, seeking a time of introspection and reflection. It was a spiritual journey in which she went to "receive the power of nature." And, even in growing beyond the ardors of active nature loving, she has continued to learn from nature.

Although nature is also a place of personal growth for Budi, he finds it not so much a sacred site as a site for exploring personal freedom. He started nature loving as a rebellious high school student. "The first time I climbed Mount Merapi," he explained, "I hardly remember it, I was drunk, I was with other high school students trying to reach Mount Vodka." He wanted to be an "outlaw," and he found free-spirited—and often drunk—community with nature lovers. Even in college, he turned to nature loving to find a good time outside the boundary of dull respectability. He jokes about it with a sense of self-mocking irony: "In my college, my friends did nothing but study. Oh shit, no fun [This in English]. So I made a connection with the upperclassmen who already were the informal power in the college. We had beautiful moments. While they were studying, I was laughing and making jokes. And I still got good grades."

I found Budi's ability to laugh at his own weaknesses—and those of his mates—to be one of his most attractive qualities. In telling his personal history with nature loving, he stressed the transgressive quality of the groups he joined, as well as the superficiality of their obsessions with oppositional style. He tells of a mountain climbing club he joined: "We were the hoodlums of the campus. We took on a tough appearance. We acted hard and stubborn. But in practice, we were lazy." When they hiked, they rarely got above the settlements of local residents. "It was just a tourist trip." But they thought of themselves as brave adventurers: "We had to go to places that were exotic and romantic." Meanwhile, the club's membership and its standing in the school grew. "We had a kind of power—social status and reasonably nice bodies." They bullied the college to give them funds for their trips: "If nothing was forthcoming, we would say, 'Take our request to the Assistant Deacon, or we will badmouth you.'" They got all kinds of funds and support, and used them to play. "At that time, we were hedonists, and we loved to have a good time."

Budi looks back on these early days and laughs at himself. He is a great commentator who has a way with words; he has something to say about every outing. In an interview about a nature lovers' expedition to Lore Lindu, in the interior of Sulawesi, he was candid about the horrors of the trip, and particularly those involving the problems of social interaction on the team. In his self-conscious style, he was willing to blame himself as much as others for the tensions and to see the working out of these kinds of problems as part of the "experience" (*pengalaman*). He began his description with an awkward admission:

"I didn't want to go because the leader was Chinese. In those days I was racist against Chinese. I didn't like them. A month before the departure, they still didn't have a photographer. . . . So I went along." Rather than a longawaited romantic quest, the trip was an almost casual last-minute concession.

The social difficulties did not end with the constitution of the team. "There was lots of personal friction that emerged. I slept outside. . . . I slept in a hammock. I wanted to listen to the radio, and the radio was inside [the tent], but I wasn't allowed inside. Saiful, a Palembang guy, didn't want to come out; he wasn't brave enough. 'If you come out, I will really slash you with a machete.' I was already annoyed but not yet insane. I smoked; I played *gableg* dominos constantly. We were almost a month in the forest. We really had to work in the forest."

"How did it feel?"

"It was alright. I had never been in the forest for so long. I had often been out for two, three, maybe four days. With the same people, looking for a new experience. Here the team interaction was different; my psychological condition was different." He began to tell stories of the weird things they did. "We arrived at the peaks of that mountain range, and we stopped. We were to do research for two or three days. There we celebrated [a Muslim holiday] by butchering a chicken. We had a voodoo ritual. . . . We slaughtered it in a ceremony: 'Wu wu wu, wu wu wu!' [He danced around, mimicking old U.S. movie stereotypes of Native American ceremonies.] We circled around until that chicken must have been dizzy, in that party. Then we roasted it."

The bizarre, the crazy, the difficult, the intense: all were gathered in his experience. Interactions with the local villagers added to the mix. "Many times when we were hiking, we got lost. Once when we came into a village, we received a kind welcome. . . . When we arrived, we wanted to bathe. 'There's no bathroom, only in the river' [the villagers said apologetically]. We went as a group down to the river to bathe, but the water was chocolate colored and nauseating. I figured they also bathed there [and bathed anyway]. When we finished bathing and went back to the village, they were laughing: 'Ha, ha, taken in by a trick, taken in by a trick.' That was crude."

Sometimes, the nature lovers purposely took advantage of the villagers, too, as in this anecdote about a church auction, in which local people donated foodstuff to raise money for the church. "When we started to bid, no one was brave enough to bid higher than we did. So we could buy a chicken for Rp. 750 when they normally sold for two or three thousand rupiah. No one else would bid, so the chicken would go to us."

In the process of negotiation of their local status, Budi did learn some important things about social and environmental problems in the area. He went on to speak about the difficulties of organizing a national park into a protected core area and outlying buffer zones in which certain economic activities were permitted. A village had to be moved from the core and reestablished, with difficulty, on other land; the villagers were appropriately worried about schistosomiasis in their new location. His new knowledge and his endurance of the difficulties went hand in hand: As Budi explained, this was "experience."

Dwi was a member of this same expedition, and the trip also forms an important memory for him: a memory of a complex organizational undertaking. Dwi and Budi are close friends, but they have quite different styles. Dwi is serious, responsible, and meticulous, with none of Budi's playful abandon. He showed me his diary from the Lore Lindu trip, which records every meal he ate, however humble, every social interaction that disturbed team dynamics, and every sleepless night spent swatting at mosquitoes. Even in his oral account, he narrated the trip as a series of technical failures and successes. He had some funny stories—a team member running from a snake; an unchewable piece of dried buffalo meat—and some moving stories, such as that of helping a "bewitched," dehydrated villager through his knowledge of first aid. He attributes the problems they had, becoming lost in the forest, to an accumulation of technical mistakes, such as their casualness in taking compass readings, which could have prevented them from circling back on their tracks.

More recently, Dwi has become excited about the project of writing about nature lovers' organizations. He has combed through available club records, compiling careful genealogies of club organization and activities. He also writes about nature lover objectives and training methods. So far, most of his writing has been circulated only internally among nature lovers; but he is thinking of other ways to use this material, not only to communicate about nature loving, but also to develop his skills as a communicator. Dwi is self-conscious about improving his writing, his management skills, and his technical knowledge through nature loving. For Dwi, nature is a site for building organizational leadership skills.

Hamam also feels a sense of social responsibility in nature. But for Hamam, the responsibility has nothing to do with the organizational features of nature lovers' clubs. Hamam wants to improve himself and the world. Out in wild nature, Hamam says he feels his daily burdens lifted; and from this sense of relief, he feels he can come back to the city with a stronger sense of personal responsibility. After some time exploring nature loving, Hamam has also become interested in Javanese mysticism and started to work with a traditional mystic in training himself in that discipline. He has food taboos, such as not eating salt, which help him focus on personal growth. Nature loving also participates in his spiritual development. When he climbs a mountain by himself, he says he feels small. There are so many mysteries of nature that are unknown and difficult to understand with logical reason, even the idea that God or some Essence made the world. These kinds of thoughts do not make him want to remove himself from society; instead, they reaffirm his commitment to society—and to nature.

Hamam feels that the term "nature loving" (*kepencintaalaman*) is a heavy burden that must be taken seriously. To love nature means to refuse to fight against nature. It means to guard nature and to unite oneself with nature. Most nature lovers, including himself, he says, are really just "enjoyers of nature" (*penikmat alam*). He, for example, still smokes; if he really would be a nature lover, he would have to give up smoking, he says. Loving nature is something to aspire to, not to claim easily.

Over the last few years, Hamam has become interested in environmental advocacy, either with established NGOs or with one he would organize himself. He has done some work with an NGO that advocates ecotourism as a socially responsible form of tourism. Mass tourism, Hamam says, drains the country's natural resources. Tourism needs to be organized with conservation principles in mind. This could include educating tourists about the importance of natural ecosystems. He sees ecotourism, too, as a possible alternative to the natural and social destruction of most rural development projects. He told me of the horrors of the grand "One Million Hectares" development scheme that was a government showcase in 1996 in Central Kalimantan. He spent several months there, working as a community organizer advocating community-based ecotourism development. Government development plans made it difficult to get people to think in terms of small-scale alternatives. Planners had mapped out a huge tract of swampy country—one million hectares—to turn into wet-rice fields. The residents had had a profitable livelihood raising water buffaloes; the water buffaloes were all confiscated and taken away, leaving the people without resources. Meanwhile, the rice would not grow, he said. When the president came for a tour of the project, project managers took strips of sod with rice seedlings in it and laid them out, making it look as if this would be a fertile rice basket. As soon as the president left, the imported seedlings died, leaving the ground bare. Hamam sees this kind of large-scale irresponsibility as the major threat to the Indonesian environment.

Hamam's interest in the NGO world brings me back to the relationship between nature loving and environmental advocacy. Nature, for Hamam, is a realm that calls up responsibility for better behavior. This is one way that nature loving can make environmental advocacy possible. But nature, for nature lovers, is a realm of many meanings and avenues for passion and growth. Sri's wisdom and healing; Budi's freedom and mobility; Dwi's organizational aptitudes; and Hamam's responsible guardianship: Each of these represents one of the ways nature comes to be a substantial thing in the nature loving community. There are diverse paths here. But each contributes to understandings of nature that might make one want to consider it an *object* of reflection, discussion, or advocacy.

Nature loving is not the same as environmental activism. The distinctiveness of student nature loving is, however, important to understanding environmentalism not only because many Indonesian environmental activists got their start in college nature loving, but also because they know how to recognize "the environment" in part because of nature loving. Further: Around the world, environmental activism depends on distinctive cultural ways of recognizing the environment. "Global environmentalism"—whether coercive or collaborative—can *only* exist in the dialogues and overlaps among these distinctive concerns about nature.

One important strain of nature appreciation in the United States naturalizes the love of nature to argue that it is a biological feature of human nature to feel refreshed in the wild (Kellert and Wilson 1993). This is the reason, many conservation biologists argue, that humans have a species responsibility to save nature. Indeed, it appears that the romance of nature is a widespread practice. Yet we need not naturalize it as a universal biology in order to appreciate its global spread. I have tried to show the formation of nature loving's national particularities as a way of knowing its cosmopolitanism. The personal force of "nature," and its appearance as an object of reflection, depends on both this localization and its cosmopolitan referents.

"This earth, this island Borneo"
[Biodiversity assessment as a multicultural exercise]

Knowledge grows through multiple layers of collaboration—as both empathy and betrayal. The process of layering is perhaps most striking in insignificant, vernacular collaborations—like the one I catalyzed in the village of Kalawan, at a moment when a much-cherished biodiversity was becoming an issue of anxious concern.

1994. It started with an innocent question about eels; I was thinking of dinner. "Are there any eels in the river?" I asked. Uma Adang, my Meratus Dayak friend and mentor, leaned back, assuming her most serious oratorical bearing. "Facing the year 2000," she proclaimed, "we must make a list of all the contents of this earth, this island Borneo." Plants and animals, their names and uses and local or foreign locations: all, she told me, should be listed. I was taken aback. I had not yet had the chance to explain much to her about my new research on global environmentalism. She was not in touch with global biodiversity experts, although surely some radio announcer or nature hiker had brought the rhetoric of environmentalism to her village. Yet she beautifully articulated the spirit of environmental prophecy: the looming, apocalyptic crisis of nature as revealed at the turn of the millennium, the chance to save the earth through proper naming, and the necessity, in doing so, of moving back and forth between "the island" and "the earth"—the minutely local and the whole globe.

Over the next ten days, Uma Adang sat with me and dictated over a thousand local life-forms. She wasn't feeling well, and she didn't want to go outside. Instead, she felt happier sitting with me on the floor of her house, telling me

Laba di ai'ing **Beings of the water**

1. iwak: the great white fish just called "fish"

2. anakan: another white fish

3. masapi: a big eel, as big around as a person's arm, it hides in holes but can be lured out at night with chicken guts
4. usei: another freshwater eel, also delicious
5. kambalang: a tasty fish
6. tilan: a thin, scaly fish, like an eel
7. manki: a green fish with red tail and fins
8. puyao: another green fish
9. lampam: a white fish with a red mouth and tail
10. bidugung: a yellow fish, 3 fingers wide
11. badaris: a small white fish
12. saluwang: a minnow
13. kanduri: a catfish
14. kihung: a long black fish

These are found in seasonal creeks and swamps:

15. alirao: a catfish
16. la'is [*Belodontichthys dinema*]: a catfish
17. sambunit: a small catfish
18. tamparisay: a fish, 4 fingers wide
19. panting: a catfish
20. puntur: a long fish
21. sanggiringan: the size of a person's thumb, it swims in schools
22. lampuk: a catfish similar to la'is
23. walut [*Monopterus albus*]: a small swamp eel

These have legs:

24. bidawang: a large turtle
25. biyanan: a small turtle
26. kuntan: a tortoise
27. kuduk: a common frog
28. kungkung: a toad
29. ambulahang: a green toad
30. i'irak: another toad
31. karantung: a frog; "the music of the deep water"
32. tangkaricak: a tiny frog that calls day and night

More water animals:

33. takuyung: long whorled river snails

about plants and animals. Every now and again, someone else in the household, feeling the pleasure of our work, would come in with a plant sample picked outside: "You haven't listed this yet." We would add a new name to our list. Or, restless, I would follow someone to gather river snails or fern fiddleheads for dinner, and another name would emerge. But most of the time we were deprived of the stimulus of the plants and animals around us and left, instead, with Uma Adang's memory and imagination. Nor had we books of flora and fauna to recall more species to mind; we had to remember an organism to place it on the list, and, in the context of this oral recitation, we almost never went back to add forgotten species to earlier categories. We missed a good many plants and animals we both knew—and, I'm sure, many more with which I am unfamiliar. Still, more than one thousand life-forms is not bad. I have been told that U.S. Americans, asked to do a similar task and with less local specificity, could not list more than several hundred. Uma Adang self-consciously limited herself to living things that were found in her local area, a karst-studded plain of small shifting fields and still-large but threatened forests at the foot of the Meratus Mountains. She excluded life-forms that she knew occurred at the coast, as that, she said, should be a different list. This was a self-conscious project of placing a local niche within a global imagining. The lists acknowledged and acclaimed global biodiversity by conserving a local space within it.

Because I had asked about eels, we began with *laba' di ai'ing*, beings of the water. Uma Adang listed the best fish to eat, and then some less significant fish, then the fish found in swamps, the reptiles, the amphibians, the mollusks, the crustaceans, and finally the water plants. Because I had watched people fish and admired their catch, the list easily evoked the everyday livelihood practices through which I, too, could call to mind these water creatures. Wading in deep river pools, young men threw hand-woven nets to catch the sweet-fleshed *iwak*. In the mountains, men bent bamboo poles, their ends craftily hooked underwater so that they sprung straight up when a fish took the bait, leaving the iwak swinging high over the river. When the iwak were big, people divided them up in small chunks, counting out equal shares for every household just as if they were game. In Uma Adang's network, boys swam underwater with home-made goggles and rubberband-powered spear-guns to bring us delicious *kambalang* and *lampam*. Woven bamboo traps caught smaller fish in fast-running streams. In muddy creek holes, we could build a tiny dam and scoop up *saluwang* minnows with our hands; we steamed and ate them, bones and all. I myself once brought home a great *panting* catfish; it had been killed by a bird, which flew away when I ran up, leaving its fresh prey. As for turtles, frogs, shrimp, and snails: We had enjoyed them all. And, of course, eels.

The taste of food was not, however, the only pleasure called up in this list. Uma Adang is alert to the colors, textures, and sounds of the beings around her. She described the *karantung* frog as "the music of the deep water" and mimicked its call. She knows plants and animals in relation to locations: She tried to remind me of the place I had just seen the water plant *tantamau*, on the rocks where we were gathering snails. Sometimes forest birds and animals become companions: I saw my first *kuntan* tortoise when I was introduced to Uma Adang's latest pet, whom she brought home from the forest to coax and protect and feed ripe bananas as it crawled around the house. As for riverside *lua'* trees, we talked as much about the animals attracted to the tree because of its fruit as about its human uses.

Meanwhile, the river was becoming a difficult place to find food. With the building of new roads, the practice of sending an electric current into the water with a car battery had been introduced to Uma Adang's area. All the fish, big and small, died. (At least one person died too, by accidentally slipping into the water while the electric current was still active.) The rivers were becoming barren. Uma Adang's worries about this situation provoked her attention to listing the river's denizens. Her list was a form of apology that soon enough we would not be eating and even encountering these fish and frogs and eels. A prospective, incipient nostalgia helped motivate the list: the same incipient nostalgia as that which motivates so much of the science of environmental conservation, particularly concerning the conservation of biodiversity.

Incipient nostalgia had caught us, enlivening our encounter. Indeed, the globalism of our exercise meant that

34. takuyung duduk: small river snails
35. takuyung bilut: small river snails
36. takuyung baba: round river snails
37. kalimbuai: large, round river snails, live in holes; the shells can be made into lime
38. kacambang: freshwater mussels
39. katam: river crab
40. katam siwao: a red swamp crab
41. hudang sungai: freshwater shrimp

Plants that grow in the water:
42. tantamau
43. tantamau panjang: looks like hair
44. halimpayao: grows around rocks in the river

Plants that grow only at the river's edge:
45. lalamas: an aroid with taro-like heart-shaped leaves
46. haris: a wild ginger, with green, fist-sized flowers
47. tigarun: a tree, leaves burnt for pain medicine
48. bayuan: a tall tree with edible fruits
49. lua' panggang: a cauliflorous tree with edible fruit
50. kasai [*Pometia sp.*]: a tree, fruits used for fish bait

our list was charged by emotions, quests, and voices originating from many sites, each buffeting us with their whiffs of pleasure, charisma, terror, dead authority, or charm. They crowd around me now, in telling the tale, bringing their eccentric habits and irascible opinions to any purpose we might have concocted.

The biologist, E. O. Wilson, fresh from communion with ants, rises to proclaim with reverence: "the diversity of life is the cradle and greatest natural heritage of the human species" (Wilson in Takacs 1996: 309).

Since the 1980s, biodiversity has developed as an object of worldwide concern: the centerpiece of global environmentalism. Public awareness of biodiversity draws from the visibility of conservation biology: the science that grows from taking the threat of species extinctions seriously. Conservation biology is self-consciously action-oriented as well as research-driven (Noss and Cooperrider 1994). Crossing lines between science and policy, it asks us to care about the abundance of species in every corner of the earth. Listing species is significant because it allows us to discover variety and to appreciate its dynamics.

My mother, the only Chinese American member of an Ohio wild flowers society, tells me: "Learning the names of plants is just like learning the names of people you meet; when you know their names, you can get to know them better."

The idea of biodiversity has proved charismatic because it combines the scientific legitimacy of biology with popular legacies of plant and animal identification. Victorian amateur collectors, particularly in England and its diaspora, were fascinated by the variety of nature (Dunlap 1999). The theory of evolution interpolated species collecting into one of the most thrilling sciences of the times. Similarly, conservation biology energizes contemporary popular practices of nature appreciation in which learning the names of species creates a vitalizing intimacy with nature (Wilson 1992). Species-oriented nature appreciation—from birdwatching to wildlife television—had a well-established place in late twentieth century metropolitan cultures. Conservation biologists were able to draw on this popularity, and build it, as they showed the importance of conserving the diversity of nature. Working together across lay and technical lines, conservation biologists and environmental activists have made attention to biodiversity—including the practice of making species lists—the first requirement of conservation itself.

The environmental activists of the Rainforest Action Network transmit the latest communiqué from the U'wa people of Colombia: "We U'wa will not cede our cultural, historic, and ancient rights. We prefer genocide sponsored by the Colombian government rather than handing over our Mother Earth to the oil companies" (Cabildo Mayor U'wa 2000).

The blossoming of the international campaign to save the Amazon forest in the late 1980s inspired a new political form: collaborations between indigenous leaders and environmentalists. Indigenous rights became entangled with conservation initiatives. Such collaborations were inspired in part by researchers who had found that indigenous people appreciated and managed the biodiversity with which they lived (e.g., Posey 1985). It seemed possible that culturally sensitive alliances among scientists, activists, and indigenous peoples might make conservation possible in some rich, not-yet-simplified patches of nature (Redford and Mansour 1996). In this spirit, conservationists have revitalized attention to the traditional knowledge of rural people. It seems hopeful that so many indigenous people are not only well-informed about biodiversity, but also willing to share their knowledge with conservationists. Yet obstructions abound.

Political ecologist Søren Hvalkof learns why the Siona Indians of the Ecuadorian Amazon refuse resource extraction contracts: "In impassioned voices they told revolting stories about how [during the early twentieth-century rubber boom] the local rubber patrons and their contractors had murdered, tortured, and abused their folks" (Hvalkof 2000: 87).

One obstruction is the terrifying history of past encounters through which indigenous knowledge has entered the metropolitan corpus of science and industry. Most of the economic products in use today for global agriculture and industry were introduced from the knowledges of rural people who knew and used these products; and this process of extraction continues (Juma 1989). This has not been a pretty history of mutual benefit. Infused with practices of enslavement, terror, theft, murder, and deceit, the expansion of European and "international" knowledge of economic products has been deeply entangled with subjugation. The current course of global capitalism suggests that such coercive and unequal collaborations will continue. Many of the most conspicuous models of conservationist collaboration (such as "rainforest marketing," in which local identification of economic plants is coupled with corporate production and distribution, and "biodiversity prospecting," in which rural people help scientists gather plants for corporate pharmaceutical development) have suffered from their refusal to repudiate this past history, instead drawing from its legacy of exploitation (Dove 1993; Shiva 1997).

Feminist theorist Noel Sturgeon offers a generous reading of the quirks and promises of U.S. ecofeminism, yet she worries that ecofeminist attention to indige-

nous knowledge, despite good intentions, reconstitutes white privilege: "One way this occurs is through the racial essentialism of the idea of the indigenous, which erases all difference between and within the categories 'Native American' and 'Third World' and constitutes them as racialized Others to a white Self that is Western, modern, and industrialized" (Sturgeon 1997: 113).

Another obstruction is the metropolitan romance that produces the categories with which we know "indigenous" people and "wild" nature. These are modernist categories in negation; they index people and places not included in "modern" landscapes, that is, landscapes in which planners have worked hard to subjugate variety for the cause of regularity, hygiene, property, efficiency, and profit. Because indigenous people and wild nature only exist in opposition to these modernist programs, any generalizations we make about them are likely to be wrong. We quickly ascend to a world of fantasy every time we imagine tribal survival or spirituality, or wild nature's competitive struggle or harmonious stability. These categories have a limited usefulness in helping us understand the idiosyncratic histories of particular social and natural landscapes. Yet it seems to me that we cannot give up these fantastical categories. It is only because of the protest embedded in them that some conservationists even imagine collaboration across cultures to preserve the variety of nature. The alternative fantasy—a falsely uniform modernism—is much worse.

Even the staunchly scientific International Union for the Conservation of Nature and Natural Resources has suggested that wilderness protection requires working with indigenous peoples: "It is becoming obvious that the key to protecting a cherished landscape lies within the communities that call it home"(Holdgate 1993: v).

While this argument can lead to oversimplifications, we do not need to reify either indigenous people or wild nature to explore its practical possibilities (Stevens 1997). The crux of the argument about indigenous people and conservation is that the regularizing modern imagination has had *such* a destructive effect on species diversity that almost any other human lifeway is likely to be better at maintaining it (Banuri and Marglin 1993). Farmers invade tropical forests when they are incorporated into modern political economies (Lohmann 1993). This attention to the historical and cultural specificity of modernist destruction is an important—and promising—divergence from more popular conservationist models, which posit all humanity in conflict with nature. It is worth attending to indigenous-conservationist collaborations just to give them some breathing room.

At a 1998 conference in Georgia, activists and scholars argued about community-based conservation. Both sides agreed that these are some of the most promising conservation programs we know. Yet the scholars insisted, "Aren't we oversimplifying 'community' and 'nature'?" (Brosius, Tsing, and Zerner 1998).

Many critical scholars have given up on conservationists' interest in indigenous people, categorizing it only as a repetition of metropolitan fantasies and imperial histories. Anthropologists make fun of activists' stereotypes about other cultures; literary critics trace these stereotypes back through a literary legacy (Ellen 1986; Slater 1995). Political ecologists show the disciplines conservationists impose on rural people and connect these to the history of colonialism (Li 2003b; Neumann 1998). These are crucial critical perspectives. Yet, taken together, they offer a historical metanarrative of imperial modernization in which nothing can happen—good or bad—but more of the same. Familiar heroes and villains are again arrayed on the same battlefield. It is difficult to see how new actors and arguments might ever emerge.

Scholars have consolidated their critical perspective on conservation by looking for *contests* in which parties with different stakes—European hunters and African herders, resident farmers and urban nature lovers, foreign activists and native tribes—struggle over the definition and use of nature (Brosius 1999a). This work usefully brings culture and politics together in understanding environmental conflicts; but there are other ways, too, to look at politics and culture. Much less attention has been paid to *collaborative* relationships through which environmental campaigns have been mounted. Collaboration is not necessarily good for all parties; to study it is not to pretend that easy solutions abound. Collaboration does, however, draw attention to the formation of new cultural and political configurations that change the arena of conflict, rather than just repeating old contests.

"Turtles and Teamsters": The unlikely—and tentative—alliance between labor and environmentalism successfully closed down the World Trade Organization's meeting in Seattle in 1999 (Berry 1999).

In this spirit, I stride cautiously but with determination into the arena of conservationist-indigenous alliances. Even as seemingly innocent an activity as making species lists can find itself enmired in condescension and theft: Does the list stereotype indigenous knowledge, limiting future economic and political strategies for the group? Does it erase nascent intellectual property rights or make information available for corporate exploitation? To care about these questions does not turn me away from multicultural environmentalism. Instead, such questions sharpen my attention to the process of collaboration.

Hewan Beasts

"Should I start with the largest and go to the smallest, or should I start with the smallest?" asked Uma Adang.

"Begin with the largest," I said, but neither of us had the commitment to pursue this systematically.

51. banting: wild buffalo; in the times of her great-grandparents they roamed these woods, but none remain
52. minjangan: Sambar deer
53. bayi: bearded pig
54. kijang: barking deer
55. landak: common porcupine
56. pilanduk: mouse-deer
57. baruang: sun bear
58. macan: clouded leopard
59. musang raya: bearcat civet?
60. musang penden: a small civet
61. tinggalung: Malay civet
62. kucing hutan: leopard cat
63. laruk: masked palm civet
64. sikik: another civet
65. sa'at: stink badger. The odor glands, placed in a field, deter pests.
66. barang-barang: otter
67. tanggiling: scaly anteater
68. tangka': squirrel
69. tupay: a treeshrew
70. angkis: long-tailed porcupine
71. bujit: a small treeshrew
72. bicing: a very small treeshrew
73. bantis: another treeshrew
74. mancungan: a treeshrew
75. salusuk: orange Malay weasel. I saw one eating a snake.
76. wagang: rat
77. ku'ung: giant flying squirrel
78. bangkoi: pig-tailed macaque
79. warik: long-tailed macaque
80. hirangan: grey leaf monkey. It laughs: "hahahaha."
81. cabang: red leaf monkey

In drawing attention to our collaborative process, my first two steps are an acknowledgment of *eclectic knowledges* and *overlapping pleasures*. List-making is eclectic to the extent that it draws on multiple, fragmentary sources. Furthermore, any list made by two or more people is a negotiated, eclectic product. To acknowledge this eclecticism allows us to admire its creative use of limited materials, rather than to grasp only for scope. It allows us to imagine the list within historically changing conversations, rather than as transcendent knowledge. My input in the species list I made with Uma Adang blended a variety of historically particular genre conventions and forms of curiosity, ranging from scholarly fashions (writing with informants) to activist strategies, from childhood passions (nature appreciation) to fragmented biological observation in Kalimantan and elsewhere. Similarly, Uma Adang brought her own mixture of historically particular goals and resources to the task. The discussion between us sparked new items on the list by juxtaposing and blending our combined intellectual stock within the limited confines of an enthusiastic oral performance, held indoors and in that sometimes awkward mixture of regional dialects with which Uma Adang always directed conversations even without my added blundering.

The eclecticism we produced is perhaps obvious—and I've tried to make it visible in the translations I offer by including Latin names only occasionally and by identifying organisms through an irregular mixture of Uma Adang's and my own commentary. I ignore questions of classification, offering only the negotiated list. I am more interested in introducing my readers to plants and animals than in adding them to a biological or cultural master list. To speak to a heterogeneous readership, I mention, for example, that *lalamas* (#45) is an aroid, like taro, for those who care; for those who don't, I hope that the image of heart-shaped leaves by the side of the stream beckons at least a little. This is, then, a motivated set of translations and not a simple addition to either universal or local cultural knowledge.

In other collaborative species lists, the Linnaean Latin name of an organism is paired dichotomously with a "local" name; the Latin name offers international information, while the local name grounds it in a particular place and discovery process. Conservationist-indigenous collaborations have sometimes used these lists to argue that local names on the list represent a codified traditional knowledge, which can match at least in form its scientific counterpart. There are lots of good reasons to codify knowledge. Sometimes such codifications are a tool for historically marginalized people to gain a place in negotiations of their resource rights. Anthropological investigations of the breadth and detail of indigenous knowledge can play an important role in facilitating this process, and I am full of appreciation for such work. However, for the specific task of understanding *collaboration*, it is necessary to draw attention to the context in which communication and codification occur. This requires acknowledgment of the inevitable eclecticism and serendipity of the knowledge-making process. The systematic study of "Meratus ethnobiology" is another task.

A concern with collaboration also draws my attention to the overlapping pleasures of list-making. If lists have anything to do with conservation, it is because they exude a certain charisma: They make people exclaim in wonder at the diversity of nature; they can inspire us to preserve that diversity. Yet for urbanites outside of the practices of nature appreciation and conservation biology, such lists often seem dead bureaucratic forms. Who cares whether there are ten species of snails or ten thousand? To ask how list-making works as a form of collaboration in nature appreciation is to make that appreciation palpable. What pleasures motivate each side of the collaboration to participate?

For Uma Adang, the pleasures have been many. Consider the pleasure of storytelling: It is impossible to tell or listen to stories in Kalimantan without saying the names of plants and animals. People encounter a large variety of plants and animals every day. It is hard to talk about what people are doing or where they have been without talking about plants and animals. One of the pleasures of Uma Adang's list was its incitement to remember and tell stories.

In Kalimantan as in other places, to talk of snakes often provokes stories. When we arrived at snakes in our list, the house began to jump with stories of snake encounters. Uma Adang's sister told me about the time she was bitten by an *ular ambularas*. She wasn't content with a casual tale. In her

82. undao: Bornean gibbon
83. bakatan: proboscis monkey, "mainly near the coast, but they sometimes come here."
84. hikuk: silvered langur, "mainly at the coast."
85. kalalawar balu: a large bat, one of many kalalawar
86. kalalawar pisang: a small bat, hangs at the top of banana trees and eats mosquitos
87. kaluwang: a large bat, sucks nectar from flowers
88. bingkarung: a lizard
89. biyawak: monitor lizard
90. inta'ang: a small lizard with a "comb" on its back
91. silat: a small lizard
92. cacak: house lizard
93. salimandan: giant millipede
94. amburakungan: a centipede with a dangerous bite
95. salipan: a smaller centipede
96. kala': scorpion
97. taki': a biting lizard?
98. silu': a tiny centipede with a mean bite
99. lingut: a tree-living millipede
100. cacing: earthworm

Ular Snakes

101–104. sawah: python. "It can swallow a person or a deer."
s. punggur: a small python
s. gading: the largest of the pythons, with clear variegation
s. batu: a long thin python

s. ripung: a large, mottled python
105–108. tadung: cobra.
t. kapayang: a grey snake
t. kumbang: a black snake that makes a lowing noise
t. ari: a snake that can leap from trees
t. mu'is: spitting cobra. It can put out your eyes.
109. ular sendok: Its head can look like a spoon. A cobra?
110. ular tampukung: a white snake with a reddish head
111. tanggal baju: a snake with a red head and tail and greenish stripes
112. ular simpay: a brown snake
113. ular tangkaliutan: changes colors from green to brown
114. ular binkarung: a small golden snake
115. ular pucuk: a green snake
116. tatak amas: a long snake with white and black horizontal stripes
117. ular puang: yellow and black; it resembles a python and eats chickens
118. ular nuna manis: a tree snake that is fed by birds, according to legend
119. ular liang: a snake that eats cave-dwelling swifts
120. ular ambularas: a mainly coastal snake with a deadly bite
121. ular lidi: a small, mainly coastal snake said to be able to soar. Perhaps it is legendary. They say one once fought the great naga snake that holds up the earth; the naga swallowed the ular lidi, but the latter fought the naga from the inside, and won.

Sayur Vegetables

796–801. kacang: green beans—k. rambat; k. sutra; k. ranggas; k. ga'ak; k. cangkul (wingbean); k. balimbing (wingbean)
802–806. bayam: amaranth—b. hijau; b. habang; b. putih; b. binuang; b. saraji
807. sasawi: Chinese cabbage

own intimate mockery of Uma Adang's oratorical style, which had been so successful in grabbing my attention, she fashioned her story with an air of officious spiritualism: "The snake was coiled around a tree, and when I passed, zap, it bit me in the calf. Another person might have died. But I had an 'anti'—to drink a tea of the roots of *tandoi* dug at noon on a Friday. The poison spread up to my head, climbing like a snake's scales, turning my body cold. It was freezing my flesh. It rose three times and fell again three times. I looked up and saw the rays of the sun spreading like a hand, and I knew I would recover."

Immersed in stories of snakes, I couldn't hold back my own story of an encounter with a king cobra outside a village in the mountains. I was standing by the river when the great dark snake came speeding out of the bushes following a frog. With a heroic leap, the frog jumped into the water. The snake stopped at the shore, by now only a few feet away from me. It was standing with its head at least four feet off the ground. We turned toward each other and gave each other a long, long look. Panicking, I turned and took two steps before realizing the impossibility of flight across the tumbled riverside boulders. I turned back. The snake was gone. Shaken, I returned to the house. "That was no ordinary snake," said my host. "If you had stayed, it would have spoken to you and given you a magical gift." Back in the United States, I came across the king cobra's picture in a book on snakes in the library, and it was only then that I found that the snakes I had come to know as *tadung* were also cobras.

The stories we exchanged about snakes focused on the unusual and the unexpected. But the pleasures of the everyday and the ordinary are also told in stories and even lists of diversity. Plants and animals figure everywhere in Meratus Dayak livelihood practices and the stories through which they are savored and shared. Discussion of cultivation and gathering, for example, is all about the diversity of plants and animals and tastes and habitats. Foods are diverse in both forests and fields: the range of food plants gathered from the forest is matched by the range of crop varieties nurtured in swidden fields. Swidden plant variety is mulled over and discussed every time something is to be planted; every time a neighbor comes to ask for one of those ripe squash; every time a young couple borrows not just one but many kinds of rice seed to extend their social networks; every time a child demands *that* variety of banana and not that other one.

For an observer used to imagining agriculture as cleanly weeded lines of corn, wheat, or tomatoes, but not all tossed together, the most amazing thing about a Meratus swidden field is the extraordinary number of plants growing together in the same small spot. There may be trees saved from the forest that was cut to make the field: fruit trees, honey trees, sugar palms. Fallen trunks and stumps, sometimes resprouting, litter the ground. Between them grow an exuberance of plants: not only grains, such as rice, corn, millet, and job's tears, but root crops, such as taro, cassava, and sweet potatoes, as well as beans crawling up the stumps, eggplant bushes five feet high, dense clumps of sugar cane, spreading squashes, gangling banana and papaya trees, gingers and basils and medicinal plants, and on and on. The field is a scene of enormous variety, and it would be a mistake to ignore this variety in thinking about the appreciation of biodiversity, although, of course, most (but not all) of this variety represents *cultivated* variety and not wild nature. A sharp line between nature and agriculture will not help here: To appreciate Meratus Dayak pleasures in biodiversity, the swidden field is an important site. And while this variety is well known to connoisseurs of shifting cultivation (Conklin 1975), it is worth giving other readers a quick look at a field.

The production of rice is the centerpiece of the Meratus swidden field: It frames the schedule for labor and forms the standard for sufficiency. Most people who make a field grow between three and thirty varieties of rice. Uma Adang and I decided not to list rice varieties because of my mistaken recollection that we had done so on an earlier occasion; I'm sure they would have added many entries to our list. But the luxuriance of rice varieties is more than matched in the diversity of vegetables grown together with rice, and here Uma Adang listed with exuberance.

Variety is at one level a matter of taste. Who would grow only one variety of bananas (and certainly not the bland and pasty giants of North American grocery stores) when more than thirty varieties beckon? Red, long, fruity bananas, or

808–810. lapang: bitter melon lapang—l. ga'ak (inedible, self-seeding); l. buluh
811. karawila: loofah
812–819. kaladi: taro—k. kihung; k. kasumba; k. iwak; k. kasih baranak; k. kalawan; k. langkat; k. dulang; k. nyiur
820–822. waluh: orange-fleshed squash—w. tanduk; w. sarasah; w. duduk
823. baluh: green-fleshed squash
824. butun: a large squash
825–826. kalimbung: another squash-like vegetable—k. buntal; k. panjang
827. kalumbay: a wild vine of the swidden with edible shoots and melon-like fruits
828–841. tarung: eggplant—t. damar; t. masam; t. baliri (not planted but encouraged); t. manggiringan (self-seeding, encouraged); t. hintalu; t. tunjuk; t. kamumu; t. humbut; t. dewata; t. kumbayau; t. malawin; t. jutut; t. pimbatu; t. janak (wild: Uma Adang says it is poisonous, but her sister says it's just sour)
842. pembaitan: a forest plant the young tips of which are good to eat; it isn't found in the swidden but just came up in the list because of its taste
843. ranti: not planted but grows in the swidden; its growing tips are a prized edible
844. capa: another self-starter, a children's medical aid
845. capa kapala: another capa used for headaches
846. akar litu: a tough-stemmed fern that is difficult to get rid of; leaves are used for curing headaches
847. kambang pukul ampat jam sore: four o'clock flower; a swidden decoration
848. kambang hiang: another decorative swidden flower
849. kambang hiang laki: another decoration
850–856. hantimun: melons and cucumbers—h. sumangka; h.

katupat; h. parupuk; h. padi; h. jalamu; h. buhaya; h. padi ulin
857. hantikup: a wild cucumber that appears in swiddens
858. ganyum: a taro-like aroid, the root is used for starch
859. bamban batawi: a tumeric-like herb, also used for starch
860–868. gumbili lancar: sweet potato—g. samiter; g. kapal; g. kantang; g. barlampung; g. bungur; g. waluh; g. saribu; g. karangan
869–874. gumbili kayu: cassava—g. timbusur; g. sapikul; g. ikal; g. pangantin; g. kuning; g. cawau
875–905. isang: bananas—i. manurun; i. talas; i. tahur; i. sarapang; i. lilin; i. mahuli; i. kalimbing; i. kapas; i. kunyit; i. burung; i. raja; i. kaladi; i. gandang lampang; i. susu; i. awa'; i. saring; i. palapah; i. nyaru; i. bantai; i. gundang gandir; i. ka'ilih; i. ambun; i. huyi; i. tampang; i. bangkat; i. talas kijang; i. jutut (self-seeding, from the forest); i. pangkaran (self-seeding, from the forest); i. sahing (self-seeding, from the forest); i. tanduk; i. sarapang
906–909. kanas: pineapple—k. bali; k. paun; k. baduri; k. balai
910. cangkuk manis: the young tips are eaten
911. silur: a bush; the young tips are eaten
912–913. timbaku darat: hill tobacco—t. sangku'; t. galawir
914. wijin: sesame
915. kopi: coffee
916. kayu manis: cinnamon
917. gatah: rubber
918. cingkih: cloves
919. kacang tanah: peanuts, a cash crop
920. kacang kadali: soybeans, a cash crop
921. kacang hijau: mung beans, a cash crop
922. jantan: millet
923. hinjalai: job's tears
924. sahang: black pepper, a cash crop

tiny, delicate yellow bananas, or bright orange, saucer-like bananas, or hard, astringent roasting bananas, or even wild bananas, sweet, but full of seeds: In these, a person can choose and vary snacks. Food habits sometimes follow health precautions: nursing mothers, for example, are careful about the varieties of beans and cucumbers they eat, lest residues passed in breast milk irritate their babies. Tastes also expand to respond to the demands of the market when vegetables are grown as cash crops. Chili peppers are a women's cash crop, picked pepper by pepper in the hot sun, but easy to ask the market-bound men to transport and not so valuable that the men are tempted to take the small gains. The tiniest varieties—which take so long to pick—are the most valuable; the longer ones take less time and bring a lesser price. Most women mix plantings and move back and forth in harvesting. Besides, some years, one variety thrives while the others wilt. Some rice varieties are more sensitive to pest damage than others. And when one rice variety after another succumbs to drought, there are hardy cassava roots and long-growing taro roots from last year and quick-growing millet at the edge of the field—not to mention plants from the forest.

Variety responds to and expands the ecological niches of the swidden field. Crops cycle, reusing the same space. Corn is sometimes planted in the still-warm ashes of a newly burnt swidden field, with rice planted later between the growing cornstalks. The corn will be harvested before the rice flowers. Banana plants take eighteen months to bear fruit; sugar cane takes more than a year to reach an edible size; papaya trees, when they finally fruit, bear for at least five years. All of these are planted early in the making of a swidden, with the expectation that they will be fruitful only while a second crop of rice grows, and perhaps long after as the swidden slowly grows back into forest. Thus, too, rattans and trees— coffee, rubber, fruits, sugar palms—are planted in the swidden, with the expectation of an even later harvest amidst growing forest plants.

Spatial niches are created as well as niches in time. Beans are planted around a stump to give the vines support. Job's tears form a line of demarcation where two fields meet. Almost any vegetable responds well to being planted in the ash heaps that result from the secondary burning of piled debris; this is a privilege not granted to the rice, the green rows of which blanket the field. Some plants, such as cock's comb and basil, are grown to add color and fragrance to this blanket. Meanwhile, self-seeding and regrowing forest plants are encouraged to provide more variety to the swidden's vegetables and medicinal plants.

For those of us more accustomed to agricultural systems that feature single crops in straight rows, the swidden is a wonderland of variety. How can a farmer keep track of so many kinds of plants, each with its own cycle of production and needs for nurturance? Meditating on this question, I recall that *plantation* agriculture, the industrialization of farming developed with European expansion, was invented self-consciously to harness coerced, and particularly slave labor. The enslaved or otherwise alienated farm worker will not keep track of variety; it is all overseers can do to make him or her care for one crop. Modern agriculture draws on the plantation heritage to create field systems that do not require nuanced attention from the farmers; field laborers and machinery can usually do the job. Under these conditions, it is difficult to grow more than one crop with one set of requirements. Before we naturalize these conditions as the only way to make plants grow for human uses, we might return to look at swiddens.

The variety of swidden vegetables also can remind us of the inextricability of aesthetics and survival. Meratus grow many kinds of crops because they value variety for its taste, for the sociability it allows, for its sheer exuberance, *and* because it increases the chances of a bountiful harvest. Crop variety guards against crop failure due to pests, climate, or soil conditions. Crop variety invites borrowing and giving of samples, seeds, and cuttings, and it ties farmers to a wide social network, near and far. Crop variety is valued for the beauty it gives the field and as a sign of the prowess of the farmer. The interweaving of aesthetics and survival here reminds us not to consider the Meratus a "spiritual" people who love nature only for its cosmic beauty, without the materialist priorities of modern urban life. It reminds us not to consider the Meratus a "hungry" people who think only of hand-to-mouth survival and, unlike modern urbanites, value

925–929. lumbuk: chili peppers, a cash crop—l. rawit; l. gandang; l. taji; l. tiung; l. salaka
930–934. katila: papaya—k. amas; k. sumangka; k. badrai; k. rambai; k. kapayang
935–945. tabu: sugar cane—t. batung; t. banang; t. lilih; t. kulipak; t. sawah; t. langan; t. hudang; t. paring; t. tanduk; t. manadar; t. pinggan
946–949. pacar: henna-tree [*Lawsonia inermis*]; the leaves are pounded with lime to make a red dye used as fingernail polish—p. halang; p. kayu; p. gandura
950. sarunai: a bush grown for its red flowers
951–954. kacang: other kinds of stringbeans—k. parang (a yard-long stringbean); k. kumak (another yard-long string bean); k. guring (self-seeding, poisonous); k. makah (a bush bean)
955. kangkung: kangkung [*Ipomea reptans*], the leaves are cooked as a vegetable
956. ginjir: a taro-like aroid with edible leaves

Kulat Mushrooms

w = grows on wood
g = grows on ground
e = edible
i = inedible

676. kulat galang: light-brown agaric with thin gills and a prominent ring, w, e
677. k. kumut: large, brown, w, e
678. k. bintalau: reddish, w, e
679. k. bintalau putih: white fruity-smelling stemmed polypore, w, e
680. k. sarang ganting: yellow, w, e.
681. k. kulibir: the color of red meat, w, e
682. k. tangka: reddish, w, e
683. k. tangka putih: white, w, e
684. k. halang: large, w, e
685. k. kumarau: black, w, e
686. k. kumarau laki: reddish, w, e
687. k. tumpu': yellow and white, medium/large, g, e
688. k. su'un: small, white, g, e
689. k. bantilung: small, black, g, e
690. k. sawar: white, g, e
691. k. ma'oi: white, w, e
692. k. haruwai: white with colored patterns, w, e
693. k. gulambang: large, white, w, e. Fast growing: another might be in the same spot the next evening.
694. k. andap: small, white, in deep woods, w, e
695. k. karikit: small, white, w, e
696. k. pakiki: large, red and yellow, w, e
697. k. hirangan: large, dark, w, e

nature only to the extent it can feed them. These are the two most common stereotypes not only of "tribes" but of rural people in general. Yet the modernist dichotomy that drives each, in which aesthetics is either higher or lower but certainly separate from survival, is of no use in describing commitments to biodiversity most anywhere in the world, and certainly not in Kalimantan. Each time we begin to be seduced by slogans such as "nature appreciation is an idea only in the privileged West," or "Third World people care about development not species conservation," or "religion X *is* a form of conservation," we might want to remember the variety of vegetables in the Meratus swidden field.

But we were speaking of pleasures, and particularly the pleasures of listing species, and I have not yet mentioned the most obvious: the making of the list itself. Uma Adang loved the idea that I was writing down the list and enumerating each item. For ease of taking notes, I started my numeration with "one" every time we switched to a new lifeform. But Uma Adang always wanted to know the total, and I added and added again each time we took a break. Making it past one thousand items became a goal. The list took on all the pleasures of writing, counting, and classifying: Uma Adang and I were pretending to be bureaucrats with the authority of state and international codification. We were ordering the world by naming it. As Uma Adang explained to me, "Everyone knows these names; but not everyone knows how to organize them properly." True enough; these names were common knowledge, but few of my Meratus friends would have had Uma Adang's memory, patience, and fun in making the list.

Consider mushrooms. With fungi (unlike snakes), I might have recognized at least cosmopolitan families and species if we had identified them in the field—or talked about them in detail. But Uma Adang was so enthralled with list-making at that point that she sped through, hardly minding my questions, building the list. We did pretty well, for a memory project. But I hadn't known most of these names, and I was barely able to get her to offer me the briefest of descriptions: whether the fungus grew on wood or on the ground; whether it was edible or inedible. The lure of adding new items was too great to be patient with questions.

Uma Adang is not alone among Meratus Dayaks in liking to make species lists. When I first began research in the area, species lists were one of the first ways I learned to have rich conversations with the people I met. I drew a blank asking abstract questions about gender or power, but I could tell right away that people enjoyed telling me which fish were in the river, which insects made noises, which fruits they hoped to harvest, which trees yielded good firewood. Sometimes I heard children teaching their younger siblings words by having them repeat a list of plants or animals. Uma Adang took this local genre and did her best to use it as a connection to international sources of knowledge. She enjoyed it both as bureaucratic form and as millenial science. She made herself cosmopolitan by making this globalism her own.

Sometimes too, the urgency and authority of the list allowed misinterpretations within the eclectic web we wove. The most striking instance occurred when I asked Uma Adang whether rocks have names. I was thinking of a conversation with another Meratus friend who had told me that he differentiated between "living" rocks and "dead" rocks: basalt and sandstone were his respective examples. He thought living rocks could reproduce themselves, although slowly and surreptitiously. Uma Adang mistook my meaning. She began to list the geographical names of the locally prominent karst formations, moving from one end to the other of the area she had demarcated as "local." I couldn't stop her no matter how hard I tried; she insisted on finishing. And, although I had a difficult time trying to put it into my list, it was a nice demonstration of the importance of *locality* in her idea of the globalist project.

Despite such reasonably irrelevant fun, there are two reasons I offer this list in the margin of my text. First, it can remind both conservationists and scholars of why we might want to reach out across cultures to understand and advocate the pleasures of biodiversity. Cultural theorists need to know that the variety of nature is an important rural concern, not

698. k. litu: small, dark, w, e
699. k. talinga ka'ar: small, red-black, w, e
700. k. runtuh: medium, multicolored/red, w, e
701. k. tahun: small, grey, w, e. Appears yearly in newly burned swiddens.
702. k. utak hundang: lit. "shrimp head fungus," w, e. On dead, scorched logs of a swidden.
703. k. hilalang: small, white, g, e
704. k. siau: lit. "quail fungus," small, red, g, e
705. k. hidung bayi: lit. "hog's nose fungus," black with a liquid inside that is used as hair conditioner, w, i
706. k. tukul: black inside, yellow outside; rubbed on children's swellings, g, i
707. k. bigi tarung: lit. "eggplant seed fungus," black and white, solid "like a peanut," a salve for children, g, i
708. k. jantang: large, hard, and white , w, i
709. k. kandasuli: large, white, red, and black; layered clusters, w, e
710. k. lidah: lit. "tongue fungus," red and white, w, e
711. k. lamak ba'ung: large, green, and black, w, e
712. k. tungkul: small but plentiful, white, yellow, and red if young, w, e
713. k. baras: small, white, w, i
714. k. kuranji: small, yellow, g, e. It regrows quickly, even overnight.
715. k. undingan: small, black, plentiful under logs, g, e
716. k. janggut hundang: lit. "shrimp's beard mushroom," g, e
717. k. hati minjangan: black and the size of a person's big toe, g, e
718. k. mangku-mangkuk: red, g, e
719. k. dadak: a basket stinkhorn, g, i
720. k. tayi hayam: lit. "chicken shit mushroom," a stinkhorn?, g, i
721. k. ari: funnel-shaped, white with crowded, decurrent gills, no ring, and a tough stalk, w, e. A

neighbor brought one but at first confused it with 676.

722. k. sejajar jantan: a red shelf fungus, w, i

723. k. jantan kacil: a brown shelf fungus, w, i

724. k. takut dilanjung: lit. "the fungus that's afraid of the basket," white, w, e. It's soft when you pick it but hardens soon (i.e., in your basket).

725. k. sarang: white, used as a hair conditioner, w, i

726. k. bintang: lit. "star fungus," puffball, g, e

727. k. tumbung: large, round, poisonous, g, i

728. k. minyak: the pink-spored deer mushroom [*Pluteus cervinus*] or something similar, w, e

729. k. pipi asah putih: white shelf fungus, w, i

730. k. pipi asah habang: red shelf fungus, w, i

731. k. kayu mati: any inedible conk; here, a general enough term to end the category

just an imposition of metropolitan scientists. Conservationists need to know that our knowledge of nature is always cultural knowledge, whether we are scientists or farmers. To be aware of the necessity for careful coalitions with those whose knowledge and pleasure comes from other sources is the beginning of a nonimperialist environmentalism.

Second, Uma Adang's list offers a vivid image of global friction. The list is self-consciously globalist: an entry into a world-making millenial project. It is self-consciously localized: following the contours of local geographies and their plant and animal residents. It is self-consciously culturally particular and cross-culturally generative: it speaks of the possibility of multiple kinds of translation. The list offers the pleasure of making a widely circulating form come to life in the terrain around one's home place, and for foreigners as well as local folks. The list builds a situated "point of view" from which to engage globalism. The ability to work from a point of view is the very thing scholars need to assess scale-making claims and practices.

But how can I end without a celebration of fungal abundance?

> *Kulat kulangit,*
> *Bintang bintangit,*
> *Kulat di tanah,*
> *Bintang di langit.*

It is a Meratus *pantun* rhyme. The first two lines are just for rhythm; read them for their sounds. Then say: "Mushrooms on the ground are like stars in the sky."

5 A History of Weediness

....

... auu.. au... kresek. kresek. grog..
cuat. cuit... breshhh... cit. cit. citt...
her. herr... haum. haumm. grasak, grusuk...
miau.. cuat.. cuit. kong. kung. kong...

> aiueo... aiueo... huah... srep.. sret. ah...
> cek. tretetet.. bremm. bremmm... blas. lush..
> jeg. jreg... kompyang.. kompreng... aiueo...
> ngeeeeeeng.... citt. grok.. aiueo....

cuat... cit.cit.. aiueo.. aiueo...
grog... groggg. duk..kompyang. kompreng
aiueo..aiueo... stt. ssttt. besh..
jreg. jug.. ngrok..ngrokk... dor.. dor...
nguik.. door.. nguik. nguik.. bum.. yeah..
cuat... cuit.. dor. bluk.. yeah..

> aiueo..aiueo.. kresek. krusek.. stt.stt..
> dor.. door... haum. haum door. bruk.. bum...
> yeah.. hmm. hmm. bras.. brush.. jep. jep. jep..
> jep. prak.. jep. kerekek.. jep.. krekep.. jep.
> krekek.. krekek.. bumm.. yeah... greg..grog..
> grek. grok.. krekek. krekek.. jep..bummm.. yeah.

cuat... cuit... dor.. haummm... haumm..
door... bruk.. miau.. door... dor..
grog... grog... dor.. jep. jep.. krekek..
bumm.. cuat. cuit. cit. cit..
don't bother us, we want to live. cit.
preserve us. cuat.. cuit.. cit..
haumm.. dor.....
—Kristiandi Tanumihardja, "Cit..Cit..Door...Krekek..."[1]

gap. *An unfilled space or interval.*[2]

Those readers used to concentrating on humans may feel tempted to skip this chapter, which requires you to attend to nonhuman species. Ironically, this would introduce you to the chapter's chief conceptual tool. Our categories and discriminations always produce zones of "boredom" and unreadability; powerful projects of categorization, including development and conservation (as well as your scholarly reading practices, whatever they may be), produce persistently uninteresting, invisible, and sometimes illegitimate zones—which I call "gaps." Universal knowledge projects cannot be understood without attention to gaps. Of course, I would like to entice you to go on despite this warning. I have assumed no technical background. Drawing on what I hope is the widely accessible charisma of nature writing, I proceed as an appreciative traveler into the simultaneously social and natural landscape of the central Meratus Mountains. Social and natural? The deeper we proceed into that conundrum, the less analytic tools we have to consider it. Thinking past our dearly held notions of the autonomy of human sociality, we must consider the interdependence of species. We must turn to the beasts and flowers, not just as symbols and resources, but as co-residents and collaborators.

Cit..Cit..Door...Krekek...

What do the creatures that make noises in the night say? According to poet Kristiandi Tanumihardja (1994), mainly, we don't know. In his poem, we hear them speaking, but we can't understand what they say. But we make a fair and generous guess if, among the many things they say, we imagine them telling us "Don't bother us; we want to live" (line 25). "Preserve us [*lestarikanlah kami*]," the poet adds in the next line, speaking for them, and using the word for environmental protection.

International conservationists, and particularly conservation biologists, the scientists most concerned with species preservation, have made this same inference about how to know the interests of nonhuman species. There is a lot we may never know about the motivation and behavior of nonhuman organisms, but we can imagine that they, like us, want to live. In this spirit conservation biologists interpret animal habits and plant growth patterns as species-specific modes of advantage for reproduction and survival. When the urge to live is all we know, we must interpret everything we learn in a calculus of population dynamics and interspecies competition. Meanwhile, the hope of this science is that even such limited understanding might bring us closer to knowing how to live in a multispecies world.[3]

In the process of mastering such ways of translating nonhuman lives, most conservation biologists simplify what they know—or what they could know—about humans. Throwing out the libraries on history and culture, they treat humans, like nonhuman species, as a homogeneous group in which every example of behavior merely tells us, "We want to live." Furthermore, this singular, unitary human calculus of reproduction and survival is based on stereotypes about the human condition created by dominant contemporary urban elites of European descent. Through these cultural assumptions, conservation biologists construct portraits in which humans necessarily threaten the existence of all species that they do not either domesticate or cordon off in preserves.

In opposition to conservationist simplifications of what it means to be human, social scientists have formed a "political ecology." Political ecology reminds us that human interactions with the environment respond to social conventions and political coercions—not just the pressure of numbers. State regulation and systems of property shape land management.[4] This seems completely right. However, it is still difficult to understand the diversity of human–nonhuman interactions as long as we learn very little about nonhumans. Social scientists extend the kind of simplification and neglect conservation biologists apply to humans to nonhumans. We rarely hear about the lives of plants and animals; we hear only how they enter human plans. We tap into literatures on symbols and meanings, on class and colonialism, on commodification and the penetration of capitalism. But these literatures do little to help us understand nature: its diversity, its power and constraints, or its multifaceted ways of entering human histories.

Since each aims to influence public opinion, it is particularly ironic that environmental social science and biology tend to speak entirely past each other. Each field creates separate conventions of reading; it is difficult to take both into account. We lose a lot in this missed communication. In particular, we lose the ability to look at the intricacies of human relationships to nonhuman species. Conservation biologists segregate nonhumans; political ecologists too often take them for granted as resources for human use. Instead, we might want to look at how species and populations slip in and out of markets, in and out of cultural attention, and in and out of a whole spectrum of not-yet-fully-described interactions between humans and nonhumans. In addressing conservation, this process of description could take us farther than the hackneyed dichotomy between use and preservation: We could study the historical and cultural variety of relations between people, plants, and animals.

One way to a more nuanced account of interactions between human and nonhuman species is to take the landscape as an object of analysis. By landscape I am referring to the configuration of humans and nonhumans across a terrain. I am interested in the material as well as the representational practices of making and maintaining the landscape. The landscape is both "social" (created within human projects) and "natural" (outside of human control; populated by nonhuman species). My emphasis on social-natural landscapes differentiates my analysis from scholars who use "landscape" to refer either to aesthetic conventions, studied apart from a particular terrain, or to the sheer physical arrangement of things, studied without attention to social and cultural programs.

Let me turn to a particular social-natural landscape: the central Meratus Mountains as I came to know it in the 1980s and 1990s. Here scattered bamboo houses sat by small swidden fields surrounded by forest regrowth mixing into big forest. The forest here was not primeval but rather "anthropogenic," human-made forest; however, it was not nearly so neatly managed as the orchards and plantations that this term often describes. When most visitors from the city, including conservation advocates, visited, they saw "natural" forest; and that was how the area was always mapped. Indeed, there was considerable old-growth forest here, but this was mixed with old-growth-enriched old orchard-forest as well as patches of younger forest, cycled with fields. This was a weedy, patchwork naturalness without clearly demarcated forest reserves. Weeds have been of little interest to conservationists; we think of them only as indicators of disturbance. Yet this kind of weedy, mixed forest landscape harbors a significant portion of the biodiversity we associate with the tropics. Much of the island of Borneo has been covered with this kind of human-modified rainforest, at least before timber corporations cut it and plantation corporations burned it to replace it with monocrops. To move beyond timber and plantation models in understanding human relations with forests, this weedy forest landscape offers a good deal of insight.

Social life in the mountains has also been thought of as "weedy." The people of the mountains, whom I call Meratus Dayaks, are regionally known as *orang bukit*, "hill people," or, one might say, hillbillies. The association of the people and the hills has all the connotations of backward, awkward, derivative, and badly grasped culture that the term hillbilly carries in U.S. English. Meratus Dayaks are regarded as the disorderly cousins of the civilized people in surrounding plains and towns. These are people whose distinctiveness has everything to do with staying out of the way: evading government authority in its various forms; evading soldiers in their continual wars and raids; evading world religion since the spread of Islam in the sixteenth century. It would be easy to ignore them in a study that looked only for the indigenous wisdom of isolated tribes; they are not isolated, only exoticized and despised. It is not tempting to search here for some unique cosmology of nature. Instead, the practical relations of people and forest can tell us about the making of complex landscapes in which humans and diverse nonhumans share space without clear demarcations of separate spheres.

The distinctive feature of the central Meratus landscape has been its confusion of zones of livelihood and zones of forest protection. The forest has been a social and productive space as well as a place for species diversity. Nor is this confusion a site of scarcity: this landscape is rich for livelihood and for species. Yet conservation and development vocabularies make it difficult to describe the central Meratus landscape without a great deal of self-consciousness. Both conservation and development take the importance of the proper demarcation of spheres of humans and nonhumans, culture and nature, as a given. It seems "natural" to the experts to assume that a good livelihood requires permanent fields just as a healthy forest requires permanent reserves. They would have us see both nature and culture in the Meratus Mountains as a weedy social-ecological roadside. Such edges are the least interesting ecologies and societies as long as we are looking for cleanly demarcated communities of plants or of people. We see only degraded spaces: weeds and hillbillies. But what if we were to turn our perspective to give careful attention to the making of this species-diverse but social landscape?

This turn of perspective shifts us into what I call "gaps." Gaps are conceptual spaces and real places into which powerful demarcations do not travel well. The gaps of the central Meratus landscape call attention to the bad transportability of demarcations of human livelihood versus nature conservation, productive farms versus forest reserves, and settled culture versus the wild, as each of these keeps us from appreciating the history of social-natural landscapes.

By taking on these categories, I find myself in dialogue with a generation of symbolic and ecological anthropologists who argue that various indigenous people do not believe in these categories.[5] But that is not my point, although it may also be partially true. These categories do not organize the landscape materially. If we release ourselves from their hegemony, we can explore how interactions among humans and nonhumans on this landscape create its patches and trajectories. We can follow how the forest becomes readable as a social space. We can make sense, too, of Meratus respect for these authoritative conservation and development demarcations, but as the rhetoric of leaders assuaging powerful outsiders, rather than as the practice of daily life. It is not that Meratus never heard of these categories; they have known them for a long time. But in the central mountains they have put them in a particular, ceremonial place for community leaders. With this placement, the categories are crippled in their mode of traveling; they organize expert ways of seeing but not the landscapes that grow up in their gaps.

A consideration of gaps turns us from a quick dismissal of weedy, hillbilly edges to explore species-rich landscapes in which human livelihood maintains forests. This switch in perspective does not convert the forests into pristine old-growth or the people into mysterious primitives; they maintain their weedy, hillbilly features. However, through the switch we can see the richness and complexity of the history of weediness, as well as the limitations of categories that are imagined to be universals that travel everywhere. And so I organize my description in the spaces these categories make unimaginable, that is, their gaps. The challenge in making this natural-social landscape come to life on paper is to give the nonhuman species as much liveliness as the humans. As in the poem with which I began, I do my best to offer sounds and words to forest creatures. I use the ethnographic present to honor the long timescale in which this landscape was assembled, and in the hope that as I write today it has not been totally dismantled by the frontier-making dynamics I came to know in other Meratus areas in the 1990s.

Inside the Gap between Cultivated and Wild

It is fruit season. A dry spell after the heavy monsoon rains has stimulated flowering, and the fruits have come in, luscious and plentiful. Turn their names over in your mouth: durian, lahung, langsat, rambutan, maritam, buku-buku, rambai, manggu, tiwadak, kulidang. . . . When the fruits ripen en masse, we can eat as much as we want.

The fruits we picked this morning are in a basket at the front of the house, where passing visitors, seeing us through the door, can come up to share them with us. In fruit season, everyone is generous with fruits: please take some home. But before that we can sit and chat and refresh ourselves with fruit. And as we eat we throw the seeds out the door into the brush surrounding the isolated house.

The seeds of many tropical fruits sprout best when allowed to grow immediately. The temperate plants that probably come to mind for most of my readers—apples, peaches—require a dormancy period, a winter perhaps, before they will sprout and grow. Not so for many tropical fruits. If you keep the seeds for more than a few days before sprouting them, they will die. But seeds thrown out the door of the house often sprout and grow.

A year or two later the household will have moved on. The bamboo and thatch and bark of the house decay quickly. If the houseposts are made of *sungkai* (*Peronema canescens*), they may have sprouted and become new, quick-growing secondary forest trees. Within a few years, it would be hard for a stranger to know that a house had been there. Yet there is a grove of fruit trees gathered together near this spot. These are the trees we "planted" by throwing their seeds out the door. The faster growing, smaller species will begin to bear fruit in five or six years. In those same years, what once was a swidden field around the house will have become a shady young forest with trees the diameter of one's arm. The fruits whose seeds we deposited will be growing amidst a large variety of self-propagating herbs and trees. The fruit trees will mature as part of a forest. And while many of my temperate-climate readers may have passed a few apple trees in regrowing temperate forest and imagined an old homestead, few have experienced a landscape in which all the fruits one enjoys—planted or self-propagating—are an integral part of the forest. There are no dedicated orchards in the central Meratus Mountains; all fruit trees there must be able to survive in the forest, whether the species evolved in this area or was transported from elsewhere, and whether the individual was planted or grew without human intervention.

The image of casually propagated fruit trees in the forest opens a way to explore a landscape in which an important number of plants fall between familiar categories of "cultivated" and "wild." These categories are the starting line for all of us who care about biodiversity protection. Since we know best the landscape of capitalist agriculture, it makes perfect sense to draw a hard line between the domestic or cultivated, whose populations rise and fall depending on the market, and the wild, so often casually destroyed without regard to future populations. Humans are already responsible for domestic populations. In contrast, environmental movements and environmental science have formed over concerns about wild things, and we think of these as the "biodiversity" we hope to protect. Yet what of landscapes in which significant numbers of organisms are neither properly domestic and cultivated *nor* wild and independent from human nurture and propagation? Might these require new approaches to biodiversity conservation? And, indeed, to conceptualizing nature in a global perspective?

Anthropologists who are asked about these kinds of questions usually turn first to the ideas of the inhabitants. Do Meratus Dayaks have categories of "cultivated" and "wild"? they inquire. This is an important question, for the nonhumans as well as the humans, because humans so often organize their interspecies practices in relation to their cultural categories. So let me begin here: Meratus distinguish between "planted plants" (*tanaman*) and plants that "grow themselves" (*tumbuh sa'urang*). I've followed the Meratus idiom above to speak of "self-propagating herbs and trees" although nonhuman animals, wind, and other agents may be required to propagate these plants. Yet it seems a useful enough way to distinguish the human-planted and the merely human-encountered herb or tree.

The Meratus distinction does not, however, distinguish between species as uniform blocks. The individuals of many species may either be planted or grow themselves; the distinction describes the practice, not the species characteristic. Different forms of planting are recognized, ranging from the deliberate burying of seeds to the more casual sprouting of a rubbish heap. Furthermore, there are many human practices other than planting that are recognized as encouraging particular plants. Some self-propagating plants, such as rattans and wild gingers, do well sprouting in the light gap of a swidden. Some, such as bamboos, are not destroyed by swidden making and flourish with new advantage in the regrowing forest. Others, such as honey bee-friendly trees, are saved when swiddens are cleared. Choking weeds, vines, and parasites are removed around some trees to maintain them. Meratus recognize this continuum of human practices involved in encouraging plant growth. While this attention to specific practices, rather than species classes, does not solve the problem of conservation in the Meratus Mountains, it is a good beginning for opening up preconceived frameworks to investigate forms of interaction between humans and plants.

Let me return to fruits. City people expect a wide variety of fruits, generated from importing fruits from around the world and by creating new variety through breeding. There are additional sources of variety in the central Meratus Mountains. The forest of the Meratus Mountains is biologically diverse; Borneo is a center of tropical fruit diversity. Most fruits that are even partially cultivated have close cousins within the Bornean forest. This variety is much enjoyed by humans and other animals. Like orangutans, civets, wild pigs, and bats, humans have become one of the ways fruit trees, in all their variety, distribute their seeds. Fruit tree biodiversity is maintained in part by those human–fruit tree interactions that fall somewhere in the gap between cultivation and the wild.

The most famous fruit of the Bornean rainforest is the durian. The ripe fruit is green and spikey and as large as an American football; inside the thick skin are the foul and fine smelling, custardy seed coverings that comprise the valued fruit. The naturalist Alfred Wallace (1962: 57) wrote: "Its consistence and flavour are undescribable. A rich butter-like custard highly flavoured with almonds gives the best general idea of it, but intermingled with it come wafts of flavour that call to mind cream-cheese, onion-sauce, brown sherry, and other incongruities."[6] In the Meratus Mountains, only fruits still hanging on the tree are the exclusive property of tree claimants. While unripe durian makes a wonderful cooked dish, and tree claimants may harvest it, it is the open competition for ripe fallen fruits that captures the most attention in durian season. Teenagers hike through the forest in the middle of the night to search under good trees at dawn's first light. They bring home baskets of newly fallen durian and pass them around for a drunkenly rich breakfast.

Durian is thought to have evolved in Borneo; certainly, it flourishes in the forest there. In a good fruit season, one can see dozens of durian seedlings growing up all around a tree, where the sated eaters, human or nonhuman, have discarded the seeds. Not many of them survive in that deep shade; but others, transported elsewhere, may have a better chance. That includes those that are carefully planted and tended. It also includes those that grow from refuse heaps and casual droppings.

Durian is such a well-loved fruit that most trees in the Meratus Mountains are claimed. Those who plant a tree, and their descendants, claim it.[7] Those who find a self-seeding tree and watch and nurture it can also claim it. Trees can also become unclaimed, usually when the claimants leave the area and stop paying enough attention to the tree to know its uneven fruiting schedule. In this state, another person can claim the tree, or neighbors who know and watch it may share its fruits. It would be rare to kill a durian tree in swidden-making; the person who killed one would have to pay a large fine to the tree's claimants. Through a combination of distributing, planting, tending, and saving trees, Meratus increase the durian population of the forest.[8]

Durian has a host of close relatives that are also valued for their fruit. The best, to me, is *lahung*, a deep-red, long-spiked globe that resembles a giant sea urchin. Lahung is somewhat less commonly planted than durian, but it is a valued fruit tree of the forest and thus commonly claimed, protected, and carefully watched for its fruiting schedule. In contrast, *pampakin*, whose bright-orange and intensely sweet arils remind me of the icing of Halloween cupcakes, is a cultivate. It is considered a new durian species for the area. On the other side of the continuum, the small fruited durians, such as "bird's lahung" (*lahung burung*), are rarely purposefully planted, although they may be gathered when encountered in a hike in the forest. Durian relatives run a full gamut of cultivated-to-wild options.

Mangos are another diverse group of fruits in the Meratus forest. They range from the sour *hambawang*, rarely deliberately planted but much enjoyed as a trailside snack, to the strongly scented *binjai*, mainly known as a planted and tended tree. There are tiny mangos (*rawa-rawa*) and huge ones (*kwini*), and they can be bitingly sour (*tandoi*) or intensely sweet (binjai and kwini are the sweetest, but with completely different tastes). Their diversity is appreciated by Meratus, who enjoy the opportunity to savor their scents and flavors. Similarly, the diversity of litchi-like *Nephelium* fruits is much appreciated—and encouraged. The red, hairy *rambutan*, grown in many parts of Southeast Asia, is planted and enjoyed, but alongside its many relatives: the subtler, smaller *buku-buku*; the juicy *siwau*; the smooth-skinned *ringkit*; the biting *maritam* (I thought of its taste as somewhere between a pineapple and a raspberry); the tiny, oblong *jari-jari*; and many more. People look forward to these fruits, learn where they grow unnoticed in the woods, claim them; watch their ripening schedules, harvest them in great quantities, and plant them, sometimes casually in refuse heaps, and sometimes purposefully, in the swidden or by the house. In the gap between cultivated and wild, they flourish.

One of the most important and most diverse groups of fruits of the Meratus forest is the *Artocarpus* group, whose best known representatives in the English-speaking world are jackfruit and breadfruit. Jackfruit (*nangka*) and breadfruit (*sukun*) are known in the Meratus Mountains in cultivation; but both are rather unimportant. A more relevant species is *tarap* (*A. elastica*), a great forest tree only rarely deliberately planted because it is rarely in short supply. The bark can be used for cloth; the sticky, milky sap is used for bird lime; and the sweet, yellow seed coverings of the ball-like fruits are eaten, both raw as a snack and cooked as a side dish with rice. Yet tarap is far from the only *Artocarpus* of the Meratus forest. I remember *binturung* and *kulidang* particularly clearly because we ate a lot of them one season when I was living with a family for whom rice supplies were low; we gathered baskets of the immature forest fruits and cooked them for lunch and dinner. We also ate them ripe. These fruits are plentiful enough in the forest and thus rarely deliberately planted. Other *Artocarpus* are planted, such as *tiwadak* (*A. champeden*), whose sweet arils sit in a long, drooping fruit. The variety of *Artocarpus* fruits spans and confuses the distinction between cultivate and wild.

The range of human–nonhuman interactions that occupy the gap between domesticated and wild is also relevant to animals. Consider pigs: Meratus households sometimes keep a pig. In the central mountains, it is unlikely that the pig will be kept in an enclosure. Instead, the pig is set out in an old swidden field in the process of regrowing into forest. The foraging in the old swidden field is good: There may be sweet potatoes, cassava, taro, bananas and papayas, sugar cane and eggplants; and there are certainly the tender weeds and herbs of the regrowing forest. Meratus told me that the pig is unlikely to stray far from this good foraging, which compares favorably, from a pig's perspective, to the more open, big forest with its sparse undergrowth. When they need the pig, they told me, they go to the old swidden and find it. Meanwhile, the chances of the pig coming into contact with migrating bearded pigs are good, especially since wild pigs, too, are drawn to old swiddens. People say that the pigs cross-breed; I am unclear what biological differences separate human-raised pigs and forest pigs in the Meratus Mountains. In any case, the rearing of the human-raised pigs involves rearing piglets enough to bond them to people, and then setting them out in good forage. If one ignores the fact that the pigs end up as food, the relationship does not seem that different than that between people and their pet hornbills, who, fed and coddled as babies, come back to visit their old owners between flights across the forest.

A more environmentally significant relationship of semi-domestication with an animal connects Meratus and giant honey bees, *Apis dorsata*.[9] Meratus call this migratory bee *indu wanyi*, and they rely on it as a source of honey and beeswax. Like European honey bees, indu wanyi build a honey-filled wax comb. Unlike their European cousins, they do not nest inside a closed space; instead, they hang their combs in a well-lighted space under a high tree branch. Unlike European honey bees, they need light to guide each other to foraging spots, and this is why they prefer open places. In the Meratus forest, this means that they build on the branches of the tallest forest trees, those we call "emergent" to mark the way they tower above the next level of the rainforest canopy. The building of combs does not, as far as I can tell, damage the tree in any way. But these trees are often covered with vines and epiphytes, and their architecturally best branches may be blocked by competing smaller growth. Meratus prepare potential honey trees (*linuh*) for the bees, cleaning off competing vegetation. The migratory bees come back again and again, in season, to the prepared trees. Meratus say that bees will not come back to a tree that has not been cared for.

Meratus know which trees make good honey trees. *Mangaris, Koompassia excelsa*, is the tallest tree of the Bornean rainforest, recorded to grow over 260 feet; it is also the most popular of all trees for the bees, and in many other Dayak languages across Borneo is known by the local word for "honey tree." Mangaris often host more than fifty colonies in a good bee season. *Binuang* (*Octomeles sumatrana*), another huge tree whose circumference may exceed mangaris, is also a good honey tree. So are a number of kinds of *damar*, the dipterocarps that dominate the Bornean rainforest. Other honey trees of the central mountains include *alaran* (another dipterocarp), *salang'ai, tampuruyung, pulayi* (*Alstonia* sp.), *mampiring* (*Agathis alba*), *jalamu, hara wilas* (*Ficus* sp.) and occasionally *lua'* (*Ficus* sp.), *kupang, mijalungan, kasai* (*Pometia pinnata*), *tikus, jalanut, simunan*, and *anglai*. Damar, salang'ai, and jalamu trees often have as many as forty colonies. Binuang and hara wilas may invite fifteen to twenty colonies. Most of the other trees are less good sites, attracting perhaps only three to five colonies at any one time.

Meratus claim, prepare, and protect these trees. In a few cases (e.g., the fast-growing binuang), they plant them in old swiddens. Most commonly, a man claims a tree by being the first to clean it, or if the tree has been abandoned by other claimants, by reviving its cleaning. He passes this claim to his children as long as they are active in maintaining the tree as a honey tree. Most women do not climb and clean honey trees; the principal claimants are men. (Sisters retain rights to honey.) A three-species relationship is set up among bees, honey trees, and people. People encourage comb-building by preparing the trees. They save the honey trees from being cut in swidden-making and other projects. Although the arrangement may not be equally advantageous for each species, each species comes to depend on it. In neighboring areas in which loggers and plantation developers have cut down most of these tall trees, people report that there is no longer a bee migration. Furthermore, the tree species are in danger. Given the diversity of the forest and the wide spacing between emergents, many of these forest giants are quite isolated, species-wise, in the forest; every emergent tree that is cut down deprives a section of the forest of a source of seed for that species. The saving of honey trees preserves the number and variety of emergents—as well as providing a nesting place for bees. Between cultivation and the wild, bees, honey trees, and humans have created a mutually productive, symbiotic relationship.

Inside the Gap between Subsistence and Market Economies

One summer day, relaxing in the shade of a field shelter surrounded by lofty forest, my Meratus friends and I decided to record the sounds that animals make, as they knew them. They imitated the sawing buzz of the *keke*, an insect from the forest that sings every day at around four in the afternoon, reminding us of the time. They sang the sweet goodnight note of the *lingut*, a nocturnal giant millipede that lives in the trees. We tried out the melodic cackle of the *haruwai* argus pheasant, which crows from its cleared "swidden" on the forest floor. We laughed at the harsh cough of the *kijang* barking deer and fell silent remembering the softly echoing hoots of the *undau* gibbon, which, they said, tell us of a death somewhere.

Immersed in the pleasures of this textured local knowledge, it was easy for me to imagine that this was a hidden world, enclosed and lost from the sounds of televisions, chain saws, and freeway traffic. After all, the trope of other cultures and natures as forgotten worlds is so much a part of the way city people are taught to think; we fantasize the beauty of pristine nature and pristine culture only, just as we arrive, threatened by the destruction of the outside world. Yet, for all its big forests and its rich lore the Meratus landscape is not, in any way, a lost world. It is a landscape made by a history of movement and connection. Instead of imagining local knowledge of biodiversity as a condition of the landscape's isolation, I found that I needed to trace it to histories of travel and trade.

Trade brings both humans and nonhumans in and out of the mountains. Trade in this area is hundreds of years old, indeed, probably as old as human occupation. Antique collectors still comb through the mountains buying up the ancient Chinese plates and engraved brass stools and trays exchanged for Meratus products in earlier times. While some trade is relatively local,[10] most trade extends outward from the Meratus Mountains, sending rare products to China, Europe, and around the world. Most of this trade concerns forest products: the resins, rubbers, and incense woods of the tropical rainforest; the exotic animal products—python skins, bezoar stones, beeswax, and edible swifts' nests; durable ironwood shingles and flexible rattan strips; herbs sold as contraceptives and aphrodisiacs; orchids and songbirds and tiny parrots taken live from the forest.

The most amazing thing about this trade is the number of different products it encompasses. Almost all of its products are available only in small quantities, sporadically encountered. The Meratus collector must keep his eyes open for the whole variety of possible products. (I use the masculine "his" because most collectors are men.) The collector must keep his ears open, too, for news of emerging markets for other products. In the 1980s, there was a rage for the gall bladders of bears, used by Korean loggers and their business partners as aphrodisiacs. There has been a growing market for antidotes to sorcery for plainsmen who believe themselves the victims of mountain magic: the hair of albino deer; oil in which particular bird feathers or insects have been soaked. Marketable incense resins come in different kinds: the diseased heart of *garu* aloes wood; fragrant *dahupa* and *manyan* benzoin; *kaladan* camphor. Aromatic barks (e.g., *sintuk*) also find small markets. Nonaromatic resins are sometimes on the market, sometimes off: the damar resins of the great emergent dipterocarp trees, classified commercially as "white," "black," "cat's eye," "stone," etc.; the copal resin of the mountain conifer, *mampiring*.[11] While synthetic resins have replaced these in most of their international industrial uses, they still have specialized market niches, as well as being used at home. Furthermore, some kinds of collecting require the gatherer to bring together many scattered plants, whether of the same or complementary species; blowpipe poison, for example, is called *ratusan*, "hundreds," to acknowledge the large number of *ipuh* trees (*Antiaris toxicana* and others) whose latex is combined to produce the poison.

Commercial collecting of forest products requires a sharp eye for plant and animal diversity and for the particularity of sites and ecological niches in the forest. Indeed, commercial collecting encourages Meratus appreciation of rainforest biodiversity, even as it sometimes allows particular species to be overharvested for the trade. This argument runs against stereotypes of indigenous knowledge; the more detailed a community's knowledge of the forest, the more it is assumed that they have *no* contact with the surrounding world. Yet the forest-products' trade creates sharp-eyed collectors, eager to recognize new species. It is also true that commercialization can ruin the forest quickly. As I described in chapter 1, the east-side forest was turned into a free-for-all of destruction in the 1990s. Knowledgeable Meratus collectors joined clueless outsiders in the rush to plunder the landscape before the imagined end. In this context, it was easy to see that the same sharp eyes and ears, attuned to market rumors and the opportunities of forest diversity, could turn to join frontier-style destruction or to enhance long-term forest maintenance. What accounts for the difference?

In the central mountains, forest collecting has been a feature of subsistence as well as an activity for the market. Collecting is integrated into the possibilities of continuing to live with the forest; it both adds to ordinary living and produces a cash income. In the east-side frontier situation, collecting destroys the possibility of continuing to live in a forested landscape; in the central mountains, collecting makes it possible to continue living with the forest. Collecting for the market does not jeopardize subsistence; it enhances it. Forest collecting in this area takes place in the gap between subsistence and market-oriented economies. Forest products go in and out of market value, but residents continue to appreciate them as landscape features because of their local, subsistence uses. That appreciation allows a quick response to new market conditions. Whether or not this promotes ideal forest conservation policies, it is certainly many times better for the nonhuman residents of the forest than the resource frontier. The fact that there are any forests at all on the island of Borneo today, indeed, attests to the long-term forest-maintenance possibilities in the gap between subsistence and trade.

Urban stereotypes guide us to think that the difference between sustainable collecting and frontier destruction is the resilience of "local culture"; yet in fact this difference has everything to do with the relation between forest collectors and downstream traders. Downstream traders buy forest products from Meratus collectors. In some cases, they sell what they have gained further downstream, distributing the products to more specialized buyers. In other cases, they *are* the specialized buyers, bringing the forest products to their manufacturing or marketing concerns. The most important characteristic of the downstream traders who buy from central mountain Meratus collectors is their willingness to buy small quantities. In contrast, the east-side frontier situation has been stimulated in part by downstream entrepreneurs who *only* want large quantities, and thus force collectors to organize for scale. The presence of arms, and the armed forces, on the east-side frontier enforces massive extractions. In the central mountains, where soldiers and police rarely venture, it is possible to collect at a slower rate and with more careful methods.

Coercion is not irrelevant in the central mountains. Collection has been stimulated by state requirements, ranging from a precolonial gold tax, through the 1930s colonial "coupons" through which Meratus were organized to plant certain amounts of rubber, to the provincial forced rattan deliveries in the 1950s, in which the Banjarmasin furniture industry was stimulated through cheaply obtained materials.[12] Meratus collectors appreciate connections between downstream traders and the coercive apparatus of the state, which make it difficult for Meratus collectors to gain any bargaining power in selling forest products. Collectors' disadvantage is enhanced by the cultural differences between collectors and downstream traders, in which downstream traders see themselves as cosmopolitans dealing with a primitive people. Blocked by their cultural distinction, Meratus collectors cannot bypass their downstream traders to negotiate directly with larger manufacturers and merchants; they are forced to accept small sums. At the same time, this cultural difference has stimulated a certain distance, which works to the advantage of collectors: Downstream traders are unfamiliar with—and afraid of—the forest. Downstream traders work with Meratus collectors because they are unable to find forest products by themselves. This ambiguous inequality stabilizes the position of downstream traders as middlemen between collectors and larger merchants and manufacturers. Without the coercive apparatus to press deeper into the forest, these traders are content to gather Meratus collections. It is in this balance that the trade has come to be characterized by exotic products, small quantities, and sporadic and changing market demand.

Meratus collectors respond to the sporadic nature of demand by flooding the market whenever prices are high. They see themselves as powerless to set the terms of the market; they ignore it or respond to it. Given that the market mainly consists of products for which there is a small demand, flooding the market tends to cause a glut; prices drop, and no one collects anymore. If the product's price stays high, its supply tends to run out, having a similar effect on the collector, although a worse effect on the species being collected. Collectors come to expect these mini-booms and busts. The effect on a particular nonhuman species depends on how it is being collected; some do badly, while others survive. For collectors, both sporadic demand and boom-and-bust cycles stimulate attention to the diversity of forest products, for when one fails, another can be sought. The collector must cultivate an awareness of the varied opportunities of the forest.

The only practical way to make this work in the central mountains is to integrate commercial collecting into ordinary life maintainence, that is, subsistence. No one tries to survive by commercial collection alone, and while the income gained from commercial collection is important, used for clothing, tools, bridewealth, luxuries, and government exactments, no cash is required for food, shelter, and everyday sociability, which are gained from local supplies in fields and forests. Commercial collecting must fit into the schedule of subsistence labor. Men are only able to wander the forest when the work of swidden agriculture is being covered by women, as it is during the seasons for weeding, guarding the rice, and harvesting. During these seasons, as well as the period between the rice harvest and the preparation of new fields, men are free to combine commercial and subsistence collecting, bringing home wild pigs, fruit, bamboo shoots, firewood, and resin for torches, as well as products for the market.

Collecting, whether for subsistence or commercial purposes, requires an intimate familiarity with particular areas of forest. A few things are best found by roaming around large unfamiliar areas, but most collecting is facilitated by knowing the terrain (Is the plant specific to montane areas?), the ecological community (Is this a riverside plant? A plant that will grow in young secondary forest?), and the very specific natural history of particular sites, which have come to be characterized by some species and not others. Although models of optimal foraging rarely take this into account, any reader who has ever tried to locate a wildflower or even an animal site probably knows that it really helps to know the *particular* places, and not just the ecologically appropriate kinds of places, that plant or animal has been seen before; that's the place to find it again. Meratus collectors know particular sections of the forest very well, and these are the starting points for their collections. They learn these sections because they go there all the time: to hunt, to look for fruit and honey, to find old cultivates in the regrowing forest that once was their swidden or that of their great aunts, and to find saleable forest products. They learn these forest places in activities that span the gap between subsistence and trade.

These familiar territories are not exactly private property, although they come to be associated with particular groups of people. The familiar territories of individuals interpenetrate and overlap; they are not exclusive or bounded. Yet these territories also limit and organize forest management, as well as collection. Familiar territories inspire a neighborly respect that keeps people from straying too far, too long, into forest territories associated with another group of people. (There one may stumble on to a disguised but deadly spring trap, set for pigs or deer. In familiar forest, one knows where the traps are.) Familiar territories inspire an alertness in one's own "home" spaces: Which tree species are flowering? Which holes in the creek contain edible minnows? Which animal tracks have been sighted? Which honey trees are being smothered by strangling vines? This alertness is a form of attention to biological diversity, not only as a list of species, but also as growth habits, population dynamics, species associations, and ecological histories. Meratus were able to tell me so much about the forest because of this kind of alertness, grown over time in familiar territories. From it, collectors have the ability to choose products for the market, to supply local needs, and to develop a sense of the diverse relations linking humans with forest animals and plants.

Let me turn to one example: rattans. Rattans are spiny, vinelike climbing palms. Their often-barbed thorns help them catch hold of surrounding vegetation, as they rise through the forest; they also tear the flesh of animals who come too near, including hikers unfortunate enough to brush against their ever-present extensions across the trail. The stems of rattans are long, flexible, and strong; people around the world have thought of many uses for them, particularly in furniture making, mats, and basketry. In the 1980s, and into the 1990s until the local supply ran out, rattan was the most important product of central mountain trade. One species dominated above all others: *huyi saga* (*Calamus caesius*). In east-side areas where rattan could be rafted out, huyi saga was often sold in long looped bundles, called *galung* "coils." In the central mountains, however, transportation of such heavy bundles was too difficult, and rattan was generally prepared by cutting it carefully into neat strips. Coarse strips (*lampit*) were sold to the mat-making industry; fine, delicately worked strips were sold for ties, baskets, and the woven-cane furniture industry.

Huyi saga is, at least ideally, a renewable resource. If the collector leaves a length of stem at the base of the plant, the rattan will regenerate. Furthermore, it has become a cultivated crop, planted in swiddens to be harvested beginning six to eight years later. Even without planting, there is a reasonable chance that huyi saga will develop in the swidden regrowth. Secondary forest, with its stronger light, is a beneficial environment for the growth of many rattans, including huyi saga. Huyi saga fruits annually and abundantly with edible, sour fruits that are widely spread by wild animals. In the central mountains, swidden-making and rattan growth do reasonably well together.

By the early 1990s, however, huyi saga had become scarce in the Meratus Mountains. How had this happened? Indonesian national policy promoted rattan exports in the 1980s and encouraged rattan buyers, who formed contacts with a greater variety of transnational manufacturers. Prices were high; a lot of rattan was wanted. Policy excitement about rattan pushed groups of adventurers from the plains into the mountains to cut rattan themselves. These adventurers cut planted and protected rattan as well as rattan in mature forest; nor did they have any motivation to cut it in such a way as to allow regeneration. Without any protection for the rattan they had planted and encouraged, Meratus began to cut their own rattan before someone else could steal it. The competition to sell rattan grew to a high pitch; suddenly, there was no more saleable huyi saga.

Luckily, huyi saga is only one of many kinds of useful rattan that prosper in the central mountains.[13] Before the 1950s, many kinds of rattan were sold on the market. The focus on huyi saga was artificially created by government working together with industry; the forced rattan deliveries of the 1950s not only stimulated provincial industry but also advised Meratus of new conditions of trade. When huyi saga ran out in the 1990s, there was some optimism among Meratus collectors that traders would pick up on other species. Handicrafts, such as baskets, made from other rattans were still saleable. Moreover, the diversity of rattans meant that the scarcity of huyi saga was not felt in relation to subsistence uses of rattan, and there was no need to cut it as it regenerated in old fields and forest.

Huyi saga is not the only commercial species. *Manau* is a thick cane rattan whose fruits and buds are favored foods and whose cane is used for the rims of large baskets. The canes, brought to market as long, thick sticks, are called *walatung*. Bent into chairs and sofa legs, they are another staple of the furniture industry. In the 1980s, the market for manau soared. Collecting boomed in the Meratus Mountains. As with huyi saga, it is possible to cut manau in such a way that the rattan regenerates, but when collecting goes wild, many collectors ignore this. One odd circumstance helped save local populations. The stem of another large cane rattan, *minung*, looks very much like manau. It is easy for Meratus collectors to tell the difference, but it is not easy for the traders who buy from them to differentiate the species. Minung has a brittle stem; it is not suitable for furniture making. According to my Meratus friends, it can "break the machine." Meratus collectors often subsisuted minung for manau in selling cane. When this happened, the market died for a while, whether because the provincial machines were out of order or because the traders had lost faith in Meratus collectors. This lent a particularly sporadic tenor to the manau market.

Rattans, in their variety, move in and out of "resource" status in the Meratus Mountains. Relations between collectors and downstream traders are an essential ingredient in making a rattan a commercial resource. This resource status, in turn, can provoke a number of different responses from Meratus collectors. Wild overcutting is one response. Overcutting depletes the product, wiping out its resource status at least for awhile. Domestication is another response. Cultivated plants can form a steadier supply for both traders and planters, but traders are tempted, too, to send their own armed men to get these more easily locatable cultivates as long as local claims are unprotected by the state. A third response is the collectors' attempt to substitute related species. Because collectors tend to know species variety better than traders do, this last response, in particular, keeps the traders wary and puzzled, dependent on their collectors. When coercive interventions become possible, as for example, with the entry of the army into the trade, they bypass local collectors altogether to guarantee the homogeneity of the re-source and interlopers' free rights over it. But thus, too, they are likely to wipe out the resource entirely.

It is within these tensions and instabilities that Meratus collectors scan the forests for useable and saleable products. The knowledge they bring to for-est collection is not a closed, traditional knowledge but rather one that is constantly augmented by their sense of their relationship with downstream traders, of changing market demands, and of the conditions under which they can claim and sell their products. While this knowledge includes an ap-preciation for biodiversity, it may or may not nurture and protect nonhuman species. Yet the one thing that is utterly clear is that central mountain col-lectors are doing a whole lot better than the development experts and agents who surround them on almost every side.

Inside the Gap between Farm and Forest

In the central mountains, swidden farms are constantly becoming forest. In 1986, when I visited the swidden field next to which I lived in 1981, I found it a dark, shady place, thick with wild gingers rising up above my head: *pati-tih, patikang, patikala, pitukun*. Each of these members of the ginger family, Zingiberaceae, is a giant herb with flowers reminiscent of colorful sea crea-tures, and tall, glossy leaves that may reach up ten or twelve feet. I saw no trace of the grasses and weedy annuals with wind-borne seeds that are the first pioneers of open places; the shade had long ago discouraged them. Eventually, the gingers would die back too. There was already a variety of young secondary forest trees, such as the gangly ground-figs, *dandali*, with their juicy red fruits peeking from the ground. On one margin, people had maintained a small clearing next to the trail, and a few papaya trees from the old swidden still stood. Most of the other light-demanding swidden plants were gone, at least to my eyes, replaced by a young forest. Meratus say that after five years, the trees in *jurungan* "secondary forest regrowth" reach a di-ameter as big as one's arm. In ten years, they reach the size of a person's leg. When I visited the same place in 1994, the trees were substantial, and, de-spite my clear memories of bends and rocks in the stream that runs along one border, I had trouble picking the area out from surrounding forest.

Regrowing secondary forests, like this one, have never garnered sympa-thetic attention among either scholars or policy makers; they are not a pop-ular place among either developers or conservationists. Developers see sec-ondary forest as abandoned agriculture or degraded timber land; it is a place of waste, where the human mastery of nature has been neglected. Conserva-tionists see it as weedy brush, full of easily spreading species that contrast in their dense homogeneity with the complex but open architecture of the mature rainforest. Yet one might also see secondary forest as a site of possibility for both livelihood and species protection. For those who have become familiar with its wild species and enrich it with their plantings, the secondary forest is not only a place of useful products but also a place dedicated to the regrowing future. Under the best conditions, secondary forest gains architectural complexity and diversity: In fifty years, pioneer species are being shaded out by mature forest species coming into their own; and although it may take centuries to gain certain kinds of complexity, within a hundred years the forest has a formidable species diversity. Now it takes a particular kind of landscape dynamic to nurture fifty- and one hundred-year old forest regrowth. We might want to know something about it. As long as both developers and conservationists divide up the land into zones of intensive agriculture and zones of pristine nature, no such patches of regrowth and possibility will be acknowledged. The central Meratus Mountains will continue to be invisible, or worse yet, criminal.

How might we learn something from the landscape of regrowing forest? Again, it makes sense to ask how its Meratus inhabitants know it. Here the key is that secondary forest is always a *social* place; to know it is to know the history of its flora and fauna in relation to socially situated human biographies. Secondary forest is always familiar forest for some group of people; people are attached to it because they once made a swidden there and because they have continued to maintain their relationship with the regrowing forest vegetation. Long-term biographical connections between people and forest regrowth are the basis of Meratus forest knowledge and management practices.

The process of forming that dense knowledge of vegetation that forges connections between people and places begins in the swidden field itself. As I have said, some large trees, such as fruit and honey trees, are saved in the process of swidden-making. These will continue to form elements of the new forest that grows on the site. Some other trees, too, do not die in the process of swidden-making. Although woody growth is cut and burned in swidden-making, burning is only rarely intense and thorough in the Meratus Mountains. Some trees sprout from their stumps and eventually resume their status in the forest. Other woody plants also resprout from their roots if they are not killed in the weeding process. Meratus weeders cut weeds back but do not uproot them; this discourages soft-stemmed herbs more than woody plants. Some shrubs, ferns, and bamboos grow back. These regrowing elements of the old forest are the most basic resources of the regrowing forest.

Weeders get to know, too, the new plants of the swidden, whether they are unwelcome pests or valued wild vegetables and medicinal herbs. Many wild plants are encouraged in the swidden, such as the sweet-bitter wild cucumber, *hantikup*, known only as a swidden intruder. (Hantikup disappears in the shady regrowing forest; but if a swidden is cleared on this site again, it predictably reappears from seeds still in the soil. A history of hantikup is one reason, people said, to reuse a forest regrowth site for a swidden.) Women and children tend to know the most about the weeds, grasses, and herbs of young regrowth. Women learn them from weeding and children from playing in and around the fields. They remember these weeds and herbs as the swidden grows into forest.

For the first few years after the swidden's last rice crop, there is still much to harvest in the old swidden: banana trees produce new suckers; papayas fruit; taro and other aroids grow in the shade; herbs planted in the swidden flourish in the forest cover. After five or six years, there will not be much left of these short-term crops, but some of the fruit trees people planted will be bearing. In the process of keeping track of such crops, women and children also acquaint themselves with the regrowing secondary forest, looking for its own distinctive vegetation. Many of the most popular snack foods for women and children are found in young secondary forest. The sour fruit of wild gingers or the sweet berries of *mampap* vines are always a welcome find. Young secondary forest is also the favored site for collecting herbs for medicines and poultices, for beauty aids such as hair conditioners, for ritual equipment, for household tools, and for children's toys. Each time a person comes to collect a particular species, she notices the other species that have taken their places beside it in the regrowth. In this close attention to species distribution, over repeated visits, the familiarity of the site and its vegetation is continually enhanced.

The light gap of swidden regrowth encourages not only the quick-growing herbs and soft-wooded trees that will soon-enough be shaded out by other species but also a variety of plants that have a reasonably long-lasting presence in the regrowing forest. Familiarity with and use of these long-living "weeds" is one source of protected diversity in the forest. Bamboos, for example, are encouraged by swidden-making—and much valued by Meratus for their many uses. Bamboos grow in exuberant variety in the central Meratus Mountains. The most common, *paring*, is used for basket-making when the plant is young, for roof tiles when mature, and for firewood when old. The much sturdier *batung* makes house poles, rafts, and the aqueducts that carry clean spring water to convenient water-collecting sites. Batung is planted in swiddens in some west-side Meratus areas where it can be rafted into lowland markets as a cash crop; its stability as a forest plant also makes it an important marker of swidden-based forest claims in areas where immigrants may not otherwise recognize land rights. Batung, planted in swiddens made in areas in which grasses such as *hilalang* (*Imperata cylindrica*) threaten forest succession, maintains the shady ecology that allows forest plants to dominate the regrowing swidden patch. In the central mountains, however, forest successions are not threatened, and batung is rarely planted. However, like other bamboos, it does not die when cut back in swiddens; it grows back with vigor.

The sweetest, freshest tasting bamboo shoots are from one batung species, *batung manis*. Other batung, such as *batung raya*, have huge stems, which can be used as large containers. Most ordinary water and food containers are made from a more delicate species group, *buluh*. Buluh has thin walls, which can be unrolled to make temporary floors and walls for houses. *Buluh kuning*, a buluh with yellow culms, is in demand for certain rituals. The thin-stemmed *tirik* is used for fine weaving and small-bored flutes. Meratus use bamboo for many purposes, and they need to know where many kinds can be found. They return to bamboo stands in familiar secondary forest to harvest the culms they need. The persistence of bamboo in secondary forest draws them, sponsoring the knowledge and long-term relationships between people and plants through which familiar forest is made.

Palms are also encouraged in the regrowing forest. Some palms are planted: coconut palms, which may die when a bear eats the (really delicious) growing bud; areca palms, which supply valued betel quids; marsh-loving *rumbiah* sago palms, whose starchy pith yields an important hunger food; and, of course, rattans. Other palms thrive in the swidden's light gap: the thatch palm *haping*; the minor sago palms *risi* and *mangkung*. A number of palms do not die in swidden-making; *bangkala*, for example, grows new stems when cut down, and after five years these can be harvested for the tasty palm-hearts. Some palms, too, run the full range of forms of encouragement. *Hanau* sugar palms may be saved, planted, encouraged, or merely tolerated in swiddens. (Sugar is made by bruising and cutting the male inflorescence, collecting the sweet syrup that emerges, and boiling it down until it is close to crystallization.) The importance of palm diversity for Meratus draws them to both learn about and enrich the secondary forest.

Secondary forest becomes familiar forest through attention applied over many years. Secondary forest forms the most basic collecting areas for the people who know it, from which they branch out to find products that grow in old-growth forest or more specialized forest niches. Hiking with Meratus friends through familiar forest, we paused and meandered continually to check the status of fruit trees and taste locally abundant snacks. In contrast, walking through forest associated with a group with whom my friends did not have close relationships, we moved along the trail at a businesslike pace, only rarely stopping to drink or rest. The relationship between social groups and forest patches structures forest management and use. When Meratus discuss their location in the forest, they talk not only of the history of vegetation in that place but also of the social connections that tie those plants to particular people. The forest, whether young or old, is never a homogeneous "wild" place; it is a finely differentiated set of simultaneously social and natural locations.

Outsiders who come into the mountains rarely see this. Most of us are trained to see nothing but a chaotic mass of green. As one of my friends in the United States put it, "Walking in the forest is boring. It's not like the streets of a city, full of shops and people; there's nothing to see." For Meratus, there is a lot to see. Yet even forest experts have immersed themselves in ways of seeing that dull their eyes to the "city streets" of enriched secondary forest. Most often, very young regrowth, such as the *belukar* "brush" of Indonesian national land use mapping, is the model for secondary forest. It is imagined as choking with weeds and grasses, a site only of the abandonment of agriculture. The varied circumstances of forest regeneration are lumped together to form an image of messy deterioration.

Regrowth can be inadequate. The timber operations I saw on the east side of the mountains in the 1980s left landscapes in which one single plant quickly came to dominate: a vine Meratus call *balaran*. These places were biologically monotonous and unusable for either shifting cultivation or forest product collecting. Without more roots holding the soil, the first severe rains caused massive erosion. The category "secondary regrowth" does not in itself differentiate between this situation and what I saw in the central mountains, where small fields surrounded by forest were reseeded with diverse forest species. Within this confusion, the landscape is misread, to everyone's detriment: Socially enriched forest is classified as old-growth production forest, to be contracted to loggers, and thus destroyed; or else it is classified as wasteland, to be contracted to plantation development, and thus destroyed.

Why is regrowing forest so persistently difficult for experts and planners to see? On one level, a widespread if misleading "common sense" is to blame: Experts and planners are most likely to recognize only the difference between "fields" and "forests" with no connection between them. They are used to fields in permanent cultivation, fields that are "obviously" sources of human livelihood. Whether they see forests as sources of commercial timber or genetic reserves, they are likely to focus only on the completed mosaic of trees, not the process of landscape formation over time. From this snapshot perspective, the difference between a neatly cultivated field and a wild forest is visually sharp. Everything between is matter out of place.

This common-sense perspective is common in Indonesia, as it is around the world. Walking through a Meratus rubber orchard (admittedly one growing amidst varied trees), one planner asked me, "How do you like this Indonesian jungle?" as if he were perfectly blind except to random greenness. This kind of blindness would still not mean much for the administration of this area if it were not inscribed into development policy. Development has organized the national exploitation of natural resources. Between the late 1960s and the late 1990s, development directed this exploitation as if the areas in which natural resources were found were, by definition, uninhabited. Development divided the country into dichotomous zones: zones of population and zones of natural resource exploitation. In zones of population, development managed communities. In zones of natural resource exploitation, people were irrelevant. The goal of development was to get out the resources.

In 1975 a national Forestry Law defined all forests as the property of the state, to be used according to state-designated national priorities. Local rights over forested lands were written out of existence. Lots of areas without trees were mapped as "forests"; many towns and villages were included.[14] Unfortunately for the residents of the Meratus Mountains, and other vast pieces of Indonesia's Outer Islands, the bureaucrats never consulted them about the definition of "forests." They just assumed that the whole area was forested. This has meant that the whole area belongs to the state to be used for natural resource exploitation as the state pleases. It has also meant that experts and planners have not been encouraged to recognize the social history of the forest. They are trained specifically to see forests outside of appropriate livelihoods and claims.[15] People in the forests are outlaws.

The effectiveness of this training still presents a puzzle: How can it be so easy to impose official "forests" on social landscapes? To answer I can only point to the cultural legacy of official forests, in which repeated policy enactments each make the category seem more necessary, more reasonable, and more a piece of common sense. National resource policy draws directly on the colonial resource policy of the Netherlands Indies. Colonial policy, in turn, drew its model of rural landscapes in part from pre-colonial kingdoms in Java. Wet-rice fields were the favored landscapes of the court; wet-rice fields symbolized not only a community of stable subjects, but also the order and prosperity that the king could bring to the land. In contrast, the forests beyond were imagined as places of wild animals, fierce bandits, and recalcitrant shifting cultivators: unruly subjects on unruly landscapes (Dove 1985; Day 1994). Colonial administrators borrowed from these courtly aesthetics in imagining the rural landscapes they could best control. The Dutch extended wet-rice cultivation, first across Java and then across the archipelago, settling their subjects properly.[16] They also imagined new ways to use the wild forest landscapes that Javanese kings despised: These would be the places where natural resources could be freely extracted by European industry. In 1871, an Agrarian Law divided the colony into two types of land: native land and land for European exploitation. Native land would be the site of colonial administration of resident communities; the rest of the colony could be regarded as effectively uninhabited, free for plantations, mines, or other enterprises.

After independence, this dualistic division between native and European zones was repudiated in the Indonesian Agrarian Law of 1960; however, it was recapitulated in the passage of the 1975 Forestry Law, which gave all forests to the state for natural resource exploitation. Once again, the country would be divided, as it had been under colonial rule, into zones of *human* management and zones of *resource* management. In the latter zones, the claims and livelihoods of local residents would be irrelevant; the ghosts of Javanese pre-colonial courts still called these people unruly, and colonial laws still criminalized them. As natural resource exploitation became a focus of state-building, logging, mining, and tree plantations spread through Kalimantan. Each of these operations required landscapes that were empty of people and their property rights, that is, in national parlance, "forests." Each drew on the precedence of the others to argue that the forests they found were, by definition, empty and wild. Each stabilized the others' understanding of forested landscapes as wild places; each made this cultural legacy more obvious-seeming and more real.

Many conservationists have accepted the definition of the rural landscape offered by this legacy without a moment of self-consciousness. To fight for nature reserves and parks, they wrench forest areas away from national development to make way for an equivalently valued national conservation. Conservation forests, like development's production forests, would contribute to the power of the nation and its elites, at least symbolically. Like developers, these conventional conservationists have seen the forests' residents as interlopers, bandits, destroyers of the nation's value. The secondary forests that follow in their wake are the sign of their destructiveness. Caught by the legacy that stretches from Javanese kings to national development, conventional conservationists never look at *landscapes*—those historical configurations of both nature and society—even as they describe the wild nature that can only be found on those landscapes.

The Meratus landscape is intelligible to neither developers nor conventional conservationists. It is in this sense that I describe it as forming within a "gap." Gaps are zones of erasure and incomprehensibility. Gaps occur where metropolitan projects do not reach so far or deep as to change everything according to their plans. Those who believe in evolutionary stories of history try to convince us that gaps are archaic backwaters, left *behind* the advancing wave of history. People without computers, people without televisions, people without plumbing: Technology, they say, has left them behind. Behind what? How are these discriminations made and maintained? Gaps are always being produced as discriminations are made. Development creates a discrimination between zones of population and zones of resource exploitation; to the extent that the Meratus landscape is made illegible by this discrimination, it occupies a gap. This gap is not a transcendent, transhistorical space of difference. Gaps are only experienced from the perspective of a particular, historically instituted line of demarcation in relation to which certain ways of being seem invalid or illegible. From another perspective, that gap may be another form of ordinariness. Yet some perspectives are more powerful than others. To the extent that categories are drawn with power, the gaps they stimulate are worth taking seriously as critical spaces and sites for emergent voices and dreams.

It has been easy for me to pick out the gaps that development policy creates because justice-oriented Indonesian environmental activists have picked them out for me.[17] Taking up the cause of people who live in state-demarcated zones of natural resource exploitation, they have argued that we need to imagine conservation and development differently: The rights of forest-living people must be respected, and their traditional systems of forest management should be maintained. With the demise of the New Order, such criticisms and suggestions may carry some weight. The early twenty-first century is a time of change and ferment in national forest policy, and some NGO models may yet become national law.[18]

This is a great moment when many things are possible. It is also a moment for reflection. As we redress the gaps of previous ways of seeing, are we developing our own distinctive gaps? What kinds of dialogues between urban policy and rural landscape maintenance are we making possible?

Justice-oriented environmental activists, both in Indonesia and internationally, ask us to imagine both conservation and development on a community scale. This is a great starting point. However, sometimes even these plans get caught in the legacy of separation between people and forests. Some of the best-laid environmentalist agendas reproduce the separation of zones of population and zones of resource management, but in miniature: The landscape is imagined as a series of enclosed communities, each with its settlements and fields, on the one hand, and its reserved forests, on the other.[19] This has many advantages over national development and conservation, but it still makes it difficult to see the forest as a social landscape. Must we always assume a distinction between settlements, as centers of sociability and livelihood, and hinterlands, as zones of resource management? Once again, Meratus landscapes are found only in the gap.

Inside the Gap between Settlements and Hinterlands

Consider the shadow communities of the Ayuh River valley. The Ayuh is a great stream that flows through the mountains. Long before it makes its way, at last sluggish, to the coast, it bores through canyons and crashes over falls: It is not a navigation channel to the plains. Instead, its mountain segment cradles a landscape of small swidden clusters surrounded by forest: familiar forest to the people who live there, who have watched and nurtured their scattered fruit and honey trees, discovered favorite hunting and fishing haunts, and retraced the tracks of an older generation's old swiddens, materialized in enriched forest regrowth. In that landscape lies a set of once and future communities: reminders and possibilities for sociality that shadow contemporary community commitments. The overlapping spheres and tracks of familiar forest are the Ayuh's shadow communities.

"Community" here means sharing food, work, and ceremony. In one of its most formal instantiations, game and big fish are divided into cubes and counted out in piles to be distributed to each household. Rice planting is done in a large group gathered through reciprocal labor exchange. The ceremony that makes newly harvested rice fit to eat gathers everyone in a great celebration. Each of these makes a named "community" real. Yet throughout the Meratus Mountains communities are flexibly reconstructed in constant negotiations. This globally common feature of social life is particularly self-evident in the central mountains, where houses are widely separated, perched adjacent to swidden fields. Households are free to affiliate with neighbors in different directions, coalescing ever-changing communities. In a year or two they make a new house and a new swidden, and, in the process, forge a new set of social ties that may replicate or transform last year's commitments. Nowhere is this more evident than in the forests along the Ayuh River.

Because the Ayuh River is not a path to the coast, households along it orient themselves, in part, along other paths: the trails that cross the mountain divide on either side, leading to market towns and government centers. These trails are various, following the Ayuh's many tributaries up into the mountains and over passes before descending into the surrounding plains. Men hike these trails to bring forest products and crops to market; they hike back with news of products, prices, and politics. They visit kin and friends who live along these trails; they find potential spouses, political allies, and new styles and stories all along the way. Orientation to these various "exits" splinter the connections among Ayuh valley households, pulling them centrifugally into the social networks along these tributaries. Ayuh River communities are unstable, contested, and constantly breaking up and reforming.

Individual households that farm along the Ayuh one year are likely to move up a tributary for next year's farm, joining the people there.

Yet the lands around the Ayuh River are a good place to farm, fish, and hunt, and, any given year, there are quite a few people living there. These people have some of their familiar forests along the Ayuh stream. Familiar forests are always in process, changing as new trees are planted and claimed, new routes for forest collection found, new swiddens cut and old ones eased back into forest. Familiar forests always overlap. Any time a group of households agrees to make adjacent swiddens, they have affirmed at least one future site of overlapping familiarity: the regrowing forest that replaces their swiddens. The more formal claims of named communities are possible because they map on to at least one segment of each constituent household's familiar forest. Next year, each constituent household may choose whether or not to continue its membership in that community; all it has to do is move or reach out to a different segment of its familiar forest to affiliate with another community.

The forest is full of the markings of past communities, and these are also potential communities. An island of fruit trees in the forest marks a past swidden cluster. The site of an old ritual hall is remembered as a once and future community center, even as the site has blended into surrounding forest. People are reminded of these nodes of sociality every time they look at the vegetation and recall its social history. People use the stories of these shadow communities to negotiate current social responsibilities: to kindle companionship, to solicit assistance with tasks, or to find allies.

I first became aware of these shadow communities when I was living with a household on the Ayuh River. A man came by whose current home was many hours' hike upstream. He was visiting a man in my household about a local political matter, a contested marriage. To demonstrate his closeness to his host, he evoked their common membership in a community I had never heard of. It turned out to be a community that had broken apart about thirty years before. The community "center" the men identified—at a point between their current locations—was long grown up in forest. Yet it was still clearly marked in the forest vegetation; they knew it every time they passed that way. Encouraged by this material presence, our visitor claimed for this shadow community both a territory and a constituency. He talked me through a sketch map of this territory: No matter that it borrowed segments from four contemporary communities; this was a community that still existed, in shadow form, in the evidence of the forest. Made from overlapping familiar forests, and read from forest histories, communities in the Ayuh valley are simultaneously fragile and persistent, overlaid yet allowing discrete claims, composed of natural forest and of social settlement.

Even where communities have more geographic grounds for stability, the importance of familiar forests in composing them allows them to stretch, split, and change their shape like amoebae. Individuals and groups bud off. Without ever leaving their own familiar forests, households may turn in another direction, away from the community's current focal point to join another community's social networks.

All of this makes it very difficult to tell the difference between settlements and hinterlands in the central mountains. Yet community leaders do their best to misrepresent this situation to regional administrators and development experts. Ambitious for their own recognition, leaders portray Meratus communities in terms that outsiders can understand. They claim distinctive community centers and fixed territories; this keeps their communities on administrators' maps. These are more than idle claims: Leaders do their best to make administrators' categories come to life on the ground, at least in tentative performances of appropriate behavior. But, in the central Meratus Mountains, they have been unable to change the daily practices of landscape-making that allow their neighbors to reaffiliate, move apart, and choose their own livelihood trajectories.

By the 1990s, conservation had become a small, if growing, outside authority in the Meratus Mountains. Some Meratus leaders learned the rhetoric of conservation, and they learned to produce its performances: They planned ecotourism and spoke of traditional benevolence toward the spirits of plants and animals; they showed outsiders their reserved forests. As with development, it was not always clear whether even the close kin and neighbors of these accomplished leaders shared their enthusiasm about these performances. Leadership claims and commitments had a minimal effect on most people's daily life projects, and on the landscape. Once again, a bad basis for dialogue was developing.

Yet many of the conservationists who visit the Meratus Mountains are committed to empowering Meratus through community-based conservation. Why might this basically great idea create some of the same troubled dynamics as militarized and corrupt development policies? Advocates are pushed into much the same position as Meratus community leaders: If they do not portray resources and communities in terms that are recognizable by the state, national elites, and international experts, their advocacy will be entirely ineffective. In this context, advocates represent rural communities in ways that are the opposite of their audiences' worst fears: The people, they say, are organized into obedient communities with a clear structure of leadership, rational management policies, and clearly bounded territories. All that remains is to offer these communities *rights*.[20]

As advocacy this is proper and important, even with its assumptions: a unified and stable community; clearly stated management plans; and traditional customary territory. I don't think advocates are able to operate without winning images and frameworks. Yet perhaps there is some room here to maneuver—and room to learn.

And so, I emphasize again the *practices* that link humans and nonhumans in creating the social-natural landscape. Practices show us how landscape biodiversity is materially appreciated; they lead us to questions about particular human–nonhuman relationships and away from barren debates about the wisdom or stupidity of primitive people. Instead of basing rights claims on equivalents to private property, we might train our vision on the overlapping socialities of familiar forests, as these empower and constrain individuals in using forest resources. For example, even planted Meratus trees of any stature have multiple claimants: the descendants, male and female, of the original planter. No claimant can expect to profit from the tree alone. Forest management is facilitated, not hampered, by such overlapping and diverse claims (for example, rights to share in the product; see Tsing 2003a). Overlapping claims are a form of "community" through which forests are maintained. Interspecies socialities are embedded in the forest landscape. Processes of forging human–nonhuman relationships within dynamic, changing forests are as important here as forest boundaries.

Landscape and Memory

The Meratus forest is full of named locations. If Meratus do not lose themselves too often in the forest, it is not because they have a spiritual gift of navigation, as some romantics have claimed, but rather because they orient themselves to known places. Ridges, peaks, and saddles have names, as do prominent rocks and even insignificant creeks and springs and the distinctive pools, falls, and confluences of rivers. Many big trees also have names, that is, not only names for the kind of tree but also individual, personal names. Hillsides are commonly referred to in relation to the name of a big tree. Through these markers, hikers learn their way in the forest and, later, craft their tales of places and events.[21]

Forest regrowth also orients the hiker: It tells the story of past swiddens as well as forest management. Even without knowing the people who once lived there, Meratus hikers learn something of the social history of the forest through observing the forest regrowth. In their own familiar forests, this regrowth is a place of memory, whether of one's own past or that of one's kin and neighbors. Hiking through familiar secondary forest, we often spoke of the stories from the past that forest regrowth told. Even relaxing at home, Meratus are likely to tell stories of their own pasts in relation to the sites they made swiddens as well as the places they traveled. The landscape becomes a medium for telling stories of oneself and others. At one point, I collected "swidden biographies," that is, narrations of the consecutive swidden sites of each household. Since old swidden sites are not exclusive property claims, I found myself surprised at how easily their sites—and sights—rolled off people's tongues.[22] They were easy to tell because the narration of personal history through landscape has been an ordinary genre for speaking about one's past.

Habits of attentiveness, practices of naming, and genres of telling make the forest intelligible for its Meratus residents. The forest appears neither particularly frightening nor wild; it is not outside the bounds of history and civility. Once one considers the possibilities of this kind of forest intelligibility, it seems likely that people all over the world must have come to know forests as social, historical, biographical spaces. How is it that this has been so hard to recognize? What work has it taken to repress the social intelligibility of the forest? These questions bring us back to habits of thinking about nature as global and transcendent, and why these habits have traveled anywhere at all, even if they have not reordered the landscape of the Meratus Mountains.

One might again recall how hard European states had to work to evict peasants from their forests.[23] Only by seizing the forests for elites, thus making forests, coercively, off-limits for peasant uses, did European forests become empty and wild. In this state they could be what one literary critic calls "the shadow of civilization," that is, nonsocial spaces that haunted European sociality (Harrison 1992). The histories and prehistories of nationalism inscribed in European forests that Simon Schama (1995) tells in delineating a distinctly European set of regimes of "landscape and memory" require forests that have already been claimed for the shadows of nationalist elite imaginations.

This notion of forests as empty, wild, and available for elite manipulation also formed part of the repertoire of colonial scientists in their quest to understand the environment at the peripheries of European empire (Grove 1995). Forests were a key component of the discovery of this environmental form of "nature," which, these scientists learned, could be used for European profit but also destroyed beyond repair. They watched European settlers cut down forests; they worried about erosion, loss of species, and climate change. But their attention both to the settlers' use of forests and to forest protection assumed forests that were outside of long-term social occupation. These could not be forests that formed social "homes" because then they would be available for neither profit nor protection. They learned to observe empty forests, spaces of a nonsocial nature.

Learning both with and against the natives whose territories they had come to occupy, colonial scientists concluded that this profitable-yet-fragile nature was transcendent, beyond the circumscribed knowledge of any given vernacular culture. Writing to each other from one imperial corner to another, they found that this universal nature was also global, that is, interconnected across the planet. The discourse on deforestation—as necessary to human enterprise yet a cause of systematic environmental deterioration—formed a centerpiece of this discussion of a "nature" that could travel across cultures and across empires.

When this imperial discourse spread in the twentieth century to inform international development and conservation expertise, the central place of forests was not disturbed. Yet these "forests" are a very particular object, inherited from European state-making and empire-building. Forests are recognizable around the world only to the extent that they are empty and wild, the shadows of civilization. Where indigenous people are recognized within them, international discussion makes the people wild things too, assimilated to the wild emptiness of the forest. Their social lives come out to meet the international public only across a deep abyss; they flit through the forest like birds. In contrast, a more recognizable set of rural people is known in the forest, but as a destructive force: poor peasants. Represented as just ordinary folks, poor people are said to destroy the forest to make their meager living. Third World elites blame them to explain why the forests are disappearing. One sees here the resiliency of the concept of nonsocial forests. If forests are being destroyed, it is society; if they aren't, it is nature: Everything can be explained by placing it somewhere in the dichotomy of social and natural.

The Meratus Mountains have not escaped the gaze stimulated by this framework, but rather are repeatedly inscribed. The Social Welfare Department saw "social" people destroying "natural" forests and tried to resettle the people out of the forests. The loggers saw empty, natural forest and came in to log it. The plantation operators saw forest degraded by society and needing to be restored to nature—in a monocrop, profitable form. I could continue. But this is not everything that is going on. There are other forests here too: the social-natural forests of Meratus residents. To see these forests, a change in perspective is required. I mark this change of perspective in the idea of "gaps." Gaps develop in the seams of universal projects; they are found where universals have not been successful in setting all the terms. While a transcendent, nonsocial, global "nature" has become a powerful thing worldwide, it is not the only kind of nature on the planet. Whenever we want to trace the limits of hegemony, we need to look for gaps. An ethnography of global connection is impossible without this tool.

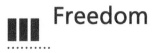

Stop!

"A hair in the flour"
[Voice and freedom]

How does one speak out against injustice and the destruction of life on earth? Words and concepts betray us. The concept of freedom is much abused, and yet the idea of freedom is still as important a tool as any for the disenfranchised. Movements split and change. What seems at first empowerment can come to seem an oppressive discipline or an empty rhetoric. To pick among the causes presented to us—as well as those hidden from our view—is a constant work of passion and judgment. It changes who we are. We imagine that we find our "voice" for that moment when a way we have learned to speak seems to fit a critical purpose. We tap into a legacy of speaking to articulate our situation within a general complaint.

The New Order regime in Indonesia came to power in 1966 by silencing one kind of voice and promoting another. The nationalist populism that had been increasingly identified with the Indonesian Communist Party was shattered in gunfire and buried in prison camps. The new state encouraged instead the voice of modernization and development. Citizens were asked to remake themselves in that modern discipline that promised future prosperity for both individuals and communities. Indeed, the greatest success of the New Order state in the countryside was the fact that so many rural people came to speak in this development voice. Their worst complaints could be solved, it seemed, by more development—that is, the expansion of the state. Most social analysts quickly naturalized this voice as the proper desire of the poor for self-improvement.

Yet even at the height of New Order rule, other voices could be heard. The echoes of Indonesia's anti-colonial struggle continued to reverberate in criticisms of corruption and calls for social justice. Critics of the state aligned themselves with varied transnational coalitions, ranging from Islam to environmentalism. Rhetorics of morality, on the one hand, and rights, on the other, came to fill the silences left by an earlier populism. Those who gravitated toward cosmopolitan, secular freedoms endorsed causes of human rights, the rule of law, and freedom of the press. Transnational political liberalism thus came to play a role in stimulating Indonesian critical voices.

Environmental protection and social justice coalesced in this current. In the environmental movement of the 1980s and 1990s, rights discourse—human rights, customary property rights, indigenous cultural rights—addressed the intertwined problems of landscape destruction and authoritarian rule. Yet the relevance of rights to the problems at hand was not self-evident; it had to be established step by step, and often in a confused dance in which even partners stepped on each other's feet. Terms were translated back and forth from foreign languages and across multiple vernacular uses. Local viewpoints proliferated, and angry debates flourished. As in any movement, it was often difficult to differentiate allies from enemies. Social criticism and political mobilization could only advance through friction.

One place to begin is with some very parochial stories. My own attempts to find a voice frame those of my companions in the Meratus Mountains.

1986. After many years of political quietude in the countryside, people are talking. In the Meratus Mountains, the talk is of timber companies, which are destroying Meratus forests. I have been spending the summer in a mountainous area not yet in the range of the loggers, but people know that the loggers are moving up the slopes on both sides. When I hike down to the Meratus resettlement village of Niwan, the renowned shaman Awat Kilay, a mentor of mine, pulls me aside. "The logging companies are ruining our land," he tells me. "When you go to Jakarta, you must tell Ibu Tien to stop." Ibu Tien is the wife of then-president Suharto, and popularly imagined as the sponsor of much resource exploitation. I protest that I don't have the status to make an appointment with Ibu Tien. He tries to talk me through it, conjuring an image of a pleasant lunch with the First Lady sipping tea. The task is urgent! I am embarrassed; I don't know how to explain my weakness and my lack of courage. I tell him that all I know how to do is write. He becomes thoughtful, taking in my explanation. He tells me to write with a critical attitude. "Be a hair in the flour," he explains. He is speaking of the rice flour used to prepare ritual cakes for the appeasement of authority. Communities offer ceremonial cakes to the spirits to keep them from taxing and troubling their human subjects; so, too, such appeasement is understood as the stuff of obedience to the state. A hair in the flour is a disturbance of everyday subservience and routine. A hair in the flour ruins the legitimacy of power. It is a benediction for my work and an inspiration for what I must continue to learn. I have repeated it to myself throughout the research for this book and its writing.

To write as a hair in the flour is to look for weaknesses, confusions, and gaps in business as usual. Without such friction, why would we bother to try to change anything? As a hair in the flour I tell of utopian social movements even where they are not victorious. These movements keep alive our sense that the forms of hierarchy and coercion we take most for granted can yet be dislodged. If I tell more about mobilizations for environmental protection and social justice than I do of suffocating development initiatives, it is to offer the former the chance to rattle the hegemony of the latter.

But let me return to 1986. One evening, when family and friends have gathered, Awat Kilay gives a rousing speech. "The timber companies are colonizers!" he declares. "We fought the colonizers in the revolution, and we can fight them again!" I am struck that he uses the rhetoric of Indonesia's struggle for independence. The timber company in this area is Indonesian, but that does not blunt its alien status. The trope of liberation seems quite right. It is a magnificent speech. But I doubt that it moves the young men whom he is trying most to impress. The young men are divided among themselves and cautious in assessing the words of Awat Kilay, who has spent many years living with the stigma of arrest and harassment for having attended a Communist-inspired land reform workshop in the 1960s. Awat Kilay's son, Ma Igul, is handsome and ambitious, but better known for entrepreneurial than political endeavor. His family jokes that he has twice converted to Islam, and twice been circumcised, to improve his connections with Muslim traders. My adopted brother Ma Salam, a nephew of Awat Kilay, aspires to political leadership in his own mountain village of Rajang but holds a grudge against Awat Kilay for an imagined slight in his childhood. The awkward relation between these three alone is enough to divide communal sentiment—and to stop me from romanticizing Meratus Dayaks as a united cultural force. Instead, I must pick through the fragments and consider my possibilities of dialogue with each.

Luckily, Meratus mobilization against logging does not depend on this little gathering. It is centered not in Niwan or Rajang, where the loggers have not yet encroached, but in the adjacent village of Manggur. Through a somewhat inadvertent coalescence of activists, nature lovers, and village elders (in this case, a tightly united sibling set), a small victory is achieved, and the logging company is asked to leave village forests in this area alone. (I tell the story in chapter 7.) The logging company is so angry at being asked to leave that they destroy the area around their base camp, dumping gasoline and strewing machinery around the forest. For the next fifteen years, logging companies attack other areas of the Meratus Mountains, but they leave this sector alone. (Niwan, Rajang, and Manggur are on the west side of the Meratus Mountains. The frontier area I describe in chapter 1 is on the east side, where logging proceeds without pause.) Only in the late 1990s does activism from this sector once again take on an important role in giving voice to Meratus aspirations. The small victories and betrayals of this time—in which the earlier history of factions, transcriptions, and voicings of freedom bear fruit—make this a story worth telling to introduce the frictions of liberal politics.

....

In the 1990s, activism grew in Manggur, Rajang, and Niwan. Village leaders worked back and forth between different kinds of regional sponsors, mixing the rhetoric of development, on the one hand, and conservation, on the other. Community strength might be gathered from development grants, ecotourism, political patronage, property registration, or environmental advocacy: The most ambitious leaders aimed to draw them all to their villages. After the New Order fell in 1998, the national political situation grew lively and confused. With their political sponsors in trouble, resource exploitation companies experienced a time of insecurity, and community options for protest widened. An archipelago-wide alliance of indigenous people gathered together in Jakarta in 1999 to demand redress for the state's nonrecognition of their rights. Manggur elders were there representing Meratus Dayaks. It was a thrilling moment for the development of new political ambitions and dreams. "If the State does not acknowledge us, we will not acknowledge the State," the delegates wrote in their report (AMAN 1999: 9). They went on to refuse state claims to their lands and resources, to reject the state's labels for them, to criticize the use of the armed forces in domestic affairs, to note the importance of women's equality, and to demand full participation in the political process.

In 1999, too, a new logging threat emerged in the central Meratus Mountains. In November, the regional government had announced an exchange of the sort misleadingly made famous as a "win-win" deal by the U.S. Clinton administration. In exchange for the conservation of a piece of logged-out forest near the east coast, the government would offer the heavily forested central Meratus Mountains to the Korea Development Company, known as Kodeco. The government planned a special economic zone on the east coast to complement Kodeco's already thriving cement and plywood factories there. Planners hoped to use a small piece of Kodeco's used-up logging concession in the area as a water catchment area for the special economic zone. But before environmental studies could be done on the feasibility of this idea, and while the special economic zone was still a gleam in a planner's eye, Kodeco was already surveying the Meratus forests they proposed as their exchange (Chamin, Maha Adi, and Hatta 1999).

Activists at multiple levels organized against the plan. Thirty-three regionally based NGOs formed the Meratus Advocacy Alliance (*Aliansi Advokasi Meratus*) to advocate for the Meratus and their forests. They pointed out that the logging plan required the government to change the classification of a forest that had long been considered a watershed protection area. They reminded the public of great floods that followed previous episodes of logging. They researched biodiversity and surveyed the opinions of Meratus residents of the forest. They contacted national and international news media, asking them to bring the eyes of the world to their campaign (Aliansi Advokasi Meratus 2000).

Meratus village leaders also became active in the campaign. Meetings were convened, bringing participants from many villages into common discussions of the problem. But as the campaign gained steam, Kodeco became active in its own Meratus patronage.[1] Kodeco representatives identified key Meratus leaders, wowed them on helicopter tours of company operations, and offered them and their communities substantial "community development" funds in exchange for their support for Kodeco's logging plans. This was money in hand, a real good as opposed to the unlikely success of environmentalist dreams. A number of leaders changed sides, offering their support for Kodeco's plan for "development."

By March 2000, the political scene was polarized. On March 13, forty anti-logging Meratus leaders gathered at the provincial capital. An NGO ally made the inflammatory statement that was used as a newspaper headline in the *Banjarmasin Post* (March 14, 2000): "We are ready to burn down Kodeco." Meanwhile, a Meratus spokesperson offered a more sober explanation of the protest: "We declare that we reject the plan to change the classification of the forest and its nature reserves for Kodeco Timber Company" (ibid.). This was not to be the last word. On March 14, almost one hundred Meratus Dayaks appeared, and this time they were demonstrating *for* Kodeco. "We are ready to accept any investor who profits from the Meratus Mountains, because we also want to be prosperous," said a spokesman (*Banjarmasin Post*, March 15, 2000).

By this time, my old friend Awat Kilay had succumbed to tuberculosis, and the next generation had grown into roles as village leaders. Naturally, Ma Igul and Ma Salam, who never had been friends, were on opposite sides of the controversy. Ma Igul stood for the right to development. He spoke for the prosperity to be ushered in by the timber company, for the benefit of all entrepreneurs. He himself was ready to gather up the forest products from soon-to-be-logged areas to bring in that otherwise wasted wealth. In contrast, Ma Salam was a leader of the opposition, speaking for the rights of villages to manage their own resources. He led mapping exercises to define village territories and spoke to regional officials about the importance of village-based conservation and development. He worked with the Meratus Advocacy Alliance, showing them how to make their work locally relevant. But local factions had taken over the debate.

Regional factions were also at play. In 2000, resource licensing was decentralized, and centralized control was replaced with negotiations among district, regency, and provincial officials and the varied blocs that aimed to influence them. Anti-Kodeco Meratus were allied with nongovernment organizations, the west-side tourist industry (which saw the death of regional tourism with the destruction of the forests), and a number of regency-level government representatives from the west side. The pro-Kodeco faction included the newly elected governor and the east-side regency officials who were already deeply involved with Kodeco's extensive operations. The governor was able to move the decision to the east-side regency, thus putting Kodeco's bloc in charge. Debate, however, continued. "Environmental minister rejects Meratus switch but provincial government persists in carrying it out," read one headline in March 2003 (*Radar Banjar*, March 18, 2003).

Conventions of news reporting would suggest I stop the story there, with the delineation of factions. Yet this would ignore everything else that has happened in the province over the last twenty-five years. During that time, Kodeco has logged most of the east side of the Meratus Mountains, creating the frontier described in chapter 1. The ecological results have been dramatic, ranging from total loss of tree cover, to its replacement with monocrop plantations, to the skimpy residual forests that were so badly burned in the great fires of 1997. One can say unequivocally that the ecological function of the forest has been badly compromised, biodiversity drastically reduced, and erosion on slopes and river silting and flooding have become major problems. (To add insult to injury, Kodeco has designated some clearcut areas "community forests.") Meanwhile, this destruction has not brought prosperity to the region and its inhabitants. Profits have been shipped out of the region. The luxury of Kodeco's compound has not been reproduced in villages. Meratus residents have been politically and economically marginalized by the flood of migrants who have followed the frontier economy. Forest-based livelihoods are no longer possible. Where compensation has been offered for forest land and resources, it in no way matches what would be required to make a living. There are now some wrist watches, televisions, and motorcycles, but these are a poor substitute for agro-forestry livelihoods. With them have come hunger, poverty, and depression. To imagine that Kodeco would take more social or environmental responsibility in its logging of the remaining healthy forest—without even being pressed—is wishful thinking.

It is with this background information that one can see that the two sides of the struggle have rather different stakes. The pro-Kodeco faction hopes to get some trace of the wealth for themselves before it slips entirely out of the province. The anti-Kodeco faction wants to change the terms of the discussion. Their protests challenge the status quo of corporate privilege, rather than trying to make a small place inside its net. The implications of each are politically different—for the forests, for Meratus communities, and for the wider public in and beyond South Kalimantan. It is a great frustration to me that nothing I can think of to write seems likely in itself to tip the balance.

Still, to write as a hair in the flour means to give the mobilization against forest destruction its due, not just to praise it, but to show how it offers a practical model to oppose global business as usual. How do we convince people that life on earth is worth saving? This is a political question as well as an environmental one. It requires a politics of working across difference in which the goal is not to make difference disappear but to make it part of the political program. Furthermore, the task requires the same breadth of global connection as does frontier resource extraction.

Thus, ironically, it seems politically as well as intellectually useful to offer a symmetrical analysis of friction in both the resource extraction industry and its opposition. To show contingencies, gaps, and slippages interrupts claims of the easy unity of the market as it also illustrates the creative possibilities of social mobilization. Each requires attention to the awkwardness of translation and the need to build heterogeneous audiences.

Politics on both sides of the Kodeco debate involved rounding up local allies by deploying a full array of transnational resources. Kodeco was only offered the central Meratus Mountains as a concession because when informed of the plan to use a piece of its land as a water catchment area, it threatened to sue at the World Court (Chamin et al. 1999). Those who wanted to preserve the forest also spoke of the international context, for example, in attracting tourists, as one spokesperson argued, "from Holland, Australia, Canada, and the United States" (*Dinamika Berita* 1999). Yet the relation between transnationalism and regional mobilization differed on each side. The pro-Kodeco faction needed to cover up their transnationalism to make participants imagine a local populism. Their transnationalism is a reminder of the alienation of profits and of control by distant elites. It must be downplayed in the making of a locally inclusive "we" who can be imagined as sharing the wealth. This is a sleight of hand, a mystification in which local and global inequalities are covered up. In contrast, the anti-Kodeco faction has the advantages of a more ready-to-hand localism: Their goal is to preserve Meratus rights and forests. Yet they must conjure a transnational "we" to amplify this small cause with enough volume to speak. Translation across difference is key to both ways of achieving political voice—but with contrasting power dynamics.

The Meratus Advocacy Alliance used translation to evoke a transnationally inclusive public who might jointly cherish the Meratus forest. For example, they argued that "the existence and holistic function of the Meratus Mountains conservation area, including biodiversity conservation, is very much tied to the life and death of many people (*public interest*) and the responsibility of the current generation to the next generation (*intergenerational accountability*)" (Aliansi Advokasi Meratus 2000: 5). The original statement is in Indonesian except for the words I have put in italics, which are in English. Indonesian is fully adequate to discuss public interest and intergenerational accountability. Translation, however, serves a political purpose, building an expansive public in the space between English and Indonesian. "Public interest" emerges in that space; the future to which generations look forward is simultaneously local, national, and global.

In contrast, consider the governor's words of encouragement to the pro-Kodeco Meratus demonstrators. The provincial newspaper goes out of its way to point out that he addressed the demonstrators in the Banjar language (*Banjarmasin Post*, March 15, 2000). Banjar is the language of South Kalimantan's regional majority. Meratus understand Banjar but have their own linguistic usages. The governor did not use Indonesian, the official language of the nation-state, but Banjar, the language identified with provincial populism. By including Meratus as if they were Banjar, he attempted to articulate populism—through translation. The newspaper's readers gather that the demonstrators are being treated, respectfully, as the voice of the common people, the populace the government must support.[2] Meanwhile, the newspaper reports Kodeco's suspicion that anti-Kodeco sentiments are spread by outside agitators (ibid.). Who's in and who's out? Where the anti-Kodeco faction must conjure virtual outsiders, the pro-Kodeco group must cover up its comprador status, while baselessly pointing fingers at the other guys.[3]

For both sides then, "voice" was built through intercultural practices, including translation. My job is to make these troublesome translations more apparent: to show that the coalitional structure of such engagements is not just a matter of adding allies, but also of remaking ideas, practices, and local, regional, and global histories. Only in this analytically symmetrical treatment can the differences between landscape destruction and the struggle for life shine through.

6 Movements

Beside the Potomac River,
at the house of George Washington
I encountered trees
that he planted.
Two hundred years from now
will you know
the tamarind trees I sowed?
  —from Eka Budianta, "Houses of Love"[1]

movement. 1. *A change of place or position; 2. A mental impulse, esp. one of desire or aversion; 3. An organization, coalition, or alliance of people working to advance a shared political, social, or artistic objective.*[2]

Travel changes the way we imagine our home places. We suddenly see them as fragile, strange, and worth savoring in new ways. In his poem "Houses of Love," Eka Budianta (2000) is struck by the fragility of his tamarind trees as he readjusts time and space beneath George Washington's trees by the Potomac River. All rural nature seems perishable in these times of cosmopolitan development. His solution—as in a number of Indonesian nature poems—is to move these cherished landscapes into his heart. After bringing us further on his travels through the blooming trees of a Tokyo spring, he returns to images of an Indonesian hillside. The poem ends with the bittersweet optimism of love and memory: "In the rainy city at the beginning of September, I have moved the bamboo house in which you were born into my heart for all time."

The poet has moved, that is, "transferred" the rural landscape into his heart, an act only possible because of his own travels. In English the term "move" has more meanings to provoke us, and these are worth exploring. To move is to travel. To be moved is to open one's heart. The travels of the poet stimulate his own heart's movement. The landscape, re-visioned through travel, is transferred to become a moving personal commitment of love. Traveling ideas often stimulate us in just this way. We see the landscapes we know in relation to other places; we are moved to change how we think at both local and global scales. Social movements—including movements to preserve rural landscapes—grow from traveling forms of activism as well as the transformation of consciousness. This chapter shows how we might think of these two meanings together in analyzing global process: movement as mobility and movement as mobilization.

What seems so simple to express in the poem, however, is not easy to explain as social science. Post–Cold War discussion of globalization glorified movement in the spread of liberalism, making the transnational travels of nongovernmental organizations, human rights advocacy, and civil society exemplars of an expanding freedom. This global movement was thought to remove layers of cultural superstition, distinction, and hierarchy to create a free—and frictionless—world. If freedom is the removal of obstructions, and movement is the fulfillment of individual desire, no mobilization is necessary.

Critics of this perspective erect its mirror opposite: movement exemplifies the spread of unfreedom. Nongovernmental organizations, human rights advocacy, and civil society spread as a transnational governmentality, a new imperial power that reaches deeply into human souls. The new subjects of liberalism are even more trapped in power because they imagine it as freedom.[3] Yet this vision shares presuppositions with liberalism's boosters. Both agree that when liberalism spreads, it is completely successful in creating the subjects it conjures, for better or for worse. Liberalism's dreams are no different than liberalism's practice in these accounts.[4]

Motion can be imagined as creating a global regime, whether of freedom or governmentality, only to the extent that motion is imagined as loosening the grip of local practice. Yet the closer we examine social and geographical mobility, the less useful it seems to think in terms of overcoming such friction. This is where movement as mobility *and* mobilization can be of use. Movement helps us visualize forms of mobility with cultural and political definition—not just transcendent freedom. The specificity of the trajectory of movement is important for what results. Furthermore, there must be mobilization—the movement of the heart—for travel to remake the world. Mobilization refigures identities even as it draws from foreign connections and comparisons.

To mobilize, a movement must offer a model of change in which individual activists as well as social groups can imagine themselves. The program must identify units of agency: What kinds of individuals and groups can make change? Two different answers organize this chapter, each keyed to the predicaments of a particular time. I first describe the careful interplay of nationalism and transnationalism under New Order repression and then turn to the mobilization of exuberant agency in the post–New Order moment of decentralization, in which ethnic, religious, and gender localizations direct a medley of transnational appropriations. In the first, the revitalized nation is the idealized agent of change; in the second, it is the charismatic package—the activist program itself—separated from national context. Each illustrates a way in which globally circulating terms, theories, and stories can be harnessed for local uses. Each requires a different model of analysis.

Under Indonesia's New Order regime, the environmental movement struggled within what seemed an endless horizon of repression. Activists asked: How might a critical opposition be possible? Transnational networks were necessary, but only as they could be made relevant to the national problem of making space for criticism. In the context of this predicament, I trace the formation of a utopian nationalism that shadowed the state even as it attempted to refigure its possibilities. I explore how transnationalism was channeled into nationalism and imperial discipline corralled for utopian dreams.

After the fall of the New Order, the nation entered a hopeful but chaotic period of reform. Political causes moved to the provinces as decentralization became a national agenda. In this moment of openness, activists considered how disenfranchised people might be mobilized to fight for their rights. They turned for precedence to transnational initiatives—and without the urgent necessity of national translations. In the jumbled creativity of turn-of-the-century Indonesia, transnational stories ricocheted here and there providing fodder for alternative dreams. Al Qaeda competed with Bollywood and Marx in shaping local visions. In this context, I trace the travels of new utopian visions. How do political models from elsewhere become relevant? Indonesia as a nation is no longer my focus; regional, ethnic, and gender dynamics come into view. Yet locations matter. Mobility means nothing without mobilization. My story retells other traveling stories, attentive to their situated uses and revisions.

In the light of these contrasts, I offer two kinds of tellings. First I explore the contradictions of liberalism as developed by brave—and privileged—critics of an authoritarian regime. Here, utopian dreams and disciplinary regimes beckon to each other, remaking the possibilities of freedom. Rather than beginning as most critics do with the contamination of utopian nationalism by privilege, discipline, and colonial discourse, I show how one might glimpse the movement's possibilities—without forgetting its limits.

In my second set of stories, activism has taken advantage of the confusions and openings of a time of reform. Regional, religious, and gender initiatives reach out to harvest allegorical packages as they zip around the globe, unmoored from their origins. Here too there is a model for understanding movement: utopian critique is commodified in allegorical packages. Scholars have had difficulty in imagining how to trace traveling forms of politics; the two most available models, national history and global circulation, territorialize and universalize, respectively, each erasing travel. My story lays out one strategy for showing how close and distant productions of politics intertwine. Together, the parts of the chapter detail varied possibilities of enmeshing mobility and mobilization.

Where Dreams Shadow Discipline

To many scholars, the nation is obsolete, a worn shoe discarded in the race toward globalization. Yet the nation continues to be a key site for political struggle.[5] In late New Order Indonesia, radical politics was nationalist politics. It was also self-consciously transnational. Nationalism and transnationalism were intertwined in forming dreams of social change.[6]

There are many reasons not to trust nationalist visions. Nationalisms have worked hand in hand with racism and coercive state power. Meanwhile, transnational politics sponsors its own coercive disciplines, forcing its categories and priorities on to reluctant nationalists. It is not easy to create a radical politics between the two.

Yet in the 1980s and 1990s, Indonesian activists built something rather exciting under the banner of environmentalism.[7] This was a time of state repression. The environment was one of the few topics open for critical discussion. Environmentalism cleared the way for other movements in the 1990s, blossoming into human rights and labor concerns, as these became possible. In its time, it was one of the most significant players in building a democratic opposition to an autocratic regime. Drawing heavily from transnational sources of funding and legitimacy, the movement worked to create a counterculture to coercive state development. In resource-rich rural areas, development meant state expansion and the expropriation of land and natural resources. Environmentalism created an alternative, however fragile. Rural community leaders were offered a new set of urban interlocutors; campaigns for local and customary rights multiplied. Global and national disciplines notwithstanding, it is hard for me not to be thrilled at the liveliness and idealism of the environmental movement of this period.

What are the forms of attention that might allow us to track the excitement of this case? We cannot focus only on traveling disciplines; we must also attend to how movements mobilize. What are the sources of passion here?

Northern readers expect environmentalism to mean the protection of wilderness or endangered species. This is not a good place to start, although these goals have not gone missing in Indonesia. Instead, the movement has been most concerned with threats to human landscapes, such as pollution, destructive development, or the theft of forests from rural communities. Indonesian environmentalism is and has been heterogeneous. I am most interested here in the prominent strand of the movement that became marked with a radical social populism. Indonesian environmental populism contrasts sharply with the elitism of many northern conservationists, and it facilitates the types of rural alliances that have not been possible in the global north. This populist strand was shaped by the goal of building a national coalition against state repression during the period of New Order rule.[8]

To make global movement matter for the nation: This was the goal for many environmentalists in Indonesia in the 1980s and 1990s. Environmental damage was both global *and* national, just as development, while a transnational project, was channeled by the state. Similarly environmental protection: Even as activists were inspired by transnational activism, they wanted a *national* movement to protect the environment. Saving the nation and saving the environment became linked causes. Yet activism could not prosper independently of the state. Only by working inside and around state forms could activists imagine alternatives to state-sponsored environmental destruction.

The Indonesian environmental movement prospered in part because certain technocrats within the state bureaucracy supported it. The New Order had come to power on the promise of Indonesian modernity, with transnational law, science, and business standards in high regard. Indonesian representatives to the United Nations Conference on the Human Environment in Stockholm in 1972 came home with enthusiastic prescriptions for environmental reform. By 1978, the state had installed a Ministry of Population and Environment, and in 1982 the Basic Environmental Management Act established Indonesians' rights to a clean and healthy environment. Environmental Study Centers were established at state universities. The nongovernmental organizations that came into being in the 1980s owed their sense of promise and their freedom of maneuver to this state sponsorship, and particularly to a few prominent bureaucrats who nurtured and protected them, building their own constituencies in the process.[9]

Environmental activists came out of the universities into a world of expanded options for young urban professionals and managers. New Order wealth allowed this class to grow exponentially. The children of this new prosperity swelled NGO ranks, creating less bureaucratic forms of public service, even as some bureaucrats feared and controlled their independence.[10] And this ambivalence was reproduced among the rising group of environmental advocates. Some developed the technical and bureaucratic solutions possible within the government. Others made issues of social and environmental justice central to their ideals. Drawing on Indonesian legacies of populism, they advocated for grassroots causes. Their organizations formulated a development counterculture, with its own claims to national legitimacy. Their structured groups and policy plans closely shadowed the state, offering alternatives even as the state's national objectives were in many ways reproduced. Meanwhile, this counterculture flourished because during the same period transnational donor organizations began to channel their funds through nongovernmental organizations around the world. In the late 1980s, Indonesian environmental organizations found themselves rich with funding and support. Dozens of groups were formed across the political spectrum. As one activist explained to me, reading a roster of environmental groups in the late 1980s it was difficult to distinguish the radical critics from the president's cronies.

Many of the most important environmental advocacy groups of the 1980s and 1990s centered themselves in Jakarta, the national capital. From there, they coordinated causes and campaigns that reached across the nation. WALHI (Wahana Lingkungan Hidup Indonesia), the Indonesian Environmental Forum, achieved a particular importance as a national umbrella group.[11] WALHI coordinated a host of specialized member groups as well as regional fora representing each of Indonesia's provinces. WALHI included national groups working on specialized issues (e.g., forests, pesticides, climate change) as well as rural community activists and provincial nature lovers. National coordination made it possible for a variety of activists to bring their causes to a wide audience and to seek *national* solutions.[12]

What was radical about this nationalism? Under the New Order, mass protests were suppressed; electoral competition meant little. Radical politics emerged as utopian critique; its goal was to raise political expectations. It questioned the inevitability of state coercion and documented the excesses of state and corporate greed. Occasionally, it was possible to change a policy; most often the goals were a longer-term transformation of public consciousness. Activists were thrilled when, even in failure, their campaigns caused people to think.

Raising political expectations was made possible by finding a critical edge between transnational and national positions. Activists found transnational standards to criticize national policies; they articulated national priorities to refocus transnational initiatives. In this play of here and there, three kinds of tactics stand out. First, liberal initiatives could be used against liberal institutions: New Order pretensions of transnationally acceptable democratic standards were challenged by taking liberalism seriously. Second, discussion within the movement about the partial successes of their own campaigns sharpened awareness about the possibilities and limitations of political coalitions at home and abroad. Third, self-conscious practices of translation focused attention on the making of a national voice. Linguistic interfaces formed sites for debating alternative visions, domesticating the foreign, and synthesizing new forms of national pluralism. Each of these tactics incorporates transnational disciplinary standards into the very techniques of national liberation. At the same time, each enlarges the confining enclosures of these disciplines to make hope possible. My next sections illustrate the conundrums of each of these three tactics.

Using Liberalism Against Itself

A 1994 courtroom vigil concretized my respect for the energy of activists working jointly for environment and nation—as it also reminded me of the specificity of this agenda. Activists had won a small victory when a sympathetic Supreme Court judge ruled that a group of villagers whose land had been flooded by the Kedung Ombo dam deserved more compensation. It was expected that—as indeed happened—this ruling would soon be overturned.[13] But before this return to the status quo, activists could use the ruling to call upon the state to live up to its promises. Adding this duty into their overextended schedules, activists entered the courtroom every morning at 8 A.M. to remind the world that justice had not yet been done. They didn't expect to win; the vigil would only prick the conscience of the nation. The vigil urged everyone to ask, Is the legal system real?

The use of liberalism to disturb the assurance of what was supposed to be a liberal state was especially apparent in movement encounters with the legal system.[14] Many environmental organizations worked hard to build a national culture of law in Indonesia. By the late 1980s, Indonesia had a number of strongly worded environmental laws; however, these laws did very little to nurture a healthy environment as long as they were never enforced. Environmentalists wanted to vitalize the legal system, to make it useful and accountable to Indonesian citizens rather than a state showcase for international relations. They hoped to push the state to live up to its laws and to inform citizens that they should make these laws their own.

Law seemed a site of possibility for expanding national consciousness in part because it was an allowable arena of discussion. Law had a special position under the New Order.[15] From the start, lawyers were important supporters of the regime, and the regime supported law. The Old Order had toyed with "revolutionary law," a system that allowed judges to decide, without regard for precedent, in the interest of the people. Lawyers were outraged, and they turned with enthusiasm to the New Order's promises to uphold consistent legal standards. The New Order's encouragement of international business also opened opportunities for lawyers. In this privileged position, a few lawyers were able to form an early and persistent source of criticism of New Order policy. In the 1980s and 1990s, Lembaga Bantuan Hukum or Legal Aid Foundations, known as LBH, formed a site for discussion of issues of inequality and justice. Through joint campaigns and lawsuits, many environmental activists directed their activism to questions of law.

In 1986 and 1987, for example, laws were passed requiring environmental impact assessments and forming implementation guidelines. But environmental impact assessments are justifications for development unless public pressure is brought to bear on assessors to consider social and environmental problems. Environmentalists wanted to make it possible for ordinary citizens to participate in the process (WALHI 1993). WALHI organized "barefoot clinics" to train community people to make a difference in environmental assessment.

Besides training programs, there were lawsuits. Perhaps the most well known was WALHI's 1988 suit, pursued jointly with the national LBH, to hold the Indorayon Company (P. T. Inti Indorayon) responsible for the environmental damage the company inflicted on the Lake Toba region of Sumatra. The company was destroying the area's forests to supply raw materials for making rayon in a pulp mill. Local residents used these forests for grazing and forest products, and they protested against having their land stolen as well as against the eucalyptus plantations with which the company replaced the forests. Meanwhile, the factory was polluting the air and water. Environmentalists' challenge to Indorayon raised issues of environmental damage in a context in which activists could also talk about social justice—as well as crony capitalism, official corruption, and popular resistance. WALHI's suit argued that the company had not conducted a proper environmental impact assessment. WALHI lost, but the suit was a victory in establishing the right of NGOs to sue on behalf of the environment (WALHI and YLBHI 1993).[16]

Lawsuits were an arena in which victory meant raising national consciousness rather than winning in court. The most striking example of this is WALHI's 1994 joint lawsuit against then-president Suharto, for giving an interest-free loan from the national reforestation fund to his close crony (and successor), Habibie, to finance his aircraft factory (Indonesian Center for Environmental Law 1994). The reforestation fund was a tax established on commercial logging and intended to support tree planting and management. It was especially bold for activists to object at this moment, because the government was closing down political expression. National magazines had been closed—for reporting critically on Habibie. The president had distributed draft guidelines for NGOs that would require them to relinquish political commentary if they received money from abroad; no one was sure the NGO community could survive. The suit was impossible; the courts refused to hear it. But assembling the suit was an organizing action, and it powerfully intertwined issues of democracy and environmental well-being.

Stirring Up Debate

Not everyone in the movement liked the priority of legal strategies. In the campaign against the Kedung Ombo dam, mentioned earlier, many activists argued in hindsight that too close a dependence on the law delayed the initiation of other strategies of protest, closed the political imagination, and formed part of the movement's terrible reliance on technical and anti-democratic solutions. Debates about politics, such as that which followed the Kedung Ombo campaign, were an invigorating part of the environmental struggle, allowing participants to reexamine their premises, and thus expanding the range of critique.

Official New Order models of social harmony had a very limited tolerance for political debate. Censorship was expected, and the sporadic punishment of public critics kept everyone feeling cautious. The dampening of public political discussion limited alliances across social sectors, isolating each group in their own caution. The promise of the environmental movement was its ability to bring together urban and rural critics of coercive development by using the strength of the alliance between foreign and domestic environmentalism. Yet the question remained: Would these coalitions reinforce power differences or overcome them in a new solidarity?

The campaign against the Kedung Ombo dam concentrated both hopes and fears about environmentalist solidarity. A review of the events illustrates the paradoxes that formed the heart of national discussion.

Peasant mobilization was slow to begin, exclusively channeled into legalism at first, and only belatedly picked up by protesters. The Kedung Ombo dam project, financed by the World Bank, the Asian Development Bank, and Exim Bank of Japan, was designed in the 1970s to provide irrigation, control floods, and generate electrical power. Some 37 villages containing up to 30,000 people would be displaced by the dam's reservoir.[17] In 1986, villagers were called together by officials and ordered to join the government's transmigration program, which would resettle them outside Java.[18] Small amounts of monetary compensation were offered to landowners, but not enough to buy other land. Threats were made against them if they did not cooperate. Yet despite promises and threats, a core group of villagers was unwilling to leave. The

Kedung Ombo campaign revolved around the stubborn refusal of these villagers to move, even when the waters began rising in 1989.

The villagers' first and most important strategy was to try to exact fair compensation for their land. Fair compensation seemed a reasonable demand: First, LBH legal activists promoted this strategy and were willing to put their time into it.[19] Second, the demand for compensation was becoming a form of New Order "common sense," popularizing the regime's rhetoric of commoditization. The kinds of demands activists later raised—that the dam should not be built, or that the government should consult people before moving them—would have been difficult. Yet the legalism of the fair compensation battle had drawbacks even beyond its weak utopianism: competing sources of advocacy, a separation between landowners and landless, and what one commentator called a "wait-and-see attitude" that delayed other efforts (Rumansara 1998: 131).

The moment of common cause was full of misunderstanding. Foreign NGO activists organized a different kind of campaign. An international NGO consortium focusing on Indonesia formed in 1985 and took up the cause. Northern NGOs (e.g., the Environmental Defense Fund, the International Rivers Network) publicized the issue and offered their criticisms of the dam to the World Bank. Southern NGO networks were also important; activists worked through the Malaysia-based Asia-Pacific Peoples Environmental Network and were in contact with Indian activists mobilizing to stop India's Narmada Valley dams. This was the period in which opposition to big dams from many countries became coordinated as an international anti-dam movement. Indonesian activists played a role in this consolidation.

Meanwhile, students began to protest. The press took notice. As the flooding began, a Solidarity Group for the Victims of Kedung Ombo formed to raise issues of government corruption, due process, and human rights. A charismatic Catholic priest turned attention to the plight of the children whose homes were being flooded. Delegations of villagers and students complained to various sectors of the government. The campaign drew national attention and raised a lot of discussion. But as one activist group put it, "Comments, both from supporters and enemies of the people are not enough. Definitely, the people are waiting for solutions" (SKEPHI 1991: 29).

Relations among the different sectors of the campaign were never smooth. Their goals diverged: The villagers wanted fair compensation for the land. The students wanted a democratic and just government. Transnational NGOs wanted to stop the ecological destruction of big dams. These goals clashed even as they found a moment of convergence. Time was short, with few chances to forge mutual accommodations. Disagreements formed problems in the coordination of the campaign. Yet the creativity of the movement also flourished through these differences. The campaign did not rely on precedent; it had to form its own connections. That these were rough and makeshift speaks to their power as well as their limitations: They made a new kind of protest possible.

Ad hoc tactics are undemocratic. The previous assessment celebrates contingency in the coalescence of the movement, but it also invites substantive criticism. Activist and analyst George Aditjondro is the most damning. He concludes one discussion of the Kedong Ombo protests as follows: "Apart from its class bias, Indonesian anti-dam struggles have brought the extra-parliamentary, patron-mediated, *ad hoc* and Java-centric nature of Indonesian politics to the fore" (1998: 47). His review of the campaign stresses the role of dissatisfied army officers in supporting the alliance between students and farmers, allowing mass demonstrations and media coverage to continue even though they were prohibited by law. Political patrons—such as Environmental Minister Emil Salim—changed their positions as the regime's winds blew. When activists took their struggle to an international NGO conference, which forwarded a petition of complaints about the dam to the World Bank, President Suharto retaliated against the NGOs, causing a retreat to more conservative strategies. Meanwhile, the movement depended on experts, intellectuals, and the media. "[T]he history of anti-dam struggles in Indonesia is a history of reinforcing global expertocracy instead of strengthening institutions of participatory and direct democracy" (1998: 48). Aditjondro's sharp criticisms were among the most important in stirring debate and reassessment in the 1990s.[20]

The campaign's successes were largely symbolic. Despite the campaign, the dam was completed and brought into operation. Because of the campaign, resettlement options for displaced villagers widened. Some were offered land in nearby national forests. Others have been allowed to farm illegally in the greenbelt established to protect the dam.[21] Yet it would be difficult to claim that justice has been achieved for the poor.

Instead, the major impact of the campaign has been in changing the symbolic valence of dam building. Big dams are symbols of human mastery over nature; they are among the most high-profile international development packages. In the second half of the twentieth century, big dams became a standard of national sovereignty. Every nation wanted its own dams, and multilateral development banks wanted every nation to have them.[22] In Indonesia in the 1970s and 1980s, big dams were seen as monuments of national development.[23] Opposing them hit a nerve.

In the hands of protesters, big dams became a symbol of the enmeshment of imperial schemes and national elites, as each disregarded the poor, nature, and the well-being of future generations. Development banks pushed big dams on the nation. Domestic elites, from construction companies to urban power consumers, benefited from their packages. The campaign discredited this combination of foreign design and domestic aggrandizement. Scientists spoke against environmental degradation, democrats spoke of corruption and mismanagement, and villagers spoke of their refusal to be displaced. In this light, foreign and domestic elites appeared self-obsessed and irresponsible. The villagers who refused to be resettled, pictured huddled on rafts and hilltops in the rising water, were compelling icons from central Java, the heartland of Indonesian populism.

However meager its practical results, this symbolic work—on the critical edge between the national and the transnational—was crucial for contesting national hegemony.

Remaking the Nation in Translation

The global spread of liberalism depends on translation. The terms through which liberalism is to be enacted must be made accessible in new locales. Liberalism is perfectly reproduced only if its language finds universal equivalents. In fact, translation carries cultural genealogies from an original language even as it takes on new genealogies of thought and action from the new language. Concepts are transformed in translation.

The environmental movement of the 1980s and 1990s worked hard at translation. Globally influential texts were made available in Indonesian. Campaigns were publicized for the world in English as well as in Indonesian. Much work was also done translating *within* Indonesia, forming bridges across regional languages and across sectors of society.[24] Problems of how to forge dialogues between elite and poor, majority and minority, and urban and rural were pressing; the question of translation stood at the center.

The challenges of translation can be seen in considering the term "indigenous." The international campaign to save the Amazon rainforest had made the cause of indigenous rights an important tool on the agenda of global environmentalism. In the 1990s, the idea of indigenous rights was spreading. Many Indonesian activists felt that the vitality of this movement would help the cause of displaced and expropriated forest residents in Indonesia. Yet how could this term become a part of an *Indonesian* movement?

One translation of "indigenous" is *pribumi*. In most areas, this term did not help activists with their cause. First, this is the term used to exclude Indonesians of Chinese origins from full citizenship; the environmental movement was not willing to endorse this racism.[25] Second, Indonesia is not a settler society; the rural victims of resource extraction are mainly of the same stock as urban elites. Except in a few areas, racial categories are irrelevant, but cultural categories are not.[26] It is in this context that activists picked *masyarakat adat* as the translation for "indigenous people." Adat refers to "custom" and "customary law"; masyarakat adat is customary or "traditional" society. In making the influential International Labor Organization convention on indigenous people available in Indonesian, for example, the translators stress masyarakat adat.[27]

The term adat, however, brings its own genealogical baggage. Who has an adat society and who doesn't? The term can be interpreted as encompassing all Indonesians. It can be limited to those places where formal litigation based on customary law has been supported by colonial and postcolonial authorities. It can be dismissed as a relic, irrelevant even to isolated rural people. It can be used to refer to subjects of colonial treaties—sultanates, chiefdoms. Or it can refer to the subjects of activist campaigns: rural minorities who have suffered from corporate and state resource exploitation.

The reason for this enormous range is the colonial heritage of the term. Dutch colonial authorities used the term to distinguish native customs and laws. For the Dutch, all of native society was ruled by adat except where regulated by European law. The question of what to do with this colonial heritage has not been settled. Modernists want to shelve it as ancient history. Culturalists want to recover it for the nation. Their arguments have been written into a contradictory set of laws. The Basic Agrarian Law of 1960 states that Indonesian law is based on adat, giving the term an important symbolic place. Yet the law does not give adat a practical role. Other laws, such as the Forestry Law of 1975, have extinguished customary rights.[28] Still others (e.g., Law 10 of 1992) have reaffirmed them.[29] Environmental activists were drawn to the term because of this contradictory legal heritage. The term could remind the public that state and corporate seizures of resources were not the only way the law spoke of property: the dispossessed were represented in those legal texts too—through adat. The term offers more than the pastoralist pleasures of the concept of "tradition" in English. It has facilitated arguments that the state is violating its own rules in refusing to respect forest dwellers' rights.[30]

The rhetoric of rights for masyarakat adat engendered fierce debate among activists. Some derided it as *romantis*, "romantic," and claimed that all traditions today are bogus. Some saw it as a feudal heritage that should be replaced by modern law. Others found it the most useful conceptual tool in their advocacy for forest dwellers, allowing them to explain why New Order systems of resource exploitation were wrong. Some spoke for migrants, arguing against the privileging of aboriginal inhabitants. Others showed the loss to conservation and human rights that followed from uprooting indigenous livelihoods. Most important, through conferences, documents, legal cases, and training sessions, the term forged a growing network linking embattled rural people.

This network of adat advocacy was particularly effective for those marginalized rural people who had not been recognized as having any rights at all—through adat or otherwise. These newly recognized masyarakat adat could now imagine themselves as more than "isolated tribes," the untutored clods of state propaganda; their difference made them, if anything, better citizens.[31] For these new citizens of adat, tradition formed a critical lens through which to de-naturalize coercive development and demand social justice.

This critique, indeed, stretched into the immediate post–New Order period. In 1999, the indigenous advocacy network gelled in an archipelago-wide alliance, the Aliansi Masyarakat Adat Nusantara (AMAN). The choice of the term *nusantara*, "archipelago," to unite the assembled representatives of masyarakat adat was carefully planned. The nation, indigenous activists argued, had discredited itself by refusing to recognize their rights; they were unwilling to use the word *nasional*. Yet they wanted a nationwide gathering to contest state policies and plan alternatives in coalition. Nusantara was an elegant way to call up and criticize the nation simultaneously, a gesture at the heart of utopian critique.[32]

At the same time, the alliance was charged with the contradictions of its invocation through adat.[33] What relations should hold between those who claimed adat through colonial treaties versus those who had advocacy causes? Opposition to the state would not hold together populist politics much longer. Did these dispersed groups have anything else in common? Would they find a negotiating point with modernists, Muslim and secular, who refused adat-based politics? Post–New Order problems emerged: political disorientation, ethnic and religious conflict, and competition among alternative future visions. The endless horizon of the New Order no longer defined the political landscape.

The Change

In May 1998, President Suharto was forced to step down, handing the government to his associate Habibie and opening the way for general elections. The beginning of the end had come earlier, in the 1997 financial crisis and the subsequent ultimatums of the International Monetary Fund, which threatened not only to open up the crony system but also to withdraw popular subsidies for rice and oil. The New Order had lost its promises of wealth—and its international backing. Without these, domestic unrest soared. Students mobilized. Demonstrations and riots filled city streets. The New Order fell.

Politics opened up. Taxi drivers speculated about what they would do as president. Repressed ideologies emerged with force. Radical Islam spread. Bookstores filled with Marxist texts. Political posturing and debate spread to the countryside, so long in silence. Community groups mounted protests. Some took over logging and mining base camps and destroyed equipment. Meanwhile, the army and gangsters spread violence. Ethnic and religious conflicts flared up. In 2000, resource policy decentralization transferred resource struggles, bribes, and arrangements to the lowest levels of the state bureaucracy. Instead of advocating for community groups, national environmentalists found themselves in a position as mediators between destructive villagers and enraged companies. Activists in Jakarta struggled to keep up with the changing situation. Sometimes they tried to make policy; sometimes they formed an opposition. Long retreats became necessary to sort things out. In the countryside, however, activism gained a new bravery and initiative. Jakarta was no longer the center of movement possibilities. In the provinces, a new dynamic of utopianism superceded national critique.

Tracking Traveling Stories

After 1998, politics moved to the countryside. Decentralization was not just a financial plan; oppositional politics, no longer centered in Jakarta, devolved to ethnic, religious, and regional struggles. Regional causes found their own transnational resources. Now that activists could take the nation apart, their biggest problem was the very caution that shaped New Order activism. How could something stronger be stirred up?

Activist stories in the provinces grew braver and wilder. My own storytelling responds: Where I have shadowed national objectives in solidarity with movement efforts, I open up to something more freewheeling. My questions move out from the anchor of the nation; hit-and-miss opportunities of mobility and mobilization are suddenly more relevant. How does political agency grow in times of flux?

In the next sections, I show how activism moves in "charismatic packages," allegorical modules that speak to the possibilities of making a cause heard. These packages feature images, songs, morals, organizational plans, or stories. They introduce us to heroes and villains; they show us how an unrepresented group can become a political force. Like all socially effective allegories, activist packages are formed in a political and cultural location that gives their stories meaning and makes them work as social interventions. This location need not be a single place; it may be a widespread political culture, or the meeting point between two or more political cultures. When an activist package is brought to a new location, it must enter new fields of meaning and of social action to make a difference in its new home. The effect of a new allegory is most striking when it inspires unexpected social collaborations, which realign the social field. We might speak of "happy collaborations"—not joyful but felicitous; in coming together, they make a difference in what counts as politics.

This model of analysis is indebted to the everyday practices of activists in transnational NGO politics, who spend much of their time in workshops trading stories of success and failure. Yet it is a difficult practice for scholars, who are properly anxious about learning enough about far-flung sites to tell globetrotting right. One can appreciate this kind of activism, however, only by taking the risk of stretching beyond one's scholarly base. Sometimes the point for activists is to borrow allegories unmoored from their home contexts and not yet bent to the niceties of local negotiation; these are allegories that can be tapped for unpopular and minority causes. To see the potential as well as the limitations of such stories, one must consider how they draw people here and there to retell them.

Let me begin by taking you with me on a trip to the Meratus Mountains with three activists from the Lembaga Pemberdayaan Masyarakat Adat Borneo Selatan (LPMA), the Empowerment Institute for Indigenous People of South Borneo. The activists are mainly urban educated Muslims, from the Banjar regional majority, advocating for non-Muslim forest dwellers. This is a challenging assignment. It is the summer of 2000. The LPMA has rented a house in the provincial capital, Banjarmasin, where activists work and talk all day and sometimes through the night. There are media events to host, conferences to plan, reports and budgets to write, grants to pursue, position papers to hammer out—and, after hours, existential and political questions about what makes all this worthwhile. The most active members have graduated from college and not yet moved to other forms of employment, so they have time—plus impressive amounts of imagination, intensity, and stamina. When I arrive at the office early in the morning for our trip, I find that my traveling companions—two young women and one young man—have been up most of the night, but still they have more energy than I can imagine, and we bounce off into the day. The public van in which we will travel refuses to leave until every seat is taken, and we sit packed, motionless, and sweating for several hours before, at last, we can feel the wind off the road. At some point, tired of chatter with strangers, I pretend to be asleep, but my activist friends still patiently explain to all the other passengers why nice, middle-class, young Muslims like themselves might expose themselves to danger and horror among the impious savages of the Meratus jungles. It is especially hard for the women, who must maintain an air of respectability while admitting that they will be beyond supervision. We will be spending most of the week in rough surroundings with no privacy. Perhaps they are thinking of this too when they tease each other playfully about potential boyfriends and girlfriends; I gather that their friendship is platonic. Besides, they are experienced travelers; being an activist involves constant travel.

After half a day in the van, we transfer to motorcycle taxis to navigate the steep and muddy hillside tracks. As evening falls, we arrive in the Meratus village of Niwan. I haven't been there for several years, and I am pleased that people remember me, although my best friends have died or moved elsewhere. Yet I press away other invitations to stick with the activists, who have moved their things into the house of one of their village allies. They are worried: they have found themselves in a dilemma. Their task here is to convene a meeting about the map-making exercise that has become an important project of the LPMA. They have trained Meratus community groups to make maps of their village territories using Global Positioning System equipment. In these times of change, it seems at least possible that these maps might influence government policy to prevent corporate theft. Yet, not surprisingly, they have run into a problem with boundaries; adjacent villages claim overlapping territorial reaches. This meeting was to have clarified the boundary between Niwan and a neighboring village. I am not at all shocked when it turns out that none of the key leaders from either village have made themselves available for the meeting; they are all reported to be sick or away on a pressing errand.

Still, the LPMA activists make the best of their time. They hand out the colorful posters they have designed for the anti-Kodeco campaign. They catch up with local gossip. After dinner, we convene an informal meeting. Some of my friends have come; others are friends of the LPMA team. We talk about the bad prices of rubber, the major local cash crop. The villagers complain that they must take whatever price comes their way. The activists have a plan: If all the villagers hoard their rubber, they can negotiate for higher prices. Their audience is not convinced. How can individuals coordinate, when everyone wants the money immediately? We go back and forth, with the activists arguing that collective action will pay off, and their Meratus interlocutors remaining skeptical. It is then that one of my activist companions launches into a story.

"There was a man named Chico," she says, "and he brought together the rubber tappers to oppose the felling of the rainforest." She is speaking of Chico Mendes, the legendary leader of the Brazilian rubber tappers movement who was murdered in 1988. We had moved from rubber prices to community rights to the forest—and the logging controversy. But even here, we all knew that there was Meratus skepticism about the power of community-based political action. Her story of Chico Mendes was an inspirational one about the possibility of effective mobilization.

I jump in, eager to stress this point. "The amazing thing about Chico was that he was successful," I say, awkwardly attempting to translate the idea of "extractive reserves." Perhaps because I am so engaged in my point, what happened next makes my head spin. The woman telling the story drives the message home. "When they came to cut down the forest," she says, "the women came out and hugged the trees." She reaches her arms out, miming the hugging of trees, and the other woman activist joins her, showing people how the women hugged the trees.

I believe we have moved from Chico to Chipko, from the rubber tappers of the Amazon to the foothills of the Himalayas where women came out to protect the forest by hugging the trees, thus the name Chipko, hugging.[34] It is an easy enough slippage. Both are famous examples of grassroots organizing for forest protection. Both are models for environmental NGOs around the world. But I can't help but smile—and pause. How have these stories arrived there? Why are international stories important to these activists? It is then that I first consider the possibility of taking apart this story, in telling more stories that precede it and make it possible. This may at least offer a sense of why two young activist women might feel empowered not only to flaunt convention in their personal behavior but also to inspire others with a sense of political direction.

In the next sections, I follow the activist allegory of Chico Mendes, with an occasional nod to Chipko. Such stories travel because they tell of conditions of solidarity, because they follow established channels of mediation, and because they augment budding conversations about the possibilities of political agency. These elements remind us that political modules can only make politics through friction. Activists are drawn to these stories about local community and global solidarity, but they cannot just replicate them. To track traveling stories is to show their transformations.

I begin by tracing the Chico Mendes story as it moved from Brazil to North America to Malaysia, and from there to Indonesia. Indonesians rejected this package in the early 1990s, only to accept it at the end of the decade. To understand why it is necessary to consider how the allegorical module was formulated—and transformed—in the specific trajectory of its movements. A Brazil–North America collaboration formed its elements, but these were repackaged in Malaysia in ways that made the package anathema to Indonesians—until after 1998.

The Uses of Alliance

How do allegorical packages form models for solidarity?

Viewed from very far away, the most important thing about Chico Mendes's fight against Amazon deforestation was the fact that it was not just a grassroots struggle, but also something larger—something that came to be referred to as *global* environmentalism. International protest against Mendes's assassination in 1988 sparked an outpouring of concern about the rainforest that leapt from one place to another; in hindsight, it was the high point of global rainforest mobilization. But what did "global" mean here? Most impressively, it referred to the possibility of a movement that could involve poor rural Brazilians, Brazilian elites, and northern advocates in a common cause.[35]

This was no easy achievement. Earlier mobilizations to save the Amazon rainforest had received a cold welcome in Brazil. At the height of the success of Brazilian development, conservationists and indigenous rights advocates were seen as inspired by meddling foreigners.[36] The military government called them subversives. The opening of the Amazon was the road to national development (Keck 1995a).

Chico Mendes and the rubber tappers came to rainforest politics from a different direction. Mendes entered politics through the trade union movement. In 1979, he joined the Workers' Party, which united church groups, intellectuals, and workers to form a progressive opposition to military government. The early actions of the rubber tappers were union actions, organized in the idioms of Brazilian workers' politics (Keck 1995b). The rubber tappers only joined with conservationists and indigenous advocates in the mid-1980s.

It was this happy collaboration, however, that opened the door for a new local/global politics, both Brazilian and transnational, combining and conflating the poetics and demands of social justice, the environment, and indigenous cultural survival. A new way of imagining what is politically possible formed within the affiliation of social groups. Workers' politics made possible a national Brazilian involvement; suddenly the movement to save the Amazon could be portrayed as a national cause. Transnational support empowered Brazilian voices. Transnational support in this case was mainly North American; this was explicitly a north-south collaboration. Mendes was an important architect of this collaboration: His trips to the United States to seek environmentalist allies and to influence policy makers were key to making protection of the Amazon an issue imagined as "global." Meanwhile, his call for extractive reserves, that is forests protected for rubber, brazil nuts, and other economic products, articulated a meeting point for conservation and economic justice (Mendes 1989).

The happy collaboration did not last long; and it is still debated how much good it has done rubber tappers. However, the charisma of this activist package was enormous, and it inspired rainforest mobilizations elsewhere. It also dragged along its own deeply located culture and politics, which were key in spreading the idea that activism could be both global and grassroots. The concept of "forest people," not just indigenous but rural *workers*, de-exoticized the rainforest, making it possible to argue that social justice rather than elite privilege was at stake. The extractive reserves model made it possible to think that preservation and profit could go together, opening an era of experimentation for environmental entrepreneurship. Finally, negotiations between Brazilian and North American activists gave new weight to the *global* claims of conservationists. The southern connection gave northerners a claim of collaborative, rather than merely imperial, globality; this was a globality that worked, the allegory said, to empower the grass roots.

Northern environmentalists took the Chico Mendes story as a mandate for their intervention wherever rainforests were threatened. The allegory for them was the story of "global" nature lovers helping vulnerable forest people. They underplayed the role of national collaborations, such as the Brazil–United States ties made possible by Mendes's union politics. This problem was particularly striking in the next "global" rainforest campaign: the movement to save the forests of Sarawak, Malaysia, and to empower the Penan hunter-gatherers who lived there. The Malaysian campaign reformulated the Chico Mendes story, making a new traveling package that was unattractive for Indonesian environmentalists.[37]

Malaysia had a strong environmental movement by the 1980s. But this was economic miracle time in Southeast Asia. Economic strength gave the Mahathir regime the authority to keep all opposition very quiet. In 1987, opposition leaders were rounded up and imprisoned. Still, groups such as Sahabat Alam Malaysia, SAM, were lively participants in publicizing the need for forest and forest people's protection.[38]

In 1987, a group of Penan blockaded timber roads to protest logging, and this caught the attention of northern environmentalists.[39] A transnational campaign ensued: Following the model set in the Amazon, northerners imagined themselves as transnational support for a local cause. Yet everything went differently in Malaysia. The transnational campaign too often ignored SAM. The Penan were nostalgic for colonial rule and asked white environmentalists to protect them (Brosius 2003a). The key interlocutor was not a Malaysian national progressive but rather a Swiss artist named Bruno Manser, who had gone into the forests and made the Penan cause his own (Manser 1996). Manser was an articulate and passionate spokesperson, but he could not make the cause a Malaysian one. Instead, he was an illegal alien, a romantic European without ties to national elites. When he disappeared in 2001, probably murdered, no Malaysians raised a public cry.

Instead, the cry of vulnerability came from the Malaysian government. This is eco-imperialism, said Prime Minister Mahathir: the imposition of a northern cause on a southern people. They are trying to deny forest people the right to development; they want to keep them in a zoo (Brosius 1999b). Malaysian progressives, disgruntled by the tactics of northern environmentalists, joined Mahathir, making this repackaging particularly strong. With this rallying cry, Malaysia led pro-development southern regimes at the United Nations' 1992 environmental summit in Rio, as Brazil had in 1972 in Stockholm. The forests would be felled for national sovereignty and social justice. The Chico Mendes story, in translation, had changed. A new allegory was created, and it, too, was traveling.

In this context Indonesian national environmentalists of the 1990s wanted nothing to do with the Chico Mendes story and its allegorical implications. Indonesians had carefully built a national environmental movement under a repressive regime. They had worked with sympathetic bureaucrats and appealed to engineers as well as social idealists. This was not a period to get involved with irresponsible northerners. The allegory would not stimulate a national social intervention. No happy collaboration was in sight.

When one northern activist tried to mount a transnational campaign to protect a group of Indonesian Dayaks in the mid-1990s, echoing Chico Mendes as well as Bruno Manser, environmental leaders in Jakarta sprang into action to stop it. Indonesian activists agreed that local livelihoods were being destroyed. But they did not want a repetition of the Sarawak campaign, with its local/global allegories. They contacted their U.S. and European supporters to stop the campaign before it could develop. Instead, they worked domestically, negotiating across government bureaucracies to advocate for the group. The disasters of the Sarawak campaign ushered in a period of careful nationalism on the part of Indonesian activists. They were willing to accept northern funds, but it was important to keep policy and politics as a domestic matter.

Everything changed in 1998 when the Suharto regime fell. Political democracy seemed possible; chaos moved through the countryside. LPMA activists were in a hurry; everything might be changed if they worked quickly, before the time of change ended. What they needed was a disciplined grassroots activism that knew how to build alliances rather than burn down camps. For this the Chico Mendes story spoke eloquently, evoking the possibility of local/global alliances that empowered communities and made possible both conservation and justice.

Chico Mendes's story established several contradictory models of solidarity, from union politics to north-south collaboration to eco-imperialism. As the story moved from place to place, its allegorical possibilities grew. Its trajectory followed power-laden circuits and squeezed into conjunctural openings. My next section turns to these.

Mediating Circumstances

A distinctive feature of the travels of the Chico Mendes story was its travel through the north. It is the story northern environmentalists made of Mendes that became significant elsewhere. No Brazilian union leaders came to organize rubber tappers in Malaysia; northern environmentalists—with their package-spreading money, media, and passports—were almost entirely responsible for making the story speak to Southeast Asians. Some translators have privileged access to making and distributing packages.

Activist packages travel when they are unmoored from the contexts of culture and politics from which they emerged and reattached as allegories within the culture and politics of those with the institutional strength to spread the word. The Chico Mendes story was transformed as an allegorical package by and for northern audiences. Mendes himself was aware of the tension between his own activist goals and northern retellings. Yet the alliance was important to him, and he negotiated skillfully between disparate positions.[40] After his death, northern uses of his story were no longer under his control. And yet it was in shedding the localizing southern attachment of Mendes's negotiations that his story became most fit to travel as a northern allegory.

The Burning Season, a popular HBO movie (1995) that dramatizes Mendes's life, and in which Mendes is played by Silvia Braga, shows some possible translations for this packaging process. The movie is made for U.S. audiences; everyone speaks in English. The rubber tappers' stand-offs against tree-cutting ranchers look suspiciously like television images of U.S. civil rights marches, with marchers linking arms and singing hymns. Masculine heroism is buoyed up by feminine communalism. The film builds its dramatic climax through juxtaposing scenes of dangerous carousing ranchers, riding and shooting and handling prostitutes, with scenes of Mendes sitting quietly among women lighting candles in church, or giving Christmas presents to his wife and children. The masculine traditions of Brazilian union politics are hardly in evidence. Here we see a key element of the northern allegory: Environmental struggles tame destructive frontier masculinity with the courage of men who represent a softer feminine or androgynous community. This allegory was written into U.S. environmental politics at the turn of the last century for John Muir (see chapter 3), and it has remained with us. Male heroics and ecofeminist communalisms strengthen each other in this story, which appeals to North Americans even as it pulls away from Brazilian roots. The Chico/Chipko pun is foreshadowed in the making of a movement of which women and gentle men might be proud. LPMA activists took their reading of Chico Mendes's story from this very movie.[41]

If the Mendes package traveled in the north particularly because of this gender story, this is even more true of the Chipko tree-hugging movement, known internationally for the presence of women as well as men supportive of women's concerns. The Chipko movement began in the 1970s in the Garwhal region of the Himalayas when the Forestry Department refused local plans for forest product development and assigned the trees to an outside company. The people demonstrated, gathering at felling sites to protect the trees. If ever a social movement has undergone multiple cultural translations, it is Chipko. The charismatic packages proliferate as both activists and scholarly portrayers vie to show the movement as a women's movement, a Ghandian initiative, a peasant insurrection, or a pro-development protest.[42] The story of the movement has become unmoored from its original context to form traveling packages. Political ecologist Haripriya Rangan (2000) argues that this unmooring has occurred through alliances with urban elites in India, who imagine the Himalayas as a sacred place for timeless nature and indigenous knowledge. The Chipko myth caters to this image. Mythic portrayals of the movement from public intellectuals in India have gained international currency. Northern activists introduce further allegorical deviations, but, in contrast to the Mendes story, it is Indian portraits of Chipko—and not rehashed northern ones—that travel most prominently.

One of the most passionate Chipko storytellers is Vandana Shiva, an ecofeminist who has written prolifically about the crimes of globalization and corporate development. For Shiva, Chipko is a women's movement, a mobilization of women's indigenous knowledge and spiritual affinity with all growing things (Shiva 1992). It is an allegory of what will be lost if we follow the demands of economists, who ignore the work of women and of nature in reproducing the earth and human well-being. Shiva's allegory has been influential in stimulating one modest but significant stream of U.N.-funded NGO and community initiatives, referred to as "Women, Environment, and Development."[43] It is on this stream that the Chipko story came to Indonesia. Yet Indonesians would never have been interested if the story had not sparked something there.

Speaking of Gender

Freed from national coordination, regional, ethnic, and religious politics emerged in Indonesia with force at the turn of the century. In South Kalimantan, the question of the role of Islam in defining politics was paramount. In the last years before the end of the New Order, a commitment to Islam and to political criticism had become tightly intertwined in the region. Islam provided a vocabulary and moral framework for demanding personal integrity and social justice. Most regional activism in those last years—including environmentalism—was empowered by the cosmopolitanism of religion. After 1998, however, political models from the international Left also seemed enticing to regional youth. Students practiced the vocabulary of revolution and liberation, citing Che Guevara or the Indonesian struggle for independence. In these globally inflected discussions of new political possibilities, the issue of *gender* stood out because of its ability to speak not only to the proper behavior of men and women but also to the interplay of their transnational and local allegiances. The dialogue between Islamic and secular Left models of politics was conducted, quietly, through negotiating gender. Without explicit reference, gender filtered into the considerations through which environmental activists weighed political options. Traveling stories of political mobilization caught the attention of local activists in part because of their gender valences.

The story of the Chipko women hugging trees—and ecofeminism more generally—sparked local attention in this context. Chipko encouraged a cosmopolitan appreciation of indigenous knowledge. It supported the notion that women could have a plurality of bases for spirituality and struggle. It offered a platform for a new kind of activism in South Kalimantan, including a happy collaboration between Muslim advocates and non-Muslim Meratus Dayaks. I don't know how to judge whether modernist Islam or spiritual pluralism offers more for Muslim women. Instead, I point to the local debates in which these varied forms of transnational inputs become charismatic. Islamic modernists and indigenous advocates respectively grasp at traveling packages to make it possible for them to do something in Kalimantan that they might not otherwise be able to accomplish. The packages offer them tools and frameworks to be political actors.

In the mid-1990s, piety was the most influential discourse of reform in South Kalimantan. The demand to clean up government was moral: public responsibility begins with one's own conscience, and the best way to end corruption is through ethical revitalization. Political meetings in these times were often prayer meetings, and brave public discussion both in and out of the university inspired heightened personal piety on the part of activists. The consequences for women were complicated. The more they joined in politics, the more drawn in they became to discourses of religious piety that required displays of modesty. There is no reason that women cannot use such discourses to further their goals, but it was challenging to form links with secular Jakarta professionals and foreign NGOs and foundations from this position.

The rising tide of Islamic activism in the provincial capital of South Kalimantan in the 1990s was exemplified in changes in fashion for women activists. In the 1980s women only covered their hair in a Muslim fashion if they were attending religious school or if they were trying to make a fashion statement, for example, wearing a green *jilbab* scarf to match a green dress. But by the mid-1990s, women activists had adopted a more pious dress style. The women I met in study groups and NGO meetings were wearing full tentlike veils. As I understood it, only such a statement of extreme piety would offer one the right to speak. While male activists did not wear special clothes, their activism too was intertwined with religious goals, including the moral protection of women.

In 1998, the fashions and precedents of the New Order began to change very rapidly. In 1997, the bravest activist T-shirt I saw in South Kalimantan read, "I am not afraid of politics." In 2000, I saw "Revolution or Death" shirts. The women LPMA activists I met were wearing T-shirts and jeans. In the mountains, we slept and even bathed in the river at night in a mixed group. These were urban Muslims, no different in background than the veiled women I had met three years before. Instead of a single road to piety, they told me about indigenous knowledge and alternative spiritualities. They were pluralists, drawing on a mix of local and foreign cultural legacies, rather than crafting a singular morality. New possibilities had opened.

My female companions in the LPMA called attention to their own stakes as women activists by reference to the term *gender*. This was a new term, adopted from English, and they were excited about it. They wanted me to tell them more about *gender*. When I asked about this, they spoke of their ability to move and travel in public despite criticisms. They wanted to walk the forest trails despite fears and stories that this was dangerous; they wanted to carry their own packs despite anxieties about their strength. *Gender* referred to a political stance, a subject position in which women could operate with secular authority.

Gender, too, formed part of a traveling package. Packages travel when they are translated in such a way as to form a significant intervention in a local scene. They are used in local debates, within which they may introduce new objects and subjects of politics. They make it possible to act within the cultural-political scenarios they promote, and they mobilize people for particular kinds of political agency.

Activist packages are allegories of political subjectivity. Packages are created in a process of unmooring in which powerful carriers reformulate the stories they spread transnationally. Unmooring is easy to condemn, but it is not always a terrible thing. Traveling packages are translated to become interventions in new scenes where they gather local meanings and find their place as distinctive political interventions. Gender has proven especially plastic as the term has been variously adopted.[44] Yet its packages, too, carry travel histories, and particularly the histories of collaboration that engender activism. Their deployment adds new layers, revising these histories: thus the contradictory variety of international feminism. To move beyond imperial models of gender and feminism, it is important to appreciate how activists borrow traveling feminisms for their own uses.

Meanwhile, it is important to appreciate how those packages went traveling in the first place. Packaging of the sort I have been describing has its own heritage. Late-colonial civilizing projects are an important model, with influence not only on post-colonial development but also on the gamut of projects of democracy, good governance, and human rights that surround us today. These packages carry the inequalities of global geopolitics even as they promote rhetorics of equality. Those who adopt and adapt them do not escape the colonial heritage, even as they explore its possibilities. Thus, too, international feminism and global environmentalism stretch this heritage but also depend upon it. In each case, adherents are committed to the spread of abstract principles. In practice, the principles come to us in allegorical bundles, marked by the culture and politics of particular moments of alliance and intervention.

"Facilities and incentives"
[Freedom for the rich]

P. T. Harvest International ["Indonesia's leading business development firm"]: *So what facilities and incentives can foreign investors expect should they want to invest in South Kalimantan?*

Governor H. M. Sjachriel Darham: *We will facilitate permits and settle land disputes. The provincial government will be proactive in settling problems. The provincial government will also help the company promote itself with the local people.*

Harvest: *How is the security situation?*

Gov. Sjachriel: *Security is very good. South Kalimantan was not even affected by the ethnic conflicts that took place in Central Kalimantan, even though it's right next door. South Kalimantan has been able to maintain security and is considered the safest region in Indonesia, according to the central government.*

Harvest: *If, for instance, a foreign company were to experience problems, would you and your office be willing to help?*

Gov. Sjachriel: *We will be glad to assist. We admit that some investors in South Kalimantan have experienced problems with claims of land ownership by local people. We have recommended the President issue a Presidential Decree that, in the event of such claims, the people must submit their legal suits against the central government, the provincial government, or the district government and not against the company or investors concerned. We are still waiting for such a policy. It is not proper to sue the businessmen or investors in such case.* (*Garuda* 2002: 54–55)

The post–New Order period has been a bundle of contradictions. Political life has revived in cities and towns. Meanwhile, a new level of chaos and violence has torn up much of the countryside. U.S.-led global war has encouraged a return of military rule, while military crimes of all sorts are reported everywhere. The sad destruction of the forests by Suharto's cronies is discussed widely; at the same time, illegal resource extraction has blossomed beyond Suharto's dreams. Corruption is criticized even as it proliferates everywhere. International conservation groups gain clout in the environmental field as Indonesia becomes poorer and more dependent: and this just at the moment radical national environmentalists worked so hard to achieve.

It is in this context that enforcement has become the dominant trope in conservation for the international organizations. Enough about community empowerment, they say: Let's get the criminals. As one foreign consultant explained, "true reform demands law, order and governance in natural-resource management" (Ivereigh 2003: 29). But how shall we create order? From the international perspective, there is only one proven formula: the recognition of the exclusive rights of national and international elites to claim valuable things. We call these rights "property."

2003. My mother sends me The Nature Conservancy's latest magazine because it contains an article on saving wild orangutans in Kalimantan (Ivereigh 2003). Orangutans are good-looking primates with their red shaggy hair and mobile faces. Unfortunately for their future, they live in lowland tropical rainforests, eating fruits, insects, leaves, and other plant material. They reproduce slowly (a female raises at most four offspring), and they require large tracts of solitary space. As the forest is felled and fragmented, orangutans suffer and die. Survivors are shot or captured for the illegal pet trade, particularly by loggers. The conservationists who inform the article are not at all optimistic that any will survive in the wild.

Privileged Americans, raised with stuffed animals and fuzzy pets, like big mammals, and it makes good sense to tell the story of Kalimantan's forests to a U.S. audience through orangutans. These American preferences can be a conservation nightmare, as when people insist on the well-being of every animal even when that animal is destroying a multispecies habitat. But the synergies between wild orangutans and rainforests are only positive ones. It is impossible to protect wild orangutans without protecting forest. Orangutans don't even steal crops or attack people; they only want to be left alone. I am willing to risk sneers about "charismatic megafauna" to support the campaign for wild orangutans; to work for wild orangutans is to work for the forest. However, the implications for the indigenous people who have lived longest with the forest are more ambiguous. Forest-dwelling peoples ought to benefit from forest protection programs. However, it is also possible to imagine conservation programs for orangutans that further rip off and displace indigenous people—even while protecting a certain amount of their socially nurtured forest. It is up to organizations such as The Nature Conservancy to determine the course. Will conservation work for or against forest-dwelling communities? Who will be conservation's allies?

Among environmental organizations, The Nature Conservancy is best known for its deep commitments to capitalism and private property. Historically, the organization imagined its mission as buying up land to protect it from development. This strategy was expanded as the Conservancy was able to solicit the donation of private lands, which either themselves become conservation lands or allow the organization to buy more ecologically valuable patches. In the 1980s and 1990s, the organization grew exponentially, becoming the world's richest environmental group (Ottaway and Stephens 2003a). The Conservancy became known for its corporate partnerships, which range from soliciting funds to urging environmental standards in exchange for the organization's imprimatur. This issue of the magazine, for example, includes an article on how the Conservancy has benefited from the generosity of General Motors, including U.S.$23 million of grant money in the last ten years (Wilkonson 2003). Still, the heart of the Conservancy is the preservation of land through ownership.

This is a strategy that depends on unquestioning confidence in private property and the political economy (e.g., law; contracts; inheritance; police protection; "interest" in several senses; transnational convertibility) that makes property worthwhile. In the United States, where this political economy is rather pervasive, it is arguably a worthwhile strategy, tapping the environmental consciousness of the landed elite and holding back the tide of destructive development. Despite their disagreements with the Conservancy's corporate policies, many U.S. environmentalists express respect for the organization's land acquisition programs. Outside of the United States it is difficult to be so sanguine. To promote private property and corporate rights in tropical rainforests is not just advocacy for the prevailing system of inequality; it introduces a new and terrible inequality, as it supports the expropriation of land and resources from the forest's old inhabitants. If worked through properly, land rights could protect forest communities; but of all the many international organizations promoting private property in Kalimantan, none, to my knowledge, have addressed the justice of a system in which forest residents, by definition, have no property. While "benefits" may be channeled to "local communities," property is for elites.

In Kalimantan, it was the Suharto regime that claimed the forests for the state, and then divided them up for the benefit of crony capitalism. Post–New Order legalities depend on this economy of theft. Companies want their fair share of the free lands created by decree; this is freedom for the rich. Some social democrats imagine the flood of immigrants, with their legal and illegal schemes, as evening out the score. But this view ignores those who already live there. From the perspective of old forest residents, legal and illegal schemes are not so different. Funded and authorized from common sources, their products find their way into common commercial pools. Legal and illegal exploiters combine forces to wrest their profits from the forest and those who depend upon it.

Resource exploitation has indeed gotten out of control. But what should be done? The Nature Conservancy suggests that legally licensed corporations, the ones with national and international clout, are the answer. They argue that the forest can be best protected by working together with logging companies, who will patrol the forest because it is in their economic interest to exclude illegal loggers. In turn, they will offer these environmentally conscious companies the benefits of ecological certification. "Our task," says the Conservancy's Scott Stanley, "is to offer a packet of incentives so compelling that companies will actually implement certification" (Ivereigh 2003: 30).

Working together with wood retailers such as Home Depot, Lowe's, and IKEA, the Conservancy's certification program would give corporate loggers better prices. Stanley tells them, "We're here to help you improve markets. We're here to make things easier for you" (ibid.: 30). Certification could increase market prices for Indonesian wood, thus offering the companies better conditions. According to the article, a number of Indonesian companies are already interested in the program.

In contrast, the Conservancy feels that parks and nature reserves are unhelpful in the current situation. Stanley explains: "Ironically it would be counterproductive to push for a protected area. It takes years to get a park approved, and, as we've seen in other areas, timber companies generally use that time to log as intensively as possible. Besides that, Indonesia can't afford to protect the parks it has now" (ibid.: 25). The article goes on to explain that police and government officials are only interested in bribes. The author comments: "So wide is the web of corruption that those officials who do prosecute illegal loggers may find themselves ostracized or threatened. Few rise to meet the challenge, especially given Indonesia's conflicting laws and the generally dismal prospects for conviction" (ibid.: 26). It is interesting that the Conservancy, which, reasonably enough, criticizes government enforcers, continues to have such faith in the private enforcers of the corporate economy. What makes them think these private militias will be any different? It is a faith that can only be interpreted as a deep, ideological conviction: privatization is always better. Even after the slew of privatization scandals that have bankrupted public funds in the United States in the preceding few years, privatization wears a halo.

Certification can be a good thing. I am pleased to see the article mention the independent and nonprofit Forest Stewardship Council (FSC), which offers the most responsible certification program of which I know. The FSC requires that certification address land tenure and indigenous rights as well as forest sustainability. If there is going to be corporate logging—and I'm sure there is—it ought to have some framework of responsibility. Yet one independent assessment has concluded that, because of land expropriation, "certification to FSC standards in Indonesia is currently not possible" (Colchester et al. 2003: 270). Indonesian environmentalists and indigenous leaders have called for a moratorium on certification (Lawrence et al. 2003).

Yet Indonesian environmentalists and indigenous leaders are entirely missing from the article.[1] The article describes a landscape populated only by foreign experts, on the one hand, and Indonesian poachers and loggers, on the other. (One orangutan survey leader is Indonesian, but the article never lets us hear from him.) The result is that we imagine an imperially mandated nature, protected for the appreciation of international elites. Indigenous communities are given a symbolic nod: a one-sentence assurance that the Conservancy will "increase the benefits of local communities from legitimate timber concessions" (Ivereigh 2003: 30) and a touristic photograph. The latter is confusingly captioned: "Meanwhile, generations of Punan people (above) have lived in and relied on the forest; their culture depends on its survival—and perhaps its on theirs" (ibid.: 29). If the Punan are necessary to the forest, why aren't they consulted in the article? Why weren't they invited to the certification workshop, which included only industry leaders and conservation authorities? And where are Indonesian activists, democrats, community spokespeople, and environmental scientists? Are these omissions just aesthetic tactics to draw the U.S. audience of the magazine, or do they reflect the Conservancy's policy? One fears the latter. One fears that the Conservancy's deep faith in capitalism and private property has overridden their ability to assess the political situation. They have chosen allies, but not those who can tell them about the social world of the forest. They will have to rely on shooting poachers—with all the terrible consequences of that decision.

I go online to find out more about The Nature Conservancy's Indonesia projects. I know they have worked with communities in other areas of Indonesia, such as Lore Lindu National Park. There, researcher Tania Li (2000) found that the Conservancy fetishized one set of local villagers as traditional tribesmen, although they were no different than farmers throughout the region. Li charges that the Conservancy has ignored the larger context of social justice in Indonesia. Given the erasure of social process in the portrayals of nature I find, I understand this worry in a new way. The Conservancy's language of community participation is bland and almost insulting: "Through a systematic and user-friendly process that uses cards, poster boards and smiley faces rather than computers and complex data sheets, village members are asked to identify what they value most about the park" (Nature Conservancy 2001). Are conservationists sales representatives with no ability to participate in conversation? I find an online account of the orangutan project that offers a new bit of information: the researchers have trained "local villagers, including a number of indigenous and forest-dependent Punan Dayaks" to conduct the orangutan survey (Nature Conservancy 2002). Perhaps there is more to say about local participation that doesn't come through in these accounts. Why are the writers so coy?[2]

Then I find a rather different source. The issue of the magazine I am reading, with its gorgeous nature scenes, must have arrived in subscribers' mailboxes just as *The Washington Post* published a major expose of the Conservancy's bad practices (Ottaway and Stephens 2003a, 2003b, 2003c).[3] The reporters detail the influence of corporate moguls on the Conservancy's environmental policies, the effects of profit-making on species protection, and the practice of selling conservation land cheaply to Conservancy officials for their summer homes. The Conservancy, they tell us, has refused to take positions on issues such as global warming and drilling in Alaska's Arctic National Wildlife Refuge to avoid criticizing their corporate sponsors. In one case, the Conservancy sponsored oil drilling on conservation land donated to protect endangered birds; bird numbers dwindled. The series raises the question of whether capitalist accumulation and conservation objectives can work together harmoniously—in the United States as well as beyond. Even in the United States, acquisition is not politically neutral. It is a struggle for freedom—for the rich.[4]

7 The Forest of Collaborations
··········

Freedom
not yet
—Ikranegara[1]

Collaboration 1. *United labor, co-operation; esp. in literary, artistic, or scientific work.*
2. *Traitorous cooperation with the enemy.*[2]

Freedom is elusive. It is easy to condemn any dream in hindsight. Yet there is something to say for delving into those bumbling moments of passion and empowerment when so much seems possible.

Freedom comes in many guises. The freedom of middle-class students to roam in wild nature contrasts with the struggle of activists for communal empowerment. Each of these in turn is barely in dialogue with the practical lives of forest residents, which depend on their ability to stay out of the way of the schemes of the ruling class. Can any cause for common justice emerge across these differences?

To ask this question well, we must move beyond the common-sense assumption that solidarity means homogeneity. Differences invigorate social mobilizations. Differences engage political abstractions, making them applicable to local situations. At the same time, differences are organized by common assumptions about political process. It is impossible to participate in a movement without representing one's demands through its ruling discourses; no one unacquainted with the concept of freedom, for example, can make claims through it. Political mobilizations mount a generalized frame for what will count as politics, including the politics of difference. Difference is thus both a pre-established frame for connection and an unexpected medium in which connection must find local purchase.

All this means that social mobilizations are facilitated by their appeal to diverse social groups, who find divergent means and meanings in the cause. Social mobilizations are also held up and redirected by their inclusion of varied groups, who disagree about what are supposed to be common causes and objects of concern. In this process, universalist causes are locally reconfigured, even as they are held by a wider-reaching charisma.

One of the best places to look for this kind of friction is in the formation of collaborative objects, which draw groups into common projects at the same time as they allow them to maintain separate agendas. This chapter considers the formation of the community-managed forest as an object of advocacy. My narrative follows how a community-managed forest emerged in one time and place through the collaborative energies of village leaders in the Meratus Mountains of South Kalimantan, nature lovers from the provincial capital of Banjarmasin, and New Order-era national activists from the Indonesian capital, Jakarta. Meratus villagers, nature lovers, and activists are, of course, the three groups I have described in some detail in the preceding three chapters. As I have shown, each group has a rather different kind of commitment to nature. In this chapter, I mix up their separate stories to show what happened when these three separate commitments came together in a short—but productive—campaign. Quite against precedent, they succeeded, at least for a while, in establishing a landscape removed from corporate destruction because it could be considered a community-managed forest.

Yet this common object, the forest, did not just hold them together; it also kept them apart. For a historian of these events, one of the most striking things about the campaign is the fact that the varied, and equally satisfied, protagonists never came to any agreement about what happened. The coupling of obviously divergent perspectives and campaign success gives us pause. Activists are used to linking disagreement and failure; if participants disagree, we think the campaign must have been a mistake. In this campaign, undifferentiated unity was not a prerequisite for success.

Difference within common cause: Perhaps this is more important than we ordinarily think. In this chapter I propose this kind of overlapping, linking difference as a model of the most culturally productive kinds of collaboration. This is not the most common connotation of collaboration; this is collaboration with a difference: collaboration with friction at its heart. Usually, scholars think of collaborators as like-minded colleagues who each contribute to a commonly conceived product. They are trained to be just alike before they begin to work together, so their collaboration is in itself culturally uneventful. Of course, there is another meaning of collaboration that opens the term in a different direction: Collaborators work with the enemy in wartime. These collaborators are not positioned in equality or sameness, and their collaboration does not produce a communal good. This is a place to start in opening up other meanings of working together. Parties who work together may or may not be similar and may or may not have common understandings of the problem and the product. The more different they are, the more they must reach for barely overlapping understandings of the situation. Their common cause is also a cultural encounter, and the objects on which they appear to agree are most successful when they appeal simultaneously to divergent cultural legacies. Furthermore, collaborators may or may not have any understanding of each other's agendas. Such collaborations bring misunderstandings into the core of alliance. In the process, they make wide-ranging links possible: they are the stuff of global ties. They are also the stuff of emergent politics: they make new objects and agents possible.[3]

Community-based conservation—which depends upon such objects as community-managed forests—has become one of the most exciting agendas in environmentalist circles: to conservationists, it is the hope for on-the-ground environmental protection; to developers and social justice advocates, it returns environmentalist energies to people. At the same time, there is much to criticize in these projects, particularly in their peculiar reifications of forests, communities, and conservation. Before we follow either advocates or critics into naturalizing the object of their debates, it seems useful to ask how this object has, in various times and places, come into being. In at least one time and place, the collaborative process joined very different perspectives on people and forests; it succeeded in part because no one stopped to realize the depth of their disagreements. Collaboration was not consensus making but rather an opening for productive confusion. Productive confusion is sometimes the most creative and successful form of the collaborative production of natural and social objects—whatever their political status.

Let me turn to the events.

What Happened in Manggur

The small village of Manggur is located in the western foothills of the Meratus Mountains. The Meratus Dayak inhabitants are shifting cultivators and forest foragers. They are a small cultural minority in both the South Kalimantan region and the nation; most Indonesians, environmentalists or otherwise, have never heard of them. Yet in 1986 Manggur people played an important role in an environmentalist drama.

In December 1986, a meeting of environmentalists was held in Banjarmasin. The meeting was sponsored by the Indonesian network for forests, SKEPHI, an issue-oriented network affiliated with the environmentalist umbrella group WALHI. Both SKEPHI and WALHI imagined themselves at that time as national coalitions of regional grassroots groups; this meeting—SKEPHI's first national meeting in the provinces—was a demonstration of and an "exercise" in that conception. A provincial nature lovers' group, Kompas Borneo, hosted the meeting, which involved activists and journalists from around the nation and abroad. Kompas Borneo further demonstrated their grassroots commitment by bringing a local environmental issue to the meeting: the conflict between the inhabitants of the village of Manggur and a timber company cutting trees on the village's traditional lands. Kompas Borneo brought a group of Manggur men to the meeting to speak, and some seventy-five meeting participants followed these men back to stay in Manggur for several days. SKEPHI and WALHI members also met with employees of the timber company, the Fast Forest Development Company; they spoke, too, with regional officials. As a result of the publicity surrounding these activities, the regional government decided not to renew rights to work the timber concession in that area. The forests returned to Meratus Dayak management. Furthermore, the newly won acclaim of the provincial group, Kompas Borneo, allowed them to garner a Ford Foundation grant to support research in the village; meanwhile, the Jakarta groups SKEPHI and WALHI moved into their strongest periods of forest and forest people's advocacy.

This was an environmentalist success. Not only was corporate deforestation halted, at least temporarily, but the process was the one radical Indonesian environmentalists most desired: A village movement enlisted the help of provincial and national activists to win rights to community forest management. Yet the closer one looks, the more confusing the story becomes.

While I was in the Meratus Mountains in 1986, I was not researching this issue, and I did not attend these meetings. It was only in 1994 that I decided to find out what happened in Manggur. I went to Manggur and spoke to various community leaders and residents. In the provincial capital, Banjarmasin, I spoke to members of Kompas Borneo who had been active in both the original exercise and the ensuing research project. I also spoke to SKEPHI and WALHI members in Jakarta who had participated in the exercise.

Everyone had a different story. The stories differed in both fact and interpretation. Who were the actors? What happened? My common-sense expectation that the versions would eventually aggregate into a neat composite tripped up against variations in how the space, time, motivation, and process of events were told. I became fascinated by the success of an alliance based on rather complete incomprehensions of collaborators' points of view.

Had I participated in the events myself, I might have such a clear opinion of what happened that I would only assess the stories I heard in relation to my version of the facts. I might have a good story to tell, but it would be a different story. Here I use the advantage of my absence: All versions seem plausible to me. For my purposes here, I have no need to worry through the question of the "real truth" of what happened in Manggur. Instead, I focus on the enigma of incompatible versions. How can it be that close collaborators have such different stories? This question brings us into the frictions of collaboration.

The stories I heard in Manggur, Banjarmasin, and Jakarta are not just varied spins on the same facts; they offer different facts. How did these accounts enter the same universe of conversation? Another story produced them as interlocutors. This is the discursive field that calls these events a grassroots environmental alliance. This discourse offered the speakers a framework for political process; it brought them into conversation and established the basis for both agreement and misunderstanding. The next part of this chapter examines the "grassroots alliance" narrative in Indonesian environmentalism to look at how it produces divergent social locations and sets them in hierarchy. Only then can I return to the divergent perspectives of each group, which go farther than what might be predictable from this hierarchy. As I have established in the previous chapters, village elder, nature lover, and national activist perspectives are produced within different and somewhat autonomously formed understandings of nature. The stories I heard in Manggur, Banjarmasin, and Jakarta spoke differently of the nature of the Meratus forest and of the role of humans in shaping its history. By reviewing these divergent perspectives through their narratives of this event, I suggest how the community-managed forest emerged in their awkward coalescence. The collaborations also produced a new kind of provincial citizen, the "environmentalist," a nonprofessional expert who is neither quite scientist nor quite politician. The nature we know is produced in such power-laden but unpredictable collaborations.

The Grassroots Alliance and the Production of the Village

The social subjects of environmentalism are as collaboratively formed as the natural objects. Consider the contrast between agendas that posit humans in nature as indigenous tribes, or as aggregate masses, or as alert villages. The tribes are the ones who are part of nature, wild and innocent as other fauna. And while this is the easiest environmentalism to make fun of, the much more powerful and dangerous mainstream agenda portrays humans as amassed atoms whose sheer density and undifferentiated drive to consumption destroys everything around them. This is the environmentalism that would limit reproduction and cordon off pure nature reserves, or in its equally scary developmentalist versions, empower southern elites in a fantasy of raising everyone's standard of sustainable living. It is in contrast to these agendas that environmentalists interested in democratic process have imagined the grassroots alliance as a structure that links policy-savvy activists and the rural or urban communities that know the most about their own environmental problems. In this frame, the village is the locus of rural environmental management. When villagers raise their voices about local environmental problems, their environmentalist allies can turn these problems into policy debates and transformations.

In Indonesia, this international environmentalist narrative assumed its particular form in dialogue with the discourse of state authority. During the New Order, Indonesian environmentalists reproduced state hierarchies in the very process of building a populist alternative. The hierarchy meant that Manggur leaders, for example, knew that they could only speak as village spokesmen. Hierarchy was not exterior to their stories, as the image of powerless people speaking back might suggest; power made possible their speaking, even if it did not determine their stories' content.

During the New Order, the hierarchy that structured the differences among village, province, and capital in Indonesia was inscribed so deeply in the architecture of state-connected organizations that it was hard to remember it as a social fact. It appeared as a natural feature of daily life. Yet it was also an imaginative construction, and this is the angle from which we must view it to see its reproduction in the environmental movement.

A "village" in this discourse is the unit of rural community. Questions of community formation and history do not need to be asked; they are taken for granted. Obviously, one assumes, rural people cohere into villages. By definition, village leaders always speak for the people. Or so it seemed during the New Order.[4] As soon as the regime fell in 1998, rural leaders all over the country demanded to be counted in units other than villages. In 1986, such defiance seemed unthinkable.

In contrast to the village, the capital was imagined as the site of policy making. National political action "of course" takes place in the capital. (To avoid the homogenizing term "national," I will use the term "capital" to refer to perspectives from the national capital.) The capital, in this logic, needs no community identity because it is the place where action is planned *for* communities, that is, other places. During the New Order, no options were apparent. Yet its artificial status emerged clearly once the New Order fell; one of the first projects for transition was the dismantling of this hierarchy through decentralization.

Finally, the provincial capital was designed as the site where the planning from the national capital is put into practice. (To differentiate these, I will use "provincial" alone to refer to the provincial capital.) Awkwardly, it was to be both agent and regional adviser of the capital; its institutional distinctiveness rested on this awkwardness. Post–New Order political thinkers are confused, indeed, about what to do with the province: Should it be a unit of regional autonomy or of national centralization, or should it be quietly dismantled?

Movements for political reform were very much limited during the New Order. Only those political parties organized by the state were approved, and even they were allowed to speak only just before elections. Workers' movements, religious movements, and regional rights movements were actively repressed. Environmentalism squeaked by at the edge of legitimacy in part because movement leaders were willing to maintain a respectful dialogue with the state. In this context, it is not surprising that environmentalism reproduced certain categories of New Order political culture—even as they challenged state policies.

The necessity of presenting itself as nonpolitical shaped the politics of the emerging environmental movement as it coalesced in Jakarta in the 1980s. The nature imagined by WALHI has always been populated, defined, and managed by people. Yet it was never possible to cast environmentalism as a form of political mobilization. Environmentalists might protect the forms of nature and natural management that already exist; but they ought not be creating political desires. The Indonesian Communist Party had mobilized across the country in the 1960s, and they had gotten killed for it. Environmentalists could see themselves as advocates for rights and management practices that already existed; but they needed to obscure any consciousness raising that their own efforts created. In this context, an already popular theme of much urban intellectual culture blossomed: the division between the wealth and alienation of urban elites, on the one hand, and the poverty, communal sociality, and wisdom of rural villagers, on the other. Jakarta environmentalists working on rural issues began to see their role as the protection of already existing rural wisdom.

This agenda was in many ways a critique of the government's development program. New Order development treated villages as units of collective ignorance to be brought up to development's progress-oriented standards. In contrast, the capital's environmentalists argued that village people have better schemes of resource management than the government. New Order development used provincial offices to execute national orders; in contrast, the capital's environmentalists invited provincial groups to raise issues. But in the classic fashion of a counter-discourse, the government's administrative hierarchy was reproduced in these reversals. Villages remained the natural units of rural community. The capital remained the site of policy decisions. The provinces remained the site of regional mediation between policies and people. Indeed, the naturalization of this division of roles has been a major subject of progressive self-examination in the post–New Order era.

During the New Order, however, the three-tiered hierarchy became institutionalized in WALHI precisely as a piece of its most populist anti-state stance. WALHI is an umbrella group, the focus point of a network, and not a monolithic management agency. Key to its functioning has been the Regional Forum in each province; provincial groups are to raise the issues that inform WALHI's central organizers. The Regional Forum should have contacts in the villages, which thus are the ultimate site of agenda setting. You can see the appeal of this democratic process for the provinces and villages: The provinces are to raise issues, not just carry out policy; village leaders are to speak for the people, not just obey orders. Working together, then, spokespeople from these different levels, with a new sense of empowerment, reproduced a hierarchy that defined their structural distinctions, forming both limitations and creative possibilities.

The activists I spoke to in Manggur, Banjarmasin, and Jakarta spoke from their roles as village leaders, provincial advocates, and capital organizers, respectively: Village leaders spoke of community rights; provincial advocates spoke of raising issues; capital organizers spoke of building policy. These roles, however, did not determine their definitions of environmental problems and of the forms of political agency that could address them. In the next sections, I propose that activists in these different locations told different stories because they had developed contrasting histories of the Manggur forest. These histories did not complement each other within the national hierarchy I have described; instead they challenged each other, and thus formed the grounds for unexpected overlaps and dialogues.

Forest History 1: Recording at the Edge of the Wild

I begin with the province, since it was here that, as was appropriate in the political hierarchy, the issue of Manggur was raised for a wider audience. Kompas Borneo was formed in the late 1970s by students at the provincial university. The group organized adventures in nature, particularly hikes in the forests of the Meratus Mountains. A first-person account can offer the flavor of Kompas Borneo's growing involvement with Meratus Dayaks in the 1980s:[5]

> Sometime in the 1970s a helicopter of the Conoco oil company crashed into a Meratus mountainside. We heard about it in an article in *Tempo* about savage murders. [Until state censors shut it down in 1994, *Tempo* was the

country's leading news magazine.] The article said that the local Dayaks cut the body of the American pilot in half. We decided to go look for the remnants of the helicopter. It took us several trips; at first, the Dayaks were suspicious of us and sent us in the wrong direction. Finally, after several expeditions, they got to know us, and a Dayak man accepted us as adopted children. They took us to the place where some rusted scraps still remain.

We began to go back to these villages as our hiking destinations, and we became interested in their social and cultural life. One of the villages was Manggur. There, we heard about their problems with Fast Forest Development Company, which had begun timbering operations in the area. The timber concession went right across village land. Besides, it was located in an area that had been zoned as a watershed-protection forest since the colonial era. We were looking for an issue then, and so we decided to raise the issue of Manggur. When the WALHI summit meeting was held in Banjarmasin, we brought down several Manggur leaders so they could explain the problem directly to the meeting. We then took the participants on a field trip to Manggur for three days. Journalists were there from all over the ASEAN region. The regent in that sector was afraid that he had a "Bruno Manser problem" on his hands, and so he refused to sign the papers renewing the timber company's right to work there.

Bruno Manser was the Swiss nature lover who made an international cause of the destruction of the forests inhabited by the Penan of Sarawak, East Malaysia. Like Manser, Kompas Borneo members saw themselves as different kinds of people than the indigenous Borneans they pledged to protect. They were able to speak for Dayaks because, unlike Dayaks, they themselves were not isolated primitives who chopped up alien helicopter pilots, but, instead, cosmopolitan citizens. It is in this framework that rainforest adventures can become social causes. Civilized people who reach out to touch the wild can speak for it at the edge of its destruction. As history comes in to threaten traditional communities and the forests they husband, environmentalists speak as critical witnesses.

The ability to speak both about and for Dayaks and their forests defined what it came to mean to be an "environmentalist" in Banjarmasin. The members of Kompas Borneo began as nature lovers but became more and more interested in environmental advocacy causes. Still, they were not, for the most part, professional activists or ecologists. When the group wrote their successful grant proposal for continuing research in Manggur (LSPMKB 1987), they identified themselves mainly through the English term "environmentalist," despite the fact that most had other jobs—as law professors, journalists, or the like. Through their role in raising the issue of

Manggur, they became experts, not by disciplinary training but by their unique positioning. They became environmentalists as advocates for nature and the people who live in it; they could stand at the edge of the wild to record and preserve it. They spoke for the people and their forests—but they were not fully of them.

How was this positioning accomplished? I'm interested here in the ways in which stories engage with and create the materiality of the world. The most developed version of Kompas Borneo's environmentalism is found in the series of documents they wrote about Manggur for the Ford Foundation, the provincial government, and the newspaper, between 1987 and 1991.[6] The most surprising thing about these documents to me was the fact that the role of Manggur people as agents in a struggle against the Fast Forest Development Company completely disappeared. Manggur became a traditional community about to enter history for the first time.

In the 1987 grant proposal, for example, Manggur is presented as a typical Dayak community poised uncertainly at the edge of modernity (LSPMKB 1987). On one side, the Fast Forest Development Company threatens to bring too much development too fast. On the other side, a proposed nature reserve requires standards of conservation that are incompatible with human habitation. This is modernity, with its segregation of culture and nature. The traditional Meratus of Manggur are caught in the middle, still outside of history, but vulnerable and confused.

The proposal waffles about the relationship between Manggur and the forest. It praises Manggur's traditional forest management for maintaining the forest. Yet it argues that local livelihood practices will destroy the natural surroundings if development assistance is not forthcoming. Tradition saves nature; tradition destroys nature: The proposal tells it both ways, combining rhetorics of development, conservation, and cultural survival. In one telling fragment, the group suggests that they build model houses for Manggur villagers to help them develop. Later, they say that the houses will be built in the local style. This cannot but raise the question: What is wrong with the houses they already have?

Manggur is presented *both* as a community living in harmony with nature, whose traditions should be recorded and preserved, *and* as a community that must be improved in order to use and conserve nature more appropriately. The role of the expert is double: to record, advocate, and revere, on the one hand, and to guide, manage, and modify, on the other. This was a challenging agenda in the authoritarian development climate of the provinces. I do not mean to slight the enormous courage and intelligence of its advocates by focusing on its contradictions. Yet these contradictions are important in examining cultural gaps and linkages. I suggest that these contradictions have been held in place, with difficulty, precisely by the moment of alliance. It is only through Kompas Borneo's collaboration with SKEPHI and WALHI, on the one hand, and with Manggur leaders, on the other, that they were able to maintain for themselves the tension of their joint role as advocate-guides and researcher-developers, that is, provincial environmentalists. In the next sections I show that the way these collaborations work to stabilize this position of expertise reverses our expectations. It is the collaboration with capital organizers that stabilizes provincial expectations of the community that should be preserved—the wise community that lives with and manages nature. The collaboration with village leaders stabilizes involvement with the government's policy hierarchy, with its rhetoric of development, which can give community advocates the strength to survive.

Forest History 2: Managing the People's Gardens

I turn briefly to the view from the capital. Briefly, because no one in Jakarta cared much about what happened in Manggur. The event was an exercise, a textbook problem that helped to establish a paradigm. Its details were unimportant in themselves. The organizer mainly remembered the problems of running a conference: making sure the arrangements are in place, worrying about the food preparation. She remembered that Manggur was a beautiful place, and that the village people were friendly. She remembered arranging meetings with the timber company management and with the regency and provincial government; she advocated a chain of negotiations, rather than any single confrontation, as the most effective strategy. Like other Jakarta participants, she had not followed up on the case and was unaware that the timber company had been turned away from that sector of its concession. Successes such as that are rare, she added, asking me to write up a version of the events to remind WALHI activists that grassroots advocacy can work (Tsing 1995).

The details of what happened in Manggur were less important in the capital than the model of forest history that Manggur helped to build for both WALHI and SKEPHI. In this model, forests are not wild places—as they were for Kompas Borneo; they are populated and managed, not by wild, primitive people but by familiar social communities. The history of forests involves not the modernization of the wild, but the struggle between resource-greedy institutions, such as the colonial and national state and the logging companies they authorize, and local communities of forest-dwelling peoples. Forest-dwelling peoples manage their environments through customary rules and practices. Deforestation is caused not, as the developers claim, by village ignorance and consumption but rather by commercial logging ventures and authoritarian resource control, which wrest the landscape away from village management. Environmentalism is populist advocacy because it is the support network for the grassroots struggle of communities for their long-established land and resource rights.

I myself like this populist narrative, which has numerous advantages over more powerful alternative forest histories. It may be the best tool we have to convince governments and international agencies that there are alternatives to handing the forests to logging companies. In describing it as a narrative, I do not mean to be unsympathetic to its claims, but rather to point to their specificity. In particular, it is important to notice that this is not a history told, like that of Kompas Borneo, at the edge of the wild.

How is it, then, that WALHI and SKEPHI were able to work with Kompas Borneo, despite their divergent understandings of the agency of the forest and its people? What they shared was the idea that Manggur was a community—a traditional, coherent, well-organized consensus of people who lived relatively stably with the forest. The kinds of community they imagined were different: The capital's village was a management unit, long engaged in histories of struggle against greedy outsiders; the province's village was a cultural unit, as yet unaware of the alienating but civilizing effects of history and struggle. In other words, in the province, history had only just begun for Manggur; the capital supported one moment in a continuous social history. Moreover, the capital's village community was united by rational resource planning; the province's village community was united by traditional ritual. But these two notions of community had enough in common to form the basis of an alliance—an alliance to let the villagers of a place such as Manggur speak. Both provincial and capital activists worked to protect the Manggur community and the forest that was central, in both views, to defining community. The Manggur drama depended on this overlap of understandings. And the subsequent strength of environmentalism in both the province and the capital drew from it.

Forest History 3: Trees Are Social Networks

Ironically, the coherence of community has been no simple matter in Manggur. Since 1982, Manggur has been the name of a village, that is, a government administrative unit, as well as the politically central settlement location in this unit. Before this reorganization, this location was part of a much wider "village" area, and not its politically central settlement. Both before and after reorganization, the groups and settlements of the area have moved around and regrouped. Here, most families maintain a residence in a jointly constructed and maintained hall, the *balai*; they also have another house on their swidden field. Balai halls are rebuilt every few years, and particularly at that point families split off with other groups, come into the group, or move the balai to another location. New swidden fields are made every year, and their shifting locations influence and are influenced by a family's changing direction of social ties. When I visited the area in 1980, many of the 1994 residents of Manggur were living in a balai site called Purun, which by 1994 no longer existed as a settlement site or a social group. In this context, in which there is little to stop individuals and families from continually reshuffling their social ties and geographical locations, pulling together a "community"—and keeping it together—is an ongoing challenge.

The landscape plays a major role in community building—as well as community dispersing—in the Meratus Mountains. As I discussed in chapter 5, groves of fruit trees, some carefully planted and some sprouting from discarded seeds, develop around settlement sites; even when people move away, these groves remain as markers of a community that may re-form in the future on the basis of its ongoing, tree-made memories. Most people maintain allegiances not only to the groves and neighbors of their current locations but also to older groves and past neighbors, with whom they may live again. Similarly, the vegetation that grows up as a rice swidden returns to forest makes this secondary forest not just a site of memory but also of ongoing use for those who tended the spot. Some of this vegetation is planted, some encouraged, some cleaned and managed, some mainly ignored. It draws its human associates back again and again into the social community of those who have farmed or tended or foraged contiguous and overlapping locations. Furthermore, many individual trees in the forest, including fruit trees, starch palms, rattans, and the forest emergents on which honey bees build their nests, are claimed. Claimed trees pass to the descendents of claimants; they draw siblings and cousins through their common claims. Collective harvests of fruits, honey, and starch, in contrast, gather friends and neighbors who may or may not be kin, and who come to the base of the tree following the tree claimants who announce the harvest. These trees, and the charismatic individuals who draw harvesters to their bases, become social as well as geographic focal points in group formation. The history of the Meratus forest is a history of social networking. The forested landscape is not just managed by social networks or a model for them; it is simultaneously the shaper of social networks and the material through which they are shaped.

Meratus social networks do not stop at the edge of the forest. Community leaders forge real and imagined ties with the officials, police, and merchants of surrounding Banjar towns; from the Meratus perspective, these regional authorities grant Meratus leaders the power to lead. Meratus leaders have long learned to submit to and to mimic the rhetoric of regional and state authority as a condition of autonomy—and of convincing local constituencies that they are powerful enough to lead. Their leadership strategies draw boundaries, paths, and shifting centers into the history of the forest. Leaders tell the boundaries of state-recognized, once-recognized, or hoping-to-be-recognized village and neighborhood communities; of course, claims overlap. People's movements toward and away from markets and centers of regional authority create directional paths. Coexisting social clusters compete for status as a local center, a drawing place for community.[7]

Given these shifting flows of community associations, Manggur had done very well in the 1980s. A sibling set of nine adults and their families formed a cohesive core, which in itself was big enough to call "community," and attracted others besides. One of the older brothers was an ambitious and charismatic man who managed to get appointed to the position of village head in the late 1960s, when the village was still a huge territory. He made good political connections, and in 1994 his words still carried much weight. His history of leadership helps explain how his residence in the early 1980s won the position of central location for the newly recognized smaller village—Manggur. (Not every settlement was so lucky. Four other hamlets, not located in the spot called Manggur, are part of the administrative village.) Meanwhile, one of his younger sisters became village head of the new village in 1982, and she continued to be village head in Manggur through the 1990s. The youngest brother was village secretary. And these three people—whose identities are so continuous with the positing of "Manggur" as a political entity at all—were consistently the main players in the environmentalist drama I have been describing.

With this background material, you may not be surprised to hear that the stories these three individuals told are different from those I heard from SKEPHI and Kompas Borneo. *My* original anxiety about contradictory versions, however, developed as I heard the village head tell the story: Although she remembered and delighted in telling me about the December 1986 meeting in Manggur, she timed the environmental victory as coming *before* this event, in 1985. That victory consisted of moving the timber company out of the forest of her social network into the forest of other Meratus social networks. Here is a piece of her story:

> In 1983, the timber company made a road near here. Ten Manggur families moved down to the road. [Moving to the road showed compliance with state civilizational standards, even as it aggravated the company.] The timber company filed an official complaint that we were cutting swiddens in the timber

concession. If they had not complained, we would never have gotten involved; they could have kept cutting for ten years. But we were forced to meet with the government. I had to go down to government offices constantly; I barely could stay two nights in a row at home. That was when I was still energetic; I would be tired of it now.

I went to the District Office and finally even to the office of the governor. I would never have been brave enough to go there except that the company had said we were at fault. The company had blamed us, saying that shifting cultivation caused succession to grassland [*hilalang*, the tropical grass *Imperata cylindrica*, which forms forest-excluding grasslands]. I argued back, that there was no proof of this; there is no grassland in Manggur, and there never has been.

The governor told me that by chance there was a meeting of Forestry Department officials from the capital there, and I should consult with them. I went to the Forestry official and I said, "Maybe we are at fault, but I would like to see the map of the timber concession." They had a map that showed that the concession was really located in the next district! They had been stealing logs from our district. The official cancelled the forestry meeting and took me back to the district; within a week the company was turned out. They moved their operations to the next district. After that, everything has been peaceful.

My starting assumption is that most of this story is true. The contradictions in timing could be produced by what counts as success: For the village head, it is a consolidation of her village territory; for Kompas Borneo, it is the growing legitimacy of environmental politics regionally; for WALHI, it is the practice of grassroots support against government coercion and corporate land grabs. However, the village head's story also needs to be considered within genres of Meratus leadership narratives, in which, in my experience, not every meeting between the narrating leader and the external authority that empowers him or her to speak could have physically occurred. Since the power to lead is granted by these ties to powerful outsiders, every leader I knew told of meetings with regional authority, for a community ideally forms around the power of this story. What really happened? This question is more puzzling still in the story I heard from the charismatic and forceful older brother, who, like his sister, put himself in the center of the action, never mentioning the other. Here is a fragment:

I went to the timber camp boss to complain about their destruction of our fruit and honey trees and rattan. The boss said, "Take your complaints to Ibu

Tien [New Order President Suharto's wife]. We have permission from the top." I was angry. I gave that boss half an hour to agree to negotiate with us. After half an hour, he was still unwilling to talk.

So I went to Jakarta, I went to President Suharto, and I asked, "Is it true that you have agreed to the timber companies cutting down our village trees?" The president said, "They are selling my name." He paid all my expenses to come back; I could have asked for any amount. I'm only sorry I didn't ask for one of those plastic cards that allows you to take money from a bank whenever you want for the rest of your life. He would have given it to me. Then the journalists from seventeen countries came to Manggur [This is the meeting I have been describing], and they gave their witness to the things I said. That's what helped us close down the timber concession and return the land to the village.

Is there any Meratus Dayak who could go to Jakarta and meet with the president? No one I spoke with in the province or the capital could even imagine the possibility. From their perspective, it isn't something village people do. It didn't happen.

I don't think I have to decide. Through whatever combination of leadership strategies and storytelling, Manggur has thrived. Furthermore, the stories have proliferated into documents. Most astounding perhaps, is a typed page signed by the leader I just quoted. The document uses all the appropriate jargon: "We, the people of Manggur, are indigenous people who protect the environment with our traditional culture. We will consider any offense against the environment to be an offense against our human rights." I don't know who wrote this document. When I read it, I had just written a document in the name of another Meratus leader, so I did not think its international literacy completely odd. It surely is a serious mimicry of authoritative rhetoric, and of the most impressive sort. Through just this kind of mimicry, Manggur has become a real village, by which I mean the kind of village other people imagine, rather than just a flexible, tentative Meratus settlement. Indeed, Manggur has become a minor ecotourist attraction, part of the international, national, and regional circuit that draws visitors to villages in the rainforest (Tsing 1999).

In the process of making this real village, the landscape also changed. In 1994, it was hard to deny that Manggur's forest was a model of community-based resource management, quite of the sort that progressive funding agencies have begun to advocate in recent years. As hundreds of ecologically minded visitors, including myself, can attest—and I counted 592 visitors in the guest book between July 1988 and July 1994—Manggur people are happy to explain their customary territory and to point out and identify the diversity of forest plants within it, the areas of mature forest that are not normally cut, and the prohibitions against unreasonable profit from harvesting timber products. Other Meratus also value vegetational diversity, maintain mature forest, and sell almost no timber. But because of the tentativeness through which communities can be defined, it is hard to know whether they fit environmentalists' criteria for community-based management or not. In contrast, Manggur created the landscape of international environmentalist desire.

Manggur has not done this by being the right kind of community all along. Instead, a number of smart leaders copied the rhetoric and symbolism of a particular sector of authority, hoping to draw and maintain a constituency with the legitimacy and aura they gained in this process. Their collaboration with SKEPHI, WALHI, and Kompas Borneo did not stem from common understandings of village community or forest history. Instead, they overlapped in understandings about the authority of knowledge and policy emanating from regional and national centers. Manggur people agreed with those from the province and the capital that elites make the rules. It is in this context that Manggur leaders almost surely prompted Kompas Borneo members to include development rhetoric in their grant proposal. Development is the wisdom of the state, and Manggur leaders took that on in the same ways they take on environmentalist wisdom.

Just a fifteen-minute hike from the central settlement of Manggur is another Meratus hamlet, a part of Manggur village. The people I talked to there were extremely eager to talk to me about other things, yet they told me that they knew nothing about how the timber concession was closed. They told me to talk with the leaders I have mentioned; that story is those leaders' business, they said. The events in Manggur were not a grassroots movement in the ordinary sense. They did not unite the people of the village in a common resistance. When I asked a Meratus friend in another district what had happened to the timber concession, he said the village head of Manggur was able to get help from important connections that allowed her to influence the officials. The borrowed authority of leaders, rather than unified community action, is the dominant Meratus model of political agency. It is hard to argue that it is wrong in describing this case.

These last Meratus stories remind us that despite its collaborative stability, the community-managed forest of Manggur had a rather tentative status. Meratus community members can undermine the best-laid plans of leaders like those who helped bring Manggur's community-managed forest into being. In general, they do this not so much by destroying the forest as by refusing to act like a community.

Furthermore, although the emergence of the community-managed forest in Manggur was locally important and effective, it did not travel anywhere, in part because few of the parties involved knew just how well this environmental "exercise" had worked. When I spoke with Meratus in other places in the 1990s about how they might deal with timber company incursions, no one imagined that they might apply the Manggur exercise to their own situation. When urban activists returned to mount a campaign against logging in 1999, they re-invented community-managed forests based on their knowledge of other places.

Yet the very limitations of the incident make it easy to think with as a model of the effectiveness of collaboration. It is possible to tell the story in its own historical bubble, with no succeeding history to undermine the promise of the initial emergence of the category. The story tells of possibility and of hope. Sometimes difference can lead to new forms of unity and struggle.

Progressive activists spend most of their time either searching for seamless consensus or making a point of their irreconcilable differences. My story suggests other political avenues. It also suggests other methods for learning about the world.

Thus, for example, research objectives: For most advocates of environmentalism, the challenge for scholars of the environment is to learn to gather compatible data sets so that we can aggregate the data to form a global picture. The issue of local perspectives, from this point of view, is a technical problem to be overcome. My story gives space for the opposite approach. What if we paid more attention to *incompatible* data sets? In other words, what if we took a look at the ways social position, genre, and practical knowledge shape the data we gather? Instead of erasing incompatibility, we need to find out where it makes a difference.

Banjarmasin, Jakarta, and Manggur activists tell different histories of the forest: the forest is a challenging wild place; the forest is a site of popular resistance and communal management; the forest is the medium of social networking. These stories do not fit together neatly; they allow us to gather different kinds of data about resources and resource management as well as different stories of environmental activism to save forests. It is only through recognizing this kind of discrepancy that we can begin to sketch the environmental history of this area. Furthermore, this history is not served by just setting these perspectives side by side. The hierarchy that sponsors but does not control their divergence, and the contingent overlaps and collaborations that mark out their effects, are essential parts of that history. Indeed, the natural objects that populate that history—including community forests, villages, and environmental advocates of various sorts—become historical agents precisely through the contingent collaborations that show us their agency from varied perspectives.

Beyond Manggur

What happens when these categories gain the power to travel?

My own story of what happened in Manggur, like those I have been relating, began as a particularly positioned oral narrative. I designed the story for academic settings, but before long it carried me into contact with program officers from the Ford Foundation, which by the 1990s had become a center for many such stories about what had come to be called community-based natural resource management. (The awkward acronym is CBNRM.) Through its Rural Poverty Alleviation Program, the Ford Foundation had become a major funder of CBNRM projects around the world—including one submitted by the members of Kompas Borneo to work in Manggur. The Ford Foundation has a reflexive streak, and program officers tend to enjoy hearing scholarly analyses of their programs. My Manggur story caught someone's attention in this regard, and for the next few years through conferences and workshops I found myself with access to a host of other related stories about community-managed forests, fisheries, wildlife, water projects, and the like. Mingling under the auspices of the Ford Foundation, these concepts were no longer just local sparks of hope; they stretched, worried each other, and traveled.

One of the first things I learned was that the excitement about community resource management at Ford drew from contingencies—rather as it had in Manggur. Once suggested, CBNRM filled a niche that had not been noticed before. It stretched between community empowerment and conservation. It fulfilled dreams of improvement as well as preservation. The idea developed, too, when it found unexpected collaborators, inexplicably drawn to each other by this small corroboration in their otherwise independent agendas.[8] The emergence of the concept at Ford resembled its moment in Manggur; yet, of course, the Ford Foundation and a short if successful gathering in an obscure Meratus village could not be more different. In Manggur, participants glimpsed the promise of community forests in the light brush of contact. No bureaucratic or commercial institutionalization marred the protean possibilities of the dream. In contrast, the goal of the Ford Foundation is to make such promising visions real—with all the power and peril of that exercise.

The Ford Foundation's promotion of CBNRM gave it the kind of universal status I began this book by discussing—the status of a universal-in-engagement. On the one hand, Ford's power and money urged NGO workers and activists from around the world to recast their projects within the emergent rhetoric of community resource management. On the other hand, each project was marked by its specific set of more or less self-conscious overlaps and compromises among collaborators. In contrast to many well-promoted globalist concepts, CBNRM is *supposed* to have a local flavor, and so it is important to remain suspicious of claims for local originality, which may only support a program's self-justification. Every international conference on the topic—however much a celebration of diversity—teaches NGO workers, as well as academics, how to cast their projects with a pitch that might get them a grant. When Ford Foundation program officers are around, participants are busy pitching standard lines. Yet when grantees go home, they must work these lines into the matrix of possibilities offered by their practical situation.

With the funds and legitimacy the Ford Foundation offers, grantees have the opportunity to show that their dreams can work in the world. Utopian critique meets realpolitik here. Projects must position themselves in relation to government bureaucracies and commercial and policy elites. New and often unsavory collaborators must be entertained. The original dream may lose its force. The question of co-optation is ever present.[9]

As projects develop supporters and opponents, the influence of the donor organization itself sparks contention. Did projects develop their ideas of "community" only to meet the standards of potential grant agencies?[10] When "community" is dreamed up and imposed by outsiders, what happens to local assessments and dreams? Issues of scale-making are crucial. "Communities" are constituted in relation to other kinds of scale-making projects, including bureaucracies, nations, and international bodies of power and expertise. Community-making projects may or may not empower local people; it all depends on just how this relation is organized. Who benefits?

Rather than deliver a definitive policy assessment of these questions, Ford Foundation program officers working with CBNRM participated in a series of discussions involving academics and advocates, as well as bureaucrats and donor organizations. The discussions in which I participated were challenging. In the late 1990s, scholarly trends were moving away from an endorsement of activist projects and experiments. Practitioners and scholars often gravitated to different styles for discussing programs. Where practitioners focused on the strengths and weaknesses of particular projects, scholars tended to place these projects in longer histories and wider geographies of knowledge and power. Scholars pointed out that "native communities" are generally imagined within colonial legacies of segregation and racism. These legacies can limit the options for village people, denying them the privileges of full citizenship. Meanwhile, government and international management programs can use community-building exercises to discipline rural people, urging them to comply with barely relevant expert orthodoxies "for their own good." These perspectives usefully enlarged the context in which we were able to discuss particular projects. At the same time, they dampened the spirit of advocacy, making those who wanted to change the world seem self-aggrandizing, if effective, or silly, if not.

In the process of discussion, I found myself provoked to think differently. On the one hand, scholarly colleagues challenged me to consider the real dangers of too easy a generosity toward programs for "community" empowerment. On the other hand, community advocates made me consider whether scholarship had stopped working well as a public interlocutor. These concerns come to a head in the task of assessing the populist and romantic commitments of middle-class urban young people such as those who gathered once in Manggur. Certainly, their commitments embody the ambivalent legacies of the concept of "community." Are these young people part of the problem or part of the solution?

To return to these particular protagonists helps to clarify the challenge. Community resource management is a charismatic idea; it is easily co-opted by powerful institutions and bureaucracies. The worst situations are those in which local options are foreclosed by the force of institutions. For example, the popularity of the concept has recommended it to the international agencies that implement structural adjustment programs. Why not use community labor to save public money while dangling the hope for community autonomy as a device to keep the populace in line? German-run forestry projects in The Gambia, in West Africa, have adopted just this perspective, according to analyst Richard Schroeder (1999). In one project, communities take over a schedule of forest labor dictated from above with the promise that after three years of good behavior, they may qualify to apply for land tenure.

The distinction between well-meaning community advocates and crassly manipulative institutions blurs, however, when we consider how village elites may remake themselves as interlocutors for international expertise.[11] In their cosmopolitan efforts to connect with powerful outsiders, village leaders may endorse forms of knowledge that are wrong or biased when considered in the context of local practices. Manggur elders have been quite capable in making their stories about the Manggur forest work to match middle-class dreams—and in the process, further their own leadership strategies. Moreover, not every local vision of "community" extends social justice or environmental protection. Some visions only build a small network of privilege. There are no simple standards of assessment here. The only way to think about the political potential of a project is to learn about its local dynamics, on the one hand, and its attempts to reach out to wider collaborators, on the other.

But this is where the best and the most critically aware scholarship fails us. Theory has followed its own specifications. In overcoming the parochialism of the case study, theory overreaches to show each local situation as nothing more than an exemplification of a self-fulfilling global scheme. As long as this is what counts as theory, we have trouble getting either to urgent local dilemmas or to far-reaching collaborative visions. In assessing environmental politics, theory has had less and less to say to activists, visionaries, and the public at large. This is because theory, in directing itself to prophetic futures, has addressed itself more to replication and planned development than to unexpected opportunities and injuries that must be addressed, however inadequately. We can do better.

Theories of globalization have been particularly bad in this regard. Because they lay out inevitable trajectories, they cannot appreciate either the contingency of nightmares or the promise of utopian critique. Why did anyone bother to claim community forests in Manggur? Corporate theft and destruction made a response urgent. That Manggur leaders were able to reach out to tap the fantasies of provincial nature lovers and national activists was a local victory. It also launched a broader vision of hope: the hope that forests could be sustained as a source of life for multiple humans and nonhumans—and not just distant corporations.

Finding hope has become more difficult in recent years. As illegal resource extraction booms, it becomes harder to imagine community representatives who want anything other than their share of the money. During the New Order, resource rents mainly bypassed local residents; when the regime fell, many forest-dwellers were willing to fight for their forests. Now payments are distributed more widely. As one businessman is said to have quipped, "In Sukarno's day, we paid under the table. In Suharto's day, we paid over the table. Now they've taken away the table" (Iverleigh 2003: 26). Everyone is free to demand a cut.

Yet the more difficult the community forestry exercise becomes, the more necessary it seems. Otherwise we resign ourselves to forest plantations with privatized security—or to total destruction of the forest and its livelihoods. The international experts have already given up. The only ones who still bother to struggle over these issues are activists, students, and nature lovers—and the rural communities with whom they interface. This seems a particularly bad time to use scholarly prediction to denigrate their efforts.

To ignore utopian potential is not just pessimistic; it is also historically misleading. Insightful criticism has somehow turned to abstract dogma.

How has it happened that in order to stay true to hopes for a more livable earth, one must turn away from scholarly theory? Dialogues across scholar-practitioner lines—such as those the Ford Foundation has supported—are an invitation to come up with something rather different. Might it be possible to use other scholarly skills, including the ability to tell a story that both acknowledges imperial power and leaves room for possibility?

Re-engaging Theory

This book has suggested how one might tell these other stories. I have shown the importance of attention to situated dilemmas, on the one hand, and the moving current of human empathy we call the universal, on the other. To capture this duality, I have focused on the engagement of universals.

Despite the standardization and consolidation of capitalism, I found it impossible to learn about resource extraction without dragging my analysis into the arrogance and despair of the Kalimantan frontier. Despite the power of calls for a singular global science, I discovered environmental knowledge only in the joints of cultural and political encounter. Despite imperial standards for civil society, I have wandered into coalitions built on awkwardly linked incompatibilities. The projects I have studied self-consciously reach across the world, drawing their substance, support, and legitimacy from global sources. They deploy the rhetoric of the universal even as they shape its meanings to their particular processes of proliferation, scale-making, generalization, cosmopolitanism, or collaboration. They require us to follow calls to the universal without assuming these calls will foster the same conditions everywhere. This means grounding one's analysis of global connection not in abstract principles of power and knowledge but rather in concrete engagements.

This is a research strategy that aims to encourage critical purchase without cutting off the springs of hope. Hope is most important when things are going badly in the world; in the face of almost certain destruction, hope is a Gramscian optimism of the will. Such "unrealistic" hope begins in considering the possibility that tiny cracks might yet break open the dam; contingent openings are sites of unexpected force—for better or worse.

Political initiatives that work to reclaim forests for forest-dwelling communities respond to the conditions of theft and violence in which forest resources have become objects of frontier desire. I'm not sure these initiatives will work, and I'm sure they won't bring justice to everyone. They embroil participants in debates about authenticity and consensus. They mess with—or displace—earlier categories and cosmologies; they realign local priorities. They require what Levi and Dean (2003) call the "risk" of indigeneity, that is, the strategic transformation of local identity to enter a wider conversation. To be taken seriously by national and imperial interlocutors requires some such risk.

Initiatives such as community resource management have gained substance through their contact with transnational institutions, such as the Ford Foundation. They have brought bureaucrats and entrepreneurs into their schemes, variously advancing, diluting, and co-opting their cause. Political gains and compromises can only be assessed through constant attention to these kinds of collaborations and their effects. There are no guarantees. An appreciation of erasure and abrasion among different forms of practical knowledge, as these create emergent solidarities and gaps, can help keep us honest. For myself, I am inclined to be generous with projects as long as I see how they strain against the common-sense forms that hold us to destruction and injustice as business as usual.

Utopian critiques are critical perspectives we cannot do without—even if they will not be realized. The struggle for community-managed forests in Indonesia is a good example of a mobilization that inspires utopian, and indeed romantic, hopes. Its most tangible product so far has been the formation of a fragile overlapping agenda among environmental activists, nature loving students, and rural community spokespeople. Occasionally, this alliance has kept the forest from being destroyed for a few years, here and there. This is not so bad: Public forests worldwide are threatened and at best tentatively preserved. Meanwhile, the alliance itself revives the promise of democracy. Critics quite correctly point to crippling class disparities between students and farmers; still, perhaps it is the best thing about the alliance that such differences have not discouraged the participants. All of us need a little of the romanticism and commitment of these urban middle-class young people. Through them, the utopianism of a mobilization for the environment as justice becomes a challenge rather than a reason to give up.

Coda

....

Contemplating the emerging triumph of free-market liberalism in his country, a Russian scholar is said to have quipped, "The future is clear and well-known. Only the past is worth studying, because only the past still has mystery." The successes of corporate consolidation, free-ranging finance, and transnational economic standardization backed by military muscle have made it difficult for people all over the world to think beyond the story of neoliberal globalization. This story is not enough. Like the apocryphal Russian scholar, this book has turned away from the sureties of a self-making future to re-open a sense of mystery that might yet enrich the possibilities for imagining the about-to-be-present.

How shall we re-open mystery in our times? To emerge from under the shadow of inevitability, it seems important to bring back the passions and the stakes of global connection. Instead of inscribing structures of self-fulfillment, we might immerse ourselves in the drama of uncertainty of global capitalism and transnational liberalism. What seems at first to be a minor skirmish may yet determine history. Since we don't know how things will turn out, it's worth attending to states of emergence—and emergency. Here hope and despair huddle together, sometimes dependent on the same technologies. Urgency springs up in ruined landscapes; utopian dreams, and crass ambitions, are formed. The guaranteed futures of globalization theory seem strange and far away in this storm.

Here, indeed, I write in conversation with other scholars who would interrupt the easy flow of global capital by conjuring a heady mixture of outrage and millenialism. In the interplay of ruin and possibility, they argue, lie alternative and more open forms of global commitment. Thinking through Indonesia's history of anti-colonial struggle and state-sponsored terror, philosopher Pheng Cheah tells of radical nationalisms that offer populist hope at the same time as they are made possible by state disciplines (2003). Life and death haunt each other in these nationalisms, he says, making them both poison and medicine. Even the most utopian initiatives—say, human rights for women of the global south—are contaminated by the logics of power, and, yet, too, they carry our dreams for justice (Cheah 1997).

If justice and repression must be grasped simultaneously, so too must exploitation and creative labor. Thus, literary scholar Neferti Tadiar (forthcoming) introduces the concept of "historical experience" to tell of the subjective labor of the marginalized and displaced, which fuels narratives of capital and nation yet falls beyond these narratives' scope of explanation. For example, the experience of Filipina labor migrants—maids, prostitutes, entertainers, all disgorged from the country to earn remittances—articulates and transforms the Philippines' global disadvantage into *both* the worst disappointments and the most heartfelt desires. Their experience exposes them to the worst terrors of the global economy, even as it articulates the possibilities of new, emergent forms of social relation. This mingling of despair and hope reformulates representations of global capital, remaking the culture and politics of globalization.

The most exciting feature of this conversation for me is its requirement that the analysis be located *inside* the world of globalization's struggles and passions. Unlike most social scientists and area studies specialists, these scholars refuse to objectify the participants from the perspective of an imagined global management. Instead, Cheah and Tadiar bring us to understand the risks, collusions, and uncertainties from the perspective of those whose well-being is at stake. This opens up the analysis to the promises and dangers of history; contingency matters because it shifts the options for justice and repression, exploitation and creative hope. In this same spirit, this book has followed the contending forms of hazard, curiosity, and zeal of natural resource entrepreneurs, environmental advocates, student nature lovers, and indigenous farmer-foragers.

This perspective of engagement also informs Cheah's argument for the importance of claims to the universal (2001). As long as area studies closes itself to the universal, he says, it will cordon off those it studies from participation in remaking the world. Only because area studies scholars have conventionally imagined themselves in the service of the all-seeing West, he argues, have they confined the scope of the non-Western dreams and nightmares they study into area-bound particularities. From inside any "area," universal claims are key to global agency. Inspired by Cheah's challenge, I have taken a close look at the universal, making it a key category for my research. I call universals "engaged" to acknowledge the fact that to be effective they must enter the fray. Universal claims allow people to make history, but not under the conditions those claims might lead them to choose.

This book has argued that we know and use nature through engaged universals. The "environment" spreads around the world through the friction of engagement, both for commercial users, who tap into its divergences for capitalist commodity chains, and for advocates, who find in these same divergences the means to study, enjoy, or preserve it. As I have shown, what seem at first to be equivalent requirements to work across difference lead to contrasting consequences for humans and nonhumans. In the spirit of scholars such as Cheah and Tadiar, I suggest that social analysis can explore these diverging scenes of possibility only through its own engaged immersion in the histories it plots.

My own ability to enter this history is that of an ethnographer—a listener and a teller of tales. Yet my project stretches and changes the practice of ethnography. As I reach to describe global connections, my ethnography necessarily diverges from the holism of more familiar models, in which each anecdote or custom forms a scrap in a larger, unified pattern. Instead, following the example of subaltern studies historians who retrieve forgotten pasts plowed over by national histories, I endorse the fragment (Pandey 2000). In this project, I have used ethnographic fragments to interrupt stories of a unified and successful regime of global self-management.

Ethnographic fragments ask us to pay attention to details. The travels that inspire global connection turn out to be less controllable than those at the top imply. Making claims about scale, including globalization, turns out to be an arena of contention.

And thus there is no reason to begin a retelling of global connections in imagined world centers such as New York, Tokyo, or Geneva. Globalization is not delivered whole and round like a pizza, to be munched and dismantled by the hungry margins. Global connections are made in fragments—although some fragments are more powerful than others. My telling of global connections has featured rural Kalimantan, where the fragmentary nature of global process is especially evident. Following global connections out of Kalimantan, I found myself exploring other sites, including powerful centers of finance, science, and policy. But these, too, produce only fragments, and my Kalimantan beginnings remind me of this. Some fragments are able to make themselves look whole. Honoring the fragment means acknowledging this power but not accepting it as a done deal. Through fragments, ethnographers can immerse themselves in the contests and engagements of the present.

Fragments need not reduce analysis to simply noticing idiosyncrasy and happenstance. This book has proposed a series of methods to enable more nuanced understandings of global connection. They interrupt dominant stories of globalization to offer more realistic alternatives. Instead of positing a triumphant global regime, these methods guide us to the disjunctions of global travel, such as those I have traced in the excesses of capitalist proliferations and the awkward conjunctures of social movement building. Here it is possible to consider the practical shape of global politics and culture without the interference of self-fulfilling prophecies.

Instead of requiring an evolutionary process of change, these methods show the pervasive effects of historical encounters. Instead of starting with the dichotomy between global force and local response, these methods show the importance of contingent and botched encounters in shaping both business-as-usual and its radical refusals. Thus, I have described how cosmopolitan nature loving—like capitalist resource use—has emerged in the crossroads of old cultural legacies. I show how well-intentioned advocacy for the indigenous peoples of the forest extends the logics of power, forging new gaps in what can be said about people and forests. Yet sometimes in the urgency of a campaign, such misunderstandings are productive as objects in common begin to coalesce in the space of partial agreement. It is these moments of conjuncture that make social activism worthwhile. Meanwhile, they interrupt and change the principles of activism, introducing further genealogies of meaning and coercion into the risky mix that signifies empowerment.

Such fragments of varied schemes and travels and encounters do create a world of global connections. These are global connections made, and muddled, in friction. Curiosity about such friction might yet re-open the mystery of our times.

Notes

....

Preface

1. I first gained familiarity with Meratus social life in a two-year "deep immersion" fieldwork experience in the Meratus Mountains between 1979 and 1981. I planned other long fieldwork stays, first to study the making of social landscape, and, later, to study environmental mobilizations, but I was unable to coordinate my research permission, my health, my grants, and my teaching job. Instead, my field research has been organized into a series of shorter periods, usually of several months. Luckily, the other groups on whom I focused—nature lovers, activists, donors, scholars—felt enough of an affinity to my own social position to make ethnographic fieldwork relatively easy to arrange. (I failed in my attempts to conduct more than superficial interviews with timber and mining company representatives. Their hostility also restrained me from seeking out active employees.) And so I found myself—mostly during North American summers—traveling from Jakarta to various provincial capitals and towns and to the Meratus Mountains, letting myself follow the connections of acquaintance, and the events and issues of rainforest politics that I could triangulate across them. My fieldwork included stints in 1986, 1994, 1997, and 2000.

Introduction

1. I think particularly of Gayatri Spivak (1999), Dipesh Chakrabarty (2000), Pheng Cheah (2003), and V. Y. Mudimbe (1988).

2. Spivak uses this double negative in several of her considerations of Enlightenment projects. See, for example, Najmabadi (1991).

3. Rates of deforestation in Kalimantan over the last twenty-five years have recently been discovered to be far higher than ever imagined. Curran et al. (2004) document increasing deforestation in officially designated "protected areas." Between 1985 and 2001, they show, Kalimantan's protected lowland forests declined by more than 56 percent.

4. "For the dialectic the universal is a conceptual construction that can never know any empirical embodiment or realization: all of its particulars are also specific and historically unique, and the function of the universal in analysis is not to reduce them all to identity but rather to allow each to be perceived in its historical difference" (Jameson 2002: 182–83).

5. In the field of indigenous rights, one might contrast the writings of Elizabeth Povinelli (2002), who stresses the disciplines of liberal multiculturalism, and Kimberly Christen (2004), who argues for new openings for critical expression. For feminism, contrast Bhavani, Foran, and Kurian (2003), who aim to reform international

development, and Riles (2000), who shows the formalist constraints of NGO politics. For more on environmentalism, see chapters 6 and 7.

6. Leslie Feldman (2001) shows how philosopher Thomas Hobbes helped inspire the liberal idea of freedom as motion. Hobbes imagined his ideas as the social application of Galileo's laws of physical motion, which self-consciously omitted friction. The omission of friction is still with us in much social theory.

7. Many fascinating books have been written about the frictions of the rubber trade. Michael Taussig's *Shamanism, Colonialism, and the Wild Man* (1987) and Lucile Brockway's *Science and Colonial Expansion* (2002) are great places to begin.

8. Thinking through the universal involves techniques of formal abstraction. One must learn to generalize from one instance to another, to see an underlying or emergent principle of commonality across apparent difference. The principle must tie both instances not just to each other but to a radically open field that could at least potentially cover all other instances. It is these habits of generalization and abstraction that make proponents of universal truths uninterested in criticisms that universals do not take the heterogeneity of the world into account. The existence of particularity does not get in the way of the universal. The point of universalism is to move from particular instances to more general laws. The abstract universal is always open; new discoveries, principles, and proponents are welcome. The mechanics of universality are discussed further in chapter 3.

9. Soroos (1997: 110–46) offers a review of national positions in forming conventions on pollution in the 1980s and 1990s. Vogel (1993) gives the context of European Community environmental policies.

10. This was a period in which transnational rights discourses seemed necessary to Indonesian activists to refute authoritarian state claims of "Asian values" (Tsing 1997).

11. We cannot assess a proposition about the universal without attention to its concrete proposals and commitments. Judith Butler discusses this point with philosophical clarity in "Restaging the Universal" (2000). My analysis is indebted to her discussion.

12. Dubois (1997) describes the use of universalism by slaves in revolt in the French Caribbean. The French Revolution and the Haitian Revolution were tightly connected in their development of notions of universal rights. (In this vein, Buck-Morss [2000] argues that Hegelian ideals of universal history were developed in dialogue with Haiti's revolution.) Enlightenment ideals and universal truths were also key to the spread of Asian anti-colonialism. Pramoedya (1991) offers a literary account of the inspiration of Enlightenment ideals on an emerging nationalism in colonial Java. Universalisms have inspired both national and transnational commitments. Duara (2001) traces the interplay between European and north Asian discourses of universal truth and civilization in early twentieth century discourses of pan-Asianism.

13. The writers with whom I began—Spivak (1999); Chakrabarty (2000); Cheah (2003); Mudimbe (1988)—variously discuss these issues.

14. The broad spectrum of universalism's appeal has inspired political philosophers in a lively discussion of universals in relation to the making of democracy, cosmopolitanism, and social change. At the radical edge of the discussion, a number of theorists offer tools for thinking through the practical dilemmas of engaged universals. Judith Butler comments on the exclusions of even the most progressive univer-

salisms that follow from "the cultural location of the enunciation of universality" (2000: 37). Pursuing this linguistic metaphor, she argues for the importance of *translation* as the process through which excluded groups struggle for inclusion within the privileges granted to universalism's unmarked subjects. Because of the specificities of language, translation is always both representation and misrepresentation. All universalisms, Butler suggests, are made in histories of translation. Ernesto Laclau (2000) points to the importance of historical *contingency* in the transformation of particular complaints into universal goals. To enter the political process, Laclau suggests, a class segment must present its aims as realizing the universal aims of the community. It is the contingent nature of this process that makes it key to political struggle.

15. For Left theories of globalization, see, for example, Hardt and Negri (2000); Jameson and Miyoshi (1998); Sassen (1998); Appadurai (1996); Hannerz (1996).

16. See Jameson (1991); Harvey (1989).

17. Dowie (1996) discusses the confusion of environmental positions in the 1990s United States. Hager and Burton (1999) describe an Australian anti-environmental public relations campaign and its undoing.

18. See Soule (1995) for an anti–science–studies polemic about environmentalism.

19. Science studies scholars have been particularly innovative in describing collaborations between humans and nonhumans. See for example Haraway (2003); Latour (1996).

20. Nancy Peluso (1992) describes colonial and post-colonial teak exploitation in Java.

21. Dauvergne (1997; 2001) and Ross (2001) offer extensive analyses of this situation. I draw from their accounts.

22. Investors from the Philippines and Malaysia, where timbering had already been molded to Japan's demands, were active. Hong Kong, the United States, Japan, and Korea also made substantial investments in timber.

23. In the earliest period of the timber boom, military officers and foundations took a large share. The military formed arrangements with foreign companies and Sino-Indonesian firms to do the logging, while the military supplied the concession. In this, President Suharto pursued an accommodation he began in funding the military indirectly through letting it control Indonesia's oil. In a later period, foreign firms were pushed out of timber. Concessionaires' off-budget contributions allowed the regime to balance and appease varied military and civilian elites (Ascher 1998; McCulloch 2000).

24. Other Southeast Asian forests were also involved in this transformation act. The sogo shosha had first approached the Philippines for dipterocarps. When Philippine forests were depleted, the traders moved to the forests of Sabah, Sarawak, and only then Indonesia. The regional sweep of these biologically somewhat similar forests allowed the Japanese traders' ambitions to grow. Unsustainable harvests are fine, because other forests await. Environmental scholar Peter Dauvergne (1997) describes Japanese trading companies as casting a long "ecological shadow" over Southeast Asia, as they moved across the region decimating forests in first one country and then another.

25. Over 100 logging firms went bankrupt, and many foreign and military investors sold off their holdings (Ross 2001: 182–83; see also Brown [1999] who argues that military investments were still significant). The new policy had the effect it

planned: By 1985, there were 101 plywood-producing firms in Indonesia—up from 19 in 1978—and the industry's production was 6.5 million cubic meters per year. (In 1978, production was only 800,000 m^3.) By 1990, production was 12.6 million m^3 (Barr 1998: 9). In 1992, the ban was replaced by an export tax (Ascher 1998: 50). In 1998, IMF agreements forced the New Order to lift the ban (Barr 1998: 35).

26. Barr's (1998) description is extensive. His analysis guides mine.

27. Quoted in Dauvergne (1997: 91).

28. Barr (1998) reports on Hasan's many excesses. In 2000, Hasan was investigated for corruption, and in 2001 he was sent to prison. A variety of sources on Hasan's rise and fall are collected in Gallon (2001).

29. Quoted in Barr (1998: 1).

30. In the 1980s, a large part of Indonesia's forests came into the hands of Sino-Indonesian logging companies (Ross 2001: 183–85). Hasan, indeed, pioneered the intimate relationship between regime officials and ethnic Chinese businessmen that became the hallmark of the New Order economy. Hasan was a business associate of Suharto from the days when they jointly used smuggling to finance a division of the army (Barr 1998: 2–4). When Suharto became president in 1967, his regime made this kind of association a model. Sino-Indonesian entrepreneurs became a convenient and controllable national substitute for foreign investors. Denied the privileges of full citizenship, they offered finance and business experience in exchange for the right to make great fortunes—some of which were funneled back to their political patrons. Meanwhile, the military also maintained an important presence in promoting both legal and illegal resource extraction (McCulloch 2000).

31. Illegal logging is described in McCarthy (2000) and Obidzinski (2003).

32. The regulations on decentralization are multiple and contradictory. Colchester et al. (2003: 249–51) review the relevant acts, concluding that "decentralization has generated more confusion than clarity and has resulted in a 'tug-of-war' between central and district level authorities" (2003: 251).

33. Conservation in Indonesia involves government bureaucrats, foreign organizations, and national environmentalists. Each of these has had very different agendas. In this book, I discuss only the last of these three. Barber (1989) offers a good introduction to New Order state forestry. Lowe (1999) offers an ethnographically informed critique of foreign conservation programs. Stone and D'Andrea (2001) discuss the World Wildlife Fund, a transnational organization with a strong domestic base in Indonesia. During the New Order, the national environmental movement organized particularly around umbrella institutions with their headquarters in Jakarta. The Indonesian Environmental Forum (WALHI) continues to coordinate dozens of regional and issue-oriented groups and speaks for the national cause in both foreign and domestic fora. In the 1980s, the Indonesian NGO Network for Tropical Forest Conservation (SKEPHI) was also a national umbrella organization; in the 1990s it became an issue group.

34. Anti-government sentiments were also expressed through Islam during this period. See Hefner (2000) for a discussion of the rise of national Islamic politics in Indonesia.

35. The conceptual vocabulary of universal liberal rights was appealing not only because of its worldwide circulation but also because of Indonesia's political history. The New Order had come to power through the extermination of the Indonesian Communist Party. The rhetorical apparatus of communism would have frightened

off most of the public during the New Order years. The minute the New Order fell, however, Marxist texts filled the bookstores and were snapped up with all the pleasures of forbidden candy.

36. I discuss the Indonesian environmental movement further in chapter 6. See also Mayer (1996); Gordon (1998); Eldridge (1989); Belcher (1993); Aditjondro (1991a). Extensive documentation of issues and campaigns is available from environmental movement sources, including the UK-based journal *Down to Earth* and the Indonesian Environmental Forum's English-language *Environesia* as well as the Indonesian *Tanah Air*. Internet mailing lists, such as "WALHI updates" (walhiupdates@walhi.or.id), provide further documentation.

37. Language facility was not described as an innate female characteristic but rather as an effect of women's tracking to humanities majors in college, in contrast to college men who majored in technical fields. The ability to speak good English was an especially important skill for leaders of the internationally oriented nongovernmental organizations of the 1980s and 1990s.

"Better you had brought me a bomb, so I could blow this place up"

1. Security officers, please note: I am referring to customary expressions of everyday frustration and not plans for violence. There has never been any agitation for violence in the Meratus Mountains.

Chapter 1: Frontiers of Capitalism

1. My translation.

2. *Oxford English Dictionary*, 2d ed. s.v. "proliferation."

3. Aditjondro (1991a) makes the claim that the poem was inspirational for environmentalism. I have retranslated the lines from the Indonesian original (Ismail 1971).

4. See Tsing (1993).

5. For an introduction to critical frontier literatures, see Limerick (1987) and Worster (1992b).

6. Despite Hasan's role in devastating large tracts of Indonesian forest, Hasan was offered three environmental awards in the United States in the late 1990s. See Gallon (2001).

7. Rather than looking for an underlying principle, I've sought precedent in histories and ethnographies. In reading about the U.S. West, for example, I notice how the rush to grab one landscape element can jump off into another, as when gold prospectors made property claims on stream water. Legal precedents unexpectedly link one region and another, and aesthetic models are carried to new homes, as colonial water works inspired U.S. big dams. See Worster (1992a).

8. For an introduction to this literature, see Bryant and Bailey (1997) and Peet and Watts (1996).

9. See, e.g., Li (1999); Peluso (1996); Dove (1999). In the last few years, Kalimantan scholars have turned much more intensively to problems of ethnic violence and resource conflict. See, for example, Peluso and Harwell (2001).

10. I am referring to the much-discussed thesis called "the tragedy of the commons" (Hardin 1968), which argued that common property—in contrast to private property—is invariably degraded by its users. Many commentators have shown that this thesis is wrong, despite the fact that it has considerable authority among policy makers. (See, e.g., McKay and Acheson 1987.) Indeed, as I suggest here, the thesis itself as applied in policy can be destructive to the environment.

11. Hill (1996: 124) discusses plantation finance.

12. This issue is discussed in Carrere and Lohmann (1996) and in WALHI and YLBHI (1993).

13. See Brookfield, Potter, and Byron (1995: 105) for a discussion of acacia plantations.

14. The quotation is from David Walsh, the president of the ill-fated gold mining company Bre-X, as reported by Borsuk (1997). For more on this company and its arrangements with the Indonesian government as well as its actions on the Kalimantan frontier, see chapter 2.

15. These are prices from the mid-1990s, before the currency devaluation of 1997. At the time, one U.S. dollar was worth a little over Rp. 2,000.

16. The 1997–98 fires are introduced in Barber and Schweithelm (2000), who show how forest policy contributed to the blaze.

17. See, e.g., Gonner (2000).

18. Peluso and Harwell (2001) describe the 1997 West Kalimantan conflict. Dayak-Madurese conflict erupted in Central Kalimantan in 2001.

19. An introduction to this conflict can be found in Human Rights Watch (2001).

Chapter 2: The Economy of Appearances

1. *Oxford English Dictionary*, 2d ed. s.v. "scale."

2. As much as any place in the world, Indonesia rode high on the wave of enthusiasm for mobile, finance-driven international investment in the 1980s and early 1990s. Between the late 1980s and 1997, economic growth averaged about 8 percent per year, and in early 1997, for economists, "there was little sign of the turmoil that was to emerge" when the economy crashed and the Suharto regime followed in 1998 (McLeod, 1999: 209). Looking back, many once-enthusiastic analysts blamed the crisis on "cronyism," residual protectionism, and bad national regulatory practices. See, e.g., Jackson (1999).

3. From the first, the Bre-X story caught the popular imagination, especially in Canada, and thousands of articles have been written about it. Most major Canadian newspapers covered the story in detail; *The Calgary Sun, The Calgary Herald*, and the *Ottawa Citizen* have had many installments of Bre-X news. Only rather late in the game did U.S. newspapers cover the Bre-X story regularly, but at the height of its fame and infamy, much of the media across North America covered the story. Indonesian newspapers and news magazines also offered considerable coverage. Indonesian nongovernmental organizations added their perspectives in flyers and newsletters. Several books have been published about Bre-X, mainly by journalists. Francis (1997) and Goold and Willis (1997) tell the story with lively excitement. Danielson and Whyte (editor and staff writer, respectively, for *The Northern Miner*) offer their expertise on the people and politics of the mining scene (1997). Bondan

Winarno's (1997) account includes useful detail on Indonesian politics and texts of a number of Bre-X documents. Jennifer Well's coverage for the Canadian news magazine *Macleans* and John McBeth's coverage for the *Far Eastern Economic Review* have also been very informative. John Behar (1997) offers a useful description of Bre-X's operations. Internet investor chat lines with Bre-X "threads" offer a wealth of both technical information and personal views on the drama.

4. For discussion of these issues, see *CFRA News Talk Radio*, August 20, 1998.

5. Bre-X lawsuits had their own website, the Bre-X/Bresea Shareholder Class Action Information Website. Key issues involved the liability of stock exchanges as well as Bre-X officials (Francis 1999); the ability of Canadians to participate in U.S. class-action lawsuits (*Daily Mining News*, March 31, 1999); and the nationwide (vs. provincial) scope of Canadian class action lawsuits (Rubin 1999).

6. The Bre-Xscam.com website peddled jokes, news, and art about the Bre-X saga on their "Bungle in the Jungle" web page. A Canadian stockholder named Ross Graham recorded a song called "The Bre-X Blues" and made the CD available for sale on the *Red Deer Advocate* web page. He claims to have made back his losses on Bre-X investment through selling these CDs (*Breaking News*, December 22, 1998).

7. Junior companies prospecting for gold in Kalimantan with "post-Bre-X" advertising of their claims include Kalimantan Gold Corporation (Vancouver); Twin Gold Corporation (Toronto); and Nevada Manhattan Mining Inc. (Calabasas, CA). See *CFRA News Talk Radio*, March 20, 1999.

8. See, e.g., Behar (1997: 121).

9. To "conjure" is both to call forth spirits and to perform magical tricks; in each case, the term highlights the intentionality of the performance, the studied charisma of the performer, and the hope of moving the audience beyond the limits of rational calculation. These features characterize the economic strategies I discuss here, in which everyday performance requirements—for contracts, marketing, reports, and the like—are made into dramatic shows of potential.

10. This version of the much-told story is taken from Goold and Willis (1997).

11. *The Privateer Gold Pages* (http://www.the-privateer.com/gold.html) reviews the recent history of government, interstate, and private uses and prices of gold.

12. The importance of Filipino geologists in Indonesian mining highlights the national and regional cultural demands of the industry, which, like other industries, operates through stereotypes about the appropriate cultural specifications of labor power. Goold and Willis (1997: 170) write, "The Filipinos have their own culture in the mining world. They are well-educated and often trained at big U.S.-owned mines in the Philippines. They are fun-loving, attuned to Western tastes and sensibilities, yet Asian." Meanwhile, the resentment of Indonesian professionals toward the access of Filipinos to Indonesian projects makes them easy scapegoats when things go wrong. Bondan Winarno says Indonesian geologists use the term "Filipino Mafiosi" (1997: 164).

13. This version draws on Goold and Willis (1997).

14. Wives: Waldman and Solomon (1997); parachute rumors: *The Ottawa Citizen* March 25, 1997. The autopsy results are discussed in *The Ottawa Citizen*, April 10, 1997; Platt (1997a, 1997b, 1997c, 1997d, 1997e). Winarno (1997: 134–35) discusses the theory that de Guzman wore false teeth while the corpse had natural teeth.

15. Bob Hasan rumors: Warmington 1997a, 1997b; New York investors: Warmington 1997c. April 2 trading: Jala 1997.

16. Strathcona Mineral Services conducted the independent technical audit. In the words of the report: "We very much regret having to express the firm opinion that an economic gold deposit has not been identified in the Southeast zone of the Busang property, and is unlikely to be. We realize that the conclusions reached in this interim report will be a great disappointment to the many investors, employees, suppliers, and the joint-venture partners associated with Bre-X, to the Government of Indonesia, and to the mining industry elsewhere. However, the magnitude of the tampering with core samples that we believe has occurred and resulting falsification of assay values at Busang, is of a scale and over a period of time and with a precision that, to our knowledge, is without precedent in the history of mining anywhere in the world" (Farquarson 1997: 27).

17. McLeod (1999) gives considerable weight to the Bre-X affair in bringing on the Indonesian financial crisis by undermining investor confidence. He writes, "Perhaps the most significant recent event to crystallize attitudes on the part of the general public, the intellectual and business elite, and the foreign investment community regarding the direction in which government had been heading was the so-called Busang saga" (215). In my view, the Bre-X saga became important because it *dramatized* issues of what came to be called, following Philippine precedent from the 1980s, "crony capitalism."

18. Rumble: Wells 1997a; bungle: Bre-Xscam.com; jumble: Platt 1997f.

19. Goold and Willis (1997: 207) write about the Canadian scene: "Because so many small investors held Bre-X stock, virtually everyone knew someone who had won or lost money. Their stories, often exaggerated, played out across the country. In this environment, any rumour had legs."

20. "On Silicon's popular net forum Techstox, Bre-X dominated for months. More than 4,000 new people a day were searching for Bre-X information, and more than 700 items were being posted about the company for all to read" (Francis 1997: 153).

21. Personal narratives of frontier gold discovery often give more clues to the interdependence of company miners and independent gold seekers than official discovery tales. Bre-X geologists were quite willing to admit, informally, that they chose their prospecting sites through the advice of small-scale Kalimantan miners, who led them to gold-rich sites. Consider, for example, the narrative Bre-X chief geologist Felderhof told reporters about how he first found Busang: "Felderhof had first heard of Busang in the early 1980s, when he and his Australian colleague Mike Bird were exploring the logging roads of Borneo on rented motorcycles. They roared from village to village, asking the locals to point out where they had found gold nuggets in stream beds" (Goold and Willis 1997: 36). Indeed, one of the earliest clouds of suspicion about the rich "southeast zone" of Busang was generated by the fact that small-scale miners did not pan for gold in this area (Danielson and Whyte 1997: 197). Despite acknowledging this interdependence, it never occurred to the geologists that it might interfere with their personal rights—or their official stories—of "discovery."

22. In April 1967, Freeport Indonesia was granted a tax holiday, concessions on normal levies, exemption from royalties, freedom in the use of foreign personnel and goods, and exemption from the requirement for Indonesian equity. The terms were changed slightly in 1976, cancelling the remaining 18 months of the tax holiday and allowing the Indonesian government to purchase an 8.5 percent share (Soesastro and Sudarsono 1988).

23. More restrictive second-generation and less restrictive third-generation CoWs were introduced in 1968 and 1976, respectively. 1986–87 marked the Australian "gold rush" in Indonesia and introduced fourth-generation CoWs, with "one year of general survey ending with 25% relinquishment of concession area; three years of exploration with 75% relinquishment by the end of the fourth year; an Indonesian partner in the CoW; and equity divestment after five years of operation so that ideally after 10 years of production the local partner holds 51%" (Marr 1993: 16). Fifth-generation contracts began in 1990, with tax incentives and low tariff property taxes. A 1992 law required foreign investors in frontier areas to reduce their equity shares to a maximum of 95 percent within five years and to 80 percent within 20 years (Marr 1993: 17). Sixth-generation CoWs, requiring environmental impact assessments, were offered in 1997 (Winarno 1997: 28).

24. Dr. Soetaryo Sigit, ex-Director General of Mines, "Current Mining Developments in Indonesia," quoted in Marr (1993: 26).

25. Rachman Wiriosudarmo, quoted by Wells (1997a: 41).

26. U.S. ex-president Bush wrote Suharto to express his "highly favorable" impression of Barrick (Wells 1997c).

27. By this time, it was clear to all the players that the Indonesian government was calling the shots. Placer Dome sent their bid directly to the president (McBeth and Solomon 1997).

28. Hasan's perspective was developed in a context in which other Indonesians were calling for greater national control of Busang. Amien Rais, for example, argued that the gold "should be kept for our grandchildren in the 21st century" (cited in Francis 1997: 130). Winarno (1997: 84–94) details nationalist claims.

29. Hasan's investments during this period are detailed in McBeth and Solomon (1997).

30. Bre-X President David Walsh said he was settling with an arrangement that reflected "Indonesia's political, economic, and social environment" (Borsuk 1997).

31. The history of Freeport McMoran is the subject of a forthcoming book by journalist Robert Bryce and anthropologist Steven Feld. For issues above, see Francis (1997: 129); Goold and Willis (1997: 113–14). Marr (1993) details Freeport's West Papuan operations, with special attention to the mine's history of environmental problems and human rights abuses.

32. David Walsh died of a stroke on June 4, 1998. He had spent the last months of his life fighting class action suits and trying to clear his name (Rubin 1998).

33. The importance of small, popular investment in Bre-X highlights the importance of this national agenda. "At its peak in May 1996, 70 percent of Bre-X's 240 million shares were in the hands of individual investors" (Goold and Willis 1997: 239). This compares to a more ordinary Canadian company, which might have 30 percent of its shares owned by individuals. In 1996, according to Goold and Willis (1997: 105), Bre-X had 13,000 shareholders, including pension funds and insurance companies. According to Francis (1997: 199), about 5 percent of Bre-X trading was from outside Canada. 90 percent of all Bre-X trading was conducted on the Toronto Stock Exchange (Francis 1997: 197).

34. It is possible to make a great deal of money from speculation even if the product comes to nothing. Bre-X shareholders made money merely by selling their shares while the price was still high. The outspoken investors Greg and Kathy Chorny, for example, sold two-thirds of their stock for C$40 million and lost a comparatively

minor sum on remaining shares (Francis 1997: 196). At the end, smart investors made money by "short selling," that is, borrowing Bre-X shares from brokers, selling them, and returning them by buying them back at a lower price. Goold and Willis (1997: 221) report that 5.5 million Bre-X shares were sold short; Francis (1997: 203) reports that the investment bank Oppenheimer and Co. made C$100 million shorting Bre-X stock. Meanwhile, other firms and individuals, including Quebec's public pension fund and the Ontario Teachers Pension Plan Board, lost major amounts of money (Goold and Willis 1997: 248).

35. Other Bre-X allegories have been suggested, for example, that greed blinds everyone's eyes (Goold and Willis 1997: 267), or that the international flow of money means business must deal with "exotic and troublesome regimes" (Francis 1997: 232). Outside of Canada, the allegorical reading arose that this was just the way of Canadian business, where stock exchanges are a "regulatory Wild West" (quotation attributed to the U.S. mass media in Winarno 1997: 208). My reading refuses the distinction between the seeing and the blind to point to the money being made even in a scam. I emphasize the exotic and troublesome nature of capitalism itself—both in and beyond Canada and Indonesia.

"Let a new Asia and a new Africa be born"

1. Longfellow (1942): "Paul Revere's Ride."
2. Danaher and Burbach (2000) introduce the issues in Seattle.

Chapter 3: Natural Universals and the Global Scale

1. *Oxford English Dictionary*, 2d ed. s.v. "generalization."
2. I am indebted to Atran (1990); Drayton (2000); and Grove (1995) for my understanding of the emergence of botanical classification.
3. Nineteenth-century evolutionary theory, indeed, retained the priority of flower and seed in the secular universal it substituted for God's plan. This happy conjunction strengthened convictions about the universal order of Nature as revealed through plants.
4. Fox (1981) calls it pantheism.
5. Muir signed one work with a global address: "John Muir, Earth-Planet, Universe" (Lankford 1991: 36). Lankford also quotes Muir explaining his commitment to moving back and forth between tiny details and the grand scheme of Nature: "If my soul could get away from this so-called prison . . . I should hover over the beauty of our own good star. I should study Nature's laws in all their crossings and unions . . . But my first journey would be into the inner substance of flowers" (38).
6. Limbaugh (1991) discusses Muir's friendship with Sarah McChesney, a leader of feminist animal rights activists. Muir's stories of the moral behavior of animals were written to this audience.
7. Muir's vision of Nature seemed powerful and convincing in part because it helped resolve an imperial problem: Was California a part of the U.S. nation or part of its global empire? Yosemite National Park was a firm claim to the national status of the still-wild western states. Nationalizing nature brought the global-imperial

agenda of travel, conquest, and awe into domestic, national space. Muir himself did not focus on this national problem; arriving in California on a boat, he could have been arriving in South America. He was not invested in the national project, but his vision articulated a new national presence for California. One reason that the parks model took off around the world is that it showed one way nation-states could incorporate the wild frontiers of their imperial ambitions.

8. See Smith (1987) and Fox (1981) for versions of this story.

9. Neumann (1998) explores African examples. Stevens (1997) offers cases that work toward dialogue.

10. The question of indigenous residents has been one of those challenges. Can advocates for nature move beyond Muir's problematic relationship with Native Americans? Native Americans enter Muir's vision in several ways. First, they are a troubling absence: the haunting absence of the dead. The genocidal murder of Native Americans in California contributed to the emptiness of Nature that Muir appreciated as the window to sacred presence. Native Americans had been hunted down and murdered; remnant groups were rounded up and forced into forts and re-settlement areas, where many died. Only then could the environment to which native livelihoods contributed come to seem the exclusive handiwork of God, laid out for the gaze of settlers. Second, Muir was not sympathetic to those Native Americans who remained. Yosemite Indians—so called by neighboring enemies—still inhabited the valley, although in small numbers. Muir's writing contains only derogatory mention of them (Lankford 1991: 234). Besides being non-Christians, the native population joined white ranchers as users, rather than students, of nature. The reservation of the valley as a park did not help the native residents. Federal marshals rounded up the native population and evicted them from their lands. Yet, third, Muir scholars have argued that Native American philosophies inspired Muir's vision of Nature. (See Fleck 1985.) This brings up contemporary challenges for the Muir legacy. In stating their support for indigenous communities, advocates of nature protection so often go directly to native philosophies. Other issues—such as subsistence and survival—are easily ignored. Indigenous leaders willing to endorse nature philosophies do well with nature protection groups; those who stress community development and resource use are drawn, instead, to alliances with developers. The common split within communities with some leaders arguing for support of environmentalists and others siding with developers is a piece of this legacy.

11. The climate change models discussed in this section are those that were widely discussed in the mid-1990s, during a period of great hopefulness for international cooperation on environmental issues. The more blatant U.S. endorsement of imperial claims in the twenty-first century has dampened these hopes and reduced the public prominence of climate modeling. To evaluate the models' use of universal frames and the global scale, I focus on the period when the models seemed most charismatic.

12. Northern industrial countries were singled out as "Annex I countries" and asked, as a nonbinding target, to scale back greenhouse gas emissions by 2000 to 1990 levels. This separation between northern and southern countries was continued in the 1997 Kyoto Protocol, which, responding to the fact that no nation had met its Rio pledges, set comprehensive greenhouse gas emission targets. Demeritt (1999) offers an insightful analysis.

13. The Kyoto Protocol goes far in converting environmental values into busi-

ness values. The Protocol allows countries to lower their emissions through business rather than environmental accounting: They can trade in emission reductions by buying figures showing reduced rates from other countries ("international emissions trade") or by supporting emissions reductions wherever they are cheapest ("joint implementation"). However, for many business leaders, these concessions were not enough. See Demeritt (1999).

14. Gale (1998) offers a comprehensive history of the ITTO in the 1990s.

15. Many conservation organizations also believe in logging as a route to forest preservation. First, it adds economic value to forests, creating the will of governments and investors to maintain forests. Second, by working with timber harvesters and wood product industries, conservationists might have the ability to influence the forest practices in which these users engaged. To withdraw from interaction would be to give up the possibility of leverage. Some conservationists also hope to insert other small conservation goals—such as the establishment of nature reserves or parks—into the forest management agenda. Despite these incentives to stay with the ITTO process, however, many environmental NGOs turned against the ITTO in the mid-1990s.

16. This was the "Non-Legally Binding Authoritative Statement of Principles for a Global Consensus on the Management, Conservation, and Sustainable Development of All Types of Forests." Even supporters of the document agree that the principles have more to do with détente than with a forest program. See Fletcher (1995).

17. The definition is repeated in many organization publications. See ITTC (1992).

18. The term is from James Ferguson (1994), writing of international development.

19. On the turnaround, see Sizer and Plouvier (1997); on the new programs, see Atya and Simula (2002). WTO and GATT bans on trade restrictions have been important presences in the negotiations.

"Dark rays"

1. In the following section, I quote from Professor N.'s articles, which he gave me as photocopies of typescript manuscript. Because I think it most respectful to discuss his work without revealing his name, I quote these without citations as personal communications. All were written in Indonesian.

Chapter 4: Nature Loving

1. In Indonesian but signed in English, "whoever." My translation, as are all excerpts and quotations not specifically identified as English.

2. Oxford English Dictionary, 2d ed. s.v. "cosmopolitan," "specific."

3. I take the term "affluent Asia" from Sen and Stivens (1998).

4. Some groups call themselves *pecinta alam*.

5. Interview August 25, 1994; Jakarta. We spoke in English.

6. For example, Bryant and Bailey (1997: 159) write that "the environment in the Third World is largely a livelihood issue."

7. Students are a talkative, reflective bunch. Many have also committed themselves to writing about nature loving in senior theses, organizational memos, expedition reports, newspaper articles, and nature lover newsletters. Most informally, log books become a forum for communication for nature lovers' groups; there members write their late-night musings, their poetry, their opinions, their observations, and their complaints. Interviews, conversations, and written materials have informed my knowledge of nature loving.

8. Siegel describes the formation of a teenage consumer culture, built particularly around tastes in popular music. High school students are at the center of the *ramaja* ("teenager") subculture of Solo. In teenage music magazines, editors and fans used foreign styles to manufacture cosmopolitan national fashions. They were engaged in a new kind of teenage identity formation; Siegel calls it "the fantasy of an integrated self" (1986: 229) and "the potential for biography" (228).

9. Caesar Sardi tells the story this way in his senior thesis (1995: 24): "Mapala UI [the University of Indonesia nature lovers' group] was the first organization of university student nature lovers. Around 1964, a group of students from the Humanities Faculty, including Soe Hok Gie, Aristides Katoppo, Rudi Badil, Herman Lantang, and others, felt tired out by the play of politics at that time. The bringing together of nature lovers represented an organization that freed itself from politicization, when most student organizations were involved in political work to influence powerful elites." Under New Order political repression, depoliticization moved way beyond their original frame of expectations. By the late New Order, the quietude of censorship was stifling, and at least some of the early nature lovers had become important activists, fighting for a wider breadth for political speech. Aristides Katoppo, for example, an environmentalist journalist, took a leading role in the independent journalists' opposition to New Order censorship.

10. Soe Hok Gie's remarkable essay "Conquering Mt. Slamet" (1995) relates his experience on one early nature lovers' outing. In sharp contrast to more recent nature lovers' essays, Soe is obviously immersed in the politics of the countryside. He describes his patriotic motives for nature loving: to get to know the country and to train to be a better citizen. He comments on the political strife that has shaped the Javanese landscape. Even at the top of the volcano, he engages in political debate— stimulated by pro-Sukarno graffiti—over freedom of speech.

11. See, e.g., Sardi (1995: 23), who says that scouting became nature loving in the 1970s, when teenagers (*ramaja*) refused the discipline of scouting in an "anti-establishment" (*anti kemapanan*) move.

12. The Kopassus record of covert operations, torture, kidnapping, and provoking riots became a subject of national and international discussion after the role of this unit in organizing paramilitary violence in East Timor was revealed (*TAPOL Bulletin* 1999). In 1997, however, Kopassus continued to have a reputation for virility, discipline, and flair among the university students I talked to. The role of Kopassus in guiding both student demonstrations and mass killings in 1966 was not discussed among the students I knew; I am unclear whether they knew about it. A Kopassus team climbed Mt. Everest in 1997.

13. The Republic of Indonesia assumed administration on May 1, 1963. An agreement between the Netherlands and Indonesia stipulated that the Papuans would have the opportunity to choose to remain with Indonesia or become indepen-

dent. In 1969, Indonesia selected 1,022 Papuan representatives who unanimously chose to remain with Indonesia in a public ceremony which contemporary Papuans call "The Act of No Choice" (Saltford 2003).

14. Eben Kirksey (personal communication) points out that this language recapitulates colonial expeditions to Mt. Jaya. These climbs employed Dayaks as well as Javanese convicts as porters. Neither the porters nor Papuans who climbed Mt. Jaya are counted here as "sons of Indonesia."

15. Edwin tells a fascinating story of national competition over the mountain during World War II. A German army unit, the Edelweiss Battalion, secretly climbed the mountain to place the German flag on its peak. The Soviets had to scramble to assemble climbers to take down that German flag (1990e: 8).

16. My translation.

17. This assistance was unnecessary in Indonesia, where no laws excluded it.

18. Bentoel held the franchise to produce Marlboros in Indonesia until 1999, when Philip Morris Indonesia became a separate corporate entity. In 1990, U.S. market share was less than 1 percent for cigarettes. However, Philip Morris had already decided to begin major advertising campaigns, such as sponsoring the Marlboro Indonesian Masters tennis tournament and the Marlboro World of Sports spectacular (an exhibition of racing cars and motorcycles) (U.S. General Accounting Office 1992: 47). By 1996, Philip Morris was spending U.S.$6.3 million in Indonesia for advertising (Hammond 1998).

Chapter 5: A History of Weediness

1. My translation.

2. *Oxford English Dictionary*, 2d ed. s.v. "gap."

3. For an introduction to conservation biology, see Soule (1986). For Indonesia, see Environmental Management Development in Indonesia Project (1996).

4. For introductions to political ecology, see Bryant and Bailey (1997) and Peet and Watts (1996).

5. See Strathern (1980); Ellen (1996).

6. Michael Dove (personal communication) first drew my attention to Wallace's description.

7. The flexibility of the concept of "planting" is suggested by the way tree claims are tied to the whole range of ways, from deliberate to casual, of sprouting the tree. A Meratus who threw a durian seed out the door of her house while eating the fruit would never describe herself as "planting." However, if the seed sprouted and grew, she would claim the tree as one of her planting, because of its timing and location next to her house. Fruit trees that sprouted in the area of someone's current house or swidden were always claimed by the householders as their trees unless they were planted with some ceremony by someone else (as, for example, when I was invited to plant durian for when I came back).

8. See Peluso (1996) for a more extensive discussion of durian management in a West Kalimantan location.

9. I discuss Meratus honey hunting and the symbiotic relationship of people, bees, and honey trees in more depth in Tsing (2003a).

10. Some trade stays within the mountains, connecting one watershed and an-

other, such as the trade in blowpipe poison; some trade connects the mountains and the plains, extending little farther than nearby towns, such as the trade in honey.

11. Damar resin was an important part of the forest products trade in the first part of the twentieth century; the trade declined until the very end of the century, when it picked up again. Damar trees are members of the *Dipterocarpaceae* family. Mampiring is an *Agathis*. Garu (also known as *gaharu*) is an *Aquilaria*; manyan is *Styrax benzoin*; kaladan probably *Dryobalops oblongifolia*; sintuk probably *Cinnamomum sintok*. Burkill (1966) is still the best source on these economic products.

12. I review this history of state requirements in Tsing (1984). See also Lindblad (1988).

13. There are many kinds of *huyi*, each with long, flexible stems that are good for tying and weaving. *Huyi lamah* and *huyi lantau* are used for tying posts and bamboo walkways. *Huyi galang* and *huyi irit* are also good for tying; before the market was homogenized, they had good market value. *Huyi lilin*, "waxy rattan," is a fine-stemmed rattan used whole, rather than split, to tie house floors. *Huyi kaningai* is similar, but it is only found in wet mountain saddles, in the kind of forest called *gunungan*. *Huyi karas*, "hard rattan," has a more brittle stem. *Huyi wariung* is a dark-stemmed rattan with excellent weaving qualities; it makes the most durable back-baskets. *Huyi dahanan* is the stiffest of the rattans called huyi; it makes superior spear handles. There are also many rattans not classified as huyi, such as *nangi*, *pikak*, and *ariwa*.

14. Other government bureaucracies mapped these lands and settlements differently; the actual situation on the ground, in relation to how the category of "forests" was interpreted, depended variously on the relation among bureaucrats and local residents, and their mutual ability to see common-sense "forests" in the area.

15. Vandergeest and Peluso (1995) introduce the idea of "territorialization" to describe the historical exclusion of residents from rights to the forest by state forestry programs in Southeast Asia.

16. I discuss the formation of colonial agrarian landscapes in Tsing (2003b).

17. The newsletters of Indonesian environmentalists, such as *Environesia*, document this history of criticism and advocacy. (See also the journal *Down to Earth*, an international attempt to follow up on these cases.) I introduce the national environmental movement in chapter 6.

18. In 1999, environmental activists worked very hard to influence the new national forestry law. Their suggestions to include community forestry and indigenous rights did not enter the law that passed. See FKKM (1999a) for an NGO-supported draft, and FKKM (1999b) for a postmortem on the version that passed.

19. Activist countermapping projects in Kalimantan have worked with difficulty to negotiate between international standards of segregated territoriality, on the one hand, and the local flexibility of land use and community. See Sirait et al. (1994); Peluso (1995); Tsing (1999).

20. Li (2002); Peluso (1997); and Zerner (1994) discuss the problem of activist reification of community and territory in an Indonesian context.

21. Rosaldo (1986) and Brosius (1986) offer insightful descriptions of place-based narration among other Southeast Asian forest dwellers.

22. In some areas of Kalimantan, shifting cultivators use such histories to establish property claims over demarcated plots of forest (Jessup 1981).

23. E. P. Thompson (1975) describes the harsh laws created in England to enclose

the forests, keeping out peasant "poachers." In a similar spirit, Peter Sahlins (1994) describes the resistance of French peasants to the exclusivity of state and industrial forest claims. Nor were such enclosures limited to Europe: Gold and Gujar (2002) tell how royalty in Rajastan claimed exclusive privilege over the forest; as soon as the king was deposed, peasants flocked into these royal spaces, destroying them. The willingness of peasants to destroy forests leads many analysts to conclude that forest users cannot conserve. Yet this conclusion ignores the political history of elite expropriation, in which peasants and forests became pitted against each other.

"A hair in the flour"

1. Kodeco was ready in part because it had become the target of many small protests. In December 1998, a group of villagers occupied Kodeco's golf course, claiming that compensation for their land had not been paid (*Banjarmasin Post*, December 22, 1998). In March and April 1999, another group occupied Kodeco's main offices, demanding compensation for one of Kodeco's coconut plantations (*Banjarmasin Post*, March 11, 1999 and April 15, 1999). Villagers felt morally empowered because Kodeco had razed a local cemetery for the plantation. Other companies across the region were similarly under attack. It was time for Kodeco to improve its image.

2. The governor may or may not have known that Banjar and Meratus languages, while close, are not identical; he also probably did not care, and this lack of attentiveness is one of the key translation practices here. He addressed the Meratus demonstrators as *pian sampaian*, "all of you [respected ones]" (*Banjarmasin Post*, March 15, 2000). Banjar language uses pronouns that differentiate listeners in terms of age and status; *pian* is respectful. Meratus language has no such status-differentiating pronouns. The governor's respect was thus contingent on Meratus willingness to consider themselves Banjar. Certainly, all the Meratus demonstrators understood the Banjar pronoun; they would have understood Indonesian, the national language, equally well. The point was not comprehension but the making of a form of populism that would work for the state, in alliance with the demonstrators.

3. This illusory share-the-wealth inclusiveness also works by appropriating the words of opponents. In supporting the pro-Kodeco demonstrators, the governor spoke the very words Kodeco's critics used to make their case. "[W]e will use [the natural resources of the Meratus Mountains] with care to the environment and conservation," he began, continuing with the claim that, of course, the government would never allow any logging to which the populace did not agree and in which it did not participate (*Banjarmasin Post*, March 15, 2000). Participatory and environmentally friendly logging would be the government's goal. Kodeco would surely agree, and then it would be left to disgruntled environmentalists and Meratus residents to contest the practice of this agreement.

Chapter 6: Movements

1. My translation.
2. *Oxford English Dictionary*, 2d ed. s.v. "movement."
3. Hardt and Negri (2000: 36) argue that transnational NGOs are at the forefront

of a new disciplinary Empire: "These NGOs are completely immersed in the biopolitical context of the constitution of Empire; they anticipate the power of its pacifying and productive intervention of justice." Other critics of global liberalism borrow the term "governmentality" from the writing of philosopher Michel Foucault, who analyzed the mechanisms of liberal power both in and out of state rule (Foucault 1991). Barry, Osborne, and Rose (1996) show the relevance of this analysis to the contemporary spread of liberalism. Readings of Foucault's assessment of social movements differ; however, many anthropologists, environmental studies scholars, and critics of NGO politics have found in the concept of "governmentality" a route to discuss the role of environmentalism, feminism, and human rights in extending, rather than challenging, coercive power. For critiques of environmental initiatives, see Li (2003a) and Ferguson and Gupta (2002). Agrawal (2003) uses the term "environmentality" to discuss the regulative power of community forest management.

4. It is not useful to overestimate the heterogeneity of liberal projects around the world; in fact, there are enormous pressures toward standardization and consolidation. The coercions of structural adjustment packages; the intimacies of international conference culture; the prestige of northern training programs; the requirements for funding and participation in transnational organizations; the threat of international sanctions: Each of these and more facilitate standardization and consolidation of liberal programs. Yet none of these has much to do with liberal theories of synchronized self-regulation and perfect replication. Understanding the spread of liberalism requires getting outside of liberalism's self-portrait.

5. For varied positions in the debate on the fate of the nation, see Appadurai (1996); Sassen (2000); Beverly (1997).

6. Keck and Sikkink (1998) discuss this kind of dynamic across transnational advocacy networks in the 1980s and 1990s.

7. My discussion focuses on social mobilizations around the environment rather than on conservation bureaucracies or organizations. Conservation organizations and bureaucracies have often focused on the *enforcement* of environmental protection without regard for the social context in which protection has been proposed. The social dynamics of conservation enforcement require an entirely different analytic treatment. For a New Order example, see Peluso (1993); for a post–New Order discussion, see Lowe (2003).

8. Elitist environmentalisms of the global north are also shaped by nation-making goals of various types, including anti-immigration politics.

9. Judith Mayer's (1996) review of the history of the Indonesian environmental movement has been particularly useful to my discussion. See also Gordon (1998); Belcher (1993); Eldridge (1989).

10. Government suspicion of the idea of *nongovernmental* organizations meant that a direct Indonesian translation of the term NGO could not be used in New Order Indonesia. "Nongovernmental" was interpreted as anti-state. Instead, the categories *lembaga swadaya masyarakat* (LSM)—"self-reliant community institutions," and *lembaga pembangunan swadaya masyarakat* (LPSM)—"self-reliant community development institutions," were used. Eldridge (1989) discusses the dilemmas of political dependence of these groups. Aditjondro (1990) discusses the community development counterculture some groups were able to promote, for example in designing alternative technology.

11. WALHI's activities are documented in its Indonesian journal *Tanah Air*, its

English-language journal, *Environesia*, and its online "updates" (walhiupdates@walhi.or.id). WALHI (1990) offers one attempt to lay out the purposes and organization of the group.

12. Transnational NGOs operating in Indonesia chose varied relations to the national cause. In the 1990s, WWF-Indonesia engaged in national environmental politics. The national branch used divisions within the transnational organization to craft self-consciously Indonesian environmental strategies, for example, in acknowledging the draw of charismatic megafauna (tigers, pandas) on northern donors but funneling these funds into rebuilding social landscapes through what WWF called "integrated conservation and development projects." In contrast, Greenpeace acted as a foreign presence in Indonesia. Young Indonesians were attracted to Greenpeace precisely because of the allure of the foreign. In contrast to WWF, Greenpeace materials were available only in English.

13. President Suharto intervened to have the ruling changed. Aditjondro (1998: 41) reviews the specifics of the Supreme Court victory and its dismissal.

14. The term "liberal" was not a New Order piece of rhetoric. New Order politicians called Indonesia a "*panca sila* democracy" in contrast to a "liberal democracy" to argue for the importance of consensus. (Panca Sila are the five official principles of citizenship.) Yet international liberalism shaped the state and its bureaucracy, including its embrace of the rhetoric of law, elections, property, and the like. Meanwhile, the term *liberal* was available in translation for varied nonofficial uses. In the late 1990s, for example, a group formed calling itself *Islam Liberal* to differentiate itself from Islamicism.

15. Daniel Lev (1992) reviews this history.

16. The strategy of suing on behalf of the environment is part of a portfolio of transnational strategies in environmental law. WALHI's suit formed part of several legal challenges and counterchallenges in the Indorayon case. WALHI's national legal challenge was particularly important because customary law had been used against local residents, since lineage elders had received a token payment for the land (WALHI and YLBHI 1993).

17. Reports vary in their statements about the numbers involved. This one is from SKEPHI (1991: 2). The anti-dam campaign began with the resistance of five villages; others joined (Aditjondro 1998: 39). There were said to be 5,000 families in danger of being flooded out in 1989 (Rumansara 1998: 123).

18. Resettlement did not seem a problem to the engineers because the environmental impact assessment, conducted in 1984, concluded that 75 percent of these people were willing to transmigrate. Rumansara (1998) explains that this result was achieved through a survey that asked people whether they would like "a better life." If they said yes, this was interpreted as a willingness to transmigrate.

19. One LBH activist conducted "legal awareness training" workshops in the area to inform people of their rights to compensation; these workshops helped shape villagers' demands (Rumansara 1998).

20. A series of articles in *Kritis* in 1990 and 1991 offers the flavor of national debate about the Kedung Ombo campaign. Aditjondro (1990) opens with a criticism of the mobilization for ignoring "structural" features of big dam building—such as bureaucratic centralization and the Green Revolution destruction of peasant agriculture—in favor of raising sympathy for dam victims. He writes of the importance of long-term "cultural critique," including appropriate technology movements, and

warns against too quick a celebration of the campaign's success. In a follow-up article, Arief Budiman (1990) picks up this last point to lambast Aditjondro for cynicism and to offer an optimistic account of the possibilities for NGOs and student activists to work together. Student activists open up issues, he says, while NGOs follow up on them. Aditjondro (1991b) replies angrily, and Riwanto Tirtosudarmo (1991) wraps up the exchange by reminding readers of the weakness of all oppositional politics in New Order Indonesia.

21. Rumansara (1998) reviews these options.

22. Cooperation among multilateral development banks, development experts, and construction companies led to the standardization of the "large dam" package. The World Bank, as well as the various Asian and Latin American development banks, have made it possible for nations all over the world to have their share of large dams (McCully 1996).

23. Aditjondro describes the dam building program in which Indonesian engineers imagined they overcame colonial belittlement by building bigger dams, even with limited equipment. He describes a political culture in which Indonesian media boasted of having the very biggest dams in Southeast Asia, even where this was not true (1998: 32–34).

24. In the mid-1990s, for example, the organization Sejati published pamphlets by and about Indonesia's cultural minorities, highlighting their strong traditions of customary law. To make them accessible to a wide audience, they made the publications beautiful with photographs and gave them Indonesian and sometimes English texts, augmented by fragments in the regional language. Sejati was particularly interested in convincing Indonesian elites that minority cultures were worth nurturing within the national plan. In one project, they worked jointly with a major bank, offering books to its customers to educate them about Indonesia's rich but vulnerable cultural diversity (Brown 1994). Films also spread their message. Other activists, however, objected to Sejati's culturalist and elitist objectives.

25. A Chinese Indonesian whose family has been in the archipelago for many generations can still never be a pribumi, a "native son." The New Order government continued a long colonial history of Chinese exclusions; anti-Chinese violence in May 1998 was only one symptom. (See, e.g., Pramoedya 2000.)

26. Race has been important in West Papua.

27. See ILO (1994). The introduction, by Stepanus Djueng and Sandra Moniaga (1994), discusses political issues in translation. Moniaga in particular has been a key architect of advocacy for masyarakat adat, and she has written extensively about this in both Indonesian and English (1993; 1994). See also Tsing (2001) for a fuller history of the term adat in colonial and national scholarship and policy.

28. The Basic Forestry Law was revised in 1999. Unfortunately, despite intense negotiations on the topic, the new law is no better at recognizing adat rights. See Colchester et al. (2003: 137); FKKM (1999b).

29. Law 10 of 1992 concerning Population Development and the Development of Happy and Prosperous Families recognizes the rights of "vulnerable peoples" to "utilize a customary territorial heritage." See Zerner (1992).

30. For example: Colchester et al. (2003) offer a summary of legislation on adat rights, opening an argument against environmental certification of timber without respect for adat forests.

31. Many forest-dwelling groups had been officially classified as *suku terasing*,

"isolated tribes," and thus deprived of any recognition of customary rights. In contrast, groups with long-established adat rights, such as the Batak of Sumatra, did not find the appeal to adat politically critical (Mary Steedly, personal communication). In some areas, such as West Papua, official adat leaders have been more closely aligned with the state than with protesters (Eben Kirksey, personal communication).

32. Some groups in the alliance were not interested in critique at this point but rather succession. Still, they joined the alliance for its oppositional solidarity.

33. For a critical assessment of assumptions about indigeneity that underlay the alliance, see Li (2003b). For a sympathetic discussion of the alliance's political difficulties, see Aditjondro (2003).

34. In hindsight, I am not sure whether this was a confusion of speech or of hearing. It turns out that LPMA activists knew the Chico Mendes story through a film, described below, *The Burning Season* (HBO 1995). This film includes a scene of Brazilian tree hugging. My discussion of the incident with LPMA activists later was inconclusive. Certainly, they knew both stories well.

35. Mendes's story is told in many places, including his own text (1989); Revkin (1990); Shoumatoff (1990); and Hecht and Cockburn (1990). Keck and Sikkink's (1998) transnational analysis of the mobilization to save the Amazon forest has been particularly useful for my discussion. See also Keck (1995b).

36. Political scientist Kathryn Hochstetler (1997) has documented how the Brazilian environmental movement shunned rainforest protection issues through the 1970s, concentrating instead on urban pollution.

37. Keck (1995b) and Keck and Sikkink (1998) open discussion of the relation of the mobilizations in the Brazilian Amazon and in Sarawak. A number of key organizers, including Marcus Colchester of the World Rainforest Movement, worked in both campaigns.

38. Eccleston and Potter (1996) introduce Malaysian environmentalism.

39. The Penan campaign is discussed in many sources, including Manser (1996) and World Rainforest Movement and Sahabat Alam Malaysia (1989). J. Peter Brosius's analysis (2003a, 2003b, 1999b) informs my description of the campaign.

40. Keck and Sikkink (1998: 142) discuss the negotiation of divergent perspectives in the Amazon campaign.

41. LPMA owned a video CD version of the movie. After the incident described above, they loaned the film to Meratus villagers, who in turn became acquainted with Chico Mendes through this medium.

42. See, respectively, Shiva (1992); Weber (1988); Guha (1989); Rangan (1996). See also Garb (1997) for northern translations.

43. Braidotti et al. (1994) introduce this United Nations initiative and explore its implications.

44. Spivak writes about the use of "gender" in World Bank supported development projects in Bangladesh; feminists have rejected "gender" there, saying that it is an imperial imposition (2000). My thinking about the "unmooring" of gender draws on her paper. In contrast with the Bangladesh rejection, in Yemen, "gender" sparked controversy because it was identified too deeply with women's sexual freedom; the women's studies center at the University of San'a was closed down because the center used this word (Abu-Nasr 2000; Seteney Shami drew this article to my attention).

"Facilities and incentives"

1. The Indonesian Minister of the Environment is quoted, explaining the omission of other Indonesian agendas by suggesting that what Indonesians need most is enforcement-oriented foreign intervention: "Combating unlawful logging should top the list of developed countries' priorities in line with their commitment to conserve tropical forests" (Ivereigh 2003: 29).

2. Worse yet, they describe the certification program in misleading rhetoric: "To protect orangutan habitat, The Nature Conservancy is facilitating the development and implementation of a locally derived model for collaborative management that will create incentives necessary to gain support from forest-dependent communities, forest industry, and the local and provincial government" (The Nature Conservancy 2002). What could this possibly mean, and why don't they tell us?

3. Follow-up articles on a congressional investigation and the Conservancy's response are, respectively, Stephens (2003) and Stephens and Ottaway (2003).

4. Meanwhile, other alliances and tactics have been in play. WALHI, AMAN (The Indigenous People's Alliance of the Archipelago), and the U.S.-based Rainforest Action Network (RAN) have called on U.S. firms to stop buying Indonesian wood. RAN has singled out The Conservancy's partner, Home Depot, for "good promises, bad results." See Rainforest Action Network (2003).

Chapter 7: The Forest of Collaborations

1. Ikranegara's poem consists only of the title and one word: *belum* ("not yet"). The poem, which appeared originally in the June 1998 special issue of *Horison* on "Reformasi," is dated May 20, 1998, the day before President Suharto's resignation and the end of the New Order. I encountered the poem in the bilingual collection *Secrets Need Words*, edited by Harry Aveling (Ikranegara 2001).

2. *Oxford English Dictionary*, 2d ed. s.v. "collaboration."

3. The process of collaboration has sparked an insightful discussion in science studies, where it has called attention to "boundary objects" (Star and Griesemer 1989) and "trading zones" (Galison 1997).

4. A uniform system of "village" administration was mandated in 1979, recapitulating earlier attempts to simplify and codify rural social order. See Colchester et al. (2003: 166–71).

5. This quotation is pieced together from notes taken during two separate interviews with the speaker. The language is my best approximation of what was said, but, even beyond issues of translation, it does not represent the words of the speaker precisely. I have written the interview in the first person despite this limitation in my attempt to better offer the spirit of my informant's communication.

6. In referring to these texts, I am caught in an awkward position in trying to protect the privacy of my informants. I have changed the names of people and places in this chapter; to prevent casual readers from disturbing the privacy of these people, I have omitted references that immediately reveal proper names. Scholars who need to know more about these texts will find the references in Tsing (1999).

7. Meratus community formation is discussed in more depth in Tsing (1993).

8. At one Ford-supported conference, Walter Coward, director of the Rural

Poverty Alleviation Program, offered his reflections on the genesis of CBNRM during his tenure at Ford. His story stresses two conjunctures through which the idea became charismatic enough to travel. The first was his discovery of small-scale, "community-based" irrigation at precisely that moment when development agencies were obsessed with large-scale irrigation. Coward relates how Philippine villagers showed him sophisticated local systems of irrigation. International developers had ignored these small-scale systems; they wanted big dams. Small-scale irrigation could be the perfect symbol for the alternative: not Big Dams, but small dams; not Big Development, but community-based development. The political will to support local forms of resource management owes a great deal to the fact that small-scale irrigation was such an apt carrier for the idea of community (Coward forthcoming).

The second conjuncture was the extension of community-based irrigation to build the idea of community-based forestry. Coward told conference attendees how he arrived in Indonesia, as a Ford Foundation program officer, with ideas he had developed in the Philippines about small-scale irrigation. There he met foresters worried about forest destruction and the loss of rural livelihoods. Thinking together, they hatched a larger domain of "community-based natural resource management": Community irrigation models could help reorganize forestry. Two kinds of charisma were gained in this articulation. First, CBNRM took off toward many resources, becoming a general resource-management model: Soon, for example, Ford was thinking about community-based fisheries. Second, a new set of allies was acquired. Conservationists were worried about forests; indigenous rights groups worried about forest communities. The Ford Foundation was not ready to endorse either conservation or indigenous rights; however, their programs gained momentum from the impetus of these overlapping causes.

9. Consider, for example, the influential Zimbabwean initiative called CAMPFIRE. CAMPFIRE offers rural communities a share of the income gained from international big game hunting if they conserve local wildlife. CAMPFIRE is a very different model of community-based conservation than that discussed so far. Rather than working to conserve resources for village use, this program offers villagers a quid pro quo: Put up with the wildlife, which compete with village cattle and destroy village crops, in exchange for a share in the sometimes considerable revenues of big game hunting. This striking arrangement brings us directly to the particularity of collaborative partners, which range from rich white hunters, willing to pay top dollars for trophies, to a national government unwilling to provide for rural citizens directly.

In a history of the program, CAMPFIRE's founder, Marshall Murphree, portrays it as a set of strategic compromises in which the "congruent objectives" of allies could be tweaked into a practical arrangement (Murphree forthcoming). The compromises, he admitted, helped explain the failures of the program as well as its successes; for example, by allowing local government to count as "community," the program became entwined with government's own corruption and inequality. Critics of CAMPFIRE have charged that the program is just too deeply intertwined with bad collaborators. Conservation for the benefit of big game hunters fits too neatly into the colonial legacy of native displacement in East Africa; government management objectives join too poorly with local empowerment (Neumann forthcoming; Matowanyika 1997). Questions about community resource management only open wider: When do contingent collaborations negate utopian hopes leaving only practical—and unworthy—solutions? When does CBNRM become a top-down management scheme?

One response to these questions assessed the influence of CAMPFIRE with a cautious optimism. Ken Wilson, a Ford Foundation program officer in Mozambique, found that the inspiration of CAMPFIRE encouraged national elites in Mozambique to support community resource management in the 1990s (Wilson forthcoming). At that time, the political climate in Mozambique differed sharply from that in Zimbabwe, in his assessment. Where Zimbabwe offered top-down management, Mozambique allowed models to "bubble up" from local sources. Community resource experiments could be worked out in relation to a more circumscribed and relevant set of players, from shamans to foresters. Communities could be negotiated closer to the ground. In Wilson's story, CAMPFIRE facilitated a combination of local initiative and international backing.

10. Agrawal (1997) offers a critical reflection on the history of concepts of "community" as these inform CBNRM. This too is a Ford Foundation supported discussion paper.

11. Leach and Fairhead discuss this problem in relation to West African forest histories (2000). See also Tsing (1999).

References

··········

Abu-Nasr, Donna. 2000. Yemen divided over 'gender' fight. Yahoo! News. http://dailynews.yahoo.com/h/ap/20000515/wl/yemen_gender_clash_1.html.

Aditjondro, George J. 1990. Dampak sistemik dan kritik kultural yang terlupakan: Suatu relfleksi terhadap kampanye Kedung Ombo yang lalu. *Kritis* 4 (3): 44–52.

———. 1991a. The emerging environmental movement in Indonesia. Occasional paper. Salatiga: Universitas Kristen Satya Wacana.

———. 1991b. Aksi massa dan pendidikan masyarakat hanya dua aspek gerakan kaum terpelajar di Indonesia. *Kritis* 5 (3): 87–104.

———. 1998. Large dam victims and their defenders. In *The politics of environment in Southeast Asia*, eds. Philip Hirsh and Carrol Warren, 29–54. London: Routledge.

———. 2003. Gerakan masyarakat adat, mengayuh di antara batu karang dan pusaran air di laut lepas. *Seputar Rakyat* 5 (Tahun I, Juni): 15–17.

Agrawal, Arun. 1997. Community in conservation: Beyond enchantment and disenchantment. Gainesville, FL: Conservation Development Forum Discussion Paper No. 1.

———. 2003. Environmentality: Technologies of government and the making of subjects. York Centre for Asian Research, Asian Environment Series, York Univ. http://www.yorku.ca/ycar/publications.htm.

Aliansi Advokasi Meratus. 2000. *Kasus alih fungsi kawasan hutan lindung pegunungan Meratus dan pencadangan kawasan HPT. PT. Kodeco Timber*. Banjarmasin: Aliansi Advokasi Meratus.

Aliansi Masyarakat Adat Nusantara (AMAN). 1999. *Catatan hasil Kongres Masyarakat Adat Nusantara, Jakarta, 15–22 Maret 1999*. Jakarta: AMAN.

Anderson, Benedict R. O'G. 1972. Java in a time of revolution. Ithaca, NY: Cornell Univ. Press.

———. 1999. Indonesian nationalism today and in the future. *New Left Review* 235 (May–June): 3–17.

Appadurai, Arjun. 1996. *Modernity at large*. Minneapolis: Univ. of Minnesota Press.

Ascher, William. 1998. From oil to timber: The political economy of off-budget financing in Indonesia. *Indonesia* 65 (April): 37–61.

Atran, Scott. 1990. *Cognitive foundations of natural history*. Cambridge: Cambridge Univ. Press.

Atya, Richard Eba'a, and Markku Simula. 2002. Forest certification: Pending challenges for tropical timber. ITTO Technical Series 19. http://www.itto.or.jp/inside/download/E-Certification.pdf.

Austen, Ralph. 1653. *A treatise of fruit trees. . . .* together with *The spiritual use of an orchard . . .* Oxford: Tho. Robinson.

Balibar, Etienne. 2002. Ambiguous universality. In *Politics and the other scene*, trans. Daniel Hahn, 146–76. London: Verso.

Banjarmasin Post. 1998. Lapangan golf Batulicin masih diduduki. Dec. 22.

———. 1999. Warga duduki PT Kodeco sepekan. March 11.

———. 1999. Kodeco didemo, kegiatan sempat terhenti. April 15.

———. 2000. Kami siap bakar Kodeco. March 14.

———. 2000. Gubernur setuju Meratus dieksploitasi. March 15.

Banuri, Tariq, and Frederique Marglin, eds. 1993. *Who will save the forests? Knowledge, power and environmental destruction.* London: Zed Books.

Barber, Charles V. 1989. The state, the environment, and development: The genesis and transformation of social forestry policy in New Order Indonesia. Ph.D. diss., Univ. of California, Berkeley.

Barber, Charles V., and James Schweithelm. 2000. *Trial by fire: Forest fires and forest policy in Indonesia's era of crisis and reform.* Washington, DC: World Resources Institute.

Barnet, Richard J., and John Cavanagh. 1994. *Global dreams: Imperial corporations and the new world order.* New York: Simon & Schuster.

Barr, Christopher. 1998. Bob Hasan, the rise of Apkindo, and the shifting dynamics of control in Indonesia's timber sector. *Indonesia* 65 (April): 1–36.

Barry, Andrew, Thomas Osborne, and Nikolas Rose. 1996. *Foucault and political reason.* Chicago: Univ. of Chicago Press.

Behar, John. 1997. Jungle fever. *Fortune* (June 9): 116–28.

Belcher, Martha. 1993. *Southeast Asia rainforests: A resource guide and directory.* San Francisco: Rainforest Action Network.

Berry, Joe. 1999. Sea turtles and teamsters together at last. *Labornet Newsline*, December 19. http://www.labornet.org/news/123199/08.html.

Beverly, John. 1997. Does the project of the left have a future? *Boundary 2*, 24 (1, Spring): 35–57.

Bhavani, Kum-Kum, John Foran, and Priya Kurian. 2003. An introduction to women, culture, and development. In *Feminist futures*, eds. Kum-Kum Bhavani, John Foran, and Priya Kurian, 1–21. London: Zed Books.

Blake, William. 1982. Auguries of innocence. In *The rattle bag*, eds. Seamus Heaney and Ted Hughes, 47–50. London: Faber and Faber.

Borsuk, Richard. 1997. Bre-X minerals defends pact with Indonesia. *Wall Street Journal*, February 2, B3A.

Bourdieu, Pierre. 1984. *Distinction: A social critique of the judgement of taste.* Trans. Richard Nice. Cambridge, MA: Harvard Univ. Press.

Braidotti, Rosi, Ewa Charkiewicz, Sabine Hausler, and Saskia Wieringa. 1994. *Women, the environment and sustainable development.* London: Zed Books with INSTRAW.

Breaking News. 1998. Bre-X investor gets last laugh with song. Dec. 22. CANOE Web site. http://www.canoe.ca/moneyBreXSaga/dec22_brexblues.html.

Bre-X/Bresea shareholder class action information Web site. http://www.Brexclass.com (site now discontinued).

Bre-Xscam.com Web site. The bungle in the jungle. http://www.Bre-xscam.com (site now discontinued).

Brockway, Lucile. 2002. *Science and colonial expansion: The role of the British botanic gardens.* New Haven, CT: Yale Univ. Press.

Brookfield, Harold, Leslie Potter, and Yvonne Byron. 1995. *In place of the forest: Environmental and socioeconomic transformations in Borneo and the eastern Malay peninsula.* New York: United Nations Press.

Brosius, J. Peter. 1986. River, forest and mountain: The Penan Gang landscape. *Sarawak Museum Journal* 36 (57, n.s.): 173–84.

―――. 1999a. Analyses and interventions: Anthropological engagements with environmentalism. *Current Anthropology* 40 (3): 277–309.

―――. 1999b. Green dots, pink hearts: Displacing politics from the Malaysian rainforest. *American Anthropologist* 101 (1): 36–57. Special issue, *Ecologies for Tomorrow: Reading Rappaport Today*, guest ed. Aletta Biersack.

―――. 2003a. The forest and the nation: Negotiating citizenship in Sarawak, East Malaysia. In *Cultural citizenship in island Southeast Asia*, ed. Renato Rosaldo, 76–133. Berkeley: Univ. of California Press.

―――. 2003b. Voices for the Borneo rainforest: Writing the history of an environmental campaign. In *Nature in the global south*, eds. Paul Greenough and Anna Tsing, 319–46. Durham, NC: Duke Univ. Press.

Brosius, J. Peter, Anna Tsing, and Charles Zerner. 1998. Representing communities: History and politics of community-based resource management. *Society and Natural Resources* 11:157–68.

Brown, Catherine Saint George. 1994. *Bajau*. 2d ed. Trans. Sasha Salim. Jakarta: Yayasan Sejati.

Brown, David. 1999. Addicted to rent: Corporate and spatial distribution of forest resources in Indonesia: Implications for forest sustainability and government policy. Indonesia UK Tropical Forestry Management Programme, Jakarta. Yahoo! Geocities. http://www.geocities.com/davidbrown_id/Atr_main.html.

Bryant, Raymond, and Sinead Bailey. 1997. *Third world political ecology*. London: Routledge.

Bryce, Robert, and Steven Feld. Forthcoming. *Corporate power and civil society: The story of Freeport-McMoRan at home and abroad*.

Buck-Morss, Susan. 2000. Hegel and Haiti. *Critical Inquiry* 26 (Summer): 821–65.

Budianta, Eka. 2000. Rumah-rumah cinta. In *Masih bersama langit*, 1–3. Magelang, Indonesia: IndonesiaTera.

Budiman, Arief. 1990. Gerakan mahasiswa dan LSM: Ke arah sebuah reunifikasi. *Kritis* 4 (3): 53–59.

Burkhill, I. H. 1966. *Economic products of the Malay Peninsula*. Kuala Lumpur: Ministry of Agriculture and Cooperatives, Governments of Malaysia and Singapore.

Butler, Judith. 2000. Restaging the universal. In *Contingency, hegemony, universality: Contemporary dialogues on the left*, Judith Butler, Ernesto Laclau, and Slavoj Zizek, 11–43. London: Verso.

Cabildo, Mayor U'wa. 2000. Communique to the national and international public: Oxy invades U'wa territory. Rainforest Action Network, January 20. http://www.ran.org_campaigns/beyond_oil/oxy/communique_000120.html.

Calgary Sun. 1997. Ultimate betrayal: Bre-X boss says pair ruined dream. October 12. CANOE Web site. http://www.calgarysun.com/.

Carrere, Ricardo, and Larry Lohmann. 1996. *Pulping the south: Industrial tree plantations and the world paper economy*. London: Zed Books.

Carter, Paul. 1987. *The road to Botany Bay*. London: Faber.

CFRA News Talk Radio Web site. 1998. TSE raises listing standards for mining and exploration companies; and TSE tightens rules for junior miners. August 20. http://www.cfra.com.

CFRA News Talk Radio Web site. 1999. Indonesia trying to recover reputation after Bre-X, says specialist. March 20. http://www.cfra.com.

Chakrabarty, Dipesh. 2000. *Provincializing Europe: Postcolonial thought and historical difference*. Princeton, NJ: Princeton Univ. Press.

Chamin, Mardiyah, IG. G. Maha Adi, and Almin Hatta. 1999. Yang misterius di Meratus. *Tempo* (December 5): 51.

Cheah, Pheng. 1997. Posit(ion)ing human rights in the current global conjuncture. *Public Culture* 9 (2): 233–66.

———. 2001. Universal areas: Asian studies in a world in motion. *Traces* 1 (1): 37–70.

———. 2003. *Spectral nationality: Passages of freedom from Kant to postcolonial literatures of liberation*. New York: Columbia Univ. Press.

Cheah, Pheng, and Bruce Robbins, ed. 1998. *Cosmopolitics*. Minneapolis: Univ. of Minnesota Press.

Christen, Kimberly. 2004. *Properly Warumungu: indigenous future-making in a remote Australian town*. Ph.D. dissertation, University of California, Santa Cruz.

Clifford, James. 1997. *Routes: Travel and translation in the late twentieth century*. Cambridge, MA: Harvard Univ. Press.

Colchester, Marcus. 1990. The International Tropical Timber Organization: Kill or cure for the rainforests? *The Ecologist* 20 (5): 167.

Colchester, Marcus, Martua Sirait, and Boedhi Wijarjo. 2003. *The application of FSC principles No. 2 and 3 in Indonesia: Obstacles and principles*. Jakarta: WALHI and AMAN. http://www.walhi.or.id.

Conklin, Harold. 1975. *Hanunoo agriculture*. Northford, CT: Elliot's Books. (Orig. pub. 1957.)

Coward, Walter. Forthcoming. Building models of community-based resource management: A personal narrative. In *Representing communities*, eds. J. Peter Brosius, Anna Tsing, and Charles Zerner. Oakland, CA: Altamira Press.

Curran, L. M., S. N. Trigg, A. K. McDonald, D. Astiani, Y. M. Hardiono, P. Siregar, I. Caniago, and E. Kasischke. 2004. Lowland forest loss in protected areas of Indonesian Borneo. *Science* 303 (February 13): 1000–1003.

Daily Mining News. 1999. Will Canadians be allowed in American Bre-X suit? March 31.

Danaher, Kevin, and Roger Burbach, eds. 2000. *Globalize this! The battle against the World Trade Organization and corporate rule*. Monroe, ME: Common Courage Press.

Danielson, Vivian, and James Whyte. 1997. *Bre-X: Gold today, gone tomorrow*. Toronto: The Northern Miner.

Dauvergne, Peter. 1997. *Shadows in the forest: Japan and the politics of timber in Southeast Asia*. Cambridge, MA: MIT Press.

———. 2001. *Loggers and degradation in the Asia-Pacific*. Cambridge: Cambridge Univ. Press.

Day, Tony. 1994. 'Landscape' in early Java. In *Recovering the Orient*, eds. Andrew Gerstle and Anthony Milner, 175–203. Singapore: Harwood Academic Publishers.

Demeritt, David. 1999. Global climate change and the cultural politics of science. Paper presented to the U.C. Berkeley Environmental Politics Seminar.

DePalma, Anthony. 1997. At end of a miner's rainbow, a cloud of confusion lingers. *The New York Times*. March 31, A1, D10.

Dinamika Berita. 1999. Bupati HSS minta pemda Kalsel tarik izin PT Kodeco. November 30.

Djueng, Stepanus, and Sandra Moniaga. 1994. Kata pengantar: Kebudayaan dan manusia yang majemuk. Apakah masih punya tempat di Indonesia? *Konvensi ILO 169,* 5–17. Jakarta: ELSAM (Lembaga Studi dan Advokasi Masyarakat) and LBBT (Lembaga Bela Banua Talino).

Douglas, Stephen. 1970. *Political socialization and student activism in Indonesia.* Urbana: Univ. of Illinois Press.

Dove, Michael. 1985. The agroecological mythology of the Javanese and the political economy of Indonesia. *Indonesia* 39: 1–36.

———. 1993. A revisionist view of tropical deforestation and development. *Environmental Conservation* 20 (1): 17–56.

———. 1999. Representations of the 'other' by others: The ethnographic challenge posed by planters' views of peasants in Indonesia. In *Transforming the Indonesian uplands,* ed. Tania Li, 203–29. London: Harwood Academic Publishers.

Dowie, Mark. 1996. *Losing ground: American environmentalism at the close of the twentieth century.* Cambridge, MA: MIT Press.

Drayton, Richard. 2000. *Nature's government: Science, imperial Britain, and the 'improvement' of the world.* New Haven, CT: Yale Univ. Press.

Duara, Prasenjit. 2001. The discourse of civilization and pan-Asianism. *Journal of World History* 12 (1): 99–130.

Dubois, Laurent. 1997. Slave emancipation and the limits of citizenship during the French revolution. Working Paper 97–32, Harvard Univ. International Seminar on the History of the Atlantic World, 1500–1800.

Dunlap, Thomas. 1999. *Nature and the English diaspora.* Cambridge: Cambridge Univ. Press.

Eccleston, Bernard, and David Potter. 1996. Environmental NGOs and different political contexts in South-East Asia. In *Environmental change in South-East Asia,* eds. Michael Parnell and Raymond Bryant, 49–66. London: Routledge.

Edwin, Norman. 1990a. Dua puluh enam tahun, antara perintis dan penurus. *Kompas* (April 29): 1, 13.

———. 1990b. Letkol Mutopo, perwira 'paling tinggi.' *Kompas* (April 29): 12.

———. 1990c. Dia hilang antara kabut. *Kompas* (July 29): 2–3.

———. 1990d. Ayam hitam di puncak gunung. *Kompas* (July 29): 2–3.

———. 1990e. Ebrus, gunung kebahagiaan. *Kompas* (October 27): 8–9.

Eisler, Dale. 1997. Sorrow in St. Paul. *MacLean's* 110 (April 14, 7): 55.

Eldridge, Philip. 1989. NGOs in Indonesia: Popular movement or arm of government? Working Paper 55, Clayton, Australia: Centre of Southeast Asian Studies, Monash Univ.

Ellen, Roy. 1986. What Black Elk left unsaid: On the illusory images of green primitivism. *Anthropology Today* 2 (6): 8–12.

Ellen, Roy, and Katsuyoshi Fukui, eds. 1996. *Redefining nature: Ecology, culture, and domestication.* Oxford: Berg.

Environmental Management Development Project in Indonesia. 1996. *The ecology of Indonesia series.* Hong Kong: Periplus Press.

Farquarson, G. 1997. Busang technical audit: Interim report. *Gatra* 17 (May): 27.

Feldman, Leslie Dale. 2001. *Freedom as motion.* Lanham, MD: Univ. Press of America.

Ferguson, James. 1994. *The anti-politics machine*. Minneapolis: Univ. of Minnesota Press.

Ferguson, James, and Akhil Gupta. 2002. Spatializing states: Governmentality in Africa and India. *American Ethnologist* 29 (4): 981–1,002.

Fleck, Richard. 1985. *Henry Thoreau and John Muir among the Indians*. Hamden: Archon Books.

Fletcher, Susan. 1995. International forest agreements: Current status. Congressional Research Service Report for Congress, 95-960 ENV, September 11. National Council for Science and the Environment. http://www.NCSEonline.org/NLE/CRSreports/Forests/for-11.cfm.

Forum Komunikasi Kehutanan Masyarakat (FKKM). 1999a. *Reformasi daerah yang terhenti*. Yogyakarta: Aditya Media.

———. 1999b. RUUK dan potensi bahaya desintegrasi. *Warta* 2 (9): 3–4.

Foucault, Michel. 1991. On governmentality. In *The Foucault effect*, eds. Graham Burchell, Colin Gordon, and Peter Miller, 87–104. Chicago: Univ. of Chicago Press.

Fox, Stephen. 1981. *The American conservation movement: John Muir and his legacy*. Madison: Univ. of Wisconsin Press.

Francis, Diane. 1997. *Bre-X: The inside story*. Toronto: Key Porter Books.

———. 1999. Brokers must pay for their role in Bre-X. *National Post Online*, May 20. http://www.nationalpost.com.

Friedman, Thomas. 2000. *The lexus and the olive tree: Understanding globalization*. New York: Anchor Books.

Fukuyama, Francis. 1992. *The end of history and the last man*. New York: Free Press.

Gale, Fred. 1998. *The tropical timber trade regime*. New York: St. Martin's Press.

Galison, Peter. 1997. *Image and logic: a material culture of microphysics*. Chicago: Univ. of Chicago Press.

Gallon, Gary. 2001. Special on Bob Hasan and Indonesian forests. *The Gallon Environment Letter* 5 (2, January 8). http://library.mtroyal.ca/archives/gallon/gallon52.htm.

Garb, Yaakov. 1997. Lost in translation: Toward a feminist account of Chipko. In *Transitions, environments, translations*, eds. Joan Scott, Cora Kaplan, and Debra Keates, 273–84. New York: Routledge.

Garuda. 2002. Investor update. August: 54–55.

Gellert, Paul. 1998. A brief history and analysis of Indonesia's forest fire crisis. *Indonesia* 65 (April): 63–85.

Gibson-Graham, J. K. 1996. *The end of capitalism (as we knew it): A feminist critique of political economy*. Cambridge, MA: Blackwell.

Gold, Ann, and Bhoju Ram Gujar. 2002. *In the time of trees and sorrows*. Durham, NC: Duke Univ. Press.

Gonner, Christian. 2000. Causes and impacts of forest fires: A case study from East Kalimantan, Indonesia. *International Forest Fire News*, 22: 35–40.

Goold, Douglas, and Andrew Willis. 1997. *The Bre-X fraud*. Toronto: McClelland and Stewart Inc.

Gordon, Joshua. 1998. NGOs, the environment, and political pluralism in New Order Indonesia. *Explorations in Southeast Asian Studies*. 2 (2). http://www.hawaii.edu/cseas/pubs/explore/v2/gordon.html.

Grove, Richard H. 1995. *Green imperialism: Colonial expansion, tropical island edens, and the origins of environmentalism, 1600–1860*. Cambridge: Cambridge Univ. Press.

Guha, Ramachandra. 1989. *The unquiet woods: Ecological change and peasant resistance in the Himalaya*. Berkeley: Univ. of California Press.

Hager, Nicky, and Bob Burton. 1999. *Secrets and lies: The anatomy of an anti-environmental PR campaign*. Monroe, ME: Common Courage Press.

Hajari, Nisid. 1997. Is the pot at the end of the rainbow empty? *Time* 149 (14, 7 April). Online version. http://www.time.com/.

Hall, Stuart. 1996. On postmodernism and articulation: An interview with Stuart Hall, edited by Lawrence Grossberg. In *Stuart Hall: Critical dialogues in cultural studies*, eds. David Morley and Kuan-Hsing Chen, 131–50. London: Routledge.

Hammond, Ross. 1998. *Addicted to profit: Big tobacco's expanding global reach*. Washington, DC: Essential Action. http://www.essentialaction.org/addicted.

Hannerz, Ulf. 1996. *Transnational connections: Culture, people, places*. London: Routledge.

Haraway, Donna. 2003. *The companion species manifesto: Dogs, people, and significant otherness*. Chicago: Prickly Paradigm Press.

Hardin, Garrett. 1968. The tragedy of the commons. *Science* 162: 1243–48.

Hardt, Michael, and Antonio Negri. 2000. *Empire*. Cambridge, MA: Harvard Univ. Press.

Harrison, Robert Pogue. 1992. *Forests: The shadow of civilization*. Chicago: Univ. of Chicago Press.

Harvey, David. 1989. *The condition of postmodernity*. Oxford: Basil Blackwell.

Harwell, Emily. 2000. Remote sensibilities: Discourses of technology and the making of Indonesia's natural disaster. *Development and Change* 31 (1): 307–40.

Hayden, Corinne. 2003. *When nature goes public: The making and unmaking of bioprospecting in Mexico*. Princeton, NJ: Princeton Univ. Press.

HBO (Home Box Office). 1995. *The burning season: The Chico Mendes story*. Videorecording. Burbank, CA: Warner Home Video.

Hecht, Susanna, and Alexander Cockburn. 1990. *The fate of the forest: Developers, destroyers, and defenders of the Amazon*. New York: Harper Perennial.

Hefner, Robert. 2000. *Civil Islam: Muslims and democratization in Indonesia*. Princeton, NJ: Princeton Univ. Press.

Hill, Hal. 1996. *The Indonesian economy since 1966*. Cambridge: Cambridge Univ. Press.

Hochstetler, Kathryn. 1997. The evolution of the Brazilian environmental movement and its political roles. In *The new politics of inequality in Latin America*, eds. Douglas Chalmers, Carlos Vilas, Katherine Roberts-Hite, Scott Martin, Kerianne Piester, and Monique Segarra, 192–216. Oxford: Oxford Univ. Press.

Holdgate, Martin. 1993. Foreword. In *Parks for life: Report of the IVth world congress on national parks and protected areas, 12–21 February 1992*, ed. Jeffrey McNeely. Gland, Switzerland: IUCN World Conservation Union—Worldwide Fund for Nature.

Human Rights Watch. 2001. Indonesia: the violence in Central Kalimantan (Borneo). http://www.hrw.org/backgrounder/asia/borneo0228.htm.

Hvalkof, Søren. 2000. Outrage in rubber and oil: Extractivism, indigenous peoples, and justice in the upper Amazon. In *People, plants, and justice*, ed. Charles Zerner, 83–116. New York: Columbia Univ. Press.

Ikranegara. 2001. Merdeka. In *Secrets need words: Indonesian poetry, 1966–1998*, ed. and trans. Harry Aveling, 344–45. Southeast Asia Series, No. 105. Athens: Ohio Univ. Center for International Studies.

ILO (International Labor Organization). 1994. *Konvensi ILO 169*. Jakarta: ELSAM (Lembaga Studi dan Advokasi Masyarakat) and LBBT (Lembaga Bela Banua Talino).

Indonesian Center for Environmental Law. 1994. Kontroversi seputar dana reboisasi bagi pembangunan pesawat terbang P.T. IPTN. Jakarta: Indonesian Center for Environmental Law.

Ismail, Taufiq. 1971. Aku ingin. *Horison* 6 (August 8): 241.

ITTC (International Tropical Timber Council). 1992. Draft report of the International Tropical Timber Council at its eleventh session, Yokohama, Japan 28 November–4 December 1991. Report XI/25. Yokohama: ITTO.

ITTO (International Tropical Timber Organization). 1990. The promotion of sustainable forest management: A case study in Sarawak, Malaysia. *Report submitted to the International Tropical Timber Council* VIII (7, May 7).

———. 2000. Measuring up: Assessing progress toward sustainable forest management in the tropics. http://www.itto.or.jp.

Ivereigh, Djuana. 2003. It takes a forest. *Nature Conservancy* 53 (2): 20–31.

Jackson, Karl, ed. 1999. Introduction: The roots of the crisis. In *Asian contagion*, ed. Karl Jackson, 1–27. Boulder, CO: Westview Press.

Jala, David. 1997. Frenzy stuns market. *Calgary Sun*, April 2. http://www.calgarysun.com.

Jameson, Fredric. 1991. *Postmodernism, or the cultural logic of late capitalism*. Durham, NC: Duke Univ. Press.

———. 2002. *A singular modernity*. London: Verso.

Jameson, Fredric, and Misao Miyoshi, eds. 1998. *The cultures of globalization*. Durham, NC: Duke Univ. Press.

Jancar-Webster, Barbara. 1993. Eastern Europe and the former Soviet Union. In *Environmental politics in the international arena*, ed. Sheldon Kamieniecki, 199–222. Albany: State Univ. of New York Press.

Jespersen, Christine. 1997. Engendering adventure: Men, women, and the American 'frontier,' 1880–1927. Ph.D. diss., Rutgers Univ.

Jessup, Timothy. 1981. Why do Apo Kayan shifting cultivators move? *Borneo Research Bulletin* 13 (1): 16–32.

Juma, Calestous. 1989. *The gene hunters: Biotechnology and the scramble for seeds*. Princeton, NJ: Princeton Univ. Press.

Keck, Margaret. 1995a. International politics in the Amazon. Paper presented at Environmental Conflicts and Movements conference, Five College Program on Peace and Security, Amherst, MA.

———. 1995b. Social equity and environmental politics in Brazil: Lessons from the rubber tappers of Acre. *Comparative Politics* 27 (July): 409–24.

Keck, Margaret, and Kathryn Sikkink. 1998. *Activists beyond borders*. Ithaca, NY: Cornell Univ. Press.

Kellert, Stephen, and Edward O. Wilson, eds. 1993. *The biophilia hypothesis*. Washington, DC: Island Press.

Laclau, Ernesto. 2000. Identity and hegemony: The role of universality in the constitution of political logics. In *Contingency, hegemony, universality: Contemporary di-*

alogues on the left, Judith Butler, Ernesto Laclau, and Slavoj Zizek, 44–89. London: Verso.

Lankford, Scott. 1991. John Muir and the nature of the West: An ecology of American life, 1864–1914. Ph.D. diss., Stanford Univ.

Latour, Bruno. 1996. *Aramis, or, the love of technology*. Cambridge, MA: Harvard Univ. Press.

Lawrence, Jessica, Noriko Toyoda, and Helvi Lystiani. 2003. *Importing destruction*. San Francisco: Rainforest Action Network. http://www.ran.org/info_center/reports.html.

Leach, Melissa, and James Fairhead. 2000. Fashioned forest pasts, occluded histories? International environmental analysis in West African locales. *Development and Change* 31 (1): 35–59.

Lev, Daniel. 1992. *Lawyers as outsiders: Advocates versus the state in Indonesia*. SOAS Law Department Working Paper 2. London: Univ. of London, School of Oriental and African Studies.

Levi, Jerome, and Bartholomew Dean. 2003. Introduction. In *At the risk of being heard: Identity, indigenous rights, and postcolonial states*, eds. Bartholomew Dean and Jerome Levi, 1–44. Ann Arbor: Univ. of Michigan Press.

Li, Tania Murray. 1999. Marginality, power, and production: Analyzing upland transformations. In *Transforming the Indonesian uplands*, ed. Tania Li, 1–44. London: Harwood Academic Publishers.

———. 2000. Constituting tribal space: Indigenous identity and resource politics in Indonesia. *Comparative Studies in Society and History* 42 (1): 149–79.

———. 2002. Engaging simplification: Community-based resource management, market processes, and state agendas in upland Southeast Asia. *World Development* 30 (2): 265–83.

———. 2003a. Situating resource struggles: Concepts for empirical analysis. *Economic and Political Weekly* 38 (November 29): 5120–28.

———. 2003b. *Masyarakat adat*, difference, and the limits of recognition in Indonesia's forest zone. In *Race, nature, and the politics of difference*, eds. Donald Moore, Jake Kosek, and Anand Pandian, 380–406. Durham, NC: Duke Univ. Press.

Limbaugh, Ronald H. 1991. Stickeen and the moral education of John Muir. *Environmental History Review* 15 (1): 25–45.

Limerick, Patricia. 1987. *The legacy of conquest: The unbroken past in the American West*. New York: Norton.

Lindblad, J. Thomas. 1988. *Between Dayak and Dutch: The economic history of Southeast Kalimantan, 1880–1942*. Dordrecht: Foris Publications.

Lohmann, Larry. 1993. Against the myths. In *The struggle for land and the fate of the forests*, eds. Marcus Colchester and Larry Lohmann, 16–34. London: Zed Books.

Longfellow, Henry Wadsworth. 1942. Paul Revere's ride. In *A treasury of great poems: English and American*, ed. Louis Untermeyer, 803–6. New York: Simon & Schuster.

Lowe, Celia. 1999. Cultures of nature: Mobility, identity, and biodiversity conservation in the Togean Islands of Sulawesi, Indonesia. Ph.D. diss., Yale Univ.

———. 2003. Sustainability and the question of 'enforcement' in integrated coastal management: The case of Nain Island, Bunaken National Park. *Jurnal Pesisir dan Kelautan*. Bogor: Institute Pertanian Bogor.

LSPMKB (Lembaga Studi Pengabadian Masyarakat Kompas Borneo). 1987. Usulan dana bantuan. Project proposal submitted to the Ford Foundation.

Lundin, Brien. 1998. International pursuit: Turning world-class potential into world-class reality. *Gold Newsletter's Mining Share Focus* 2 (1): 4.

Manser, Bruno. 1996. *Voices from the rainforest*. Selangor, Malaysia: INSAN.

Marr, Carolyn. 1993. *Digging deep: The hidden costs of mining in Indonesia*. London: Down to Earth.

Massey, Doreen. 1995. *Space, place and gender*. Cambridge: Polity.

Matowanyika, Joseph. 1997. CAMPFIRE: An enigma? Paper presented at Representing Communities conference, June 1–3, Helen, GA.

Mayer, Judith. 1996. Environmental organizing in Indonesia: The search for a newer order. In *Global civil society and global environmental governance*, Ronnie D. Lipschutz with Judith Mayer, 169–213. Albany: State Univ. of New York Press.

McBeth, John. 1997. The golden boys. *Far Eastern Economic Review* 160 (10, 6 March): 42–44.

McBeth, John, and Jay Solomon. 1997. First friend. *Far Eastern Economic Review* 160 (8, 20 February): 52–54.

McCarthy, John. 2000. 'Wild logging': The rise and fall of logging networks and biodiversity conservation projects on Sumatra's rainforest frontier. Occasional Paper 31 (Oct.), Center for International Forestry Research, Bogor.

McCulloch, Lesley. 2000. Trifungsi: The role of the Indonesian military in business. Paper presented at the International Conference on Soldiers in Business. Jakarta, October 17–19. http://www.bicc.de/budget/events/milbus/confpapers/mcculloch.pdf.

McCully, Patrick 1996. *Silenced rivers: The ecology and politics of large dams*. London: Zed Books.

McKay, Bonnie, and James Acheson. 1987. *The question of the commons*. Tucson: Univ. of Arizona Press.

McLeod, Ross. 1999. Indonesia's crisis and future prospects. In *Asian contagion*, ed. Karl Jackson, 209–240. Boulder, CO: Westview Press.

Mendes, Chico. 1989. *Fight for the forest: Chico Mendes in his own words*. London: Latin American Bureau (Research and Action) Ltd.

Mitchell, Timothy. 2002. *Rule of experts: Egypt, techno-politics, modernity*. Berkeley: Univ. of California Press.

Moniaga, Sandra. 1993. Toward community-based forestry and recognition of *Adat* property rights in the Outer Islands of Indonesia. In *Legal frameworks for forest management in Asia*, ed. Jefferson Fox, 131–50. Honolulu: East-West Center. Occasional paper 16.

———. 1994. The systematic destruction of the indigenous system of various *Adat* communities throughout Indonesia. In *Seminar on the human dimensions of environmentally sound development*, ed. H. P. Arimbi, 31–36. Jakarta: WALHI.

Mudimbe, V. Y. 1988. *The invention of Africa*. Bloomington: Univ. of Indiana Press.

Muir, John. 1915. *Travels in Alaska*. Boston: Houghton Mifflin.

Muir, John. [1894] 1988. *The mountains of California*. Golden, CO: Fulcrum Press.

Murata, Sachiko. 1992. *The Tao of Islam*. Albany: State Univ. of New York Press.

Murphree, Marshall. Forthcoming. Congruent objectives, competing interests, and strategic compromise: Concept and process in the evolution of Zimbabwe's CAMPFIRE programme. In *Representing communities*, eds. J. Peter Brosius, Anna Tsing, and Charles Zerner. Oakland, CA: Altamira Press.

Najmabadi, Afsaneh. 1991. Interview with Gayatri Spivak. *Social Text* 9 (3, 28): 122–34.

Nature Conservancy. 2001. Community consultations provide key to Lore Lindu success. http://nature.org/wherewework/asiapacific/indonesia/news/news803.html.

Nature Conservancy. 2002. The Nature Conservancy discovers large population of orangutans in Borneo. http://nature.org/magazine/winter2002/orangutans/.

Neumann, Roderick. 1998. *Imposing wilderness: Struggles over livelihood and nature preservation in Africa.* Berkeley: Univ. of California Press.

———. Forthcoming. Model, panacea, or exception? Contextualizing CAMPFIRE and related programs in Africa. In *Representing communities*, eds. J. Peter Brosius, Anna Tsing, and Charles Zerner. Oakland, CA: Altamira Press.

Newman, Peter. 1996. Peter Munk: A dreamer who became a king. *Maclean's* 109 (50, 9 December): 42.

Noss, Reed, and Allen Cooperrider. 1994. *Saving nature's legacy: Protecting and restoring biodiversity.* Washington, DC: Island Press.

Obidzinski, Krystof. 2003. Logging in East Kalimantan, Indonesia: The historical experience of illegality. Ph.D. diss., Univ. of Amsterdam.

Ottawa Citizen. 1997. Rumors swirl around Bre-X. March 25. http://www.ottawacitizen .com.

———. 1997. Buried body not geologist: Report. April 10. http://www.ottawacitizen .com.

Ottaway, David, and Joe Stephens. 2003a. Nonprofit land bank amasses billions. *Washington Post*, May 4, A01.

———. 2003b. How a bid to save a species came to grief. *Washington Post*, May 5, A01.

———. 2003c. Nonprofit sells scenic acreage to allies at a loss. *Washington Post*, May 6, A01.

Pandey, Gyanendra. 2000. Voices from the edge: The struggle to write subaltern histories. In *Mapping subaltern studies and the postcolonial*, ed. Vinayak Chaturvedi, 281–99. London: Verso.

Peet, Richard, and Michael Watts. 1996. *Liberation ecologies: Environment, development, social movements.* London: Routledge.

Peluso, Nancy Lee. 1992. *Rich forests, poor people: Resource control and resistance in Java.* Berkeley: Univ. of California Press.

———. 1993. Coercing conservation: The politics of state resource control. In *The state and social power in global environmental politics*, eds. Ronnie Lipscutz and Ken Conca, 46–70. New York: Columbia Univ. Press.

———. 1995. Whose woods are these? Counter-mapping forest territories in Kalimantan, Indonesia. *Antipode* 27 (4): 383–406.

———. 1996. Fruit trees and family trees in an anthropogenic forest: Property rights, ethics of access, and environmental change in Indonesia. *Comparative Studies in Society and History* 38 (3): 510–49.

———. 1997. Mapping against power, to create power, or in the shadow of power?: Counter-mapping texts and images. Paper presented at Representing Communities conference, June 1–3, Helen, GA.

Peluso, Nancy, and Emily Harwell. 2001. Territory, custom, and the cultural politics of ethnic war in West Kalimantan, Indonesia. In *Violent environments*, eds. Nancy Peluso and Michael Watts, 83–116. Ithaca, NY: Cornell Univ. Press.

Platt, Michael. 1997a. ID challenged. *Calgary Sun*, April 5. http://www.calgarysun.com.

———. 1997b. Dead or alive? *Calgary Sun*, April 11. http://www.calgarysun.com.

———. 1997c. Foul play fears haunt geologist. *Calgary Sun*, April 19. http://www.calgarysun.com.

———. 1997d. Family accepts autopsy. *Calgary Sun*, April 21. http://www.calgarysun.com.

———. 1997e. Print identified as De Guzman's. *Calgary Sun*, April 24. http://www.calgarysun.com.

———. 1997f. Rush hour in the jungle. *Calgary Sun*, May 23. http://www.calgarysun.com.

Posey, Darrell. 1985. Indigenous management of tropical forest ecosystems: The case of the Kayapo Indians of the Brazilian Amazon. *Agroforestry Systems* 3: 139–58.

Povinelli, Elizabeth. 2002. *The cunning of recognition: Indigenous alterities and the making of Australian multiculturalism*. Durham, NC: Duke Univ. Press.

Pramoedya Ananta Toer. 1991. *This earth of mankind*. Trans. Max Lane. New York: Morrow.

———. 1996. My apologies, in the name of experience. Trans. Alex G. Bardsley. *Indonesia* 61 (April): 1–14.

———. 2000. Rasionalisme anti-Tionghoa dan usaha menyikapinya. *Mitra* (March 4): 3–6.

Pratt, Mary Louise. 1992. *Imperial eyes*. London: Routledge.

Rabinow, Paul. 2002. Midst anthropology's problems. *Cultural Anthropology* 17 (2): 135–49.

Radar Banjar. 2003. Menteri LH tolak tukar guling Meratus tapi pemprov tetap akan melakukannya. March 18.

Rainforest Action Network. 2003. Lumber and paper giants to announce ban of Indonesian wood and pulp. *Old Growth Forest News*, May 15. http://www.ran.org/ran_campaigns/old_growth/indonesia/.

Rangan, Haripriya. 1996. From Chipko to Uttaranchal: Development, environment, and social protest in the Garhwal Himalayas, India. In *Liberation ecologies: Environment, development, social movements*, eds. Richard Peet and Michael Watts, 205–26. London: Routledge.

———. 2000. *Of myths and movements: Rewriting Chipko into Himalayan history*. London: Verso.

Ray, John. 1686. *Historia plantarum generalis, I*. London.

Redford, Kent, and Jane Mansour, eds. 1996. *Traditional peoples and biodiversity conservation in large tropical landscapes*. Arlington, VA: The Nature Conservancy.

Revkin, Andrew. 1990. *The burning season: The murder of Chico Mendes and the fight for the Amazon rain forest*. Boston: Houghton Mifflin.

Riles, Annelise. 2000. *The network inside out*. Ann Arbor: Univ. of Michigan Press.

Roesdianto, Victor. 1994. Hutan Kalsel [The forests of south Kalimantan]. In *Cerita dari hutan bakau*, ed. F. Rahardi, 181–82. Jakarta: Pustaka Sastra.

Root, Terry, and Stephen Schneider. 1995. Ecology and climate: Research strategies and implications. *Science*, New Series, 269 (5222, July 21): 334–41.

Rosaldo, Renato. 1986. Ilongot hunting as story and experience. In *The anthropology of experience*, eds. Victor Turner and Edward Bruner, 97–138. Urbana: Univ. of Illinois Press.

Ross, Michael. 2001. *Timber booms and institutional breakdown in Southeast Asia*. Cambridge: Cambridge Univ. Press.

Rotmans, Jan. 1995a. Integrated assessment. Plenary comments delivered at the First Open Meeting of the Human Dimensions of Global Environmental Change Community, June 1–3.

———. 1995b. *Targets in transition*. Pamphlet issued by Rijksinstituut voor Volksgezondheid en Milieu (National Institute of Public Health and the Environment). Bilthoven, The Netherlands: GLOBO.

Rowley, Anthony. 1990. Logged out: Sarawak report criticized by conservationists. *Far Eastern Economic Review* (December 13): 72–74.

Rubin, Sandra. 1998. Obituary: David Walsh. *Financial Post*, June 5. CANOE Web site. http://acmi.canoe.ca/MoneyBreXSaga/jun5_obituaryda.html.

———. 1999. Let all Canadian Bre-X shareholders in class-action suit, court urged. *Financial Post*, February 11. CANOE Web site. http://acmi.canoe.ca/MoneyBreXSaga/feb2_letallbrex.html.

———. 1999. Felderhof still insists Bre-X site has gold. *Financial Post*, March 10. CANOE Web site. http://acmi.canoe.ca/MoneyBreXSaga/mar10_felderhof.html.

Rumansara, Augustinus. 1998. Indonesia: The struggle of the people of Kedung Ombo. In *The struggle for accountability: The World Bank, NGOs, and grassroots movements*, eds. Jonathan Fox and David Brown, 123–50. Cambridge, MA: MIT Press.

Sahlins, Peter. 1994. *Forest rites: The war of the demoiselles in nineteenth-century France*. Cambridge, MA: Harvard Univ. Press.

Saltford, John. 2003. *The United Nations and the Indonesian takeover of West Papua, 1962–1969*. New York: RoutledgeCurzon.

Sardi, Caesar. 1995. Motif gratifikasi media dan pajanan media surat kabar mingguan. B.A. thesis, Universitas Gadjah Mada.

Sarmiento, Domingo. 1998. *Facundo, or civilization and barbarism*. Trans. Mary Mann. New York: Penguin. (Orig. pub. 1845.)

Sassen, Saskia. 1998. *Globalization and its discontents*. New York: New Press.

———. 2000. Spatialities and temporalities of the global: Elements for a theorization. *Public Culture* 12 (1): 215–32.

Schama, Simon. 1995. *Landscape and memory*. New York: Knopf.

Schmink, Marianne, and Charles Wood. 1992. *Contested frontiers in Amazonia*. New York: Columbia Univ. Press.

Schroeder, Richard. 1999. Community, forestry and conditionality in The Gambia. *Africa* 69 (1): 1–22.

Scott, Peter Dale. 2000. Minding the darkness (IV.xi). In *Silenced Voices*, eds. Frank Stewart and John McGlynn, a special issue of *Manoa* 12 (1): 224–29.

Sen, Krishna, and Maila Stivens. 1998. *Gender and power in affluent Asia*. London: Routledge.

Shiva, Vandana. 1992. *Staying alive: Women, ecology and development*. London: Zed Books.

———. 1997. *Biopiracy: The plunder of nature and knowledge*. Boston: South End Books.

Shoumatoff, Alex. 1990. *The world is burning*. Boston: Little, Brown.

Siegel, James T. 1986. *Solo in the new order*. Princeton, NJ: Princeton Univ. Press.

Sirait, Mertua, Sukirno Prasodjo, Nancy Podger, Alex Flavelle, and Jefferson Fox.

1994. Mapping customary land in East Kalimantan, Indonesia: A tool for forest management. *Ambio* 23 (7): 411–17.

Sizer, Nigel, and Dominiek Plouvier. 1997. Increased investment and trade by transnational logging companies in ACP countries: Implications for sustainable forest management and conservation. Draft of a Joint Report of WWF-Belgium WRI and WWF-International, 1997. http://www.rainforestfoundationuk.org/JointReport.pdf.

SKEPHI (Indonesian NGO Network for Tropical Forest Conservation). 1991. *Kedungombo: Between development myth and marginal reality.* 2d ed., Jakarta: SKEPHI.

Slater, Candace. 1995. Amazonia as edenic narrative. In *Uncommon ground: Toward reinventing nature*, ed. William Cronon, 114–31. New York: Norton.

Slotkin, Richard. 1992. *Gunfighter nation: The myth of the frontier in twentieth century America.* New York: Atheneum.

Smith, Michael L. 1987. *Pacific visions: California scientists and the environment, 1850–1915.* New Haven, CT: Yale Univ. Press.

Soe Hok Gie. 1995. Menaklukkan gunung Slamet. In *Zaman peralihan*, 31–49. Yogyakarta: Yayasan Bentang Budaya.

Soesastro, Hadi, and Budi Sudarsono. 1988. Mineral and energy development in Indonesia. In *The minerals industries of ASEAN and Australia*, eds. Bruce McKern and Praipol Koomsup, 161–208. Sydney: Allen and Unwin.

Soroos, Marvin. 1997. *The endangered atmosphere.* Columbia: Univ. of South Carolina Press.

Soule, Michael, ed. 1986. *Conservation biology: The science of scarcity and diversity.* Sunderland, MA: Sinauer Associates.

———. 1995. The social siege of nature. In *Reinventing nature? Responses to postmodern deconstruction*, eds. Michael Soule and Gary Lease, 137–70. Washington, DC: Island Press.

Spivak, Gayatri Chakravorty. 1999. *A critique of postcolonial reason.* Cambridge, MA: Harvard Univ. Press.

———. 2000. Gender. Paper presented at Social Science Research Council workshop on Words in Motion, New York City.

Star, Susan Leigh, and James Griesemer. 1989. Institutional ecology, "translations," and boundary objects: amateurs and professionals in Berkeley's Museum of Vertebrate Zoology, 1907–39. *Social Studies of Science* 19: 387–420.

Stephens, Joe. 2003. Charity's land deals to be scrutinized. *Washington Post*, May 10, A02.

Stephens, Joe, and David Ottaway. 2003. Nature Conservancy suspends land sales. *Washington Post*, May 13, A03.

Stevens, Stan, ed. 1997. *Conservation through cultural survival.* Washington, DC: Island Press.

Stone, Roger, and Claudia D'Andrea. 2001. *Tropical forests and the human spirit.* Berkeley: Univ. of California Press.

Strathern, Marilyn. 1980. No nature, no culture: The Hagen case. In *Nature, culture, and gender*, eds. Carolyn McCormack and Marilyn Strathern, 174–222. Cambridge: Cambridge Univ. Press.

Sturgeon, Noel. 1997. *Ecofeminist natures: Race, gender, feminist theory and political action.* New York: Routledge.

Sukarno. 1983. Let a new Asia and a new Africa be born. *Collected Documents of the*

Asian-African Conference, April 18–24, 1955. Jakarta: Agency for Research and Development, The Department of Foreign Affairs.

Tadiar, Neferti. Forthcoming. *Things fall away: Historical experience and the makings of globalization.* Durham, NC: Duke Univ. Press.

Takacs, David. 1996. *The idea of biodiversity.* Baltimore, MD: Johns Hopkins Univ. Press.

Tanumihardja, Kritiandi. 1994. Cit..cit...door...krekek.... In *Cerita dari hutan bakau,* ed. F. Rahardi, 122. Jakarta: Pustaka Sastra.

TAPOL Bulletin. 1999. The Kopassus-militia alliance, 154 (5). http://www.melanesia.org/views/tapolNov1999.htm.

Taussig, Michael. 1987. *Shamanism, colonialism, and the wild man.* Chicago: Univ. of Chicago Press.

Thompson, E. P. 1975. *Whigs and hunters: The origin of the black act.* New York: Pantheon Books.

Tirtosudarmo, Riwanto. 1991. Mampukah LSM menjadi 'counter-hegemonic movement'? *Kritis* 5 (3): 105–8.

Tourefort, J. P. 1719. *Institutiones rei herbariae.* 3rd ed. Paris: Imprimerie Royale.

Tsing, Anna Lowenhaupt. 1984. Politics and culture in the Meratus mountains. Ph.D. diss., Stanford Univ.

———. 1993. *In the realm of the diamond queen.* Princeton, NJ: Princeton Univ. Press.

———. 1995. From the village to the capital: A successful environmental alliance. Report prepared for the Indonesian Environmental Forum (WALHI).

———. 1997. Transitions as translations. In *Transitions, environments, translations: the meanings of feminism in contemporary politics,* eds. Joan Scott, Cora Kaplan, and Debra Keates, 253–72. New York: Routledge.

———. 1999. Becoming a tribal elder and other fantasies of green development. In *Transforming the Indonesian uplands,* ed. Tania Li, 159–202. Amsterdam: Harwood Academic Publishers.

———. 2001. Land as law: Negotiating the meaning of property in Indonesia. In *Land, property, and the environment,* ed. John F. Richards, 94–137. Oakland, CA: Institute for Contemporary Studies Press.

———. 2003a. Cultivating the wild: Honey-hunting and forest management in southeast Kalimantan. In *Culture and the question of rights,* ed. Charles Zerner, 24–55. Durham, NC: Duke Univ. Press.

———. 2003b. Agrarian allegory and global futures. In *Nature in the global south,* eds. Paul Greenough and Anna Tsing, 124–69. Durham, NC: Duke Univ. Press.

Turner, Frederick J. 1994. The significance of the frontier in American history. In *Rereading Frederick Jackson Turner,* ed. John Mack Faragher, 31–60. New York: Henry Holt.

U.S. General Accounting Office. 1992. International trade: Advertising and promoting U.S. cigarettes in selected Asian countries. GAO/GGD-93-38. http://www.gwjapan.com/ftp/pub/policy/gao/1993/93–38.txt.

Vandergeest, Peter, and Nancy Lee Peluso. 1995. Territorialization and state power in Thailand. *Theory and Society* 24: 385–426.

Vidal, John. 1990. High stakes in the rainforest. *The Guardian* (October 19). http://www.library.ohiou.edu/indopubs/1990/10/19/0005.html.

Vogel, Daniel. 1993. Environmental policy in the European community. In *Environmental politics in the international arena,* ed. Sheldon Kamieniecki, 181–98. Albany: State Univ. of New York Press.

Waldman, Peter, and Jay Solomon. 1997. Geologist's death may lie at heart of Bu-sang mystery. *Wall Street Journal*, April 9, A10.

WALHI (Wahana Lingkungan Hidup Indonesia). 1990. Special Double Issue: WALHI's tenth Anniversary. *Environesia* (September/December).

———. 1993. *Strengthening EIA capacity in Asia.* Jakarta: WALHI.

———. 2000. 7 Momentum utama di bumi. *Warta Bumi* 1 (2): 1–2.

WALHI and YLBHI (Yayasan Lembaga Bantuan Hukum Indonesia). 1993. *Per-jalanan secarik kertas.* Jakarta: WALHI and YLBHI.

Wallace, Alfred Russel. 1962. *The Malay archipelago.* New York: Dover Publications. (Orig. pub. 1869.)

Warmington, Joe. 1997a. Bre-X takeover claim. *Calgary Sun*, April 6. http://www.calgarysun.com.

———. 1997b. Bank on more intrigue. *Calgary Sun*, April 8. http://www.calgarysun.com.

———. 1997c. Yanks waiting: Americans ready to gobble up Bre-X shares. *Calgary Sun*, April 13. http://www.calgarysun.com.

Weber, Thomas. 1988. *Hugging the trees: The story of the Chipko movement.* New York: Viking Penguin.

Wells, Jennifer. 1996. King of gold. *Maclean's* 109 (50, December 9): 39–40.

———. 1997a. Rumble in the jungle. *Maclean's* 110 (5, February 3): 38–39.

———. 1997b. Gunning for gold. *Maclean's* 110 (7, February 17): 52.

———. 1997c. Greed, graft, gold. *Maclean's* 110 (9, March 3): 38–45.

Wilkonson, Todd. 2003. Natural ally. *Nature Conservancy* 53 (2): 32–37.

Williams, Nick Jr. 1988. Boom time along 'rim of fire': Indonesian miners revive gold rush spirit of 49ers. *Los Angeles Times*, December 12, sec 1, 1+.

Wilson, Edward O. 1992. *The diversity of life.* Cambridge, MA: Harvard Univ. Press.

Wilson, Ken. Forthcoming. Of diffusion and context: The bubbling up of community-based natural resource management in Mozambique. In *Representing communities*, eds. J. Peter Brosius, Anna Tsing, and Charles Zerner. Oakland, CA: Altamira Press.

Winarno, Bondan. 1997. *Bre-X: Sebungkah emas di kaki pelangi.* Jakarta: Penerit In-spirasi Indonesia.

World Rainforest Movement, and Sahabat Alam Malaysia. 1989. *The battle for Sarawak's forests.* Penang, Malaysia: World Rainforest Movement and Sahabat Alam Malaysia.

Worster, Donald. 1992a. *Rivers of empire: Water, aridity, and the growth of the Ameri-can West.* New York: Oxford Univ. Press.

———. 1992b. *Under western skies: Nature and history in the American West.* New York: Oxford Univ. Press.

Yanagisako, Sylvia. 2002. *Producing culture and capital: Family firms in Italy.* Princeton, NJ: Princeton Univ. Press.

Zerner, Charles. 1992. Indigenous forest-dwelling communities in Indonesia's outer islands: Livelihood, rights, and environmental management institutions in an era of industrial forest exploitation. Report prepared for the World Bank.

———. 1994. Through a green lens: The construction of customary law and envi-ronment in Indonesia's Maluku Islands. *Law and Society Review* 28 (9): 1079–1122.

Zgodzinski, David. 1997. Bre-X: The battle between bulls and bears on SI. May 4. Silicon Investor Web site. http://www.siliconinvestor.com/.

Index

....

accumulation: capitalist, 244; flexible, 75; spectacular, 72–73, 75–77
activism: environmental, *see* environmentalism; generations of, 22; grassroots, 233; Islamic, 237; mining, 140; in New Order, 227; social, 272
adat, 225–26, 291n.27
Aditjondro, George, 223, 291n.23
agency, 6, 214–15, 227, 230, 238, 252; of destruction, 26; global, 270; Meratus model of, 261
agriculture, 165; capitalist, 177; plantation, 167
Aliansi Advocasi Meratus, 209–10, 212
Aliansi Masyarakat Adat Nusantara (AMAN), 226, 293n.4
Al Qaeda, 11, 215
Americans: indigenous, 6, 91, 100, 283n.10; middle-class white, 142, "Native," 160; privileged, 240; stereotypes of "Native," 151
Anderson, Benedict, 128
APHIDS, 76
Aristotle, 91
armed forces. *See* military
articulation, 77
Asia-Africa Conference, 81–87
Asia-Pacific Peoples Environmental Network, 222
Asian Development Bank, 222
Asian tigers, 36
Asosiasi Panel Kayu Indonesia (APKINDO). *See* Indonesian Wood Panel Association (APKINDO)
axiom of unity, 89–90, 96, 106, 111

Barrick Gold, 61, 71–73, 281n.26
Bauhin, Gaspard, 92
biodiversity, 155–58, 182–83, 190, 209–10; conservation of 157–60; cultivated, 165; discourse of, 95; of fruit, 178; local knowledge of, 182, 186, 189; in mixed forest landscape, 174, 177–78; of rattans, 188; as rural con-

cern, 169–70; in secondary forest, 190
biodiversity prospecting, 159
biopower, 5, 30
bioprospecting, 95
botany, 6, 90–95, 96, 99
Bresea Resources, Ltd., 60, 279n.5
Bretton Woods, 60
Bre-X Minerals Ltd., 56–57, 60–67, 69, 71–73, 75–77, 278 nn. 3 and 14; 279 nn. 5 and 6; 280 nn. 16, 17, 20, and 21; 281 nn. 30 and 33
Budi, 147, 149–51
bureaucracy, 35, 85, 217, 263–65
Burning Season, The, 234, 292n.34
Bush, George H. W., 64, 281n.26
Butler, Judith, 274–75n.14

Campus Normalization Law of 1978, 129, 132
capital, 11, 42, 44, 59; global, 269–70; finance, 59–60, 75–77; financial, 57; investment, 70
capitalism, 1, 11–12, 35, 100, 173, 282n.35; of Asian Tigers, 21; in crisis, 42; crony, 56, 220, 241, 280n.17; cultural specificity of, 3–4; global, 2, 11–12, 43, 56, 159; and the Nature Conservancy, 241, 243; universalizing quality of, 3–4; and war, 12
Cesalpino, Andrea, 91
charisma, 33, 38, 64
charismatic megafauna, 240, 290n.12
Cheah, Pheng 269–71
Chipko, 230, 235–36
Christianity, 9; and European botany, 91–92, 94; and Muir's nature worship, 97
Christians, 48
civil society, 214, 267
civilization, xiii, 48–49, 131, 274n.12; end of, 82; "the shadow of," 201
citizens, 253; of adat, 226; environmentalists as, 249; global, 103, 108; in New Order, 205, 219; U.S., 99

citizenship, 264–65; of Indonesians of Chinese origin, 224, 276n.30; in New Order, 131; of transmigrants, 41; and U.S. national parks, 96, 99
class, 13, 135, 173, 223; in Muir's cause, 98; in New Order, 130
climate change, 7, 101–6, 109, 114, 201, 218, 244
Clinton administration (U.S.), 208
coal, 24, 51–54, 114
coalition. *See* collaboration
Cockburn, Alexander, 32
coercion, 4, 6, 9, 75, 184–85, 188–89, 259
collaboration, 5, 13–14, 155, 226, 238, 245–47, 255, 262, 267–68, 293n.3; and axioms of unity, 89–90; in botany, 94; Brazil-North American, 230; in CAMP-FIRE, 294n.9; coercive, 159; conservationist-indigenous, 159, 160, 163; contingent, 262–63, 294–95n.9; frictions of, 249; frontier, 27, 33; in global climate modeling, 103; in globe making projects, 56, 76, 111–12; happy, 228, 231–33; in ITTO, 107; and Muir's vision of nature, 100–101; north-south, 231, 234; process of, 162; between student nature lovers and armed forces, 133; between student nature lovers and village leaders, 18, 255; transethnic/translocal, 35
colonialism, 9, 81, 83, 94, 161, 173; anti-, 274n.12; Dutch, 184–85, 194–95, 225; legacy of, 294n.9; struggle against, 269
commodity, 51–52
community, xi, 197–200, 250, 256–58, 264–65, 287n.20, 293n.7, 294n.9, 295n.10; forest, 241; forest-dependent, 293n.2; indigenous, 283n.10
community-based natural resource management (CBNRM), 22, 260–62, 263–66, 294 nn. 8 and 9; 295n.10
companies: coal, 54, 140; construction, 224, 291n.22; logging, x, xi, 29, 67, 242, 255–56, 275–76n.25, 276n.30; mining, 29, 32, 63–64, 67; oil, 158–59; plantation, 29, 44–45, 174; timber, x, 174, 206–7, 242, 248, 255, 258–60, 262; transnational, 67
conglomerates. *See* companies
conjuring, 57–59, 63–65, 68, 75
Conoco Oil Company, 252
conservation, 116, 157–58, 195, 241, 294n.8; biocentric nature, 119; biodiversity, 212; of charismatic megafauna, 240; community-based, 161, 199, 247, 263,

294n.9; and development, 202, 208, 290n.12; in Indonesia, 276n.33; in ITTO's mandate, 107–8, 284n.15; and livelihood, 175; of Meratus forests, xi, 174, 199, 254, 288n.3; in the salvage frontier, 32; and "science wars," 12–13
conservationists, 12, 189, 195, 199, 240, 244; in Brazil, 231; international, 172; and ITTO, 107–8, 110
conservation biologists, 154, 158, 172. *See also* conservationists
conservation biology, 158, 163, 173
consumption, 130, 142
contingency, 3, 60, 263, 270, 275n.14
contracts of work (CoWs), 69–72, 74, 281n.23
corporations. *See* companies
corruption, 59, 222, 239–40, 242, 276n.28; in politicians, 15; in New Order, 37, 56, 236; official, 220
crisis, 41, 42; Asian financial (1997), 21–22, 41, 55, 64, 226–27, 280n.17; logging, x
crony system, 226
cronyism, 55, 278n.2; franchise, 59, 69, 71, 75, 77
cultural relativism, 7
culture, 25, 35, 40, 74, 122, 234, 271; destruction of, 23; as element of global climate modeling, 105; frontier, 50, 59, 68, 75–77; *kebudayaan*, 49; "local," 184; Meratus Dayak, 174; political, 228, 251, 291n.23; survival of indigenous, 231; teenage consumer, 285n.8; traditional, 260; youth, 129
cultures, 4, 25, 31, 35, 122, 169, 161; indigenous, ix, 32

damage. *See* destruction
dams, 222–24, 290–91n.20, 291n.23; Kedung Ombo, 219, 221–23; Narmada Valley, 222
Dayaks, 31, 49, 253, 286n.14. *See also* Meratus Dayaks
deforestation, 18, 107, 202, 248, 255; in Amazon, 231; rates of, 273n.3
degradation. *See* destruction
democracy, 22, 100, 117, 233, 238, 268, 274–75n.14; and *ad hoc* tactics, 223; and environmental well-being, 221; in finance, 56; and the frontier, 31; "*panca sila*," 290n.14; Western liberal, 11
deregulation, 55; zones of, 45
desire, 32, 51, 261

forestry, 100, 107; community, 266, 287n.18; 244; German-run, 265; Indian department of, 235; New Order state, 276n.33; state institutions of, 107; state programs of, 287n.15; traditional agro-, 31

Foucault, Michel, 289n.3

franchise cronyism, 69, 71, 75, 77

free trade, 86, 106, 109

freedom, 10, 205, 208, 245, 274n.6; Enlightenment concept of, 14; and the frontier, 31; and New Order environmentalism, 17; and new social movements, 4–5, 214; personal, 149; for post-colonial nations, 81, 83; for the rich, 241, 244; sexual, of women, 292n.44; of speech, 285n.10; of transnational political liberalism, 205–6; as universal truth, 8, 84–85; and unfreedom, 214

Freeport McMoRan, 62–63, 69, 72–73, 280n.22, 281n.31

friction, 1, 18, 89, 207, 214, 220, 272, 274n.6; between aspirations and political achievement, 85; in contingent articulation, 77; in collaboration, 13, 245–46, 249; in the commodity chain, 51; among contested universals, 87; cultural, xi; in global capitalism, 12; in global connections, x, 3; global, 170; of liberal politics, 208; in the market, 21; metaphor of, 5–6; in rubber trade, 274n.7; symmetrical analysis of, 211

frontier, 17, 30–36, 42–43, 65–69, 72, 210; capitalist, 27; closing of, 65; critical literatures of, 277n.5; emptiness of, 72, 280n.21; human face of, 33–35; Latin American, 31; masculinity in, 39–41; mining and investment, 73; and national parks, 283n.7; resource, 28–29, 184; salvage, 32; techno-, 31–32; as a traveling theory, 31

GATT, 284n.19

gender, 13, 215, 236–38, 292n.44; in Muir's writing, 98;

General Motors, 241

genocide, 158–59

global warming. See climate change

globalism, 101, 170; in spectacular accumulation, 73

globalization, xii–xiii, 3, 55–56, 85–86, 214, 270–71; corporate, 11; neoliberal, 269; Philip Morris' campaign for, 142; theories of, 75, 266, 269

gold, 2, 47, 56–57, 63, 114, 279 nn. 7 and 11; 281n.28; Bre-X's discovery of, 61–63, 65–67, 280 nn. 16 and 21; price of, 60

governmentality, 107, 214, 289n.3

Green Revolution, 21, 290n.20

Greenpeace, 290n.12

Grove, Richard, 93

Guzman, Michael de, 61–62, 65–66, 71, 279n.14

Habibie, 220–21, 226

Hall, Stuart, 76

Hamam, 147, 152–53

Hartwell, Emily, 43

Harvey, David, 75

Hasan, Mohammed "Bob," 16, 32, 44, 63, 71–72, 276n.30, 277n.6, 281n.28

Hayden, Corinne, 95

Hecht, Susanna, 32

hegemony, 12; of development, 17, 207; European, 94; and friction, 6, global, 60; limits of, 202; national, 224; partial, 76

hillbillies, 174–76

history; environmental, 12, 262; Hegelian ideals of universal, 274n.12; natural, 95, 186

Hobbes, Thomas, 274n.6

Home Depot, 242, 293n.4

human nature, 153–54

human rights, 76, 84, 121, 205–6, 222, 225, 238, 260, 269; abuses of human, 72–73, 281n.31; in New Order, 17, 216; and new social movements, 4, 14, 214, 289n.3

Humboldt, Alexander, 96–98

Hvalkof, Søren, 159

hybridity, 26

IKEA, 242

immigrants, 46–47, 241

independence; frontier, 64; Indonesian, 128, 195, 207, 236

indigeneity, 267–68

indigenous people, 225, 260; and biodiversity conservation, 159, 240; and cultural categories, 175, 202; political alliance of, 208

Indonesian Dayaks, 233. See also Meratus Dayaks

Indonesian Environmental Forum (WALHI), 145, 218, 220, 247–48, 251–52, 255–56, 259, 261, 276n.33, 293n.4

Indonesian Wood Panel Association (APKINDO), 16
Indorayon Company, 220, 290n.16
inequality, 220; mystification of local and global, 211; and the Nature Conservancy's strategy, 242; north-south, 56
Inhutani, 34
International Labor Organization, 225, 291n.27
International Monetary Fund, 226, 275–76n.25
International Rivers Network, 222
International Tropical Timber Organization, 106–11, 284n.14
Islamic Party, 128–29
Islam, 9, 174, 207; as critique of New Order, 205, 236, 276n.34; and gender politics, 236–37; liberal, 290n.14; among nature lovers, 125; radical, 227; and science, 115–17

Jameson, Fredrick, 4
jungle, 64, 72, 229
justice, 9, 87, 117, 269; and community-based conservation, 247; economic, 231; and Empire, 289n.3; Enlightenment concept of, 14; environmental, 119; in Kedung Ombo case, 219, 223; rhetorics of, 5. See also social justice

Katoppo, Aristides, 123, 285n.9
Kedung Ombo dam, 219, 221–24
Awat Kilay, 206–7, 209
Kodeco. See Korean Development Company
Korean Development Company, 47, 208–12, 229, 288 nn. 1 and 3
knowledge, 10, 81, 136, 265; in collaboration, 89, 155, 161–63; cultural, 170; cultural analysis of, 122; environmental, 113, 267; European, 94; global, 93; globally traveling, 8, 12, 87; indigenous, 8, 35, 93, 159–60, 235–36; interdependence of, 66; "international," 159; local, 68, 93, 182; Meratus, 189, 190; nature as, 12; as produced in dialogue, 92–93; stereotypes of indigenous, 183; universal, 112, 172; women's, 235
Kompas Borneo, 248, 252–56, 258–59, 261
Kopassus, 128, 133–34, 285n.12
Krishnan, Mr. 52–54
Kyoto Protocol, 105–6, 283n.12, 283–84n.13

labor: alienated, 167; creative, 269; organized, 161; slave, 167; standards for, 86
Laclau, Ernesto, 275n.14
landscape, 177, 213; colonial agrarian, 287n.16; destruction of, 206, 212; frontier, 68, 74; as genre, 201; human, 217; Javanese, 285n.10; Meratus, 175, 182, 195, 257; as object of analysis, 173; of resource extraction, 67; ruined, 269; rural, 194, 213–14; social, xi, 29, 194, 273n.1, 290n.12; social-natural, 174, 175, 200; uninhabitable, 2; unruly, 194
law, 33, 225, 290n.14; colonial, 195; customary, 48–49, 225, 290n.16, 291 nn. 24, 28, and 29; environmental, 219, 290n.16; and environmental activism, 117–19, 219–21; forestry, 119, 194, 225, 287n.18, 291n.28; in New Order, 121, 129, 219–20; property, 86; "revolutionary," 219; transnational, 217
Legal Aid Foundation (LBH), 220, 222, 290n.19
Lembaga Bantuan Hukum (LBH). See Legal Aid Foundation (LBH)
Lembaga Pemberdayaan Masyarakat Adat Borneo Selatan (LPMA). See Empowerment Institute for Indigenous People of South Borneo (LPMA)
Li, Tania, 243
liberalism, 214–15, 218–19, 224, 289 nn. 3 and 4; 289n.4; 290n.14; economic neo-, 1; free market, 269; political, 206; transnational, 269
liberation, 207, 236
Linnaeus, Carl, 93–94
livelihoods, 28, 284n.6; destruction of, 2, 23, 41, 110, 153, 233, 266, 294n.8; forest-based, x, 29, 210; indigenous, 225–226; and parks model of nature preservation, 100, 283n.10; in secondary forest, 190; zones of, 175, 193–95
logging, 28, 41, 283, 208–12; campaigns against, xi, 209–12, 227, 229–30, 232; commercial, 31, 220, 255–56; and conservation, 242–43, 284n.15; frontier, 30, 33–35; illegal, 17, 110; in New Order, 15–17, 275n.23; "reduced impact," 110. See also timbering
Lowe, Celia, 94
Lowe's, 242

Ma Igul, 207, 209
Ma Salam, 34, 207, 209–210

magic: "black," 137; of finance, 57; invulnerability, 39; masculine, 38; mountain, 183; of nature, 126, 147

Manser, Bruno, 232–33, 253

Marxism, 9

masculinity, 38–40, 144, 234–35

men, 144, 277n.37; and environmentalism, 234–35; in frontier, 38–40; Meratus, 156, 166, 181, 198; and sports, 117; white, 31

Mendes, Chico, 296–235

Meratus Advocacy Alliance. See *Aliansi Advocasi Meratus*

Meratus Dayaks, xi, 29, 33, 174, 210, 252–56; activism of, x, 199, 207–12, 247–48, 256–61; and cultural categories, 177; dispossession of, xii; in frontier, 40; livelihood practices of, 164–65, 178–82, 185–86, 190–92, 286n.7; Madurese conflict with, 49–50, 278n.18; and propriety, 48–50

migrants, 23, 41, 68, 210, 225

military, 33, 128, 208, 275n.23; and forest product collecting, 184; in frontier, 29, 34, 39, 47, 67; and the market, 37; and nature lovers, 132–33; post–New Order, 54, 227, 239

mining, 31; for Canada, 65, 73; coal, 51–54; and conjuring, 57; and Filipino geologists, 279n.12; gold, 23, 40, 60, 66–68; illegal, 17

mobilizations, 5, 22, 214–15, 230, 289n.7; for the Amazon, 292 nn. 35 and 37; across difference, 245; against forest destruction, 211; through friction, 206; global rainforest, 231; against Kedung Ombo dam, 221; liberatory, 9; against logging, 207. *See also* movements

modernity, 141, 160, 254; and development, 21; and New Order, 217

modernization, 84–85, 205; imperial, 161

Moffett, Jim Bob, 72–73

movements, 214, 271; Brazilian environmental, 292n.36; Brazilian trade union, 231; Chipko tree-hugging, 235; environmental, xii, 177, 215, 224; Indonesian democratic, 5; international anti-dam, 222; Malaysian environmental, 232; Meratus anti-logging, 261; in New Order, 251; new social, 4–5, 289n.3; utopian, 207; youth, 128

Muir, John, 95–101, 282 nn. 5, 6, and 7; 283 nn. 7 and 10

Mulroney, Brian, 64

Munk, Peter, 61, 71

Murphree, Marshall, 294n.9

Muslims, 48, 228–29, 236

Narmada Valley dams, 222

nationalism, 216, 218; anti-politics, 146; post–World War II, 83–84; and nature loving, 131–32; nonpolitical, 129, 131; in public schools, 129; radical, 269; utopian, 215

nature, 100, 103, 148, 153–54, 282n.5, 283n.10; global, 95–98, 107, 111–12, 177; imperial discourse on, 202; as religion, 97; rural, 213; as system, 93–95; universal, 88–92

Nature Conservancy, The, 240–44, 293 nn. 2 and 4

nature lovers, x, 16, 125–26, 266, 270, 285n.7; and cigarette marketing, 142, 144–46; citizenship of, 249; environmentalism of, 152–54, 207, 218, 246–48, 252–55; expertise of, 136–37; "global," 232; and Kopassus, 133–35; and "local people," 140–41, 151; nonpolitics of, 131–32; North American, 97, 98, 100; and outdoor sports, 117, 122, 138–41; and personal freedom, 149–51; and the romance of nature, 123–24, 147–49; and spirituality, 116, 152; and the supernatural, 137–38; urban, 161; youth of, 128–31. See also *pencinta alam*

non-governmental organizations (NGOs), 76, 278n.3; in anti-dam campaign, 222; in anti-logging campaign, 209; environmental, 117, 230, 284n.15, and nature loving, 147; in New Order, 217–18, 220–21, 236–37, 289n.10; transnational, 289n.10, 290n.12

oil, 114, 275n.23

orangutans, 240

orchards, 16, 46, 47, 177; Meratus rubber, 194

Orta, Garcia de, 93

Overseas Private Investment Corporation, 72–73

"packages"; activist, 232, 234–35, 227–38; allegorical, 231; charismatic, 227

pagans, 48

pan-Asianism, 274n.12

patriotism, 132; anti-politics, 133; business-oriented, 16; state-led, 8

peace, 82–84
peasants, 6, 124–25, 201–2
Penan, 232, 253
pencinta alam, 122, 125, 137. *See also* nature
  lovers
Pentacostals, 41
piety, 22, 48–49, 236–37
Pinchot, Gifford, 99–100
Placer Dome, 71–72, 281n.27
plantations, 30, 36, 41, 43, 45–46, 124, 167,
  194–95; acacia, 278n.13; developers of,
  182; eucalyptus, 220; forest, 266; industrial tree, 15, 32, 36; Kodeco, 43, 288n.1;
  monocrop, 210; operators of, 202
plywood, 2, 15–16, 30, 275–76n.25
poachers, 243, 287–88n.23
policy, 158, 187, 291n.27; development,
  194; European Community environmental, 274n.9; and forest fires, 278n.16;
  makers of, 103, 278n.10; resource, 194
political ecology, 173, 286n.4
politics, 2, 216; adat-based, 226; anti-
  globalization, 86; anti-immigrant, 289n.8;
  Brazilian union, 234; coalition, 13; Cold
  War, 85; and culture, 232, 234; ethnic
  identity, 4; environmental, 7–8, 95, 112;
  in-friction, 14; Islamic, 276n.34; in
  Kodeco debate, 211; liberal, 1; local/
  global, 231; in New Order, 218; NGO,
  273–274n.5, 289n. 3; non-, 129; post–
  New Order, 226; rainforest, 231; revolutionary, 129; techno-, 21; U.S. environmental, 99, 234–35; youth, 128–29
pollution, 119, 140, 217, 274n.9; as transboundary issue, 7, 101; urban, 292n.36
populism, 288n.2; Indonesian, 217–18, 224;
  nationalist, 205; pro-Kodeco, 211;
  through translation, 212
power, 3, 259, 264, 267; coercive, 289n.3;
  European colonial, 9; and friction, 6; imperial, 214, 267; logics, 269, 272
preservation, 99, 241
privatization, 12, 21, 34, 242; U.S. model
  of, 15
privilege, 265; corporate, 211; elite, 232;
  white, 160
property, 18, 23–25, 39, 46, 74, 160, 173,
  225, 290n.14; claims to, 277n.7, 287n.22;
  common, 35, 278n.10; and conservation,
  240–241; destruction of, 86; and freedom,
  10; intellectual, 161; private, 35, 106, 186,
  200, 241, 243, 278n.10; regimes of 47; of
  state, 194

prostitution, 39–40, 234
P. T. Harvest International, 239
Punan Dayaks, 243–44

race, 13, 225, 291n.26, in Muir's cause, 98.
  See also racism
racism, 83–84, 160, 216, 224–25, 264
Rainforest: Amazon, 101–2, 158–59, 292
  nn. 35 and 36; and ecotourism, 260; Indonesian, 2, 14; loggers' view of, 15–16;
  marketing of the, 159; and Nature Conservancy, 240–41; "Run for the," 32; social making of, 35. *See also* forests
Rainforest Action Network, 158–59, 293n.4
Rangan, Haripriya, 235
rape, 33, 40
rat poison, 45–46
rationality, 138; market, 10
rattans, 16, 187–89, 287n.13; claimed, 257;
  forced deliveries of, 185; Indonesian national policy and, 187; in swiddens, 166,
  178
Ray, John, 93
Reagan, Ronald, 143
reason, 138; and faith, 116, 118; universal, 9
reforestation, 36; fund for, 220
regulation: environmental, 34, 65; government, 66
religion, 25, 114, 117, 215; cosmopolitanism of, 236
remittances, 270
reserves: extractive, 230–31; genetic, 193;
  nature, 195, 209, 242
resettlement, 31, 100, 206, 223, 290n.18
resource exploitation. *See* resource
  extraction
resource extraction, xi, 14, 22–23; and
  CoWs, 69; in "forests," 194; frontier, 28,
  59, 67–68; illegal, 17, 240, 266; and indigenous advocacy, 224–25; and Nature
  Conservancy, 242; in New Order, 206,
  225; post–New Order, 208; and terror,
  159
revolution, 236; American, 82; French,
  274n12; Haitian, 274n.12
rice, 23, 45, 153, 194; bottom of the barrel,
  42; in swiddens, 165, 186, 191, 197
rights, 10, 17, 251, 280n.21; adat, 291 nn.
  28, 30, and 31; 292n.31; to a clean and
  healthy environment, 217; customary,
  67–68, 75, 181, 216, 225, 291–92n.31; to
  destroy forests, 108; to development, 86,
  233; of disenfranchised people, 215; gay,

tourism; adventure, 130–31, 139; eco-, 152–53, 199, 208, 260; mass, 153; nature, 100; and U.S. citizenship, 99
tradition, 21, 225, 254
transmigrants: Javanese, 23–24, 41, 47; local, 24
transmigration, 23, 30, 221, 290n.18
transnationalism, 211, 216
translation, 31, 274–75n.14, 288n.2, 291n.27; in activist work, 18, 215, 219; of Chico Mendes story, 233; of Chipko, 235; across difference, 212; globalism and, 170; of term "indigenous," 224–26; of Uma Adang's species list, 62
tribes, 42, 161, 168–69, 174, 226, 249, 291–92n.31
Turner, Fredrick Jackson, 32

Uma Adang, 25, 48–49, 155–57, 162–65, 168–70
United Nations, 84
United Nations Conference on the Human Environment (1972), 217
United Nations 1992 Environmental Summit in Rio, 105–6, 109, 233, 283n.12
United Power, 52
United States, 86, 231, 241, 275n.22; and Bretton Woods, 60; government of, 72–73, 143; imperial claims by, 283n.11; and Kyoto Protocol, 106; military globalisms, 101
unity, axiom of. *See* axiom of unity
universals, 1, 4–5, 6–9, 274 nn. 8 and 11; business-oriented, 106; contested, 87; cultural specificity of, 111–12; engaged, 8, 10, 263–64, 267, 270, 274–75n.14; and

Nature, 88–92, 95–96, 97–100; secular, 282n.3
Usman, Professor N. 117–19, 284n.1.

violence: anti-Chinese, 291n.25; Dayak-Madurese, 49–50; ethnic, 277n.9; frontier, 32–34, 44, 267; and ownership, 67–68; post–New Order, 227, 239

Walsh, David, 60–62, 64, 69, 278n.14, 281 nn. 30 and 32
war, 6, 64; U.S.-led global, 239; nuclear, 83; religious, 85
Wild West, 31, 59, 65; regulatory, 282n.35
wilderness, 100, 124; protection of, 160; U.S., 95–96, 99
Wilson, E. O, 158
Wilson, Ken, 295n.9
women, 103, 114, 117, 228–29, 234, 236–38, 269, 277n.37; activism of, 230, 235; equality of, 208; in frontier, 39–40; Meratus, 166, 181, 191; peasant, 124–25; sexuality of, 48; white, 98
Women, Environment and Development, 235
Women's Studies, 292n.44
Wood, Charles, 33
World Bank, 221–23, 291n.22
World Court, 211
World Trade Organization, 86, 161, 284n.19
World Wildlife Fund, 276n.33; Indonesian, 290n.12

Yeutter, Clayton, 143
Yosemite, 97–99, 282n.7, indigenous residents of, 283n.10

matic plant with grass-like leaves and white flowers. P 361. **kunyit**: tumeric, *Curcuma domestica*. P 36
ngal, *Languas galanga*. P 363. **lahiya**: ginger. P 364. **sarai**: lemon grass. P 365. **kambang ba'ingi**: sweet
6. **kambang habang**: cockscomb. P 367. **kambang kuning**: yellow cockscomb. P [810]. **waluh**: orange
uash. P [840]. **sumangka**: watermelon. P [841]. **hantimun**: cucumber. P 368. **hubi**: greater yam, *Dioscore*
[802]. **kaladi**: taro. P [930]. **tabu langan**: a variety of sugar cane that is green stalked. P [871]. **isang kali**
ariety of banana. P [870]. **isang ma'ulih**: another banana. P 369. **kambat balik**: a decorative bush with var
ves. P 370. **titi'is**: a decorative plant with broad leaves. P 371. **hati-hati**: *Coleus*. P 372. **kayu tulak**: a de
nt, perhaps *Graptophyllum pictum*. P 373. **halinjuang**: a decorative plant with red leaves, *Cordyline frui*
4. **nyiur**: coconut. P 375. **pinang**; areca palm. P 376. **hanau**: sugar palm, *Arenga pinnata*. P 377. **wa-wa**
est tree, whose wood is medicinally useful. 378. **pulayi**: a forest tree, *Alstonia sp.*, with soft white wood u
emonial boards. 379. **buluh**: a thin-walled bamboo, very useful, e.g., for carrying water and cooking.
tung: a heavy-haulmed, strong bamboo with delicious shoots and many uses (*Dendrocalamus asper*?).
uh kuning: a yellow-haulmed bamboo. P 382. **haur**: another large bamboo (*Gigantochloa scortechinii*?)
mbang kati kapur: a vine with a fragrant white flower; medicinally useful. P 384. **kambang malati**: jasm
num sambac. P 385. **kambang tuak**: a shrub with fragrant white flowers, waxy leaves, and medicinal uses
mbang papanggil putih: a shrub with white flowers and medicinal uses (*Clerodendron sp.*?). P 387. **kamb**
ng: an herb with red flowers used by shamans. P 388. **kambang kandasuli**: a shrub whose roots and flow
dical uses. P 389. **kandawastu**: a grass-like herb whose fragrant roots are used as a skin-cleansing powde
yu tangkan: a small tree whose roots are used for medicines. P 391. **kambang ai'ing mawar**: its fragrant
used to scent the hair, and in a tonic. P 392. **kambang tatawa**: a fragrant orchid; it is found in the forest
raised at home. 393. **janjarum putih**: a shrub with white flowers. 394. **papanggil habang**: an herb with
e flowers on square, red stems. 395. **rumput sadip**: a weed of the regrowing forest. 396. **rumput janggut**
herb with white flowers grown for its herbal uses. P 397. **akar pamulangan**: a tall, climbing vine used in
es. 398. **tantapung nasi**: a small tree of secondary growth whose roots are used in herbal cures. Its whi
are bunched "like rice." 399. **balimbing tunjuk**: a tree with sour edible fruits whose roots are used in
es (*Connaropsis sp.*?). 400. **akar gita'an**: a forest vine with a white latex whose roots and stems are u
rbal cures; it has a delicious orange fruit (*Willughbeia sp.*?). [907]. **gatah**: rubber, *Hevea brasiliensis*. Its r
ed for herbal cures. P 401. **kambang campaka**: a small tree with an aromatic blossom (*Michelia sp.*?). Its r
ed for herbal cures. P 402. **pudak**: a screw-pine (*Pandanus tectorius*?) with fragrant flowers and many uses
ndan: another useful screw-pine (*Pandanus sp.*). P 404. **pudak satugal**: another screw-pine, used to
sserts. P 405. **tabusalah**: a decorative cane, used for rituals. P 406. **tabusurung**: another ritually importa
407. **pihaung**: another ritually important cane, rather like 405, but currently out of style. P 408. **tibarau**
t grows by the side of streams and is used for herbal cures (*Saccharum arundinaceum*?). [45]. **lalamas**: a
e plant used for herbal cures. 409. **tamiang ngalis**: a vine found in rocky places and near streams, used fo
es. Birth aids and drinking vines: 410. **kurawanglu**: a ginger family rhizome used for women giving bir
nput kamuyang: a red-stemmed herb whose stem is used as a poultice for birthing mothers. 412. **upas**:

d for timber. **552. anglai**: its wood is valued highly on the market. **553. ulin**: Borneo ironwood, the r
wood most valued for building posts and shingles, *Eusiderocylon zwageri*. **554. ulin danau**: It looks like
nger leaves, but the wood is soft. **555. pijalungan**: another forest tree that has become commercially va
amar Dipterocarps: **556. d. balahung**: a big forest tree. The following damar are called **meranti** in the ti
de, which usually indicates *Shorea* spp.: **557. d. takuyung**: it can be tapped for illuminant resin. **558. d. lii**
makes great rice bins. **559. d. bilai**: valued by commercial loggers. **560. d. tampuk ranggas**: also valued
. **561. d. pungkangan**. **562. d. bangkiray**: its bark is good for flooring and rice bins. The following dan
ful for resins: **563. d. putih**: its light-colored resin was once an important trade product. **564. d. kapau**:
ree with good resin for illumination. **565. d. tulang**: its dark resin is good for torches. The set of damar t
I gathered higher in the mountains is equally extensive but almost entirely non-overlapping, suggest
ariety. **566. pulayi kuning**: like pulayi (378) but yellow, larger, and not so soft-wooded. **567. kayu kaca**
tree with commercially valued timber. **568. madang**: the wood is used for house posts. A laurel? **569. b**
big tree that is not good for commercial timber because the wood rots easily; it can be used for roof s
570. sinampar: a big tree with commercially valued timber. **571. masahangan**: another big tree. [50]. **Ka**
ia pinnata?) good for floor boards. **572. sungkai**: a fast-growing straight tree, *Peronema canescens*. Ho
ade from it sprout. Commercial plantations have been made. On the west side it is a small-holder cash cr
lua' katam: useful for boards (*Ficus sp.*?). **574. lua' panggang**: small-scale commercial loggers log it. [45
Artocarpus elastica; small-scale loggers log it, depriving residents of its many uses. **575. lua' manis**: the fr
od to eat (*Ficus sp.*?). **576. binuang bini**: a tall straight tree that grows quickly if planted; a site for hor
77. **binuang laki**: similar, except the leaves are smaller. Rice-pounding mortars are made from binuang. (
s sumatrana?) **578. jumit**: a big tree good for boards or rice bins. These trees have fruits beloved by anim
jaling: the fruits, which grow directly from the bole, are eaten by barking deer and mouse deer. **580. s**
mountain oak, whose acorns are much loved by wild pigs. **581–88. kariwaya**: strangling figs, *Ficus* spp. Th
re eaten by birds. **k. nasi**. **k. ganggaram**. **k. tampuk biru**. **k. kampayau**. **k. masak malam**. **k. lamak**.
in. **k. tangga datu**. I collected different strangling fig names higher in the mountains, again suggest
ariety. **589. kangkalayau**: another big tree whose fruits are eaten by birds. [452]. **kangkala'**: the birds l
it just as people do. **590. langsat tiung**: a big tree whose fruits are eaten by porcupines. **591. kupang**
ee with edible fruits, sold at market; wild pigs love them. P Fruits that are good fish bait: **592. pampahit**
with bitter red berries; the young sprouting leaves can be eaten, but they are bitter. **593. ganggaram**
plant with red fruits that fish eat. **594. pilancau**: a tree with black fruits that make good fish bait. Trees
secondary forest: **595. ma-manik**. **596. ya-yami**. **597. tantapung**. **598. gigingah**. **599. binjai hayam**. 6
n: an herbal cure can be made from its roots. Trees that make good firewood: **601. mambaratan**: found
ary forest and big forest. **602. ambaratisan**: a log made from this tree will burn all night. **603. niwai**: a
o useful for roof supports. **604. bilayang kiyatan**: its wood is not strong enough for boards. [489]. **bilaya**
p. **605. bilayang riwat**. **606. bilayang tabas**. **607. bilayang buah**: its fruits are sweet. **608. jawaling**: a sm